Ambiguous Cinema

For Ella, and the loving family she gave me

For Patrick, always and forever

Ambiguous Cinema

From Simone de Beauvoir to
Feminist Film-Phenomenology

Kelli Fuery

EDINBURGH
University Press

Edinburgh University Press is one of the leading university presses in the UK. We publish academic books and journals in our selected subject areas across the humanities and social sciences, combining cutting-edge scholarship with high editorial and production values to produce academic works of lasting importance. For more information visit our website: edinburghuniversitypress.com

© Kelli Fuery, 2022, 2024

Edinburgh University Press Ltd
The Tun – Holyrood Road
12 (2f) Jackson's Entry
Edinburgh EH8 8PJ

First published in hardback by Edinburgh University Press 2022

Typeset in Ehrhardt MT Pro by
Cheshire Typesetting Ltd, Cuddington, Cheshire

A CIP record for this book is available from the British Library

ISBN 978 1 3995 0423 2 (hardback)
ISBN 978 1 3995 0424 9 (paperback)
ISBN 978 1 3995 0425 6 (webready PDF)
ISBN 978 1 3995 0426 3 (epub)

The right of Kelli Fuery to be identified as author of this work has been asserted in accordance with the Copyright, Designs and Patents Act 1988 and the Copyright and Related Rights Regulations 2003 (SI No. 2498).

Contents

List of Figures vi
Abbreviations of Featured Works by Simone de Beauvoir viii
Acknowledgements ix

Introduction 1

1. Beauvoir's Ambiguity, Cinema and Feminist Phenomenology 9
2. Must We Burn Cavani? Moral Ambiguity in *The Night Porter* 35
3. Moments of Moral Choice in Debra Granik's *Leave No Trace* 61
4. Habit the Cinematic Encounter: Cheryl Dunye and the 'Dunyementaries' 91
5. A New (Ethical) Face on Love: Bad Faith and Claire Denis's *Let the Sunshine In* 121
6. A Cinema of the Borderlands: Lucrecia Martel's *Zama* 146
7. Sensuous Co-Performance: Lynne Ramsay's *We Need to Talk About Kevin* and Beauvoir's Aesthetic Attitude 177
8. Femme Desire and the Reciprocal Gaze in Céline Sciamma's *Portrait of a Lady on Fire* 201

Conclusion: Make Your Choice – Ambiguity Beyond Beauvoir 227

Filmography 233
Bibliography 235
Index 248

Figures

1.1	Julie clasps her arms around herself, a gesture of self-protection in *The Souvenir*	20
1.2	Julie's insecurity is shown via comportment	20
1.3	Julie stands on the threshold, between her past and her future	22
1.4	Julie's direct address to the camera	25
2.1	Max caresses Lucia's wound in *The Night Porter*	51
2.2	Lucia finds a pink dress which reminds her of the one Max gave her	52
2.3	Max gives Lucia a pink dress in the death camp	52
3.1	Close-up, shallow focus of a spider in a web in *Leave No Trace*	65
3.2	Granik focuses on gesture, an example of 'phenomenological filmmaking'	67
3.3	Extreme wide shot, low angle, of Will and Tom crossing St John's bridge	71
3.4	Close-up, shallow focus of Will and Tom approaching Portland Aerial Tram terminal	72
3.5	Granik's focus on hands conveys Tom's need and want for community	86
4.1	Cheryl Dunye's habit of direct address	105
4.2	Cheryl hesitates when describing what she does for a living	112
4.3	Diana assumes first go of the joint without invitation in *The Watermelon Woman*	115
5.1	Close-ups of Isabelle focusing on her emotional state in *Let the Sunshine In*	124
5.2	'A view from within'. Isabelle's POV of the window and outside world	130
5.3	'A view from without'. Isabelle's POV of David's apartment	130
5.4	Isabelle visits Vincent in his apartment	140
6.1	Adults lazing around the pool in *La ciénaga*	148
6.2	Zama looks out to sea	160
6.3	Zama listens to women speaking	161
7.1	Scene of the chaotic *La Tomatina* festival in the beginning of *We Need to Talk About Kevin*	191

7.2	Kevin's new bedroom, all in the colour blue	197
8.1	Mikäel wins a wrestle with a friend in *Tomboy*	208
8.2	Footballers in *Girlhood*	210
8.3	Marianne and Héloïse discuss the inequality of marriage on the beach in *Portrait of a Lady on Fire*	217
8.4	An expression of ambiguity during Sophie's abortion	223
8.5	Héloïse reconstructs Sophie's abortion so that Marianne can document it via painting	224

Abbreviations of Featured Works by Simone de Beauvoir

ADD   *America Day by Day*, translated by Carol Cosman, Berkeley: University of California Press. 1999.

ASD   *All Said and Done*, translated by Patrick O'Brian, Paragon House Publishers. 1993.

CA   *The Coming of Age*, translated by Patrick O'Brian, New York: W.W. Norton and Company. 1996.

EA   *The Ethics of Ambiguity*, translated by Bernard Frechtman, New York: Open Road Integrated Media Inc. 2018.

FC   *Force of Circumstance*, translated by Richard Howard, New York: G. P. Putnam's Sons. 1965.

LM   'Literature and Metaphysics', in Margaret A. Simons (ed.), *Simone de Beauvoir: Philosophical Writings*, translated by Marybeth Timmermann, Urbana: University of Illinois Press. 2004.

MWBS   'Must We Burn Sade?', in Margaret A. Simons and Marybeth Timmermann (eds), *Simone de Beauvoir: Political Writings*, translated by Kim Allen Gleed, Marilyn Gaddis Rose and Virginia Preston, Urbana: University of Illinois Press. 2012.

PC   *Pyrrhus and Cineas*, in Margaret A. Simons (ed.), *Simone de Beauvoir: Philosophical Writings*, translated by Marybeth Timmermann, Urbana: University of Illinois Press. 2004.

PL   *The Prime of Life*, translated by Peter Green, Cleveland: World Publishing. 1962.

TSS   *The Second Sex*, translated by Constance Borde and Shelia Malovany-Chevallier, Introduction by Judith Thurman, New York: Vintage Books. 2011.
Also translated by H. M. Parshley, Alfred A. Knopf Publishers. 1953.

WCLD   'What Can Literature Do?', in Margaret A. Simons and Marybeth Timmermann (eds), *Simone de Beauvoir: 'The Useless Mouths' and Other Literary Writings*, translated by Marybeth Timmermann, Urbana: University of Illinois Press. 2011.

Acknowledgements

I wrote *Ambiguous Cinema* during the COVID-19 pandemic, a global experience that exposed ambiguous and complex situations for us all. Fully aware of the privilege in being able to focus on research when others were navigating new learning technologies and rapidly reconfiguring their work and life balance, I immersed myself in the writings of Simone de Beauvoir and her commentators to complete this project. The stay-at-home order in California meant I was not able to visit archives, movie theatres, or discuss ideas and chapters with colleagues in person. My family became my captive audience and they bore my chatter with their usual good humour (most of the time). Noah and Joshua, I am so lucky to have sons who care enough about what their mother does to argue so passionately with her. Thank you, Noah, for working so hard on the filmography and happily doing the jobs that always take more time than you think. Joshua, thank you for gaming quietly in the room next door.

One of Beauvoir's gifts was her exhaustive account of her life available through her autobiographies, diaries, essays and articles. I cross-referenced these with well-known and highly regarded biographies, which are wonderfully meticulous and extensive in their own accounting of Beauvoir's work and life. Read in combination with the posthumous publications of Beauvoir's letters (to Aldgren, Sartre, Leduc) and with the scholarship on her philosophy, it felt as though there were many perspectives and voices helping me even in lockdown. While I have unfortunately not met most of scholars cited in this book, it is without doubt that their works have helped me use my time in ways that made writing this book both possible and pleasurable. I am so thankful for the collective passion and rigour present in the feminist philosophers cited throughout this book, enabling such diversity on the thinking and writing about Beauvoir's ideas.

My thanks to Chapman University for honouring my sabbatical, providing me with the time and space to concentrate on a single research project. Without this, I would not have been able to finish the book in the time that I did. A very special thank you must go to Dana Polan, whose generosity of time and attention in finalising this manuscript meant more to me than I can fully convey, helping to navigate the tensions between

Beauvoir and cinema, and articulate the differences in my film choices. I'm looking forward to sharing a scotch in person one day soon.

Thanks to Julia-Hammett-Jamart and Walter Tschacher who provided clarification with translations in relation to *The Night Porter*. Thanks to Federico Pacchioni who sourced hard to find Liliana Cavani films during lockdown. Thanks to Sam Girgus and Will Brown who also offered comment and criticisms on drafts of the book, which helped me to shore up my own position on many points. Thanks also to the anonymous reviewers who were very supportive of the book and offered suggestions that helped me clarify future applications and directions of Beauvoir's notion of ambiguity. Thank you to Gillian Leslie who is an exceptional editor – professional, helpful and kind – and who showed great interest in the project from day one. Thanks also to Sam Johnson and Caitlin Murphy – it is an absolute pleasure to work with people who are friendly and respond so quickly to emails. Thank you to Lilies Films for the permission and honour to use an image from Céline Sciamma's *Portrait of a Lady on Fire* (*Portrait de la jeune fille en feu*) for the cover.

Amber Power was a formidable graduate research assistant, offering an eagle eye on draft chapters. Thanks also to the students in my spring 2021 Film, Gender and Sexuality class who were introduced to many of the ideas present in this book. Even in the world of zoom, their discussion and feedback on the links between Beauvoir's philosophy and film choices were instructive and helped affirm the longevity as well as the limits of her ideas in the twenty-first century.

Toward the end of writing *Ambiguous Cinema*, my mother-in-law, Ella, passed away from cancer. I loved her very much. In *A Very Easy Death*, Beauvoir wrote of her own mother's death to cancer, saying that no-one dies 'from being born, nor from having lived, nor from old age. You die from *something*' (1965: 105). Ella taught me what it is to die *with* something – dignity and a refusal to release your agency. As I write this, I can hear her saying: 'I don't know about that', fingers tapping and all. Thanks to Linda and Paul, who have shown that while this past year has been hard, distance is only ever geographical. And thanks to Fiona for her special friendship and trustworthy feedback on my image choices.

Lastly, thank you to my Patrick. You have read this book in all its many versions, seeing it transition from its early focus on adolescence to something quite different, and were so supportive every step of the way. We worked together writing our respective books side-by-side for close to a year and this experience has become one of my most cherished memories. This book is also dedicated to you, once again, with all my love.

Introduction

A challenge in writing *Ambiguous Cinema*, one that often rears its head in the field of film-philosophy, lay in crafting the right balance between an exposition of philosophy and its relevance or application to the study of cinema, and our lived experience with the moving-image. How much philosophy is too much? When and where is the right moment to introduce and engage with film? If the project is to break new ground, or illuminate a fresh or overlooked philosophical approach, where should the emphasis lie? In the outline of philosophical concepts? In the illumination of how such concepts can help us think more ethically or morally with film as exemplar? Or in demonstrating that films themselves are works of philosophy, which, when merged with the right tools (or philosophical thinkers), make it possible to twist our eyes and bodies to more reciprocal and moral perspectives and/or behaviours? There will be the desire to find a neat and tidy definition of ambiguity in the opening pages of this book, but I encourage the reader to resist that yearning and accept a slower working through of Simone de Beauvoir's idea so that the entire notion of ambiguity can become a more personal, embodied, debated, self-defined concept and experience as it relates to the study of one's relationship with film.

However, it is worth highlighting the several interconnected themes that operate throughout this book as a way to ameliorate the frustration a suspended definition incurs. At times, the elaboration of Simone de Beauvoir's philosophy of ambiguity (and the philosophy of other thinkers) takes centre stage, delaying a discussion of the selected film. This might seem as though the film part of 'film-philosophy' is left behind but given that Beauvoir's philosophy has had slight attention within the field of film studies, I felt it necessary to spend time establishing the different inflections of how her notion of ambiguity evolved, rather than provide a strict, and therefore limiting, definition. This is so readers might determine for themselves the ways in which Beauvoir's thinking impacts their own film experience alongside the films I have elected to examine.

Firstly, and primarily, I situate the specific notion of ambiguity as a thread that runs through Beauvoir's varied body of work. Ambiguity, as Beauvoir devises it, is not to be understood as a definable concept, rather she draws attention to it in order to unhinge our way of thinking and relating to others in the world. Her idea of ambiguity evolves as she specifically thinks through the ways in which each of us make choices and relate to the world around us, foregrounding situations and sensations of uncertainty that frame how 'ambiguous experience' comes to be recognised, or perhaps more accurately, felt and sensed. What is ambiguous for me, may not necessarily be ambiguous for you, and even further, there are differences between individual and cultural experiences of ambiguity which are dependent on turbulent histories related to cultural identity politics (such as race, gender, sexuality, age, class, ability, and so on). At the heart of Beauvoir's idea of ambiguity, what drives her philosophy of existentialist ethics, is an understanding of freedom that is dependent on recognising the role others play in our lives – not just the act of recognition, however; Beauvoir says that in order for our freedom to exist, we must reciprocate our recognition of the other's freedom. To paraphrase her, we cannot rely on the past to determine our future and if we accept this uncertainty, this ambiguity, we can see that relations with others are an important (if not the most important) part in becoming and acting ethically. In its own modest way, this book aims to continue that project with a specific study of ambiguity as it transpires within the situation of film experience.

Therefore, in each chapter of this book, a particular aspect of ambiguity is discussed in terms of Beauvoir's writing, where her different works are explored to examine how we might think about the implications her idea of ambiguity holds for film and film experience. As I note in several places throughout *Ambiguous Cinema*, the specificity of Beauvoir's idea of ambiguity underwrites her philosophical innovation, establishing a legacy that is often overlooked in favour of the bias for men doing philosophy (in film studies, and the particular area of phenomenology, this is typically Jean-Paul Sartre, Maurice Merleau-Ponty, and to a much lesser degree, Frantz Fanon). For the valorisation of these male thinkers, particularly Sartre, Beauvoir was often there first, even at times publishing under his name. Consequently, a second theme of *Ambiguous Cinema* is an emphasis on the difference between close Beauvoirian readings and close feminist readings of key films, which are not always the same thing. If feminist action is seen to be taken here, it lies in the prioritisation and questioning of Beauvoir's phenomenology, even if her concepts are not always specifically feminist themselves.

In writing about the connection between Beauvoir's philosophy and cinema, several widely held assumptions about her and her work tend to cloud or intrude upon efforts to showcase the complex and diverse phenomenological reach of her thinking, specifically how her idea of ambiguity helps us to think critically and philosophically about film experience. Given the strong and very popular association of Beauvoir's name with feminism, expectations of *Ambiguous Cinema* might be that it concentrates solely on classical feminist film theory or provides an outline of Beauvoir's own love of film. It does neither. While I do integrate and inflect Beauvoir's feminist politics throughout the book as an important hermeneutic of film analysis, the primary goal is to foreground her idea of ambiguity as the cornerstone of her phenomenology, and consequentially of her feminist and political ideas. Ambiguity, therefore, is shown to be a consistent formal praxis particular to Beauvoir's philosophy, as well as being a subject of lived experience to which she gives considerable attention throughout her many works. This dual aspect of ambiguity is argued as an unspoken but consistent presence and aesthetic in the films of the women filmmakers referred to throughout this book. While this acknowledgement is important in and of itself, *Ambiguous Cinema* uses Beauvoir's specific conception of ambiguity as a starting point upon which to build. The limitations of Beauvoir's own thinking around race and ethnicity are addressed, as even though she did not deal enough with non-White experience, her phenomenology leads me to the writings of Gloria Anzaldúa, María Lugones and Mariana Ortega whose different works speak to the ways in which a notion of ambiguity can be decolonised. In their own phenomenological arguments, these Latina feminists offer a more fruitful conceptual development of embodied and ambiguous emotional experience.

There is a tension in bringing Beauvoir and cinema together that deserves direct comment, particularly as the main method used here is the application of her phenomenological thinking to reflect on, and at time describe, film aesthetics and experience. Cinema involves embodied, lived experience which intermeshes our thoughts and feelings into a dreaming often engaged with an appeal to rethink life from new moral or ethical points of view. Obviously, not all cinema does this, but it is argued throughout *Ambiguous Cinema* that many independent women filmmakers do repeatedly tell stories that revolve around themes of individuation and freedom, as well as our desire for them – certainly those discussed in the following chapters do. Beauvoir's philosophy of ambiguity emerged as a response to the global turmoil of the Second World War, where the world found itself torn apart by violence, and where divisions of action and inaction quite literally resulted in life or death. For Beauvoir, it was literature not cinema that offered the means of liberation, establishing 'emotionally significant *communication* between readers and writers rendering freedom supportable and morally worthwhile' (Hengehold 2011: 193). But it is evident in *America Day by Day*, a diary that documented her four-month trip across the United States in 1947, just how much cinema had become a significant part of the way she included everyday life into her philosophical thinking. Oftentimes, Beauvoir turns to film to articulate how she feels: 'Next to my hotel, they're showing *Henry V*, with Laurence Olivier. I go in. I love the film, but when I leave the movie house, I feel unsatisfied. Those colored images didn't speak to me of America' (ADD 21). She notes the value and necessity in taking popular cinema more seriously, addressing the obstacle of censorship during the Hays code era in relation to the making of John Steinbeck's *Wayward Bus* (ADD 119). She also made efforts to view silent films by Douglas Fairbanks and D. W. Griffith at the Museum of Modern Art (ADD 341). Despite Beauvoir's enduring love of literature, it is very clear how important cinema was for her, particularly its role in thinking through the affective, and ironically, more psychoanalytic aspects of lived experience.

As women's lived experience continues to be impacted by ideological, physical and political dangers, I have chosen to focus only on films by independent women filmmakers in this book. If there is a simple, explicit point to be made in *Ambiguous Cinema* by linking Beauvoir's idea of ambiguity to the study of film experience, it is to recognise the appeal within women's filmmaking regarding our responsibility to face difficult emotional experience so that we might successfully realise an embodied ethical freedom – certainly for women, but hopefully the appeal will transcend such gender specificity. The key to understanding what is included as ambiguous experience within the context of cinema – a task taken up in various ways by the forthcoming chapters – is to understand how Beauvoir's notion of ambiguity offers us the critical tools to determine the connections between ethics, politics and emotion as involving choice, recognition and reciprocity. But most importantly, to understand that the interconnection between choice, recognition and reciprocity is always already tumultuous because it relates to freedom. Our choices (how we feel, what we think, how we act) are not solipsistic. They involve and depend on others. Are choices made within the context of film experience made independently from the film, or in collaboration with the film, as part of cinema's coloniality? Or are choices made in response to the invitation within a film, its appeal to introject and hold multiple, and at times opposing, points of view? The ethical questions raised during ambiguous cinematic experience emerge through recognition of a film's ability to appeal through its uncertainty (and oftentimes emotional turbulence) and to choose to think it, think with it, respond to it or not. As a result, Beauvoir's thinking helps to conceptually locate key philosophical themes that relate to and inform the affective aspects of film experience, feeling the political properties and ethical appeal of film. In this book, the selected films mainly concentrate on women's lived experience, but readers are encouraged to travel with these ideas and their implications.

On the topic of film preference, Beauvoir and I would certainly not agree. She avoided French comedies 'that claim to be funny' (ASD 179) because she thought them vulgar or boring; she found documentaries didactic (ASD 190) and believed 'seeing a film generally calls for less effort than reading a book' (ASD 177). And yet somewhat paradoxically, she was attuned to the political potential of cinema:

> a director who wishes to set up a real communication with the audience will take the greatest care not to arouse a mental disturbance that might cloud their vision: like a good writer, he will make his appeal to their freedom. (ASD 177)

It is the premise of this last comment that orients my thinking on Beauvoir's theory of ambiguity and the role I see it playing within lived film experience – even if I disagree with her about a director's intention to avoid mental disturbance. Beauvoir appears to contradict herself here, given she had previously argued for the necessity of interference in determining being: 'No project can be defined except by its interference with other projects' (EA 76). I propose a much closer (albeit at times, implicit) association between Beauvoir's phenomenological conception of ambiguity and the emotional unrest she saw it causing, with a contemporary object relations psychoanalytic focus on relationality and emotional turbulence.

The films I discuss concentrate on this notion of emotional turbulence as a central component of ambiguity. As such, several films appear to work from what might be seen as negative example. Liliana Cavani's *The Night Porter* discusses the need for ethical vision in order to disclose the negative reality of patriarchal privilege within heteronormative relationships. Cavani's film explores the ways ambiguity is embodied within traumatic experience, where the body as well as the mind is altered in situations of total fear and uncertainty. Similarly, in my discussion of Lucrecia Martel's *Zama* I discuss the tensions involved in situations of patriarchal dominance so that Beauvoir's idea of ambiguity is understood as necessarily involving difficult emotional experience. Yet, this is perhaps the precise point where I see connections between phenomenology and psychoanalysis as being worthwhile. If we do not have the capacity to acknowledge such difficulty then the potential for growth and new possibilities is denied – even further, the ethical action of reciprocal recognition is thwarted. In later chapters I discuss other films which illustrate more positively the role emotional tension plays in determining ethical freedom – in Debra Granik's *Leave No Trace*, Claire Denis's *Let the Sunshine In*, Lynne Ramsay's *We Need to Talk About Kevin*, and Céline Sciamma's *Portrait of a Lady on Fire* – but which equally emphasise the need to assume responsibility and confront the sensations inherent within emotional turmoil.

In the phenomenological–psychoanalytic link (two approaches often seen as oppositional to one another), the struggle for the expression of the self – its agency, freedom, and mental growth – is the key concern. I am convinced that an intermeshing of psychoanalyses and phenomenologies represents a core and vital value of cinema, being the opportunity to explore difficult, disturbing and ambiguous lived experience that we cannot think alone. The project of *Ambiguous Cinema* lies in examining Beauvoir's concept of ambiguity to consider the ways in which it is affected aesthetically through the cinema of selected independent women filmmakers. It also asks if the emotional turbulence disclosed in their films extends to a closer understanding of the links between phenomenological and psychoanalytic thinking regarding film experience itself. If successful, *Ambiguous Cinema* will contribute to the discussion of ethics, reciprocity, emotional tension and difficulties involved in the pursuit of freedom so prevalent within independent women's filmmaking.

The term 'emotional turbulence' is taken from psychoanalyst Wilfred Bion's 1976 article, wherein he describes it as the content and sensoria of latent lived experience ('what is latent is *emotional turbulence*' 1976/2008: 295), ostensibly within the context of borderline personality. However, to sequester emotional turbulence only to the limitation of this psychic pathology would mean to misunderstand Bion's aim. Bion understood states of mind as contiguous, linked and (potentially) evolving from one state to another, as though previous proto-mental states of being carried microchimeric elements in their future iterations. For Bion, emotional turbulence is demonstrative of resistance to change or the demand of psychological growth, such as when we face an existential hurdle and encounter turbulence which we can either choose to confront and attempt to work it through or avoid it altogether. Any life event that marks a change from one state to another 'would always determine a state of turbulence' (López-Corvo 2005: 237) and asks we make the choice to either tolerate or avoid 'the emotional turmoil' (Bion 1976/2008: 297). If we choose to bear the difficulty of complex emotional life, we facilitate mental growth. If not, we adopt what Bion called magical thinking, and what Beauvoir called bad faith.

In their introduction to *Existentialism and Contemporary Cinema: A Beauvoirian Perspective*, Jean-Pierre Boulé and Ursula Tidd observe that Beauvoir's fascination of cinema speaks directly to the thought and felt aspects of film experience: 'as she [Beauvoir] describes it, [cinema] activates unconscious psychic fragments of the past and mobilises them into present lived experience' (Boulé and Tidd 2012: 2). While I disagree with Beauvoir's view that one leaves their 'actual self ... as a conscious entity' (ASD 177) at the cinema door, I take her reflection on film-going to be more descriptive of the intermeshed psychoanalytic-phenomenological aspects of film experience than a straightforward philosophising about what happens when we watch movies. Beauvoir acknowledges cinema's capacity to communicate thoughts and feelings to others that people themselves might not be able to perceive, which is similar to Bion's view of the artist as someone who is able to convey meaning through images 'to those with less capacity to intuit' (1976/2008: 303). While we might be aware that emotional turbulence exists, we are much less able to specify what exactly it is.

> It is hard to penetrate what we 'all know' and to suggest that there may be something that has not yet emerged from the turbulence, just as there may be something – we do not know what – that led to the turbulence. Are we then to inhibit the turbulence? Or are we to investigate it? (Bion 1976/2008: 303)

On these terms, Beauvoir's idea of ambiguity helps to consider the affective and political impact of films made by specific independent women filmmakers, which critique present social tensions by exploring our ethical and ambivalent relations with others. Ambiguity does not simply (or only) identify difficult, turbulent or indeterminate moments of moral choice in lived experience; it also recognises their ripe political possibility. Feminist issues and concerns are not always at the forefront of the films discussed throughout this book, despite functioning along such clear political lines. Instead, the overarching sense of ambiguity observed within the films themselves permits a more effective investigation of the important role emotional turbulence plays in women's cinema, highlighting its political, sensory potential.

The following chapters do not, therefore, couch, concentrate or develop Beauvoir's thinking within the context of Sartre's or Merleau-Ponty's phenomenologies, although I do discuss how Beauvoir's thinking differs in response to them where relevant. Similarly, when Beauvoir's idea of ambiguity hits its limit, most evident in her lack of adequate attention to emotional lived experience of women of colour, the more productive avenues of Latina feminist phenomenologies help continue and diversify the embodied and political significance of ambiguity. Ambiguity then also functions as a critical tool that helps us to understand how Beauvoir's own thinking can be expanded and developed. By acknowledging its diffuse and labile qualities, ambiguity is positioned as integral to both the structure and argument of the book, tracing its continuous evolution as an affective concept throughout Beauvoir's varied body of work – philosophical, literary, political, autobiographical and feminist – to study its applicability for our emotional and political film-going experience.

It is hard not to be drawn into the history of Beauvoir's personal life as one reads her work, but *Ambiguous Cinema* is not intended as a contribution to the commentaries on her life. There are other works that already excellently provide such material (Bair 1990, 2019; Bakewell 2017; Kirkpatrick 2019; Moi 2010; Vintges 1996). The interrelationships between ambiguity (as a difficult but inexhaustible emotional component of lived experience), womanhood and cinema are presented here as a feminist phenomenological questioning. As such I have emphasised themes of choice, erotic experience, reciprocal recognition, emotional storms and ethics of relationality over those more often seen in feminist film-theory (such as desire, representation, identity, etc.). My references to object relations psychoanalysis, via Bion and Donald Winnicott, are likewise more interested with emotional and relational lived experience than classical libidinal drive gratification models, so to explore a different (and perhaps for some, unrecognisable) model within film and media studies.

Judith Butler writes,

> relationality is not by itself a good thing, a sign of connectedness, an ethical norm to be posited over and against destruction: rather, relationality is a vexed and ambivalent field in which the question of ethical obligation had to be worked out in light of a persistent and constitutive destructive potential. (2021: 10)

Examining Beauvoir's idea of ambiguity within the context of film experience intends to indicate the value and relation of her ideas to other fields of work, but also to acknowledge its limits and perhaps its destructive potential. *Ambiguous Cinema* takes up the interdisciplinary character of feminist theory, starting from Beauvoir's idea of ambiguity as an 'outsider' philosophical concept for film-studies, and moves toward contemporary feminist film-phenomenology. In doing so, it allow us to benefit from the slippery quality of ambiguity and its intertwining with emotional lived experience, so that we do not inhibit it with definition, but instead investigate it.

CHAPTER 1

Beauvoir's Ambiguity, Cinema and Feminist Phenomenology

Simone de Beauvoir rejected and avoided categorisation throughout her life, particularly regarding her identity and her writing, choosing to express alignment with a label only if it furthered her philosophical thinking on the lived experience of freedom. Specifically, it was through her writing that Beauvoir sought to inspire revolution. Yet, at different points throughout her second autobiography, *The Prime of Life*, she writes of feeling unable to act even while aware of the responsibility required in realising freedom. She reflects on her own inaction against the capacity of her friends, Colette Audry and Simone Labourdin, to participate in support of a general strike against the rise of fascism:

> For my own part, I was such a stranger to all practical political activities that it never occurred to me that I might join them. There was, too, another reason for my abstention. I shrank from any action that would have forced me to acknowledge my actual status; what I was refusing, now as on previous occasions, was to act as the teacher I was. (PL 132)

In this disclosure, Beauvoir shows what I see as her greatest strength – her capacity to reflect on her life and political position to rethink and remake it. She does not shy away from the cost of her mistakes, if indeed she agrees they occurred; rather, she demonstrates her ability to embrace ambiguity despite the struggle it so often entails.[1] Here, Beauvoir credits her experience of the war period as igniting a commitment to put action over ideas and is no longer satisfied to keep 'situation in life at arm's length' (PL 342). She saw her writing as the creative means through which she might exercise political action, which later evolved into more public engagements (such as interviews with television and radio, and participation in political marches). This new mode of embodied political action pulled her into more visible and vulnerable situations, confirming her early philosophical idea (first expressed in *Pyrrhus and Cineas*) that ambiguity is central to the development and evolution of an ethical life, and at the same time, foundational to rich but unavoidably tumultuous emotional experience.

After publishing *The Second Sex* in 1949, a ground-breaking work that obliterated long-essentialist myths of womanhood and presented a revolutionary perspective on White European women's sexual freedom, Beauvoir is said to have declared herself a feminist in a 1972 interview with Alice Schwartzer in *Le Nouvel Observateur*. 'I would say that today I am a feminist *in that way* [aiming to change conditions for women in society], because I have come to understand that we must fight for the concrete condition of women before our dreams of socialism can come true' (Beauvoir in Simons and Timmermann 1972/2015: 194, my emphasis). Margaret Simons notes, however, that Beauvoir's 'decades-long feminist engagement' (2015: 10)[2] is evidenced throughout most of her work and was specifically addressed in an interview as early as November 1949,[3] as well as in her many public essays for popular magazines throughout the fifties and sixties (2015: 12). Beauvoir herself complicated matters: 'I was apolitical and would not have availed myself of voting privilege had I possessed it, it hardly mattered to me whether my rights were acknowledged or not' (PL 173). It is hard to imagine this being true, as Beauvoir was not one for being ignored or unheard, and her work is dedicated to thinking through and supporting sexual and political freedom and equality for others.

Accepting that Beauvoir's work was interpreted as a radical philosophising of women's situation,[4] we might ask why Beauvoir made her statement as she did in 1972. In her interview with Schwartzer, she says she decided to be a feminist '*in a certain way*', suggesting it wasn't being feminist that was under question, rather that a particular inflection was now being emphasised. Her 'being-feminist' responded to changing cultural and political issues, as one might expect when comparing 1949 to 1972. There are certainly issues within Beauvoir's phenomenology of lived experience that she neglected to explore but it is to be stressed that she exacted a critical assessment of her own work often and without hesitation if she thought it warranted it.

Another possible answer is that throughout much of her work, both before and beyond *The Second Sex*, Beauvoir viewed ambiguity as fundamental to human existence; indeed, her experience of 'the pathetic ambiguity of our human condition' is what she sees as the catalyst for her writing becoming political action: 'I felt the need to write, in order to do justice to a truth with which all my emotional impulses were out of step' (PL 479). To acquiesce to a label readily, even one as revolutionary and contentious as 'feminist', would have been to submit to institutional thinking that prevented one's own capacity to think and act authentically, to be responsible for one's own freedom. In addition, Beauvoir never intended *The Second Sex* to be a work of or for feminism, despite it presenting a clear radical feminist politic in itself. It was her way of reflecting on the existentialist question: 'What is Woman?' (in Part One), which she explored in Part Two, via an examination of the lived experience of becoming woman: 'for the woman there is, from the start, a conflict between her autonomous existence and her "being-other"' (TSS 294–5).[5]

Beauvoir similarly initially opposed the classification of 'existentialist'[6] and 'philosopher', stating in an interview with Simons that 'Sartre is a philosopher, and I am not; and I never really wanted to be a philosopher … I have created a literary work' (Beauvoir in Simons 1981a: 168). She did however enjoy the notoriety that accompanied her publications and the place it afforded her in the public eye: 'I wanted to be widely read in my lifetime, to be esteemed, to be loved. Posterity I didn't give a damn for. Or I almost didn't […] I enjoyed seeing my name in the papers, and for a while the fuss about us [Sartre] and my role as a "Parisian Figure" gave me a good deal of amusement' (FC 46). Given her equivocality on being a feminist, it might appear odd to apply Beauvoir's philosophy to a consideration of women's cinema, yet the persistent question of what constitutes women's cinema also remains ambiguous. Ivone Margulies and Jeremi Szaniawski question whether the categorisation of 'women's films' still makes sense in an increasingly global world, stating

> the concept of women's cinema inevitably sparks arguments split between a politics of identity and activism bolstered by the explicit presence of the author or a manifest suspicion of any literal equation between extratextual and textual presences, or even the usefulness of gendered signatures. (2019: 5)

Margulies and Szaniawski sidestep 'grand assessments on the situation of women's cinema' (2019: 7), electing to look more closely (and productively) at women's use of cinema, specifically how their engagements with film through gesture, aesthetics and thought speak to the diversity within women's lived experience. Yet despite the fruitful and critical thought presented within their collection, there is no discussion or engagement with Beauvoir's philosophy.

Another reason for questioning Beauvoir's 1972 declaration is that it had political purchase; she had become a member of the MLF (*Mouvement de Libération des Femmes*, The Women's Liberation Movement) and was now a part of the 'concrete and collective struggle of women' (1972/2015: 192), who were protesting for abortion and contraceptive rights. When asked by Schwartzer: 'Should the women who fight for their liberation limit themselves to the individual plane, or move on to collective action?', Beauvoir was resolute in her support: 'They must move on to collective action' (1972/2015: 202). Her early resistance to the identifiers 'feminist', 'existentialist' and 'philosopher' has received much discussion elsewhere (Bergoffen 1997; Kirkpatrick 2019; Marso 2017; Moi 2010a; Simons 1981a, 1981b), underlining her phenomenological attitude. As Sara Heinämaa explains, Beauvoir's approach was 'not to turn towards oneself but to become conscious of our true existence, that is, our relations with the world and others' (1999: 117). In many respects, Beauvoir's application of existentialist phenomenology in her study of women's lived experience and situation helps to address the key qualities and attentions of women's cinema which Margulies and Szaniawski note as 'bodies grappling with the status of their visibility ... the burden and exposure of their exploitation; with states, affects, and how they configure identities and desiring subjectivities in flight or subjection' (2019: 8). Beauvoir writes of women's bodies as situations, looking beyond the literal interpretation and limit of biology. If a body is a situation, it responds to, interprets and intervenes in the world it is a part of. The physicality of the body is not ignored; rather, it is contextualised as a responsive materiality to the world in which it exists. This 'responsive materiality' is explored throughout this book, looking at both Beauvoir's conceptualising of women's lived experience and the ways it has been extended by other feminist phenomenologists.

Beauvoir's thoughts on women's experience, the body as situation, and the inherent ambiguity contained within such situations and identities mirror the attitudes, themes and orientations within the selected cinema of the following women filmmakers: Joanna Hogg, Liliana Cavani, Debra Granik, Cheryl Dunye, Claire Denis, Lucrecia Martel, Lynne Ramsay and Céline Sciamma. Through the sensoria of their cinema, each filmmaker explores and affects ambiguous situations that articulate women's lived experience, their films showcasing various instances and experiences of ambiguity: moral ambiguity, emotional unrest, resistance to societal expectations, or indeed an overlap of all three. In each case, the narrative ambiguity within each film is exacerbated through its style, where cinematic aesthetics further complicate easy classification. Importantly, what we also find in these filmmakers is not solely the representation of these issues of ambiguity, but also the very experience of making each film an ambiguous situation in its own unique process. Often kept outside dominant financing and distribution models, these women filmmakers have been able to produce historically critical and aesthetically innovative work that is either deeply perceptive of women's living experience (and, at times, human experience more generally) or that succeeds precisely because of its capacity to foreground the affective emotional turbulence of ambiguous existence. This has enabled their films to share similar characteristics as those seen in Beauvoir's own philosophy concerning approach and format in her metaphysical writing. In effect, each of these filmmakers enacts a form of Beauvoirian ambiguity precisely because of the environment in which they must operate to make their films.

As women filmmakers are less likely to receive the same access and financial support in the film industry as men (Setoodeh 2017), they are less beholden to producer dictates; they can deviate from traditional and historically narrow genres and narrative structures, much like Beauvoir's own philosophical and novelistic works did. Indeed, with filmmakers like Claire Denis, her unorthodox style, inclusive of esoteric characters and complex narratives, has become her signature. It would feel quite 'un-Denis' if any of her films adhered to popular, Hollywood formats. Although, admittedly as her films have continued to become more widely known, her casting of A-list actors has increased – Juliette Binoche in *Let the Sunshine In* (2017) and *High Life* (2018), also starring Robert Pattinson. Similarly, Lucrecia Martel's film *Zama* (2017), her most creatively and critically daring film to date, had a budget of $3.5 million dollars – regarded as very low for feature filmmaking – despite the thirty or so international producer investors it took to make the film. This isn't to suggest that women's cinema, or Beauvoir's phenomenology, is more effective if it is intentionally obscure or difficult (although perhaps it might be), or to denigrate accessible and variable avenues for phenomenology and cinema, rather it is to acknowledge that rejecting labels and being able to exist outside conventional and easily recognised genres affords greater potential for risk taking and inquiry of lived experience. The films examined throughout *Ambiguous Cinema* argue that the usual prioritisation of financial profit is side-lined in favour of becoming something other than their textual materiality, similar to Beauvoir's novels which were also something other than literature or philosophy.

Additionally, the non-traditional format and approach of Beauvoir's existentialist phenomenology evident in her novels (for example, *She Came to Stay*; *The Blood of Others*, *All Men Are Mortal*; *The Mandarins*), popular essays and series of autobiographical writings foregrounds the significance of ambiguity in human existence as well as its relationship to becoming. For Beauvoir, philosophy was to be lived and not limited to reading or writing (though for her, both were inextricably linked). Ambiguity was a core component within her oeuvre; a constant notion that grew richer over the course of her writings. In *The Prime of Life* she claims:

> If a theory convinced me, it did not remain exterior to me; it changed my relation to the world; it coloured my experience. In short, I had a sound capacity to adopt, a critical sense to develop; for me philosophy was a living reality. (PL 178)

From this we can interpret that it was not enough for Beauvoir to simply observe and write about ambiguity structuring human existence; she had to respond completely, in full embodied orientation to live a new ambiguous worldview.

This awareness, and the struggle it often entails, is very much present in the films discussed throughout this book, albeit via different yet distinctive aesthetic means. It is a convenient classification, given the intention of this book, to group the films of these women filmmakers as being exemplars of film-philosophy, or more specifically as examples of feminist film-phenomenology. The range of films, however, acknowledges the difficulties associated with labelling as previously highlighted and intends to combat any prescriptive classification. Instead, the aim is to enlist Beauvoir's own diversity in form, genre and focus to suggest that a feminist film-phenomenology is a state of (constantly) ambiguous becoming, and this is part of the appeal of Beauvoir's writing – to apply her ideas to cinematic experience, particularly attending to women filmmakers to echo a resistance of what 'women's cinema' might mean and to foreground the role ambiguity plays in the becoming of women's cinema. *Ambiguous Cinema*, therefore, centres Beauvoir's phenomenological concept of ambiguity as a defining feature of women's cinema, drawing heavily on her original thinking regarding the embodied situation, introduced in her early works such as *Pyrrhus and Cineas* and *The Ethics of Ambiguity*, later examined more comprehensively in *The Second Sex* and with further nuance in 'Must We Burn Sade?' While I explore some of Beauvoir's smaller pieces of writing, these are the core texts to which I return throughout the book.[7]

A core argument of *Ambiguous Cinema* is that the varied styles of independent women filmmakers (specifically those discussed in this book) act as political action, given the portrayal of difficult and tense emotional experience that is so often central to their stories, concentrating on responsibility, freedom and feminine becoming. Cinematic aesthetics (editing, cinematography, sound design, etc.) affect the ambiguity of a film's story, the film-going experience, and facilitate 'freedom in the encounter' (Marso 2017). The encounter is not just something that we experience *in situ* but is also emotional experience that returns to us affectively post-event (if at all).

Jenny Chamarette's emphasis on intersectionality shows that 'Phenomenolo-*gies* extend far beyond the field of philosophy ... feminist phenomenologies "inform" the study of film no more and no less than the study of film informs the development of feminist phenomenologies' (2018: 187). While Chamarette does not specifically concentrate on Beauvoir's phenomenology or the idea of ambiguity, she does foreground the necessity of addressing complex embodiment (inclusive of diverse and divergent disabilities) when theorising subjectivity within phenomenological approaches, noting that 'films become, in effect, a form of phenomenological praxis, which is feminist, intersectional, and complexly embodied' (2018: 196).[8] [9] Such arguments balance out previous scholarship regarding film-phenomenology which has historically been framed by canonical voices, staying close to the works of Edmund Husserl or Maurice Merleau-Ponty, rarely focusing on specific feminist or queer identity politics or ethical critique.[10] Works that move away from Husserl or Merleau-Ponty within film studies[11] do engage more directly with feminist and queer perspectives, and such research has been instrumental in igniting a new wave of feminist film theory that merges with feminist phenomenology, yet there is still work to be done.

While Beauvoir is located as a point of origin for feminist film-phenomenology throughout *Ambiguous Cinema*, I have accentuated her philosophy of ambiguity so that I can include perspectives from other pivotal authors of feminist phenomenology such as Lori Jo Marso, Gail Weiss, Iris Marion Young, Sonia Kruks, Sara Heinämaa and Debra Bergoffen (among others), whose research has sought to establish an association between ambiguity and political significance for sensory lived experience. To continue 'interference with other projects', I extend the significance of Beauvoir's notion of ambiguity through the writing of Latina feminist phenomenologists, such as Gloria Anzaldúa, Linda Martín Alcoff, María Lugones and Mariana Ortega whose work has also acknowledged the critical importance of ambiguity within lived racial experience as embodied and emotional tension. These authors have included greater multiplicity regarding women-of-colour's situation much more effectively, drawing attention to key existential principles, such as intersectionality and intermeshedness, in ways that Beauvoir did not. Therefore, while *Ambiguous Cinema* situates Beauvoir as a key figure for film-phenomenology, it also indicates other projects that help contextualise and concretise the link between the scholarly perspectives of feminist phenomenology, film theory and intersectional and intermeshed feminisms more broadly.

I focus on a phenomenological rather than specifically feminist line of inquiry, further linking these areas of thought within film-phenomenology. In this way, I take up Constance Penley's question posed in *The Future of an Illusion: Film, Feminism and Psychoanalysis*:

> Phenomenology [is] permeating all the new writing on avant-garde film, what consequences might this have for developing a methodology (or methodologies) of film analysis? And further, how does this kind of criticism relate to current developments in theoretical work on film? (1989: 35)

While Penley viewed the phenomenological approach as 'limited to a descriptive mode and an overly confining model of film as an "analogue of consciousness"' (1989: 37), she nevertheless acknowledged its relevance in addressing the life and critical function of cinema. This is the work that is left to do for film-phenomenologists – to account for the political and ethical purchase of a phenomenological approach to the study of the moving-image and its cultures, particularly addressing films that explore ambiguous lived experiences of selfhood and subjectivity so often seen in women's filmmaking.

While my intention throughout is to focus on women's ambiguous situation and experience in/with cinema, I also view the cinemas of the women filmmakers collated here as a 'seriality', with their films offering close and sustained study of the ambiguity specific to women's embodied situation. In some respects, this responds to Beauvoir's 1972 'declaration', wherein she emphasised collective feminist action. I am mindful of associating films whose main point of similarity appears to be that they are made by women, thereby unintentionally invoking an essentialist frame. Instead, these women filmmakers are brought together for the specific purpose of examining themes and tensions of ambiguity as they manifest in aesthetic, narrative and emotional contexts, presented through varying filmmaking praxes that evoke different versions of social critique on being and becoming woman, not always in the direct or overt ways one expects. The distinct and separate narratives of women discussed throughout this book are to be regarded individually, but at the same time they also appear as indicative of Beauvoir's concept of collectivity.

Sonia Kruks notes that Beauvoir 'anticipates the notion of [Sartre's] "collective"' (2012: 67), and her use of the term 'collective' is extended here to follow the Sartrean conception of 'an anonymous "series" of individuals who are unified passively and "externally" to their own intentions and practices [...] [the concept of collective] does not produce shared internal and intentional bonds among its members' (Kruks 2012: 68). Indeed, Kruks works through the political significance of Beauvoir's theory of ambiguity by accentuating the importance of being aware of how a sense of collectivity informs and structures our capacity to confront our own individual ambiguous existence: 'Although our ambiguous ontological condition must be assumed by each individually it is also a collective one, and ambiguity will also suffuse our social relations' (2012: 33). Each of these women's films, either through aesthetic or narrative structure, assume respective ambiguities, and in the act of bringing them together I argue that women's filmmaking offers greater potential in examining one's existence and the vulnerability it entails. These women filmmakers have been chosen specifically for their focus on emotionally turbulent ambiguous situations. By foregrounding ambiguity as emotional lived experience, the aim is to bring together feminist phenomenology and existential ethics with other areas of film scholarship that have often been said to lack resonance or applicability.[12]

Helen A. Fielding and Dorothea E. Olkowski (2017) offer directions that take up more active political and ethical differences than the limiting descriptive mode Penley identified. In her chapter, *A Feminist Phenomenology Manifesto*, Fielding claims that a feminist phenomenology, in addition to its ontological bases that account for embodied experience, also includes critique of 'embodied perception [that] underlies the production of knowledge and grounds politics' (2017: ix). This emphasis emerges from Merleau-Ponty's concept of flesh (1968) so to articulate our relational and material enworlding.[13] In order to advance a film-phenomenology as a relevant, ethical and politically nuanced methodology, it must involve feminist, collective and intermeshed dimensions. It must also attend to emotional experience. Fielding writes, 'the political is about what belongs neither solely to the world of ideas nor to that of empirical facts but is instead enacted in the realm of unpredictable human relations, which is the intertwining of ideas, experience, materiality and action' (2017: ix). Fielding's claim is as convincing as it is timely, particularly as it underscores the interrelational and intersectional world, concurrently situating such potential encounters as actions of responsibility and freedom. Fielding further applies Merleau-Ponty's phenomenology of perception as a method of responsibility, citing from *Humanism and Terror* and suggesting that for phenomenology to transcend its limiting descriptive mode it must 'confront ideas with the social functions they claim to articulate, to compare our perspectives with others, and to relate our ethics to our politics' (Merleau-Ponty 1969: 177). Merleau-Ponty's phenomenology illustrates an existentialist and temporal emphasis which attends to the unavoidable presence of the Other in our enworlded situations, '[t]he phenomenal subject inhabits a world that has already been constituted by others and other forces that in turn shape the subject ... reality is creatively brought into appearance in the in-between of points of view and world(s) we inhabit' (Fielding 2017: x). Fielding is, of course, referring to the lived subject rather than a field of study but there is much to be gained by extending her ideas to the field of cinema studies and indeed film-phenomenology. In Chapter 5, I discuss the extent to which Merleau-Ponty's phenomenology of situation influenced Beauvoir's own philosophy of ambiguity, which she intricately tied to ethical action.

Ambiguity and Emotional Turbulence in Joanna Hogg's *The Souvenir*

In the cinemas of the women filmmakers discussed throughout *Ambiguous Cinema*, I focus on their engagement with women's turbulent emotional experience so often overlooked or fetishised within cinema. These women filmmakers creatively and boldly incorporate ambiguity (determined here via Beauvoir's philosophy) as a central thrust in their films, the consequences of which are complex, nuanced and diverse statements about the personal lived experience of women, going beyond normative, and in some cases, Western, cis-gendered, and White experience. As an introductory example, Joanna Hogg's semi-autobiographical film *The Souvenir* (2019) helps to situate the core themes of this book – ambiguity, becoming, and emotional turbulence in women's lived experience.

Julie (Honor Swinton Byrne) is an upper middle-class, twenty-something woman at film school, working on her first feature film about a boy, his mother and their existence in Sunderland, England. Sunderland, a heavy-industry city known for coalmining, shipbuilding and car manufacturing in the mid- to late 1980s (the period when *The Souvenir* is set), is juxtaposed against the economic security and reality of Julie's situation. It is an early signal in the film of the importance of ambiguity and its reliance on aesthetic tension, particularly in terms of the clash between perceiving and being perceived. Julie's film, as an extension of her desires, draws on the adolescent boy character, sixteen-year-old Tony, to negotiate memory, location, family and selfhood. We never see this film or fictional boy, Tony, and it is implied that Julie ends up making a different film. However, it is enough that her story of Tony introduces the film and establishes its motifs of ambiguity and becoming within the experience of moral choice and existential action, extending from Julie herself. *The Souvenir* opens with Julie being interviewed by a Sunderland radio station, where she speaks about her film, specifically the character of Tony:

> JULIE
> He is very insecure and he's shy and he's lived in Sunderland his whole life and he has this overwhelming affection and love for his mother. He absolutely adores her; he almost has an obsession with her and has a constant dream of her dying. This fear inside him, he just can't bear the idea of losing her and of course, in the end, she dies.

Told via voiceover, Julie's plot summary is laid over a series of still black-and-white photographs that are understood to be images of Sunderland; as a visual treatment, they suggest the aesthetic Julie wishes to capture in her film.

Julie's being-in-the-world (first foregrounded as her privilege, later extending to include her femininity) is therefore introduced immediately at a distance. We hear her but don't see her until two minutes into the film. The opening sequence allows a situated tension to emerge, the reality of Julie's social class and home – heard in her voice over the radio, and then seen via a party in her Knightsbridge flat – is far removed from the economically depressed Sunderland of the 1980s. Class is also a key ambiguity between her and Anthony (Tom Burke), the man she falls in love with. Anthony is a civil servant for the British Home Office (or so we are led to believe) and the film follows their relationship, most specifically from Julie's point of view and experience. While Julie's student film fades to the background in terms of narrative importance, its resonance and tension are transposed on to her and Anthony's relationship and the unstated divide in their socio-economic statuses.

An effective layering of film within film and character within character is established throughout *The Souvenir*, subtly leading us to pay close attention to Julie's inner world. Hogg's use of reflective pauses in dialogue is visually echoed via the multiple reflective surfaces of mirrors and windows. We slowly become aware that Julie's wish to make her Sunderland film is an unconscious comment on her own desire as something that impedes her capacity to be authentic with herself, indeed, to come to terms with her own situated, female, desiring and emotional self. Over time, we see the security and persona of Anthony for the facades that they are. The secrecy and deceit regarding his heroin addiction is revealed but instead of focusing on the moral issues surrounding his drug abuse, Hogg's film concentrates on Julie and the ambiguity of her suffering and, most significantly, her capacity to confront and act in response to her anguish. We witness Julie struggle with her tensions quietly, often through gesture, predominantly her clasped arms (Figures 1.1 and 1.2), but equally through the fractious and awkward conversations she has with Anthony. For these reasons, *The Souvenir* is an effective example of cinema's potential to engage with existential ambiguity in ethical and political terms, where it does not privilege personal experience as belonging entirely to the pre-discursive and affective realm. There are many places throughout the film where verbal and audio-visual language are critical to furthering the evocative impact of ambiguity, whether this be through dialogue, vococentrism or pregnant pause.

In another scene, Anthony and Julie are in bed together, playfully fighting over who has more space. It is not a sexually explicit, or even overtly sexual, scene; instead, they talk of sharing the bed and the dialogue between them is fun and suggestive, establishing a flirtatious indeterminacy. If this

Figure 1.1 Julie (Honor Swinton Byrne) clasps her arms around herself, a gesture of self-protection in *The Souvenir* (Hogg 2019).

Figure 1.2 Julie's insecurity is shown via comportment as she speaks with Anthony on the phone.

weren't enough to showcase the use of visual space and verbal language to foreground contradiction within their situation, the following sequence most certainly does. Anthony is leaving Julie's apartment; the scene takes place in-between the door to Julie's flat and the lift. As we wait with them for the lift to arrive, not a word is spoken in this interstitial zone. Anthony enters the lift and just before the doors close, he says, 'I'm going to be in Paris for a while.' Julie replies with a soft, non-committal, 'Ok. See you soon.' The sequence continues the visual play with space, which is now awkwardly filled with other frames of apartment and lift doors. The dialogue remains expectant with things left unsaid and uncertainty occupies the space between them.

Julie's capacity to act, to become an agent of her own freedom, is consistently shown as limited in her relationship with Anthony. The tension that emanates from them is predominantly a social critique of (heteronormative) romantic relationships, confronting the negative affect that occurs, but at the same time *The Souvenir* is willing to confront such difficult emotional experience to think it through. As such, it negotiates the necessity of ambiguity in lived experience and stories of relating. Tension is crafted through a range of forms: narrative structure, hesitant dialogue, and other sensoria such as gesture, space, sound or light. Julie is eventually confronted with Anthony's addiction in stark reality and subsequently ends the relationship, only to reunite with him later in the film on his promise of rehabilitation. Anthony is unable to overcome his addiction and eventually dies from an overdose in a public bathroom. The film ends with Julie in the final moments of completing her student feature film and embracing her future, albeit with a significantly ambiguous outlook. She stands at the opening of a sound stage door, her indeterminate condition evident in her vulnerability; she is dwarfed by the size and scale of the door and the space both inside the sound stage and the area surrounding it (Figure 1.3). Standing exactly in the doorway's threshold – neither inside nor outside – the final shot of Julie indicates just how far she has come in her ability to confront her own ambiguity rather than constantly flee from it. She stands in-between the escapist world of cinema and faces the exterior world; she is neither consumed by one nor the other and it is her body that establishes this situation. Beauvoir famously writes 'if the body is not a *thing*, it is a situation: it is our grasp on the world and the outline for our projects' (TSS 2010: 46). Here we can consider Beauvoir's use of the word 'if', as it suggests two ways of recognising how ambiguity might work in this scenario, relevant to the body. First, if the body is not a thing, we must say that it is therefore a situation, or second, if the body is not a thing, it becomes a situation. The first of these propositions can be read as a type of either/or situation (per Kierkegaard). The second suggests a type of switching or transitional status, so 'if' becomes a type of 'when'. Julie's situation thus embodies a Beauvoirian ambiguity; we have followed her bad faith of her own suffering throughout the course of her turbulent relationship with Anthony, and we arrive at the end the film with

Figure 1.3 Julie stands on the threshold, between her past and her future.

her – aware of all the contingent facts about her life that have shaped her newfound sense of self and action.

While I refer to other films by women filmmakers in a more detailed manner throughout *Ambiguous Cinema*, Hogg's *The Souvenir* exemplifies the book's main theme: an existential phenomenological investigation of the emotional conflict within women's films and the ambiguities in which they trade. Women in these films are not judged for their action or inaction. Like Hogg's portrayal of Julie, the women characters discussed throughout this book suffer from indecision, bad faith, traumas, cruel consequences or downright miserable events but they are not moralised or denigrated for their choices, at least not within each respective film story world. Indeed, each filmmaker makes a clear effort to craft an ethical hermeneutic, opening the intersubjective field of spectatorship to choice and responsibility. Viewers are free to accept the singularity of the women characters and their actions without necessarily adhering to their individualistic worldview. Claire Denis's film *White Material* (2009) is another good example. Maria Vial (Isabelle Huppert), a French coffee plantation owner, resists engaging with or responding to the civil unrest that surrounds her, despite the increasing danger to herself and her family. Maria's only focus is her upcoming harvest and the dwindling profits that she believes will come from it. Denis's film encapsulates the existential rupture of unrest through a fictitious civil war, situating both Maria and Cherif (William Nadylam) as two elements of complexity within a colonialist situation. Neither is offered the privilege that their view is all that exists or that their actions exist apart from others. Neither Maria nor Cherif emerges as victorious and therefore no moralism is asserted above the other. Instead, an ethics of ambiguity is maintained throughout, preventing any closure or unification of negative experience. Viewers are left to determine the meaning of the film for themselves, albeit using the materiality of the film to reach such a decision.

Contextualising Beauvoir's Notion of Ambiguity

One of the inheritances embedded within Beauvoir's philosophy of ambiguity for an analysis of cinematic experience is her conception of adolescence. I interpret her reference to adolescence as a shorthand for the first concrete experience we have of highly turbulent emotional unrest that is specifically associated with the demand for responsibility and ethical action. While this appears in different forms in her earlier writings, for example via the character of Françoise in *She Came to Stay*, and is briefly mentioned in *Pyrrhus and Cineas*, adolescence is outlined more critically in *The Ethics of Ambiguity* and *The Second Sex*, with Beauvoir assigning this period of life a highly significant role. As Kruks puts it: 'Ambiguity is the central theme on which, over time, she [Beauvoir] develops a set of variations' (2012: 21), and twinned with this evolution of ambiguity is the period of adolescence that remains at the core of ambiguous existence and the paradox with which humanity constantly wrestles.

For Beauvoir, we are occupied with a 'tragic ambivalence'; we are aware of our consciousness and being-in-the-world – it is paramount to the idea of the self (the view from within), against which we are defenceless from the action of others (the view from without). This awareness is not simply psychical; it is felt as it is known. The human 'asserts themselves as a pure internality against which no power can take hold'; we experience ourselves 'as a thing crushed by the dark weight of other things' (EA 5). The paradox we wrestle with – what constitutes humanity's ambiguity – exists in emotional turbulence, which results from the assertion of one's inner world against their experience of being ('a thing crushed by the dark weight of other things'). Toril Moi reads this fundamental ambiguity as a tension that must be accepted in order to act morally or authentically, '[t]he positive acceptance of failure is what Beauvoir calls *conversion*' – a negativity of being is to be converted into a 'positive source of our existence' (2010a: 297 fn 4). The ambiguity, then, lies in holding contradictory perspectives within our ways of being. When we see and embrace tension, we can find its potential meaning and freedom to act, the only problem is that we don't want to face it and instead prefer to avoid thinking or feeling difficult and abrasive emotional experience. This is the cornerstone of bad faith (*la mauvaise foi*), a term Beauvoir and Sartre applied 'to anyone who feigned convictions or feelings that they did not in fact possess: we had discovered, under another name, the idea of "playing a part"' (PL 128).[14] Beauvoir views adolescence as the period of life where we begin to negotiate our relationship to our worldviews and situation, where we either take up responsibility for our freedoms or elect to avoid them.

As Beauvoir conceives it, the term adolescence is much more about the lived experience of ambiguity, rather than simple biological teenage development. She refers to the interstitial phenomenal period of mental, physical and emotional growth that follows childhood, where ethical ambiguities are negotiated to determine one's own moral freedoms. To a certain extent, the figure of the adolescent body bears some significance, as invariably each woman filmmaker discussed here includes adolescents as central or peripheral characters within their films. More often than not, these characters are female adolescents. The adolescent body, then, is considered in terms of situation rather than strict biological, narrative or figurative representation. As situation, adolescence marks a period of reflection or negotiation of being and becoming. In existentialist terms, it is 'adolescence which appears as the moment of moral choice' – a lived embodied situation that involves the determination of one's freedom and most significantly, the decision of how to respond, 'in the face of it' (EA 42). While Julie is clearly not an adolescent, she does reflect a way of being similar to Beauvoir's conception of adolescence, embodying the tension involved in her moral choices throughout *The Souvenir*. As observed, she is often shown holding herself, with arms clasped around her body as though she were protecting herself against the actions of others; or she is quiet, pensive and avoids meeting their gaze. The tension of Julie's bad faith within her relationship with Anthony is stressed via these gestures and evades reciprocity. This is why her final direct address to the camera is so poignant (Figure 1.4). In this moment, it is clear that Julie has made a moral choice and assumes her ambiguity, able to face it directly and not avoid it or the emotional conflict it contains. In Moi's view, Julie has affected a conversion, a capacity to confront failure, endure it and turn it into authentic, positive experience.

Beauvoir writes,

> if what is called women's futility often has so much charm and grace, if it sometimes has a genuinely moving character, it is because it manifests a pure and gratuitous taste for existence, like the games of children, it is the absence of the serious. (EA 40)

Figure 1.4 Julie's direct address to the camera.

She argued that the complicity expected from renouncing freedom is imposed on children, 'whereas the woman chooses or at least consents to it' (EA 40). Children are able to resist the seriousness of the world; their lifeworld is the 'absence of the serious'. The serious, for Beauvoir, is the relinquishing of one's freedom in exchange for the false comforts offered by society, 'he loses himself in the object in order to annihilate his subjectivity' (EA 49).[15] By placing ambiguity as fundamental to human existence, Beauvoir is saying that our struggle for freedom will entail frustrating and difficult emotional experience, 'the world becomes present by his presence in it ... the disclosure implies a perpetual tension to keep being at a certain distance, to tear oneself from the world, and to assert oneself as a freedom' (EA 23). Being aware of this tension is part of our ambiguous existence, and therefore part of the emotional turbulence within our embodied situation.

Kruks notes that our 'ambiguous ontological condition' is individual as well as collective, incurring a social and relational aspect in our 'embodied subjectivity' (2012: 33). The emotional turbulence I am equating with the perpetual tension of Beauvoir's idea of ambiguity identifies the way in which freedom becomes action. These intertwined themes of ambiguity and emotional turbulence inform the structure of this book and are directed toward a discussion of feminist film-phenomenology, including other perspectives that relate ethics to politics within women's cinema. Beauvoir's early work on ambiguity explored the tumultuous relationships between moral freedom and choice, and in part this is why her attention on adolescence is noteworthy. An identification of the emotional struggle, unrest and embodied tension manifests in highly ambiguous moments where we feel the interpellative appeal to confront difficult moral or ethical choices. Further, adolescence functions as an embodied template which affectively (that is unconsciously) reverberates in response to the turbulent aesthetics, appeals for empathy and emotional experience we experience in cinematic spectatorship. Consequently, it is through recognising the inevitability of ambiguity in lived experience and the disturbance it engenders within the human condition – evident in the cinema of the women filmmakers in this book – that the films' political, ethical and emotional force works better as a collective than as individual films.

Foregrounding Beauvoir's attention on adolescence in her philosophy of ambiguity also highlights the potential lure of bad faith which relieves us of the responsibility of moral choice. Adolescence-as-situation, however, asks that we acknowledge the longevity of this responsibility as well as its emotional unrest. Beauvoir outlines adolescence as a period of awakening, or as she puts it, 'misfortune', which is the realisation that freedom 'was first concealed to him and that all his life he will be nostalgic for the time when he did not know its exigencies' (EA 43). 'Nostalgic' is a curious word choice here, implying fantasy and projection for what was or could be based on what currently is. Beauvoir's use is indicative of its meaning in the 1920s, when nostalgic narrative and sensibility was a trend in French literature. Here she positions nostalgia as the motivation for moral choice or moral attitude. Adolescence, then, is not simply an awakening of the links between freedom, responsibility and action, but also the period where character and situation intertwine, forever ambiguous in their relation. Adolescence as time and as existence works with ambiguity together producing tension. Gail Weiss notes that the inherent ambiguity of existence 'refers to a tension that arises through our making ourselves what we are (existing beings whose existence is defined as *lack*) by trying to be what we are not' (1995: 46). This tension demands a response through action, not for resolution but to '*live* this ambiguity in meaningful ways' (1995: 45). The situation of adolescence suggests a temporality for the negotiation of tension – a reflective or turbulent period wherein agreement with absolutes is resisted. Cinema offers multiple experiences of similar affective situations and false freedoms[16] or negotiations of tension, of contentious morality, of accepting or refusing responsibility. While such situations often occur diegetically, it is argued here that such negotiation, typical of a Beauvoirian adolescent situation, is interrelational, intersubjective and intersectional within cinematic experience. The ontological premise of such cinematic experience exists on the acceptance of these existential ambiguities and their related affective sensoria.

Time, a determining quality of cinema, is also critical for adolescence and our capacity to recognise ambiguity as Beauvoir outlines it. In no way, then, can an adolescent situation typify or account for a collective cinematic experience or even prescribe an ethical relationship within visual culture. Instead, as a veritable ethical ambiguity, an adolescent situation would identify emotionally complex experience and recognise variable pathways of action. Within an adolescent situation, there is plurality (or multiplicity) rather than paternalism regarding moral choice, or as Weiss puts it:

> between two mutually incompatible but mutually compelling alternatives, and this gives rise to ethical ambiguity in the fullest sense of the word, an ambiguity that must be decisively reckoned with, but which cannot ever be satisfactorily resolved one way or the other. (1995: 47)

Taking Beauvoir's emphasis on adolescence in her philosophy of ambiguity into account, I foreground the existential and affective lived experience of emotional turbulence over the ontological specificity of 'adolescence' when discussing the broader context of cinematic experience. However, it is worthwhile thinking about how situations of emotional struggle, and the being-in-between states they often throw us into, bear close resemblance to the moments of moral choice in Beauvoir's view of adolescence. A key point of this book is the idea that cinema allows us to recognise ambiguous lived experience as it is aesthetically affected through emotionally turbulent films, and most significantly, it is the films of women filmmakers that engender such ethical ambiguities.

At the core of Beauvoir's existentialism lies an emphasis on living experience – situations that can be rethought and remade, where woman's being is the key to engendering such 'becoming' or transformation. Eleanore Holveck notes that Beauvoir's 'emphasis on freedom of action is more radical, more existential, more grounded in the world, than Sartre's' (2004: 200) and women who grow up conforming to myths of womanhood might necessarily confront ambiguity so as to unmake and remake their sense of self. The films of the women filmmakers discussed in *Ambiguous Cinema*, in different ways, present characters who struggle to be free, where their actions in the world, both corporeal and psychical, are negotiations of ambiguity involved with determining authentic moral freedoms, responsibilities and the emotional tumult this causes (see for example my discussion of Granik's *Leave No Trace* in Chapter 3). Cinema does not exist solely as a singularity, but as a singularity it depends on an understanding and hope of community. In our confrontation of complex, unsettled moments, we affirm the existence of others and the possibilities of our moral freedoms. Cinema therefore makes possible intentional consciousnesses in the normative external world. The films examined throughout this book contain ethical ambiguities in their styles and stories, particularly in sensory and aesthetic terms. The aim here is to link the very real tension and anxieties of existentialist ambiguity that forms and informs women's situation in cinematic experience.

An Overview of *Ambiguous Cinema*

While Beauvoir's idea of ambiguity informs the theme of this book, the following chapters explore its variations throughout her work via the frameworks of film analysis and film-going experience.' Chapter 2 looks at two core features of ambiguity: Beauvoir's emphasis on the interdependence of others in *Pyrrhus and Cineas*, and her later emphasis on reciprocal recognition in 'Must We Burn Sade?' within the context of Liliana Cavani's *The Night Porter* (1974), specifically the erotic experience of Max (Dirk Bogarde) and Lucia (Charlotte Rampling). Arguably Cavani's most famous film, *The Night Porter* was vilified on release in the United States, with its political significance overlooked by many reviewers and filmgoers. Teresa de Lauretis defended the film, saying it was a consciousness-raising work that exposed the 'bondage' of woman's situation, 'a measure of woman's alienation ... from herself' (1976: 38). I argue that a similar defence (though not specifically about woman's situation) was made by Beauvoir on behalf of the Marquis de Sade's life and his writings, wherein she lauded the value of Sade's capacity to disturb his readers, so that we might confront more honestly the structure of our relationships with each other (MWBS 95). I draw a parallel between Beauvoir's defence of Sade and the political function of violence in Cavani's film through the frame of ambiguity, concentrating on Lucia, her gestures, movements and choice.

In Chapter 3, Beauvoir's framing of adolescence as political and ambiguous living experience guides my analysis of Debra Granik's film *Leave No Trace*. I argue that Granik's cinematic consideration of adolescence, resonant of Beauvoir's many phenomenological reflections, presents a productive, political comment on feminine becoming in the twenty-first century. For both Granik and Beauvoir, ambiguity forms the foundation of human experience, shedding light on ethical and political aspects of lived experience. As a cornerstone of their respective projects, each uses the textures and nuances of their creative expression to foreground the phenomenological impact of oppressive situations, drawing specific attention to individual situations to make plain the consequences for society at large.

Using *Leave No Trace* as example, I explore Lori Jo Marso's notion of the encounter, extending her discussion of the relationship between affect, politics and emotion within lived experience. While Marso refers to films, such as Lars von Trier's *Antichrist* (2009), it is her treatment of emotion as a political experience that is of particular interest to me. I consider her emphasis on emotion as a character of the encounter within the specific frame of a cinematic encounter and affective economy of adolescence. Chapter 3, then, furthers Beauvoir's notion of adolescence in *The Ethics of Ambiguity*, where the intertwined notions of ambiguity and adolescence are proposed as a means of theorising the sensory lived experience within cinema, specifically how this works at conscious and unconscious levels.

Chapter 4 explores films by Cheryl Dunye, specifically her 'Dunyementaries', which are a collection of experimental films that purposefully blend Dunye's personal intermeshed lived experience as an African American lesbian woman with a hybrid style of filmmaking – part documentary, part fiction (hence the Dunyementaries). Dunye's films exemplify Beauvoir's philosophy of ambiguity but offer a critique of viewing habits in terms of film content and manner of spectatorship. I discuss Beauvoir's phenomenology of habit in connection with other feminist phenomenologists (such as Martín Alcoff and Alia Al-Saji) to think through the relationship between racialised vision, situation and freedom within film experience, ending with a consideration of how Dunye's disruptive, experimental style realises Al-Saji's (2014) phenomenology of hesitation as ethico-political action that interrupts complacent viewing habits in the cinematic encounter.

Chapter 5 examines the existential concept of bad faith in specific relation to the ambiguity that infuses patriarchal love relationships, via Claire Denis's *Let the Sunshine In*. Beauvoir was highly critical of marriage and patriarchal love, arguing that if women look to such love as giving them everything (as a means of self-fulfilment), they put themselves at risk of losing everything (TSS 703) and can never achieve authentic love. She believed placing marriage (as a definitive expression of the love relationship) on a pedestal was an act of bad faith, a 'refuge in delirious imaginings' (TSS 705), and in this chapter I argue that Denis discloses the common experience of bad faith in patriarchal love relationships as a causal factor for the anxieties women feel resulting from the ambiguity of the lover's discourse (exemplified through the character of Isabelle (Juliette Binoche)). Denis's films often explore morally ambiguous situations, which the audience is left to negotiate for itself on its own terms (often in spite of the film) and *Let the Sunshine In* looks specifically at patriarchal love as an exemplar of difficult emotional experience.

In Chapter 6, the theme of moral freedom as a marker of ambiguous cinema continues via analysis of Lucrecia Martel's film *Zama*. However, instead of continuing primarily with Beauvoir, I examine work by Latina feminist phenomenologists Anzaldúa, Lugones and Martín Alcoff to extend and develop Beauvoir's notion of ambiguity. Ortega, drawing on Anzaldúa's (1987/2012) notion of the new *mestiza*, discusses the 'multiplicity of the self' and 'the multiple positions we all inhabit, but also the experiences of selves in borderlands' (2016: 3). Latina feminist phenomenologies open fresh avenues to understand some of phenomenology's key concepts (such as being-in-the-world and bad faith), pluralising our understanding of our sense of self and other. Ortega's work emphasises multiplicity in ourselves, what she terms a 'sense of *mestizaje*' (again via Anzaldúa), focusing on the lived experience of in-between space.

I explore the protagonist's, Don Diego de Zama (Daniel Giménez Cacho), incapacity to confront failure, which is his primary problem, and the consequences this bears for those who are marginalised and oppressed within his world. The chapter outlines how Latina feminist phenomenologies extend Beauvoir's notion of ambiguity through consideration of key terms from Anzaldúa's *Borderlands*, such as *la nepantlera* (a different sense of self), and the *Coatlicue* state. *Nepantleras* are cornerstone characters in Martel's films, being 'boundary-crossers, thresholders who initiate others in rites of passage' (Anzaldúa and Keating in Ortega 2016: 19), and the term *Coatlicue* refers to an inability to think or tolerate emotional conflict. Lastly, I discuss Lugones's notions of 'world'-travelling and playfulness (1987) to argue that a shared attention on the emotional experience of inner struggle is more effective in determining the anxieties and ambiguities involved with the 'sense of being an "I"' (Ortega 2016: 18), and this informs my analysis of Martel's film and style of filmmaking.

Chapter 7 outlines Beauvoir's position on the aesthetic attitude and examines it via Lynne Ramsay's *We Need to Talk About Kevin* (2011). The aesthetic attitude is not specific to Beauvoirian phenomenology; rather, it refers to the frame of interest that structures a relationship to and with reality. When we look at a film, we can adopt a moral attitude and therefore watch it through a moral frame of interpretation, or we can adopt other attitudes, such as the aesthetic attitude, meaning we view the film through detached contemplation. This is a version of phenomenological framing. Attitude therefore refers to a frame of consciousness; an 'aesthetic attitude' has meaning (when and only when) we consciously regard it aesthetically. Beauvoir writes that the aesthetic attitude 'claims to have no other relation with the world than that of detached contemplation;

outside of time and far from men, he faces history, which he thinks he does not belong to' (EA 80). On this basis, it is an attitude that withdraws, 'fleeing the truth of the present' (EA 82). The aesthetic attitude, therefore, presents a paradoxical position, an ambiguous experience within which we are compelled to consciously determine our intention and attention.

Ramsay's films purposefully disrupt normative attitudes of spectatorship and yet equally share a similar aesthetic and narrative. Her films revolve around morally contentious situations, stories of women (or men who look after women as with *You Were Never Really Here*, 2017) and their lived experience of traumatic situations. Ramsay's films often privilege characters that are disconnected to others, possessing ambiguous attitudes toward the people and world which surrounds them, yet at the same time do not judge characters or establish any moral position regarding their actions. This is left up to the spectator to determine, or in Beauvoirian terms, to disclose. Ramsay's films are particularly helpful in explicating Beauvoir's notion of ambiguity and relatedness, that human beings are equally dependent on each other as much as they are separate from them.

Of all the chapters in this book, Chapter 8 is the one that might be considered to be most reflective of Beauvoir's magnum opus. In *The Second Sex* Beauvoir famously wrote, 'One is not born, one becomes, a woman',[17] subsequently establishing her pioneering position that woman is not fixed but instead constantly negotiated and disclosed on the basis of power and behaviour. In addition to discussing Beauvoir's argument on becoming, that is the phenomenological and moral aspect to her 'becoming woman', I explore the notion of the reciprocal gaze through an analysis of Céline Sciamma's films as an expression of femme desire, ambiguity and female body movement. This idea of a Sciammian ambiguity is identified both in terms of visual aesthetic and narrative structure as a key tactic of acknowledging the body in/as emotional turbulence within lived experience. I draw on Bergoffen's notion of 'erotic generosity' to trace how Sciamma's films devise a feminist ethic by foregrounding the importance of the bond between women.

I acknowledge that the project of *Ambiguous Cinema* is ambitious, seeking to situate Beauvoir's foundational concepts (situation, ambiguity, freedom, ethics and responsibility) more firmly within the context of cinematic experience, and to think of ways in which her work might be extended and put in conversation with other thinkers. I argue that Beauvoir's notion of ambiguity and its constitutive part in lived emotional experience, when considered in terms of film experience, helps to disclose broader anxieties and ambiguities in life that we are not able to think through on our own. As I reflected on which filmmakers to include, it became clear that I found the cinema of independent women filmmakers to be most effective in engendering a sense of ambiguity, either through style or story. Of course, it isn't always or only women filmmakers who craft such affective ambiguous aesthetic experience, but few others do so half as well, and it has certainly suited the purposes of this book to only look at women directors.

Extending Beauvoir's concept of ambiguity and putting it in conversation with the work of contemporary feminist phenomenologists has enabled a discussion of embodied lived experience of race and intermeshed identities to emerge, as their work offers a far greater emphasis on multiplicity, diversity and inclusion than Beauvoir's did. I hope readers of *Ambiguous Cinema* will find more examples of ambiguous film experience beyond those discussed here, continuing to experience disclosure of emotional experiences that are unsettling and uncomfortable but creative and challenging, and through such turbulence facilitate a capacity to confront failures so that we might better tolerate the anxieties of our ambiguous existence.

Notes

1 See Deirdre Bair's bio-memoir *Parisian Lives*, wherein she recalls Beauvoir's sister Hélène confirming Beauvoir's adherence to the pursuit of truth: '"She will tell you the truth as she knows it, or as she believes it to be. *Not*," she insisted with some vehemence, "not as she *wants* it to be"' (2019: 254–5). Bair also observes this character trait when reflecting on Beauvoir's affair with Bianca Bienenfeld Lamblin. Bair speaks of Beauvoir's 'reluctance' and shame in seducing Bianca, believing her choice to include letter correspondence with Sartre as evidence of Beauvoir never evading 'her own unsavory behavior' (2019: 292).
2 See also Sara Heinämaa (1999: 119–20) and Kate Kirkpatrick (2019: 361).
3 See Kirkpatrick (2019: 450, fn 31) who references a radio interview Beauvoir did with Clodine Chonez (1949) on the programme 'Les jours du siècle', *France Inter*, 17 February 1999.
4 Stephanie Rivera Berruz (2016) points out that Beauvoir's assumption (in *The Second Sex*) of the 'typical' woman in France equates to White, middle-class French women and therefore in her application of Hegel's master-slave dialectic to the situation of woman-as-other, ignores the multiplicity of women-of-colour, their situation and intersectional and intermeshed lived experience. In Chapter 6, I address the gaps within Beauvoir's philosophy regarding women of colour and introduce the very important work of Latina feminist phenomenologists into the book's argument on ambiguity and cinema.

5 See Moi (2010a) and Arp (2001) who both discuss the historical and social contexts that need to be considered as mitigating factors in Beauvoir's decision to write *The Second Sex*.
6 See Beauvoir (PL 433), who is asked by Jean Grenier at the Café de Flore 'Are *you* an existentialist?' Beauvoir initially expresses insecurity at this question but at Grenier's invitation and insistence that she publish in his anthology, ends up exploring 'the relationship of individual experience to universal reality' in *Pyrrhus and Cineas*. It takes her three months to write it. The term 'existentialist' was originally coined by Gabriel Marcel, who along with Søren Kierkegaard, Karl Jaspers, Albert Camus, Martin Heidegger, Fredrich Nietzsche, Jean-Paul Sartre and Maurice Merleau-Ponty is argued to be one of the early philosophers of existentialism. Beauvoir's reason for distancing herself from the term 'existentialist' is indicative of the philosophy itself – avoiding acceptance and alignment with an identity that one does not choose for themselves is tantamount to conforming to systematic, institutional thought. See also Sarah Bakewell's *At the Existentialist Café: Freedom, Being & Apricot Cocktails* (2017).
7 Recent scholarship on Beauvoir's phenomenology and its relevance for the study of film experience includes Jean-Pierre Boulé and Ursula Tidd's edited collection *Existentialism and Contemporary Cinema: A Beauvoirian Perspective* (2012); Kate Ince's *The Body and the Screen: Female Subjectivities in Contemporary Women's Cinema* (2017), which lays out a context for Beauvoir's feminist as well as existentialist legacy and identifies new areas of thought for feminist film theory, and Lori Jo Marso's *Politics with Beauvoir: Freedom in the Encounter* (2017), which spotlights the term 'encounter' to show Beauvoir's phenomenology is best understood – is most effective – if we see our interactions with others as a series of happenstances that are always emotionally and politically determined. Marso foregrounds 'the language of encounter to supplement that of situation and ambiguity' (2017: 3), arguing that 'freedom cannot be experienced elsewhere than in encounters' (2017: 4), fitting well with a study of film experience and its affective resonances.
8 Significantly, Chamarette conveys the critical importance of an intersectional feminist methodology, arguing that any account of living experience must inclusively address the impact and barriers of socio-political, cultural and ethical life. With respect to film, we might further argue that if a study of the moving-image is to effectively evaluate how screened stories and representations of bodies 'create narratives about bodies and embodied sensation' (Chamarette 2018: 203), it must also ask what the consequences are of experiencing these screened body representations. Such phenomenological questions must include: in these films, are all bodies the same? Do they come together to offer something concrete about living experience? What happens to attitudes toward bodies if screens deny complex body difference? With respect to women's bodies, we might ask if a collection of women's films is

able to say something about the diversity and ambiguity inherent in living experience, female or otherwise, precisely because they lack direct coherence.
9   See Lauren du Graf (2018) who has written brief articles on Beauvoir's interest in and love of cinema.
10 See Casebier (1991); Sobchack (1992); Walton (2016); Yacavone (2016).
11 See Chamarette (2012, 2015, 2018); Hole (2016); Ince (2011, 2012, 2017, 2019); Lindner (2012, 2017).
12 Primarily this refers to psychoanalysis, referred to in the introduction and discussed later in the book with specific reference to the writings of Wilfred Bion and D. W. Winnicott, two object relations psychoanalysts whose methodologies emphasised emotional experience in terms of thinking, feeling and becoming.
13 See Jennifer M. Barker's *The Tactile Eye: Touch and the Cinematic Experience* (2009) which utilises Merleau-Ponty's notion of flesh to challenge fixed sites of film spectatorship, and even 'an empirical spectator, for whom the meaning of the film is determined solely by personal, cultural and historical circumstances' (2009: 27). Flesh becomes the experience of enworlding, what establishes the intersubjective, and as I argue later in the book, the ambiguous, emotional experience with cinema for audiences. In Chapter 8 I consider the notion of embodied femme desire and reciprocal recognition through specific analysis of Sciamma's *Portrait of a Lady on Fire* (2019) to emphasise ambiguity in visibility and sensation through our subjective encounters with the world.
14 See Chapter 5 where I discuss the concept of bad faith (and the difference between Beauvoir's and Sartre's versions) in greater depth via Denis's *Let the Sunshine In*.
15 Beauvoir's use of the masculine throughout her writing is retained throughout only for posterity in quotation. When I discuss her concepts outside direct quotation of her work, I amend the gendered expression as appropriate.
16 Beauvoir refers to false freedoms as 'alibis' in 'Existentialism and Popular Wisdom' (1945a), a synonymous term for bad faith.
17 For a discussion on the issues in Borde and Malovany-Chevallier's translation of *The Second Sex*, see Moi (2010b) 'The Adulteress Wife'.

CHAPTER 2

Must We Burn Cavani? Moral Ambiguity in *The Night Porter*

In *The Second Sex*, Simone de Beauvoir writes, '[t]he erotic experience is one that most poignantly reveals to human beings their ambiguous condition; they experience it as flesh and as spirit, as the other and the subject' (TSS 416). A woman's sexual life is dependent on her 'social and economic situation' (TSS 415) and therefore, in order to reach an independent experience of pleasure, she must first work to overcome objectification. As a consequence of her struggle, a woman is exempt from the myth of privilege that the erotic experience begins and ends with her sexual activity, whereas inversely, man 'lets himself be duped' (TSS 416). As Beauvoir sees it, a woman can embrace her ambiguity because she sees herself first as flesh, then as subject; she is aware of the difficulty and imbalance in her situation. Reclaiming her freedom and subjectivity, of course, is relative to situations wherein they are both reciprocated and recognised.

In her essay, 'Must We Burn Sade?',[1] Beauvoir looked closer at the interrelationships between privilege and violence, considering more seriously the situated freedom involved with intimate erotic experience, although her attention on emotional experience has often been overlooked in favour of her ethical and political arguments. While Beauvoir sought to emphasise the ambiguity within the sexual act where 'Through emotional intoxication, existence is grasped in oneself and in the other as at once subjectivity and passivity' (MWBS 60), Sade was 'absolutely ignorant' of such experience (MWBS 59). Instead, he could 'rejoin the other only through representations', (MWBS 60) finding confirmation of his self in the other's orgasms he believed he engendered.

Through an examination of the Marquis de Sade's life and works, Beauvoir explores the fundamental imbalance of privilege and the cruelty that is required in order to sustain the violence it incurs through spectacle. Ultimately, she arrives at the conclusion that Sade failed in his project of living an ideologically defensible life based on egotistical pleasure, acknowledging that while his privilege enabled him to valorise cruelty in his acts of oppression – 'he chose cruelty over indifference' (MWBS 94) – he was not able to recognise a capacity for action outside of violence. Sade 'had the merit of strikingly demonstrating that privilege can only be willed egotistically, that it is impossible to legitimate in the eyes of all ... [the Western bourgeois] wants *his* justice to be *the* justice' (MWBS 95). Beauvoir saw Sade's greatest legacy as being his capacity to disturb his readers and the general public so that authenticity in our relationships with others might be known: 'He obliges us to call into question once again the essential problem which under many faces, haunts these times: the true relationship of man to man' (MWBS 95). In 'Must We Burn Sade?' Beauvoir shows how ambiguity operates within the human condition by looking at Sade, his life and his works, and the spectacle of embodied erotic experience; ambiguity becomes relative rather than remaining abstract. The correlation she makes between how Sade lives and writes his ethics is a political action, one I argue is mirrored in Liliana Cavani's *The Night Porter* (1974).[2]

Beauvoir demonstrates how Sade, while guilty of torturous and debasing sexual acts, valued the subjectivity of his victims, 'it is immediately apparent that if there is nothing in common between the torment of the victim and the torturer, the latter cannot draw any pleasure from it' (MWBS 91). The pleasure Sade gained from his sordid acts was not in the act itself but in 'knowing that he had authored it' (MWBS 91). Beauvoir's essay foregrounds the politics of ambiguity as revolving around a central paradox. The torturer requires coerced recognition from their victim and from this they experience pleasure. As Sonia Kruks writes, this false reciprocity 'must acknowledge, however inequitably, the distinctly human, embodied subjectivity of its victims, endeavoring through their suffering flesh to harness their subjectivity to the will of the dominator' (2012: 57). The contradiction lies in the intimacy within such a relation that was absent from any real emotional intoxication,[3] and in addition to this there is a collapse between the spectacle of the erotic experience and its actual, embodied reality.

In this chapter, Beauvoir's philosophy of ambiguity is explored through the interplay of privilege and violence as it occurs within the erotic experience screened in *The Night Porter*. These two concepts are treated as embodied phenomenological, political experiences, via the ambiguous, sadomasochistic relationship of Max (Dirk Bogarde) and Lucia (Charlotte Rampling). If *The Night Porter* requires justification for the violence shown between the two lovers (and this requires us to assume the ambiguous situation of what 'love' is in such a context), then it would be to ethically respond and attempt to repair the wounds of any system that impinges on the freedom of others. This is the value Beauvoir saw in Sade's work, and what I argue exists within *The Night Porter*. Cavani's use of violence illuminates the destruction and oppression enjoyed by those in positions of power and privilege and to which they are oblivious; further, it can be read as making an appeal, a demand for ethical action.

The parallel narrative between Max and Lucia's past and present reflects a sentiment inherent in Beauvoir's existentialist ethics, where an appeal is a claim for accepting responsibility through recognition of how one's past affects and shapes their present and future. The different types and intensities of violence used in Cavani's film are necessary if we are to respond to the appeal presented in the film, to take up an ethical existence that requires a negotiation of our freedom and those of others, 'the fact of having a past is part of the human condition … We must try, through our living projects, to turn to our own account that freedom which was undertaken in the past and to integrate it into the present world' (EA 100). To observe another's bad faith is a call to confront our own. Beauvoir's interest in the role of privilege and violence within Sade's own erotic experiences connects well with Cavani's own cinematic project. In an interview with Gaetana Marrone, Cavani explains, 'Ambiguity lies somewhere between thought, fantasy, and the places we are used to seeing. They convey emotions that drive the story forward' (Cavani in Marrone 2000: 83). Marrone notes the significance of Cavani's style over story, particularly with respect to the centrality of emotion, and conducts a thorough formal analysis of *The Night Porter* in her book *The Gaze and the Labyrinth: The Cinema of Liliana Cavani* (2000). What emerges from Marrone's work is the interrogative and existential quality of Cavani's film, whose 'visuality entails a certain ambiguity, which is reflected onto the formal complexity of her mise-en-scène' (2000: 83).

My reading of *The Night Porter* explores its political and ethical interplay to show how Beauvoir's existentialist philosophy of ambiguity contributes to feminist film-phenomenology. Lori Jo Marso comments that Beauvoir's fascination with Sade's work was bound up with 'his politics [that] begin and end with the body' (2016: 61) and Cavani also centres the body within a similar context. She uses dance, a predominant aesthetic in the film, as a mode of embodiment to rework normative cinematic codes. Kate Ince notes that increased diversity in filmmaking, particularly with respect to 'female subjectivity is to undo and rework the codes that embed male subjectivity into film narratives, substituting for them new forms of cinematography and narrative' (2017: 49). In *The Night Porter*, the project of dance is critical to the provocative politic and ambiguity of erotic experience, especially in terms of understanding how it represents an imbalance of power and privilege in Max and Lucia's relationship. Drawing on Iris Marion Young's (1980/2005) work on female body experience and Susan A. Reed's (1998) anthropological study of women, sexuality and dance, I argue that Lucia's infamous dance, as a sexual politic of movement, is an example of women's ambiguous embodied expression. The existential and phenomenological aspects of Lucia's dance movement are then read through two examples of 'choice', exemplifying further her ambiguous being-in-the-world. I end by discussing how Ince's concept of ethical vision illuminates Cavani's aestheticisation of violence as an act of disclosure, making visible the necessity of reciprocity in our relations with others. In addition to Beauvoir's work on Sade, I refer to her early philosophical essay, *Pyrrhus and Cineas* (1944), wherein we find the formative features of her notion of ambiguity as it relates to our moral and immoral treatment of others, to the question of violence and its association with ethical action and the situated freedom of the self. Drawing on these two essays, written eight years apart,[4] I outline how Beauvoir's notion of ambiguity, a foundational part of her phenomenological ethics, helps to accentuate the political message within Cavani's film.

By looking specifically at the lived experience of one man, his choices, actions and writings, Beauvoir demonstrates how ethical principles are interlinked with our situation and connections with each other. Her attention is firmly placed on relations with others and how such relations impact us emotionally, often in unsettling ways. It is through her close examination of Sade that she evokes a universal comment on the role of privilege and its relationship to cruelty and violence within an individualist context. Using the particularity of Sade's stories and situation, she suggests that the circumstance of human cruelty, while uncomfortable and disturbing, is nonetheless a fundamental ambiguous element of our intersubjectivity. While Beauvoir ultimately rejects Sade's argument that violence is justifiable she does approve of his efforts to demystify the narratives of how we relate to each other, vulgar and unsettling though they may be. She does not deny cruelty is powerful and 'devouring' (MWBS 79), but rather for her, it is more significant that it exposes the inherent ambiguity between freedom and flesh, 'what [Sade] essentially required of cruelty was that both singular individuals and his own existence be revealed to him at once as consciousness and freedom as flesh' (MWBS 54). Indeed, this was Sade's failure – he lacked the ability to separate the spectacle of his abuses from the reality that they were. By confusing one for the other, he was not able to legitimately rationalise his relationships with others as anything other than exploitative and false situations of reciprocity.

The Night Porter evokes a similar Sadean situation of cruelty and false reciprocity through Max and Lucia's affair. Set twelve years after the Second World War, the film shows Max, an ex-SS Nazi officer, now working as a night porter in a Viennese hotel; Lucia, formerly imprisoned in a death camp, is now married to an American orchestra conductor. They rediscover each other through a chance encounter at the hotel, where Lucia and her husband are staying during his orchestral tour. The couple soon recreate the situation of their destructive relationship that first began in the extermination camp, now played out in the confines of Max's apartment. Their inability to abandon their co-dependent and tragic torment renders them incapable of surviving in the outside world. Even in the final moments of the film when Max and Lucia leave the apartment, they assertively uphold their concurrent past and present identities; Max in full Nazi SS officer uniform, and Lucia, in her 'little girl' pink dress. It is in such moments, where both characters stubbornly maintain the master-slave dialectic,[5] that the film incites a strong audience reaction. As Marrone notes, Max and Lucia 'unveil their most hidden feelings and thoughts in an interior that becomes the theater of greater historical realities; they are themselves the spectacle that stimulates the viewers' unconventional responses' (2000: 82). Cavani's films are renowned for exploring turbulent emotional experience, their narrative ambiguity, and being unsettling to watch. *The Night Porter* typifies the complexity inherent within an ethics of ambiguity and for such reasons, it has been widely misunderstood.

US film critics, past and present, have labelled the film as 'nasty as it is lubricious, a despicable attempt to titillate us by exploiting memories of persecution and suffering',[6] 'humanly and aesthetically offensive',[7] 'too bland even to hate',[8] and 'a piece of junk'.[9] Such negativity is countered by Marrone who regards Cavani's film as one that transcends the 'objective world, [and] gradually dissolves into an examination of characters whose existence is regulated no longer by philosophical truth but by aesthetic authenticity' (2000: xiv). Similarly, Teresa de Lauretis noted the film's 'reception in America was a disgrace' revealing 'a total lack of historical, social, and artistic awareness in the critics who, alas, set the tone for most bourgeois viewers' (1976: 35). The hostility conveyed in the reviews shows a vehement rejection (and ignorance) of Cavani's investigation of Max and Lucia's relationship, provoking significant anxious reaction. The intensity of the reviews went beyond any straightforward analysis of cinematic narrative structure or form (which ironically, when noted, was applauded); collectively the critics' responses indicated an inability to register the complex socio-political function of violence in the film, specifically the interplay between ambiguity, emotion and ethical existence. The derision further highlights Cavani's success in critically effecting cruelty typical of Sadean experience – *The Night Porter* disturbed its audiences and denied easy, comforting answers just as it intended to.

In her interview with Claire Clouzot, Cavani explains the influence of Sade on her film:

> In the world, it is not virtue that comes first, but crime. This is why Sade's work is fundamental for me. I think that Sade should be distributed as an elementary book in schools. At the heart of *The Night Porter* is a pseudo-masochistic story made possible by the extreme situation of women and men. It is the detonator that allows them to express themselves. And the two protagonists accept their situation, their relationship, even taking responsibility for it right up to the end. (Clouzot 1974: 42)[10]

Beauvoir's essay on Sade helps scrutinise Max and Lucia's specific singular relationship, and more broadly the ethical and moral ambiguities that exist within our relationships with others. In particular, their relationship both portrays and helps us to explore Beauvoir's specific conception of ambiguity as an emotional as well as ethical and political issue, directing us to a consideration of cruelty as an exercise of privilege, and the need for reciprocal recognition if ambiguous unity is ever to occur within loving, equal relationships. Cavani's use of violence is intentional; instead of side-stepping it, she utilises physical and interpersonal violence to evoke ambiguity, seeking to demystify the naturalisation of relations with others, particularly between man and woman.

Lauretis defended *The Night Porter*, arguing that it is a woman's film because it stresses the ambivalence and bondage within the 'female condition' (1976: 39). Marrone, too, states that Lucia 'controls the narrative movement' (2000: 94) within the film, to which I would add she embodies and directs much of its ambiguity. Aesthetically, it is Lucia's experience and situation that sparks the incertitude of events. She chooses to stay at the hotel and not join her husband on tour; she goes shopping, buys a pink dress similar to the one Max gave her in the death camp; and she leaves the hotel, lying to her husband about joining him in New York, choosing instead to go and stay with Max in his apartment. This 'victimization, initiation, and subsequent unbreakable bondage to her oppressor-Father-lover' (Lauretis 1976: 35) is explicable in the totalitarian situation of the death camp, but in the seemingly liberated circumstances of 1957 Vienna, where Lucia appears happy in her marriage and is economically wealthy, it is not so easy to comprehend. Lucia's economic wealth is shown through costume: her gowns are tailored, her nightwear is silk, she wears pearls, her hair is coiffured – all of which degrade significantly as the film progresses, regressing to mimic the extermination camp aesthetic. Max's situation is far clearer; he is someone who follows orders, either as a Nazi officer or night porter. The rationale behind his abuse of Lucia is evidently driven by a desire for power, for control and egoistical pleasure. Max is Sadean to his core, and like Sade he does not 'understand that social inequality affects the individual even in his ethical possibilities' (MWBS 93). Regarding Lucia, however, we must come to understand her through gesture, facial expression and body movement more so than through her dialogue.

Ambiguity in Lucia's Dance

The infamous dance sequence that confirms the ambiguity fundamental to the film, predominantly defining Lucia's situation, is told via flashback as the manifestation of Max's description of the biblical story regarding Salome and Herod.[11] The previous scene shows Max serving dinner to Countess Stein (Isa Miranda) in her room, one of the permanent guests at the Hotel zur Oper. On hearing Max's rediscovery of Lucia and his love for her, she says, 'what a romantic story'. Max, as is often the case throughout the film, is very clear, sniggering as he corrects her: 'No it's not romantic', then more indignantly, 'It's a biblical story!' qualifying (as if it were in any way uncertain) 'It is not very pleasant'. This brief dialogue is important because it juxtaposes the ambiguity within Lucia's dance that immediately follows. Max expresses so definitively how he feels about Lucia, the actuality of their relationship as existing on his terms only (he consistently refers to Lucia as 'my little girl'), demonstrating that he is cognisant of his desire, his egoistical pleasure and its fulfilment. It is one of the surest moments in the film that we see him 'fully aware that he is perpetrating emotional violence on the woman. That is exactly what he set out to achieve' (Cavani in Marrone 2000: 104). Like Sade, for Max to find pleasure in humiliating and torturing Lucia, he must first valorise her. Beauvoir notes that for Sade, 'flesh has neither meaning nor price if one can, in full tranquility, treat men as things' (MWBS 55), therefore, despite Max showing emotion in his declaration of love for Lucia to the Countess, the value of her suffering only fulfils Max's pleasure as oppressor, hence his allegory of a coercive situation, casting Lucia-as-Salome.

The flashback begins with a medium, slightly tilted shot of a Nazi officer wearing a plastic face mask, Cavani formally signifying the questioning perspective we are to adopt in watching Max's recollection. Nazi officers have gathered to celebrate something (it is not clear what beyond their own existence; this appears to be Cavani's point); there are streamers and glasses of champagne all around. The atmosphere has a greenish-grey tint, symbolising the uniformity and totalitarianism within the environment and subsequent coercion of behaviour, much like prison. We see a violinist, accordionist and pianist playing the song *Wenn ich mir was wünschen dürfte*;[12] other women prisoners are in the room, entertaining the Nazi officers. The first woman prisoner we see is dressed as a clown. Lucia-as-Salome begins to sing in German, and the camera moves to a deep focus wide shot showing the spectacle of her performance as belonging both to the film's story world and the intersubjective world between audience and screen. Her dance is viewed by two primary audiences here: the Nazi Officers (including Max) and the film audience. The shot establishes the objectification of Lucia through the violence and cruelty of Nazi privilege, which by extension forms part of the erotic experience. It also represents the inability of escape; Lucia is literally surrounded by fascist men. Nevertheless, throughout the vocal performance her voice is confident, deep and seductive, conveying an entirely different (indeed oppositional) persona to what we have seen of her personality throughout the film. She is topless, her small breasts and prominent ribcage demonstrating her vulnerability and exploitation; she wears a Nazi cap, suspenders, trousers and elbow-length gloves, the latter being the only item of clothing that feminises an otherwise overtly masculine costume.

As she sings the cabaret song, Lucia-as-Salome moves seductively and confidently around the room, her movements sexually suggestive and alluring. Reed argues that historically regulated movement in women's dance offers 'accurate indices of prevailing sexual moralities linked to the regulation of women's bodies' (1998: 517). Dancing is ambiguous; as female body movement it is concurrently empowering and objectified, initiating seduction and responding to the fetishising gaze. Reed's cross-cultural examination of multiple examples of women's dance compares the diversity of movement to foreground the politics of embodiment and cultural expression. Her ethnographic survey[13] complements Young's oft-cited phenomenological study of female body movement, as it observes the intentional and ambiguous sexual characteristics of women's dancing across a range of cultures and related movements. Reed points out the transmissive potential within the politics of dance, arguing that it is a movement that both interprets space and incorporates it as an expression of resistance and subversion, 'space is not an inert backdrop for movement, but is integral to it, often providing fundamental orientation and meaning' (1998: 523). She notes that dance is a cultural expression where 'women are encouraged to display their beauty, energy, skill, sensuality, and even seductiveness' (1998: 517) but not to go too far, 'dancing is also considered risky for a woman's reputation' (1998: 518). Reed further discusses ambiguity in women's dance in Islamic societies, linking theatricality with erotic movement as a form of dance-play. These performances are simultaneous sites 'of bawdry, erotic expression and also a social critique that reinscribes a patriarchal system in which women are defined primarily through their husbands' (1998: 518). These anthropological observations on the structured body movement of women's dance help to extend Young's description of female body movement in 'contemporary advanced industrial, urban, and commercial society' (2005: 30), identifying the ways in which the situation of dance might act as an embodied political reworking of identity, specifically women's situation.

The ambiguity of the scene is two-fold: firstly, Lucia-as-Salome's movement is fetishised, the dance is perceived diegetically as sexually explicit and inviting. The song's lyrics are juxtaposed against her gestures; the words express the melancholy of not being able to know how to be happy or sad: '*was ich mir denn wünschen sollte, eine schlimme oder gute zeit?* (what should I wish for, a bad or a good time?)', while her hand moves in a sexually provocative way down the front of her body, past her breasts to her vagina. Secondly, the environment for the dance is forced. Lucia, a prisoner of the death camps, has no option but to dance for her Nazi oppressors. In both instances, ambiguity is observed as a response to the violence(s) imposed upon Lucia's body.

The seeming confidence in Lucia-as-Salome's voice, matched with her apparent assured movement around the room, contradicts her situation as prisoner/victim echoed in the lyrics of the song. Lucia-as-Salome is ambivalently recognised as both object and subject as her dehumanised body is turned into a fetishised object of desire; the cinematography and *mise-en-scène* subtly affirming the false reciprocity of her performance. Throughout the sequence, we are shown how her movement occurs within the circle of men; she never moves beyond, behind or in-between them. Marrone notes that the camera 'tilts from left to right, a subtle move that conveys the distorted reality of the spectacle' (2000: 111); Even as Salome, Lucia is offered no transcendence, and as she is unable to free herself of her situation, she is condemned to endure it.

At the end of the performance, Lucia slumps in a chair, face turned away, her right hand covering her right breast. The camera, continuing its tilt, pushes into a close-up of Lucia's face returning to sadness, fear and resignation of one who is not offered reciprocated agency. This camera movement and attention on Lucia's gestures is a highly informative part of the dance sequence. As the song comes to its close, the point of view has shifted, narrowed to that of the audience so that her despondency can be weighted as it is observed. Lucia's frozen expression, submissive and detached from the power just seen in her performance, destabilises the stereotypical meaning of eroticism within dance. While I agree with Marrone that Lucia's dance is disturbing because of the cruelty seen in the exercise of privilege and the false reciprocity within the situation, it is less clear how this dance can be understood as a 'practice of transvestism' which 'operates as a symbolic disavowal of the gazer/master' (2000: 113–14). Rather, it is better understood through Beauvoir's view, that in such 'incommensurable' moments, '[t]o escape the conflicts of existence, we take refuge in a world of appearances and existence itself hides. Believing we are defending ourselves, we annihilate ourselves' (MWBS 93). Young writes that our lived experience of space is sensed through movement and that our relations with the world around us depend on 'the capacities of the body's motion and the intentional relations that that motion constitutes' (2005: 39). Lucia's dance is constitutive of an effort to escape the 'incommensurable' moment of her imprisonment (figurative and literal). It is a refuge of movement in 'a world of appearances' and as she presses herself up against different Nazi officers, playfully moving up and down their bodies, or sits on their lap, her feminine body movement in this closed circle of Nazi men exemplifies Young's argument regarding feminine spatiality: 'Feminine existence lives space as *enclosed* or confining, as having a *dual* structure, and the woman experiences herself as *positioned* in space' (2005: 39).

The sequence ends in a series of close-ups, returning the audience to the closed Sadean world of Max and Lucia; the rest of the party is excluded from the frame. A box is brought in and placed on a table, a gift from Max to Lucia. The camera slowly pans from Lucia to a close-up of Max, who like a selfish little boy, wriggles in excited anticipation of his own fulfilment. Max opens the box to show Lucia the head of another prisoner – Johann – who had been troubling her in the camp. As with the end of the dance, the camera repeats its slow push into an extreme close-up so that we might observe, through gesture, Lucia's emotional reaction – her horror, terror and rage. As the frame constricts, we are drawn ever closer into their sadomasochistic world, the sequence ending in disillusion and failure; Max sees that Lucia is not pleased with his gift and Lucia has changed nothing of her situation through her dance.

The Night Porter refrains from prescribing women's experience; it does not 'propose a female experience as a myth of origins or metaphor for The Human Condition' (Lauretis 1976: 35). Rather, Cavani's film uses the ambiguity within Lucia's situation to say something of the false reciprocity that exists in heterosexual relationships. It is a film that exposes the oppression of women's situation in marriage and in patriarchy. As Lauretis puts it:

> Cavani's love story is not only the story of the relation between two individuals, but of the world around them, of the culture and history in which they exist, of the values, conflicts, and inner contradictions of a society which is, whether we want to see it or not, our own (1976: 36).

Clearly, the US critics did not want to see it. Lucia's choice to return to Max post-war is not evidence of complicity or free will; after all, even Sade's accomplices and victims 'kept silent' about their torture (MWBS 57). Instead of asking ourselves 'what other choice did Lucia have?', we should ask 'why does she make the choice she does?' Unable to forget and transcend the dehumanisation she experienced in the extermination camp, Lucia is condemned to repeat her trauma and regress into the relationship with Max, a world that was once all she knew.

Speaking on why people re-enact situations of traumatic experience, psychoanalyst Judith Herman writes:

> Reliving a traumatic experience, whether in the form of intrusive memories, dreams, or actions, carries with it the emotional intensity of the original event. The survivor is continually buffeted by terror and rage. These [ambiguous] emotions are qualitatively different from ordinary fear and anger. They are outside the range of ordinary emotional experience, and they overwhelm the ordinary capacity to bear feelings. (1992: 42)

In the Freudian model (1914, 1920), repetition compulsion is thought to represent attempts at (unsuccessfully) healing the initial trauma, with the primary sense of powerlessness establishing the lived experience and damage trauma does to the embodied self. In re-enacting traumatic situations, the aim is to work through what has been lost, surrendered or ripped away (the sense of agency) and repair the harm. On this basis, it is possible to argue that Lucia, on re-encountering Max, is confronted immediately with her past, thrown aggressively back into a situation wherein she had no control. Herman argues that traumatic recovery begins with establishing safety for the self, and Max's presence, of course, denies any sense of safety Lucia could possibly know. 'Survivors feel unsafe in their bodies. Their emotions and their thinking feel out of control' (Herman 1992: 160). From this moment on in the film, Lucia's adolescent and adult inner worlds collide, spontaneously leading her to recreate her persecuted position in an effort to unconsciously reintegrate the event.

An alternative psychoanalytic reading of traumatic experience, through the work of Wilfred Bion's and his notion of catastrophic change, offers a stronger focus on emotional, lived experience. Bion is renowned for using words in new ways, requiring us to let go of previous meanings and iterations. This is certainly the case with his use of the word 'catastrophic'. In *Transformations*, he states that the main concern within the analytic experience 'must be with ... the emotional experience of the analytic sessions themselves' (1965/1977: 7). Any change that occurs from such experience he terms 'catastrophic' (1965/1977: 8), defining it through three features. Firstly, catastrophic change is recognised 'in the restricted sense of an event producing a subversion of the order of system of things' (1965/1977: 8), indicative of any situation involving traumatic experience. Max and Lucia's sadomasochistic relationship is a distortion of a loving relationship. Even in the context of their historical and physical environments, their ability to be together is restricted to either the confines of the extermination camp or its present-day configuration – Max's apartment. Both are inversions of the social order. Secondly, emotional change is catastrophic 'in the sense that it is accompanied by feelings of disaster in the participants' (1965/1977: 8). Max and Lucia's self-imposed starvation is evidence of such feeling within their situation, as though they have reached the end of days. The third feature of Bion's notion of catastrophic change includes 'the sense that it is sudden and violent in an almost physical way' (1965/1977: 8). What is significant here is the emphasis Bion places on corporeality and what it *feels* like to experience trauma, rather than the psychical reason that leads to the action of repetition.

These three features of Bion's concept of catastrophic change, when considered together, help to speak of the embodied and volatile lived experience of trauma. What is shared between the Freudian and Bionian models of trauma is the sense that an experience of transformation occurs, whether it is to repair and regain what has been damaged or lost (Freud), or is an embodied transformation that is felt rather than known (Bion). Placed within the context of *The Night Porter*, this would mean that we are able to recognise the trauma within Lucia's situation without actually having to experience it personally ourselves.[14] And by extension, we are able to recognise the bondage in female experience without having to experience Lucia's specific circumstances.

The Political Purchase of *The Night Porter*

Debra Bergoffen views Beauvoir's essay on Sade as an 'examination of the politics of writing' (2012: 39), with Beauvoir being less interested in the textual analysis of Sade's literary works and even the specificities of Sade's sexual exploits (although she does go into some phenomenological detail with regard to 'knowing' when asking if Sade was a 'sodomite' (MWBS 61)) than in considering how he reconciled contradictory 'aspects of himself' (MWBS 45). Beauvoir's interest in Sade is political – evident in her title – which echoed previous essays published with similar sentiments.[15] Bergoffen notes, 'Beauvoir's readers would have been struck by its allusions to other authors who, like Sade, were judged to be threats to liberal democratic values' (2012: 43). This sentiment can be extended to Cavani, whose threat to democratic values was mentioned in the US film critic reviews. *The Night Porter*'s notoriety resulted from a misinterpretation of its use of violence, Max's sexual exploitation of Lucia, and its overt statement that such moral transgression is paralleled in the bondage of women's situation.

Beauvoir interprets Sade's writing as political action, his stories unsuccessfully defending his debauchery as ethical action in the public domain: 'Sade is clowning when he claims that in mistreating girls, he serves morality' (MWBS 84). Even though Sade makes the effort to convince others of his actions as justifiable, he is inherently unconvincing. His aim is to demonstrate an ethics in his wickedness and thereby justify his torturous acts. Sade's aristocratic privilege is made plain in such an attempt to justify his cruelty as an ethical choice, and yet, his actions speak to what Beauvoir sees as the conflict between universality and individualism: 'in Sade, we encounter in its most extreme form the conflict that no individual can evade without self-deception' (MWBS 45). This ambiguity, what Beauvoir refers to as the 'paradox' of Sade's triumph, is how he helps to expose the conflict of our own pleasures against the demands and exploitations of the collective, 'to define human drama in its generality' (MWBS 46).

With respect to *The Night Porter*, Cavani uses the situation between Max and Lucia in a similar way, compelling us to look beyond traditional relations of morality to question human behaviour – specifically to observe the capacity to inflict cruelty, damage and trauma on another. Beauvoir's essay asks what Sade can show us, and as Bergoffen says, it is to examine what acts of cruelty reveal: 'It reveals us to each other in our particularity and in the ambiguity of our conscious and fleshed experience' (Bergoffen 2012: 41). Yet, to properly grasp the political purchase of Cavani's Sadean project that lies at the heart of *The Night Porter*, it is useful to locate the beginnings of Beauvoir's notion of ambiguity, found in the most formative of her philosophical works, *Pyrrhus and Cineas*. It was in this essay that Beauvoir began to develop an existential ethics, with ambiguity at its centre, as a means to reflect on our relationships with others.

Ambiguity, to recall from Chapter 1, refers to the uncertainty of human existence, the interdependence of the self on and with the other, and the inability to definitively reconcile our inner and outer worlds between the past, present and future. Ambiguity is a feature of Beauvoir's existential ethics because it speaks to the socio-political discontent of society, particularly within the war period when Beauvoir wrote *Pyrrhus and Cineas*,[16] evolving in her subsequent works on ambiguity. Even now, within different but equal global turmoil, ambiguity remains a concept that addresses the lived experience of persistent disparity that exists within our ethical and political relationships with others: racism, sexism, misogyny, homophobia, transphobia, and so on. Ambiguity, then, helps to identify situations of tension, specifically the tensions that result from contradictory experiences; the human is both a subject for the self and an object for others. Ambiguity recognises the concomitance of two possible and simultaneously lived existences within the human situation. As subjectivities, we are never just one, we are always multiple, always dependent on our relations with others.

From this foundation, Beauvoir builds a series of features to explain ambiguity, and to eventually outline in *The Ethics of Ambiguity* the paradox of violence and freedom: 'There is an ethics only if there is a problem to solve' (EA 17). As ambiguous experience cannot be avoided, we humans must choose whether or not to act. This is the predominant question in *Pyrrhus and Cineas*; as Bergoffen puts it:

> Why act? ... the matter of ethical action cannot be separated from the matter of action itself; for it is within the context of determining the distinct structures of human activity that Beauvoir discovers the parameters of moral and just action. (2004: 82)

Beauvoir's existential focus reverberates in *The Night Porter*. Instead of looking specifically at the propriety of Max and Lucia's relationship, what is and is not morally permissible, Cavani creates a situation that invites us to ask *why* such a situation might occur, why is it repeated? What sociopolitical circumstances make it possible?

Pyrrhus and Cineas begins with a contrived conversation between the Greek king Pyrrhus and his advisor, Cineas. They are discussing the decisions and action of going to war; it is an exchange of rationalising choices through action. Pyrrhus outlines his strategy, listing countries and continents he seeks to conquer. (Knowing the political Beauvoir that was to come, it is hard not to read this as a playful comment on the grand ambitions of the privileged.) Once Pyrrhus has achieved world domination, he 'will rest', to which Cineas asks 'why not rest right away?' (PC 90). It is a short exchange of a few lines which Beauvoir uses to establish core elements inherent in ambiguity: choice, action and reciprocity. The ethical inflection she proposes lies in the rationale for these three things. Why choose to act if we cannot be sure of the outcome? The sense of uncertainty is unavoidable. 'Pyrrhus must decide. He stays or he leaves. If he stays, what will he do? If he leaves, how far will he go?' (PC 91). Choice is necessary, and any action that exercises his choice will involve others; no matter the decision, it will impact on others and their situation. Beauvoir positions choice, action and reciprocity, therefore, as ethical concerns: 'If I myself were only a thing, nothing indeed would concern me. If I withdraw into myself; the other is also closed for me. The inert existence of things is separation and solitude' (PC 92). The significance of *Pyrrhus and Cineas* is the importance Beauvoir places on our relationship with others, more precisely how our choices and actions (or inactions) will always impact another's situation and freedom. Ambiguity is a necessary, essential aspect of human existence because we do not live alone, completely separated from other human beings. 'Only I can create the tie that unites me to the other. I create it from the fact that I am not a thing, but a project of self toward the other, a transcendence' (PC 93). Beauvoir outlines an emergent ethics of ambiguity, one that at this point in her writing relied heavily on Sartre's model, which claimed that no matter the act on the facticity of the self, the freedom of the other remained inviolable; the slave is as free as the master. Mercifully, over the course of her following works, *The Ethics of Ambiguity* and *The Second Sex*, this would change considerably, and 'Must We Burn Sade' reflects how far Beauvoir had moved away from Sartre's position.

Kruks notes that despite Beauvoir echoing Sartre's 'insistence on the "infinite," and indeed "sovereign," quality of freedom' (2012: 12), she made efforts to distinguish between different experiences of freedom: ontological and practical. It is fitting to note that Beauvoir wrote *Pyrrhus and Cineas* toward the end of the Nazi Occupation and the desire to work through the traumatic situation of wartime and the feelings of hopelessness and disempowerment clearly influenced the driving concern of the essay, which asks whether or not 'our conduct toward the other' matters (PC 125). In many respects, the spirit of her questioning in *Pyrrhus and Cineas* is echoed in *The Night Porter* – how are we to make sense of the emotionally destructive experiences of war? What legacies do they leave behind? Can we ever overcome them? We do not know anything about Max and Lucia beyond the war; our knowledge of them is each other, existing within the confines of their oppression and trauma.[17] This lack of knowledge of who they are beyond their sadomasochistic world exacerbates the ambiguity of their relationship. Further, we do not know of their sexual tendencies outside each other, or even what they are like as people beyond the

Nazi/fascist power dynamic. We have Max as man and Lucia as woman, and this consequence of *The Night Porter* is why Lauretis views it as a template for the heterosexual relationship. This is the result of the facticity of the film and what determines the ethics within the film, indeed Max and Lucia's transgressions within such a relationship.

Kruks views Beauvoir's distinction regarding types of freedom as signalling a move away from Sartre's account, where her attention began to concentrate on the interdependence in our relations with others. Kruks writes:

> Beauvoir insists, it is only from others that we can obtain an affirmation of our existence. For although others do indeed annihilate or objectify me, it is they alone who also can give my being the necessity I seek. I can to some degree escape the contingency which threatens to devour my actions through the recognition of others. (2012: 12)

There are many moments within *The Night Porter* where we see Lucia make choices that appear to exemplify the practical freedom Beauvoir stipulated in *Pyrrhus and Cineas*. However, Lucia's choices and her actions only affirm the subjectivity that Max values (she returns to being his 'little girl'). I would like to focus on two sequences where Lucia appears to make a choice about her situated freedom, because they appear as most ambiguous given the oppression of her situation. These include when she goes shopping and finds a pink dress, and when she refuses release from Dr Hans Vogler (Gabriele Ferzetti), the Nazi officer who meets with her in Max's apartment.

After Lucia's husband leaves Vienna to continue his orchestra tour, she explores the city: she visits Mozart Haus, stops for a drink in a bar and shops in an antique store. As Lucia enters Mozart Haus, she is tightly framed in shot via an extreme low angle, exacerbating her sense of isolation. The room is suggestive of a prison cell and the low-angle shot makes Lucia appear small, adolescent-like, similar in body size to when she was in the death camps. The scene continues via a medium-wide shot with Lucia wandering Vienna's streets, alone and dwarfed by ornate buildings on either side. Compared with the claustrophobic rooms of the hotel and (later) Max's apartment, Lucia appears at risk and unsure in this open, urban environment; her camel coat is worn snugly, looking like a defence against other possible spaces and futures that may be available to her in the world. She stops for a drink in a darkly lit bar, the camera pans across a mosaic of brown, opaque leadlight glass windows before settling on Lucia, who is sitting in a corner, recalling the past.

Her face is expressionless throughout the sequence, making it difficult to interpret exactly what she is thinking and feeling. Parallel editing interweaves the past with the present, the low-key lighting creating a gloomy sensibility. Very little dialogue occurs between Max and Lucia as their past is what directs the present. The audience is left with the 'uneasy awareness of the extended and multiform creative game of the trapped couple' (Marrone 2000: 95). At this point, the film cuts to flashback, a death camp hospital where Max treats an open wound on Lucia's arm. The colour of the flashback is similar to that of Lucia's dance sequence, green and prison-like. The sequence is ambiguous, inverting a space intended for healing and care with desire and eroticism. A tightly framed two shot returns us to the closed-off sadomasochistic world of Max and Lucia (Figure 2.1).

Returning to the present day, an extreme close-up attempts to establish Lucia's reaction, but it remains unreadable. She continues to an antique shop, browsing in a seemingly indifferent state without any sense of looking for anything in particular, until she settles on a pink and lace dress (Figure 2.2). Subsequently, the montage gains pace and is spliced with images of a similar pink dress that Max gave Lucia in the camp (Figure 2.3). The score, previously playing *The Magic Flute*, has ceased, leaving only the sounds of a clock ticking and passing traffic. Cavani has placed us aurally and visually in the interstices of ambiguous experience.

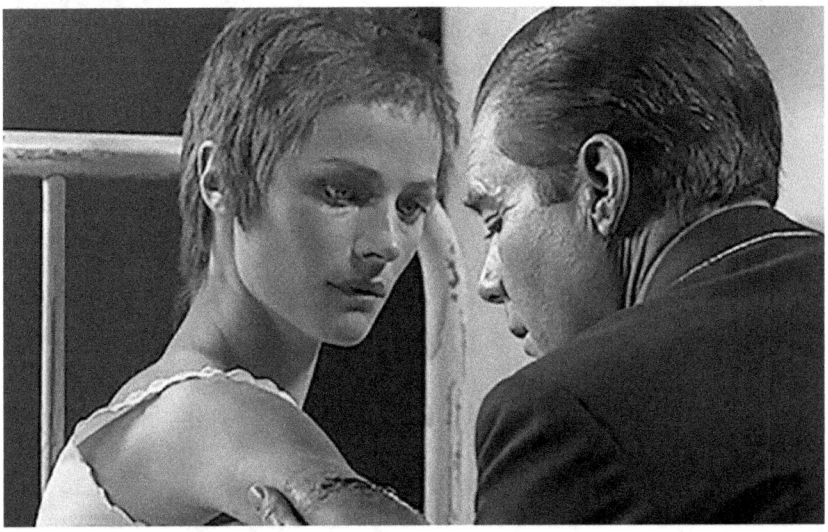

Figure 2.1 Max (Dirk Bogarde) caresses Lucia's (Charlotte Rampling) wound in Liliana Cavani's *The Night Porter* (1974).

Figure 2.2 Lucia finds a pink dress which reminds her of the one Max gave her in the death camp.

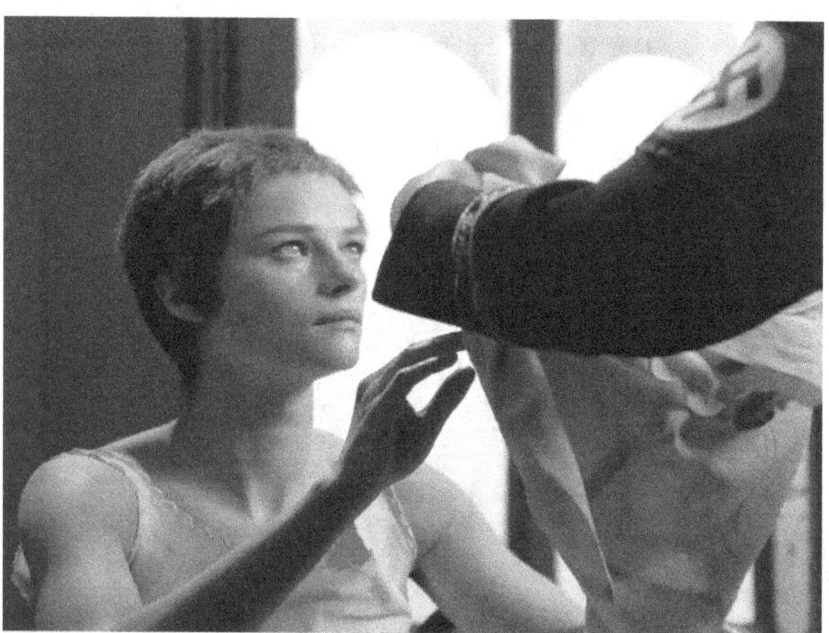

Figure 2.3 Max gives Lucia a pink dress in the death camp.

We might ask at this point why Lucia bought such a dress, but to seek a definitive answer to that question is to miss the point. Instead, Lucia's choice is an action that hinges on a sense of reciprocal recognition, which in the Sadean situation of her and Max's relationship is unlikely.

As long as she conforms to his idealisation of being 'his little girl', authentic reciprocal recognition cannot happen. Nancy Bauer argues that Beauvoir's interpretation of reciprocal recognition includes a sense of contingency, 'requiring an acceptance both of the reifying (objectifying) nature of one's own judgment of the other and of the inevitability of one's being judged, in a reciprocally reifying way, by that other' (2006: 69). Lucia's choice signifies women's ambiguous position in relationship to men and the risks that are required for genuine freedom in a loving relationship to occur. Crucially, however, Beauvoir did not see violence as linked to desire (unlike Sartre),[18] instead, authentic loving relationships were only possible through reciprocal recognition and a denial of the violence in dominance. What Beauvoir did value was the capacity for violence to alert us to uneven and disempowering social situations, such as that between woman and man, and this is the political purchase of Cavani's film.

The second example of choice which reflects Lucia's ambiguous being-in-the-world is unusually heavy with dialogue, quite different from the aforementioned scene wherein which she says next to nothing. Hans, one of the Nazi officers, has come to Max's apartment to determine whether Lucia presents a threat to the Nazis' anonymity. The sequence is shot in a combination of close-ups, medium shot, and shallow focus, making clear Hans's affective distance from Lucia and Max's inner sanctum. Cavani's medium-wide shots often use deep focus, sustaining our attention on the character's situation relative to their surroundings. Here, for most of the conversation, while Lucia is under the table, Hans remains blurry in the background. Our attention is directed to Lucia's face throughout her interaction with Hans, and the camera follows her at eye-level on the floor of the apartment. Hans tells Lucia he is there to ask her if she wishes to testify at the Nazis' mock trial, and 'to see if the situation in which you [Lucia] find yourself is entirely of your own choice'. She replies: 'I'm alright here'. This conversation takes place with Lucia on her hands and knees under a round table, with Hans sitting on a sofa behind her, out of focus. Lucia's avowal that she is there of her own free will, that it is her choice that she is chained to a radiator and subjecting herself to Max's sadism, appears to exemplify Beauvoir's early position on freedom, where she argues that despite the threat and action to one's facticity, inner freedom cannot be impaired. She writes that one 'is free in situation' (PC 124); 'One must not believe that I could elude the responsibility for that situation on the pretext that the other is free. That is his business, not mine. *I* am responsible for what I can do, for what I am doing' (PC 126). In *Pyrrhus and Cineas*, Beauvoir does not yet acknowledge that those who are in circumstances of oppression cannot be held responsible for the facticity of their situation (her perspective shifts in *The Ethics of Ambiguity* and most significantly in *The Second Sex*, where she acknowledges women's limited situation within patriarchy). What she establishes here is that one's freedom is dependent on the other, that without equal relationships with others our freedoms can never be assured.

Hans and Lucia's conversation is as much about her choice to return to Max as it is about his appeal to secure the Nazis' anonymity. As long as Lucia remains a witness of the past, the Nazis are in danger of being discovered. Hans tries to convince Lucia to remain silent and his implicit threats are immediately acknowledged by Lucia: 'Dr Vogler I remember you well. You gave a lot of orders'. Hans fails to recognise that his (and the other SS officers') fascist past of dehumanising prisoners has generated the situation he now finds himself in. The mock trial will never result in the absolution the Nazis seek, because for them to be excused from their deeds (their 'guilt-complex' as Hans puts it), they need to eradicate any possibility of recognition of their acts – to destroy any witnesses. There is no genuine effort to respect or reciprocate recognition of the other's (Lucia's) subjectivity. As Kruks puts it:

> If I am to have relations of reciprocal generosity [the capacity to choose freely] with others, and if my existence is to be given meaning through others taking up what I create, they must be my equals ... they cannot be *less free* than I am. (1990: 88)

Lucia's 'choice' to be with Max, however, is also one that Beauvoir would view as not freely made. Beauvoir points out, 'only the impoverished man can declare himself free in the midst of his misery' (PC 126) and therefore any choice that Lucia says she makes freely is still one made on unequal terms. Despite Max's (and even Hans's) offer that Lucia can call for help whenever she wishes, there is never any real sense that this is possible. Violence as a mechanism that either appeals for or forces recognition is a technique Cavani uses to her advantage throughout the film. As Marrone states: 'the spectator is constantly made to *see*, to participate in a poetic gaze that encompasses the characters' transgression and ambiguity' (2000: 86). In this second example of choice, the audience is made to see the limit of Lucia's situation, the bad faith of her 'choice' and the inescapable oppression of her facticity. Cavani cleverly avoids raised voices or performances of anger, keeping the dialogue measured and restrained. Hans speaks to Lucia as though she were an adolescent girl rather than a grown woman who has experienced significant trauma. Even the timbre of his voice refuses to recognise her on an equal footing and to acknowledge his own role in the creation of her situation.

Ince's 'Ethical Vision' and the Necessity of Reciprocity

In this final section, I address Ince's concept of ethical vision, defined via Beauvoir's notion of *dévoilement* (translated as 'disclosure') as a 'mode of unveiling, of making-visible' (Ince 2017: 89) and connect it to Beauvoir's emphasis on reciprocal recognition as a way to discuss the political function of Cavani's aestheticisation of violence. I have discussed how Beauvoir refuted Sade's justification for violence as a means to affirm our relationships to the other, and yet at the same time, how she admitted the inevitability of violence within situations of inequity (PC 138). Ince outlines the activity of disclosure being 'not a conscious or intentional act undertaken by a subject' despite existing at the heart of Beauvoir's theorising of subjectivity (2017: 89). In *Pyrrhus and Cineas*, Beauvoir says that to achieve being, 'I must reconcile myself to the struggle' (PC 135), identifying struggle as the action that affirms subjectivity, 'I therefore struggle in order to be' (PC 136). Disclosure, then, is not concurrent with the act of looking but exists through the conflict that occurs in our interdependence with others. The ethical vision of *The Night Porter* does not exist within the film itself (it is hardly Cavani's goal to entertain her audiences in the conventional sense); instead it exists within the struggle that emerges from the film's appeal to the audience.

The sadomasochism of Max and Lucia's relationship is confrontational precisely because we witness immoral treatment recurring. This exacerbates its provocation, and the shock of their abusive relationship recurring is aligned with the recognition that such abuse exists (persists) in other situations; specifically, the film acknowledges the limited freedom in women's situation. The violence of the film brings forth the struggle, to acknowledge and confront the inequality it portrays. Beauvoir writes: 'The artist cannot lose interest in the situation of the men around him. His own flesh is engaged in others. I will therefore struggle so that free men will give my actions and my works their necessary place' (PC 136). Cavani uses violence in this way, to disclose the inequality of women's situation and to make an appeal, demanding that we see this persistent inequity within society. Lucia's ambiguity must be acknowledged by the audience for Cavani's appeal to succeed. If the audience can register the inequity of Lucia's situation, and thereby acknowledge her oppressed subjectivity, then *The Night Porter* possesses the capacity to further reflect on the reality of women's situation more broadly. This isn't to suggest a universality but rather to highlight the potentiality of cinema to draw attention to a lack of freedom that might otherwise be ignored or avoided.

As noted, Beauvoir's argument in *Pyrrhus and Cineas* is limited because she had not yet moved beyond the individual's situation or acknowledged the different circumstances and conditions that exist between the historically and socially privileged and those they oppress. Nevertheless, in this essay she associates violence with her concept of appeal, recognising our need for others as well as the importance of how we treat them. Ince's concept of ethical vision, modelled on Beauvoir's concept of disclosure, draws attention to the political appeal within the films of women filmmakers, like Cavani, where the demand for reciprocal recognition and action is more effective than the 'hierarchical division of the gaze into active-sadistic and passive-masochistic forms' (Ince 2017: 92). As such, foregrounding the ambiguity within women's situation appears as a specific project of women's filmmaking, a more compelling political intervention.

The ethical vision within Sade's project operates on a similar premise of disclosure, in that his plays and novels as well as his defence of his sexual perversions, make visible the ambiguity of human existence and the cruelties within the hypocrisies of privilege. Just as Sade's aristocracy facilitated the violence of his privilege, and the brothel his torture of women, so too did the extermination camps enable Max's abuse of Lucia. The ethical vision of Cavani's film, therefore, directs us to the parallel she makes between Max and Lucia's past and present. Such abusive space, not always the brothels or death camp, are common to the privileged of their time. The erotic experience which structures Max and Lucia's relationship is fundamental because sexuality is the most intimate and fleshed of experiences, simultaneously invoking relationships of power and knowledge in human existence, between self and other. Quoting Sade, Beauvoir writes:

> The intoxication of tyranny leads immediately to cruelty because the libertine [for our purposes, Max], by molesting the object [Lucia] that serves him, 'experiences all the charms a nervous individual enjoys when he makes full use of his strength [privilege]: dominates, he is a tyrant'. (MWBS 48)

The fervour we see in Max's attention toward Lucia contradicts his position as a night porter in a small Viennese hotel, yet it does underscore Hannah Arendt's (1963/2006) idea of the banality of evil; he continues to obey orders of the mock trial (for a while) and service the Nazi hotel guests. Here we see an analogy between Sade and Max; Sade fulfilled his duties as husband, fathering children while also orchestrating cruel, sexual acts.

> That Sade ... was capable of audacious extravagance [which] does not contradict the hypothesis of his fearful timidity with regard to his equals, and, more generally

because the reality of the world ... he subordinated his experience to his eroticism because eroticism seemed to him to be the only possible accomplishment of his existence ... he chose the imaginary. (MWBS 49)

The Nazi party offered Max a privileged and therefore excused space to exact cruel and dehumanising acts on others. If privilege goes unchallenged, there is the danger of it no longer seeming like privilege. The violence toward others is naturalised and justified in the order of things. This is why on seeing Lucia again, twelve years later, Max shows no remorse, only excitement, whereas Lucia demonstrates fear, then resignation and lack of expression.

On the one hand, Lucia symbolises an aversion of responsibility of Max's bad faith, his inability to admit to the atrocities he was responsible for and enjoyed (he ends up refusing to take part in the mock trial; we see his show of glee in giving Lucia the decapitated head of another prisoner). On the other hand, Lucia also represents a false future for Max, similar to any act of bad faith, which results in the annihilation of the self. By recreating the anxiety and ambiguity in their situation, Max never confronts his responsibility for causing it. He knows that as long as their relationship exists under the conditions it does, he and Lucia (especially Lucia) can never be free. The grey rain, the closed interior spaces of the hotel, and later Max's apartment, grow increasingly smaller through the prevalent use of medium shots and 50mm lens, indicating the suffocation and impossibility of Max and Lucia escaping their mutual destruction. Max also fails in his Nazi/porter servitude, what has clearly been a significant ethical structure for him. By abandoning the project of the mock trial, Max throws the continuation and sustainability of fascist privilege – its spaces, its behaviours and its hidden mechanisms – into disarray. The other Nazi officers become worried and feel under threat. There can be no ambiguity of Nazi ethics; privilege discontinues as its systems crumble.

As an ambiguity for Max, Lucia is a break from his fascist institutional service, but at the same time enables his indulgence of cruel and oppressive private pleasures. His sovereignty is lost in one system only to be found in another. Max has lost the privilege of self-sovereignty within the fascist Nazi system that sustained patriarchal advantage, but he recoups similar sovereign existence in another patriarchal-approved institution and system – the domination of woman (systems such as marriage, the family, sport, etc., are ones which themselves abide by such patriarchal rules). Lucia represents Max's culpability, and like Sade, he is a 'culprit for life' (MWBS 50). Lucia further embodies this recognition for the remaining Nazi officers.

Should we condemn Lucia as an abettor? Throughout this chapter, I have shown how Beauvoir's notion of ambiguity developed from the necessity for reciprocal recognition, to view the other as an equal so that situations of freedoms can be shared. Lucia is never afforded such subjectivity by Max; she is his possession, his 'little girl'. Beauvoir writes, '[t]o inflict *jouissance* ... can be a tyrannical violence; and the executioner disguised as a lover is enchanted to see his credulous lover swoon with pleasure and gratitude, confusing wickedness and tenderness' (MWBS 51). Max and Lucia are shut away, 'normal existence [is] no longer permitted to' them. Beauvoir argued that what Sade 'essentially required of cruelty was that both singular individuals and his own existence be revealed to him at once as consciousness and freedom and as flesh' (MWBS 54). To reduce Max and Lucia's relationship to an expression of sadomasochistic pornography and burn the critical significance of *The Night Porter* is to miss its political and ethical potential in raising consciousness about oppression in privilege, particularly in our relationships with others.

Notes

1. 'Must We Burn Sade?' formed part of a three-article volume, titled *Privilèges* (1955). The other two articles were 'Right-Wing Thought Today' and 'Merleau-Ponty and Pseudo-Sartreanism'. All three are found in Simons and Timmermann's (2012) edited collection, *Political Writings*. Page references will be taken from this text.
2. See Cavani's interview with Claire Clouzot, where she states: 'Cinema is for me a form of psychoanalysis that I do for myself' (1974: 42). Thanks to Julia Hammett-Jamart for helping me with the translation.
3. See Kruks (2012: 56–8) who discusses Beauvoir's reading of Sade through Hegel's master-slave dialectic. She argues that on its own it is not 'sufficient to account for how oppression operates in a great many situations' (2012: 59). My interest here focuses on emotional experience within a politics of ambiguity as portrayed within Cavani's *The Night Porter*.
4. *Pyrrhus and Cineas* was published in 1944; 'Must We Burn Sade?' was first published in *Les temps modernes*, 7: 75 (Jan 1952), 1197–230.
5. See Marrone (2000: 81–115) who discusses this aspect of Max and Lucia's relationship to a great extent. For specific discussion on Beauvoir's treatment of Hegel's thought see Eva Lundgren-Gothlin (1998: 93–108); Shannon M. Mussett (2006: 276–93); with respect to oppression and Sade see Sonia Kruks (2012: 56–60).
6. Roger Ebert, 'The Night Porter', *The Chicago Sun Times*, 10 February 1975.
7. Pauline Kael, 'The Current Cinema: Stuck in the Fun', *The New Yorker*, 7 October 1974.

8 Mike D'Angelo, 'Despite risible subject matter, *The Night Porter* is more tedious than vile', *The AV Club*, 17 December 2014.
9 Vincent Canby, '*The Night Porter*' [sic] Is Romantic Pornography', *The New York Times*, 13 October, 1974.
10 My translation. Thanks to Julia Hammett-Jamart and William Brown for helping me with the nuances in translation.
11 The Bible story is one of power, cruelty and entrapment. Herod Antipas has married Herodias, the widow of his late brother Herod II and mother to Salome. As the story goes, John the Baptist spoke out against the marriage and was imprisoned by Herod Antipas. Salome danced for Herod and his guests at a banquet and for her reward, he vowed to fulfil whatever she requested. In an effort to avenge the public embarrassment of her mother (who was unhappy at John the Baptist's condemnation), Salome asked for the Baptist's head. Herod, cornered, agreed and Salome presented the head to her mother. See Mark (6:14–29) and Matthew (14:1–12).
12 Friedrich Hollander's song, previously sung by Marlene Dietrich, was reinterpreted in *The Night Porter* by Lucia (Marrone 2000: 229, fn 67). The song's title translates as 'If I could wish for something' and its sentiment shows the incapacity to distinguish between good and evil, right and wrong, sad and happy. In the version Lucia sings, the song expresses a wish to be loved but at the same time, reflects an ambiguity in knowing how to feel it, act or show it. She sings '*Leben liebe ich zu leben/ich kann euch sagen ich liebe zu gefallen/wenn auch nicht immer liebe ich zu lieben/ich weiß nicht was ich will und doch erwarte viel/wenn ich mir was wünschen dürfte/käme ich in verlegenheit/was ich mir denn wünschen sollte eine schlimme oder gute zeit*' (Translation: Life I love to live/I can tell you I love to please/if not always I love to love/I do not know what I want and still expect a lot/If I could wish for something/I would be embarrassed/what should I wish for, a bad or a good time/If I could wish for something/I'd want to only be a bit happy/because if I were too happy/I'd long for feeling sad). Thanks to my colleague Walter Tschacher for assisting me with the translation.
13 Reed's (1998) comprehensive study compares dance movements from northern Europe, the Middle East, Latin America, South America, Africa and the Pacific Islands.
14 There is room to discuss the emergence of empathy in the art of filmmaking here, as Bion also goes on to consider the similarities between artist and analyst. Gérard Bléandonu notes that Bion believed the artist was able to 'communicate an emotional experience in a universal and durable way' (1994: 200). It is beyond the scope of this work to outline the import of Bion's ideas here, and I have written on this elsewhere (Fuery 2018: 141–5), but briefly I wish to indicate how alternative psychoanalytic models that focus on emotional experience can help evaluate embodied reactions, such as the trauma seen in *The Night Porter*.

15 Bergoffen writes that Beauvoir's title 'repeats the title of a 1946 symposium in *Action* dedicated to a literature noir titled "Must we Burn Kafka"?' (2012: 23). This in turn copied a *Combat* article on Sartre: 'Should We Burn Sartre?'. See also Lori Jo Marso's 'Must We Burn Lars Von Trier?: Simone de Beauvoir's Body Politics in *Antichrist*' (2016). By echoing the title once again here, I aim to foreground the implicit ambiguity within political questionings of freedom with regard to the use of violence in women's filmmaking, particularly with respect to its examination of the 'relationship between the self and its other(s)' (Bergoffen: 2012: 43).
16 In *The Prime of Life*, Beauvoir says that she wrote *Pyrrhus and Cineas* in three months, after being invited by Jean Grenier to contribute to an anthology he was editing (PL 433).
17 This is signalled at the start of the film through an interplay of looks and power. We are first introduced to the adolescent Lucia, more specifically Max's memory of her, through extreme close-up. The sequence goes on to recall Max's invasive study of Lucia with a movie camera. See Marrone (2000: 99–100) who writes on the aesthetic differences between Max and Lucia's recollections. Such differences are a good example of Ince's discussion of Beauvoir's concept of disclosure, which I discuss at the end of this chapter.
18 See Eva Gothlin (2006), 'Beauvoir and Sartre on Appeal, Desire and Ambiguity', pp. 132–45.

CHAPTER 3

Moments of Moral Choice in Debra Granik's *Leave No Trace*

Beauvoir's thinking rarely strayed far from the experience of adolescence and its legacies for freedom, either in her literary stories[1] or her philosophical works. And even though her position evolved over time, she saw adolescence as a foundational, highly significant and demanding encounter with the politics of our freedom. She argues that adolescence is the first thought and felt experience of ambiguity, 'between the past which no longer is and the future which is not yet'. At first, she extends this living experience to all 'fellow men' (EA 6), but later, in the second volume of *The Second Sex*, Beauvoir becomes more attentive to sexual difference, outlining various situations of girlhood development.[2] Beauvoir's framing of adolescence as political and ambiguous living experience guides my analysis of Debra Granik's film *Leave No Trace* (2018), where I argue that Granik's cinematic consideration of adolescence, resonant of Beauvoir's many phenomenological reflections, presents a productive, political comment on feminine becoming in the twenty-first century. Granik and Beauvoir appear to have a lot in common. For both, ambiguity forms the foundation of human experience, shedding light on ethical and political aspects of lived experience. As a cornerstone of their respective projects (for Granik, this is seen through her films; for Beauvoir, it is her essays, novels and plays), each uses the textures and nuances of their creative expression to foreground the phenomenological impact of oppressive situations, drawing specific attention to individual situations in order to examine the consequences for society at large.

Beauvoir's thinking on adolescence is peppered throughout her immense body of work, often informing or supporting her more substantial discussions on philosophies of freedom and action in our relations with others. It is widely known that Beauvoir, like other existentialist phenomenologists, did not regard psychoanalysis favourably (TSS 49–68), and yet most of the criticism is set against the classical (that is, Freudian) psychoanalytic model that relegated women's desire to the margins. As I discussed in

Chapter 2, fundamental to existentialism is the notion of choice, and because psychoanalysis 'systematically refuse[s] the idea of choice and its corollary, the notion of value' (TSS 55), Beauvoir saw it as not offering a convincing method of freedom. In her view, Freud replaced 'the notion of value with that of authority' (TSS 55). Yet, at the end of her chapter on the psychoanalytic point of view, she returns to what can be regarded as an object relations focus by concentrating on 'the body, sexual life, and technology ... insofar as he grasps them from the overall perspective' of one's existence (TSS 68). Object relations psychoanalysis does not centre sexuality in its methodology, rather its emphasis rests on the intersubjective experience, that is, the awareness of emotional lived experience as dependent on and inextricably linked to others. Indeed, it is precisely Beauvoir's attention on reciprocity as the foundation for her existential ethics – the recognition of the other being separate to that of one's own ego – that aligns with theories of thinking as emotional experience which rests at the heart of object relations psychoanalysis.

For this reason, I see Beauvoir's position on ambiguity as being somewhat at odds with her criticism of psychoanalysis[3] because she does link ambiguous experience with unconscious or unrepresentable emotional unrest (as existential angst), focusing on the clash that arises between the view from within and the view from without. Her philosophy of a woman's becoming, as Jacqueline Rose points out, 'is an experience that plunges a woman into the deepest recesses of herself' (2018: 136). Consequently, I put Beauvoir's notion of ambiguity in conversation with object relations psychoanalysts Donald Winnicott and Wilfred Bion whose work focuses on affective, embodied experience. Placing Beauvoir's ideas in closer connection with these thinkers highlights their shared recognition of existential and emotional turbulence. Beauvoir's work is more aware of the embodied and political relationship adolescent bodies have with society, particularly girls, whereas Winnicott helps to flesh out the unspoken and anxious ambiguities adolescence evokes in us all, even those who have left their teen years behind. By combining the two approaches of phenomenology and psychoanalysis via film analysis I demonstrate the importance of gestural, embodied lived experience for interpreting the affective and emotional resonances on which visual storytelling depends.

Working from Beauvoir's deceptively simple claim, that adolescence is a 'moment of moral choice' (EA 42), Winnicott's view that it is 'a living experience, a problem of existing' (1961/1999a: 79), and Bion's claim that '[w]hen two personalities meet, an emotional storm is created' (1979/2008: 321), Granik's *Leave No Trace* evokes sensory states of ambiguity via form and content to wrestle with the thought and felt complexities of ethical decisions. Such cinematic praxis can be viewed as non-confrontational political action. Though situated within a broader male-dominated film industry, the work of independent women filmmakers often deviates from formulaic content and generic style, alerting us to living experience that often goes unacknowledged and under-explored. Granik's films are especially effective in this regard as they present reflective stories that are wholly attentive to individuals, who more often than not are in the throes of feminine becoming. It is no surprise then, that vulnerability is centred as a theme throughout *Leave No Trace*, and that like Beauvoir, Granik highlights how the ambiguity in states of becoming and vulnerability compels us to recognise that freedom is not an egotistical act that results from choosing to live as one wishes, independent of others. Instead, freedom 'is to *make oneself* a lack of being; it is to cast oneself into the world', by which Beauvoir means freedom cannot exist without everyone sharing in similar situations of freedom (EA 45), and this orientation is an ethical one. She says we are defined through our relationship to the world, to each other, 'our freedom can be achieved only through the freedom of others' (EA 169). *Leave No Trace* embraces individuation, a period and process that Beauvoir sees as the formative experience of moral choice, valorising adolescence as a difficult, anxious and ambiguous stage, but shies away from any damaging, prescriptive tropes so often seen in teen cinema. Instead, Granik's film illustrates a strong Beauvoirian sense of freedom: possible when others can share in an equivalent sense (though perhaps not the exact same circumstance or expression) of freedom as others, and that this freedom is dependent on recognising our own ambiguous embodied situation as being connected to those experienced by others. Adolescence, then, can be viewed as a recurrent affective state to which we return in moments of turmoil, an embodied emotional regression that affords us the opportunity to reassert our responsibility and our decision to act in order to realise our freedom.

Leave No Trace

Granik's fourth feature, *Leave No Trace*,[4] tells the story of thirteen-year-old Tom (Thomasin Harcourt McKenzie) and her father Will (Ben Foster), a veteran of the Iraq war who suffers from post-traumatic stress disorder. Will manages his illness as best he can and has attentively and lovingly raised Tom in an environment that seeks to shelter her from the destruction of his own trauma. Granik commendably presents a family situation that is as devoted as it is alternative, without critique, by focusing on Tom's living experience. Like Beauvoir, Granik sees female adolescents as autonomous, desiring of connection with family and friends, but does not necessarily share Beauvoir's pessimism, of feeling excluded from social experiences that surround her. Despite these two phenomenologists of female living experience responding in different times and through distinctive mediums, both embrace girlhood authentically, respectfully and earnestly, choosing to rigorously observe and address conditions of women in their own time.

We first meet Tom and Will in Forest Park, a national reserve in the Pacific North-West of the United States, just outside Portland, Oregon. The film opens with faint birdsong and a close-up, shallow focus, of moss-covered branches. It immediately sets up environment as a theme of the film; the natural world of the forest has been Will and Tom's domain for some time (the moss on the branches) – the sense given is that the forest is their home, equally safe and restrictive. The next shot, wide and in deep focus, shows Tom at ease in the green wilderness of the forest fern floor. The camera is fluid, following her as she weaves through the verdant reserve, almost blending into the foliage. It cuts to another close-up, shallow focus, of a spider in its web (Figure 3.1), another home that presents a safe but limited environment. There is no threat here; Tom is shown to be comfortable and knowledgeable in her surroundings. This is followed with a further wide shot, deep focus, of Will carrying wood. He is shown smaller in scale than Tom, no less at ease or peace within the park, for he too is part of this environment and it is part of him. The cinematography, through its scope and depth of field, indicates that Will and Tom belong to this space, they are not just familiar with it; the wilderness is not menacing or alienating for them. This sense of safety and security of the surrounding environment mimics their intimate father-daughter world. Both are foraging, eating greenery, humming in harmony the song, 'You Are My Sunshine'. The opening sequence ends having established a sense of intersubjectivity – the forest is their home and they are happy, with their minds and bodies in tune with each other and the natural world around them.

It is clear within the opening of the film that the forest has helped Will to function in a capacity that facilitates Tom's well-being. However, the contingency of their situation increases with each encounter Tom has with other people. While these are indirect meetings (Tom doesn't speak to them, she just sees them in the park), the perceived threat of other people to their isolation is made clear. Will practices drills where they run and hide themselves in the greenery to avoid being caught, keeping their survivalist skills (and Will's mistrust of outsiders) sharp. Not long after we have been introduced to the pair, they are found by park rangers and are taken into social services. From this point on, their life paths begin to slowly diverge

Figure 3.1 Close-up, shallow focus of a spider in a web in *Leave No Trace* (Granik 2017).

as each wants a different way of living, and the film artfully navigates the tensions of adolescent individuation and subsequent moments of moral choice (most of which revolve around Tom and her desires for her future). In an interview with Maria Garcia, Granik states:

> The plot of *Leave No Trace* is rudimentary. Being discovered creates a change for Tom and Will. When they are discovered, something is ruptured. Isolation was their chosen method of existing and they are now going to be asked to come back into the fold. How they fare is where the drama is ... The suspense is how does anyone stay outside that [mass consumer culture]? How do you 'think your own thoughts'? (Granik in Garcia 2018: 39)

Granik therefore places the hardships involved with responsibility and action at the core of the film, centred around Tom's experience and view of the world, which I argue is reflective of the ambiguity Beauvoir identifies as beginning within adolescence and what Winnicott sees as a problem of existence.

In *The Ethics of Ambiguity*, for example, Beauvoir says that childhood presents a 'natural situation' that is 'common to all', representing a limit of possibility that is transcended during the child's development.

Adolescence is the living situation where 'new possibilities are won' (EA 152), where their future must begin to be recognised by others (adults) 'considering it as a freedom' that 'must be opened' (EA 153). Her emphasis recognises that the adolescent's emergent freedom is bound to their body; the politics of this period (the growth of their freedom) cannot be separated from the physical growth of the adolescent body. Ambiguity, for Beauvoir, is corporeal; the adolescent throws themselves into the world in every respect, 'the body is not a brute fact. It expresses our relationship to the world, and that is why it is an object of sympathy or repulsion' (EA 44). These two emotive reactions illustrate the affective relationality of ambiguity as the adolescent visibly negotiates their encounter with the world, as a being that seeks affirmation as much as individuation. In *The Ethics of Ambiguity*, Beauvoir points to the philosophical and political importance of adolescence as living experience in order to establish an existential ethics for being responsible for one's own freedom. As Kristiana Arp explains, this was a new approach to the consideration of freedom within existentialist thought; Beauvoir introduced a moral freedom distinctive from Jean-Paul Sartre's ontological freedom, 'developing moral freedom requires assuming a certain sort of relation to other people' (Arp 2001: 2), and Beauvoir's existential ethics claims that such freedom is realised through our interaction with others who support it.

Beauvoir's literary works tend to follow girls and women in situations of frustration, by which I mean often within love relationships or triangles where she pursues her thinking on ambiguous experience.[5] *Leave No Trace* is different as it examines Tom's ethical, existential and ambiguous frame of mind regarding where and how she wants to live for herself, without any narrative of amorous or erotic love. The ethics developed in Granik's film are shown in an empathic and conscious manner using realist stylistic devices and intentional cinematography. Granik's predilection for the medium shot showcases her attention on how we relate and respond to our environment. Cinematographer Michael McDonough's use of 35mm and 32mm lenses best mimic how audiences normally see the world, how we take in events as well as how we view events as being connected to the environments in which they occur. This cinematographic style is reflective of what Lucy Bolton has referred to as 'phenomenological filmmaking' (2016: 77),[6] electing to focus on the body-as-situation and the way it relates to others. Granik describes it this way,

> I much prefer including gestures of the body. Hands are very important to me. I love to see what someone is doing, how they relate to someone else, how they have to fix or pick up something, or what they stow in their pocket. (Granik in Garcia 2018: 38)

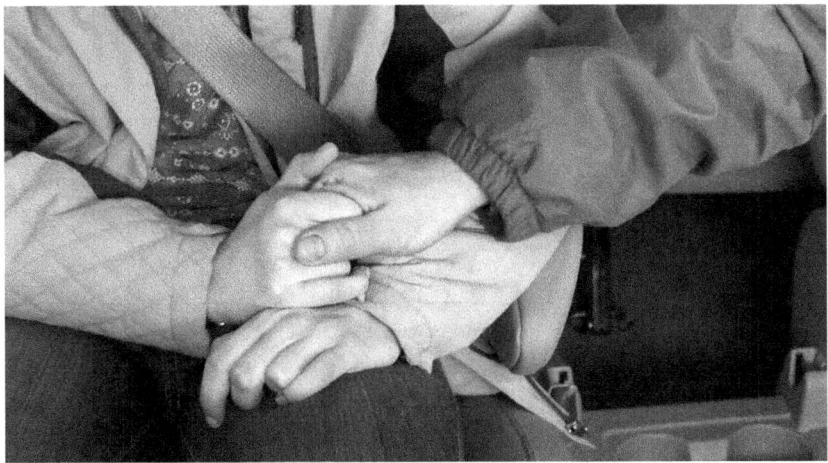

Figure 3.2 Granik focuses on gesture, an example of 'phenomenological filmmaking'.

Through the visual distance of the medium shot, the audience can focus on gesture and movement, emphasising Tom's experience of experiencing rather than the bracketed emotion she feels, normally conveyed through close-ups or portraits of the face (via a 50mm lens) (Figure 3.2). Granik wants to sustain our attention on how Tom feels and relates to others in situations, not exploit emotional reaction for its own sake.

Will and Tom are shown to live harmoniously together in the forest, with their concord built on mutual respect of the other in spite of Tom's learned sensitivity to her father's emotional fragilities. The extensive use of medium and medium-long shots during their time in the forest has directed audience awareness to ways in which the two characters relate to each other as well as their surroundings. The distance created by the medium shot also contributes to a style of 'phenomenological filmmaking' as it captures the movement of characters' gestures as well as their reactions. Tom sees a group of prison inmates installing an information sign in the forest while she is collecting wood for their campfire. On returning to the camp, she watches Will try to start kindling for the fire, but it is too damp to ignite. Despite the drizzle, Will persists. Seeing his behaviour grow slightly more intense, Tom tells him not to worry: 'Dad, it's okay. We can use the propane.' This is the first moment in the film that we see a flash of Will's traumatic neurosis; a slight dissociation from Tom (he ignores her) and from his connection to his surroundings (we hear the rain on the tarpaulin, making the irrationality of his actions obvious – it really is too wet to start a fire). Tom's attentive regard for her father's fixation is suggestive of previous experience in similar situations and she acts quickly, jumping up to start the propane grill (controlling the 'fire', the combustible aspect of this moment), even though Will tells her not to waste the gas. Tom takes responsibility in the encounter and asserts herself, an assertion displaced through foregrounding her appetite, and cooks them lunch. There is a quick shot of Will looking over his shoulder at Tom, showing that he is aware of what has just transpired. Harmony is restored soon after; the rain has stopped and Will compliments Tom, thanking her for the meal.

This sequence, despite its minimal dialogue, subtly illustrates the emotional health (and its fragility) between father and daughter; two people who might see things differently but are able to return to calm and loving states fairly quickly. Here, we can also say that it affirms Beauvoir's view of adolescence as being a series of tricky and ambiguous moral choices and confirms Bion's psychoanalytic idea that when two people meet, an emotional storm is created. Tom sees her father's neurosis and knows she must contain it to maintain equilibrium, but at the same time we note her fear and frustration. Tom, only thirteen years old, is frightened about having to contain the anxiety and internal torment of her father, yet it is a fear not consciously acknowledged. The frustration she shows is a response to this fear, having to address the contradiction in their parent-child relationship. Her choice to act (and indeed Will's accepting reaction of her choice) indicates her desire and ability to enact her own freedom by taking responsibility for her world and herself. In 'Making the Best of a Bad Job', Bion says psychoanalysis hasn't paid enough attention to the communication of body-thoughts and suggests that a closer look at the hormonal and affective machinations of the body might more effectively address a patient's emotional ambiguity:

> we have not considered the part that is played, if any, in the communication of thought, or the anticipation of thought by the glandular system [endocrine system which regulates hormones] ... perhaps the thoughts which we are accustomed to associate with the cerebral spheres could likewise be communicated to the sympathetic [fight-flight response] or para-sympathetic [state of calm]. (Bion 1979/ 2008: 326)

In other words, paying closer attention to the ways in which the body moves might be more effective in recognising how a body thinks and feels, that is, the emotional lived experience of the person.

Bion writes of 'physical anticipation', a term he coins to link body-movements with body-thoughts, as a means to observe the way in which the self communicates with the self, 'a bodily anticipation making possible the later *functional* operation of a mind' (1979/2008: 324). In the psychoanalytic context, this would help address why a 'patient says that he is terrified or is very anxious, and has not the slightest idea what it is about' (1979/2008: 326). In *Leave No Trace*, the prevalent use of medium shots, coupled with minimal dialogue and focus on characters' gestures, is one way in which attention to body-movements and body-thoughts supersedes the meaning of spoken words. Looking to what Tom or Will does, how they move, and listening to changes in vocal tone – *how* over *what* words they speak – facilitates greater insight into their emotional and ambiguous state. This is certainly the case for Will, who throughout the film communicates his self far more through gesture and movement than words.

Adolescence represents a formative experience of complex emotional development matched with political action. It is where we find our voice, where we test out our rebellion against the authorities that have pressed upon us up until this point; it is the adolescent's primary struggle of becoming, where they experiment with just how capable they are in terms of 'transcending the innocence of childhood and [becoming] competent to challenge the myths that place them in a predetermined world' (Bergoffen 1997: 144). Debra Bergoffen sees Beauvoir's discussion of adolescence within *The Ethics of Ambiguity* as the precursor to the becoming of woman argued in *The Second Sex*. In *Ethics*, Beauvoir views the adolescent's moral choices as indicative of their decision to assert subjectivity, reflecting a struggle against the world and the contexts in which it is made. We make choices against and within a world that pre-exists us. Bergoffen uses this to show how Beauvoir associates the complicity of childhood with womanhood, arguing that the adolescent girl is never afforded the promise and potential of revolt, as the myth of femininity hides 'a system of exploitation so pervasive and invisible that no social critique has targeted it and no liberation movement has taken up its cause' (1997: 144). This is Beauvoir's position in 1947, and of course today women's situation is significantly different thanks in part to her own work in *The Second Sex*. Exploitation certainly remains pervasive, particularly in historical and material systemic practices and institutions, but there have been many movements which have taken up the cause of women's liberation, often with legislative outcomes (such as the most recent #MeToo movement), and others that express progressive situations and positive resistance (such as #BlackGirlJoy).[7] Even so, the female adolescent body and its prevalent image still represents the struggle against myths of femininity. In the case of Tom, however, we see a different assertion of subjectivity, an expression often seen as the central story in the films of independent women filmmakers discussed throughout *Ambiguous Cinema* – a clearly distinctive, if unusual, echo of Beauvoir's political appeal in her work on women's becoming.

Tom's world is not Beauvoir's world of adolescent girls. She is not 'consumed by waiting [for a man]' (TSS 341); she is not a 'stranger to herself'; she does not 'open up her future ... by passively and docilely delivering herself into the hands of a new master' (TSS 342); indeed, throughout the film, Tom is not sexualised at all. Instead, the film's narrative explores the authentic and intense living experience of girlhood without resorting to Hollywood tropes. Tom is not a disturbed or rebellious delinquent (although she does rebel and resist) and she is not 'tamed by the healthy brutality of a lover or husband' (TSS 363). Rather, Tom actively seeks out connections with others, embracing her ambiguity by making 'significances and goals appear in the world. [She discovers] reasons for existing' (EA 45), finding it easier to adapt to the changes imposed on their living situation, and holds dear her ability to think 'her own thoughts', a turn of phrase she returns to Will, reminding him of his own capacity for resilience. While Tom's world differs from that of Beauvoir's girl described in *The Second Sex*, it affirms much of the tumult involved in wrestling with one's personal freedom and the sense of becoming first outlined by Beauvoir in *The Ethics of Ambiguity*. Through her character, Tom, Granik encapsulates the personal ambiguity and struggle for freedom of Beauvoir's earlier writing on adolescence and manages to showcase the possibility of a girlhood Beauvoir was wishing for in *The Second Sex*. Via Tom, Granik involves early Beauvoirian concepts of personal ambiguity and freedom in her exploration of the great untapped potential of girlhood envisioned in *The Second Sex*.

By looking specifically at Tom's experience of being caught between wanting to stay with her father and be more in the world, join communities and discover new things, Granik diversifies expressions not just of girlhood but of adolescent living experience in general. One of the sensitivities of *Leave No Trace* is its sustained but respectful and unlaboured attention on Tom's capacity to cope with her father's PTSD, predominantly conveyed through aesthetics so subtle that they almost entirely depend on an intuitive and empathic interpretation similar to Bion's 'physical anticipation'. Tom and Will take a day trip into Portland's city centre on the premise of getting more food for Tom's growing appetite, but in order to afford the food, Will must first get medication from the Veteran Affairs hospital, which he then sells for money. Sound design is important here, establishing what a difficult emotional task it is for Will to leave the forest and come into the city. The medium shots used during their time in the forest give way to an extreme wide shot, low angle, of the pair crossing

Figure 3.3 Extreme wide shot, low angle, of Will and Tom crossing St John's bridge.

St John's bridge (Figure 3.3); the audio layers combine traffic noise with a low thunder-like score to convey the foreboding sense of their journey. Compared to the opening sequence, this is a very different, much less safe environment for Will. The faint track of Tom's humming embedded into the sound design suggests that the journey is not as ominous for her as it is for her father and arguably, without his need to provide for her, Will would not cope half as well with the trip.

As Will and Tom travel in the Portland Aerial Tram above the city's freeway system, they do not speak. It is a brief sequence underlining their displacement within an urban environment and the cinematography returns to medium and close-up shots which also return the audience's awareness to the intimacy of their world. On approaching the tram's terminal, a close-up, shallow focus (Figure 3.4) reminds us of the affect between situation and feeling. It is a similar shot to the spider in the web (Figure 3.1), first seen in the film's opening sequence, but here the shot is matched with the pathetic fallacy of rain on the glass, demonstrating that this situation brings uncertainty and distress for the two characters. As they disembark, Will pays close attention to a helicopter, representing the evocation of unrepresented memories. Once again, in this short sequence of coming to the city (about one minute), where there is no dialogue, the audience must rely on sound design, performance and cinematography as the key aesthetics to convey the feeling of the characters, specifically Will's trepidation and Tom's care for her father's well-being.

Figure 3.4 Close-up, shallow focus of Will and Tom approaching Portland Aerial Tram terminal.

Not a Teen Film

In considering adolescence-as-ambiguous encounter, I am privileging two dominant interpretative frames: 1) Beauvoir's politically inflected existential-phenomenology; and 2) emotion-oriented object relations psychoanalysis, foregrounding the ambiguity of feminine becoming within independent women's cinema. This is to address the notion of adolescence quite differently to how it has previously been discussed within film studies, arguing that a comprehensive consideration of adolescence cannot be divorced from the aesthetics of cinema; filmmaking praxis is the engine of cinema's affective, political and emotional influence. Catherine Driscoll (2011) makes the necessary distinction between the 'teen film' and 'adolescence', noting the close constructive relationship it has historically had with industry and audience, and in doing so produces a critical history of teen film's beginnings and evolution. Driscoll points out that conceptions of adolescence have been informed, if not curated, through industry marketing practices of teen cinema, 'film and modern adolescence emerged at the same time and have consistently influenced each other' (2011: 5).[8] This is not the approach I pursue here; instead I focus on the important interrelation of film aesthetics, the phenomenology of adolescence, and the ambiguities it gives rise to by recognising the importance of Beauvoir's political intentions in her existential ethics.

Despite *Leave No Trace* fulfilling several key elements often used to categorise the cinema of adolescence, it defies easy classification as an example of 'teen cinema'. The film focuses on Tom's youthfulness and her intense emotional life, indicating some trouble in associating with the wider, outside world. The clash of her worldviews with her father, Will, is further set alongside the tricky socialisation with other community members, churchgoers, teens, and so on, exemplifying the affective, political and emotional turbulence such lived experience entails. Thematically, there is also the motif of Tom's wanting to connect and be accepted into a group of her own choosing. David Considine notes that '[t]he cinema of adolescence exists as an intersecting triumvirate of image, industry and influence' (1981: 123), identifying the genre of teen film as representative of being in-between and overlapping areas of film experience (industry, audience and story). Adrian Martin has said the teen film 'refers not to biological age, but a type, a mode of behaviour, a way of being' (1994: 66), and Driscoll explains that specifying the boundaries between 'teen' and 'adolescence' is notoriously difficult. Driscoll identifies three core features of teen cinema scholarship: 1) it is US-centric; 2) it is reflective of adolescent life and issues; and 3) it 'fails to represent teenagers accurately' (Driscoll 2011: 5). Her distinction between teen cinema and the inquiry of adolescence is useful for the phenomenological and psychosocial emphasis I am adopting here. She explains that the term 'teen' is narrow and limiting, identifying 'a set of tendencies and expectations rather than an identity mapping onto the years thirteen to nineteen', whereas the term 'adolescence' has been viewed within film scholarship as liminal experience (2011: 2). As the idea of adolescence evolved over time, so too did its reach and diversity in representation. As Driscoll explains, it 'was produced by interactions between social and cultural theory, public debate, and popular culture' (2011: 11). This intertwining experience of emergence, between adolescence and a growing film industry and its audience-dependent relationship, established a visual and narrative structure that has continued ever since. If we see a teenage body in a film, we are likely to think it belongs to the teen film genre; this view, that representation equals content, prescribes an idolisation of adolescence rather than effecting any adolescent sensibility for its audiences.

Driscoll's examples come from pre-1950s cinema, such as *The Kid* (1921) and *Love Finds Andy Hardy* (1938), before 'teen film' was first manufactured as a genre classification and indeed before the identity of 'teen' existed. Despite the socio-cultural and historical differences between such films and Granik's *Leave No Trace* (and arguably other examples of contemporary independent cinema), Driscoll's four notable conditions remain the best and most concise method for distinguishing between 'teen film' and 'adolescence'. These conditions include: 1) the recognition of modern adolescence as a period of 'personal and social crisis' (2011: 12), though not necessarily of adolescents and their behaviour; 2) the ways in which film industry regulations and policies of censorship were integrated into film narrative and production; 3) the increased industry awareness between film-going and the necessity of successful film marketing; and lastly, 4) an ability to adapt – cinema needed to respond to the evolving identity of adolescence in such a way that it became part of adolescent identity (and whatever that typically meant – namely ideas of rebellion, risk, tension, rejection of authority, violence and sexuality). 'Teen film', then, identifies films with teenagers in them (a category of films about teenagers for teen audiences), rather than depicting the existential ambiguity of an adolescent frame of mind and emotional sensibility.

Therefore, while inclusive and aware of the teenager and their body, adolescence (as discussed here) does not focus on representation of the teen film or films about teenagers, even though it so happens that *Leave No Trace* (like Granik's earlier *Winter's Bone*) follows the individuation of an adolescent girl and the evolving relationship with her father. By examining the affective and political encounter of adolescence, Beauvoir's claim that it is the period 'of moral choice' is reinforced through *Leave No Trace's* aesthetic sensoria and the audience's film-going experience. In some ways this speaks to Mary Ann Doane's questioning of the relation between aesthetics and politics, which she sees as fundamental to 'the entire project of feminist film criticism' (2004: 1231). Doane places her question within the context of radical or avant-garde filmmaking, *apropos* Jean-François Lyotard, to query the connection between feminist film practice and 'the avant-garde through a project of negation, a systematic interrogation and undermining of classical codes of sexual looking and imaging' (2004: 1231). She argues that this negativity led to 'collapsing politics into aesthetics' (2004: 1232). The experimentation within Granik's film doesn't revolve around the same project of negation that Doane identifies but it does advance an interrogation and undermining of classical codes of looking from the situation of the marginalised, where *Leave No Trace* 'sees' adolescence and those abandoned and disenfranchised by society (such as war veterans).[9] It isn't that Granik's film, as an object of art itself, functions as 'an outlet from capitalist reification' (Doane 2004: 1233) or that it is intended to be a specifically feminist film (Tom's desire for her own moral freedom notwithstanding); rather, Granik's choice to focus on the emotional turmoil of those residing at the outskirts of society, using direction that rejects generic representation of characters, promotes the ambiguity within mimesis, making further room for ambiguity in the cinematic encounter.

Ambiguity in the (Cinematic) Encounter

Throughout this chapter my discussion of adolescence as living experience goes beyond a literal account of a physiological or psychological period of development, arguing that it represents a sensorium of emotional turbulence often felt in moments of upheaval, uncertainty and frustration. Lori Jo Marso's notion of the encounter also connects situation and ambiguity in order to capture Beauvoir's understanding of collective freedom. As Marso sees it, and I agree, the encounter is a more effective way of speaking to the political aspect of situation and ambiguity in our relationships with others. She writes, '[f]or Beauvoir, to encounter others is not only a fact of existence it is also the *only way* to produce and experience freedom ... Ambiguity, contingency, situation, and nonsovereignty characterize encounters, and each produces, diminishes or destroys freedom' (Marso 2017: 2). The encounter, then, unites the sensory, felt tensions of ambiguity with the systemic, historical and social aspects of situation. Marso emphasises the interstices of our intersubjective, intersectional relationships with others and the struggles they contain, encapsulating 'the ontological and political fact that our lives are always entangled with others' (2017: 4). Critical to the political significance of the encounter, the psychosocial and phenomenological aspects within emotional experience occur and recur within our embodied search for freedom, emphasising the tumult and ambiguity it often evokes.

Much of Marso's work discusses the integrated affective and political life of the encounter, stating that 'emotions flow through us collectively as well as individually' (2017: 18), presenting a revolutionary way of thinking about Beauvoir's writings as being a 'series of encounters' that enable us to go beyond borders, limits and roles to realise freedom. In particular, she refers to the difficulty of such behaviour and choices, noting that Beauvoir stressed the demand and exertion felt in striving for one's freedom in a system that works hard to exclude it, '[j]ust thinking of it triggers the (psychological, emotional, material) burdens that always accompany making a choice and especially accompany agonistic interaction' (Marso 2017: 31). In *The Second Sex*, Beauvoir refers to classical psychoanalytic models to think through the reasons for the introjection of an oppressed identity, where a woman turns herself 'into a thing' (TSS 10). As mentioned, in 1949 her primary references would have been Freudian psychoanalytic models (the second volume of *The Second Sex* leans heavily on the work of Helene Deutsch, the first Freudian psychoanalyst who wrote about woman's sexuality). One wonders what Beauvoir's conclusions might have been had she encountered the work of Winnicott or Bion, two prominent object relations psychoanalysts whose interests are more focused on emotion, its materiality, and intersubjective, affective lived experience.

Rejecting the False Solution: Beauvoir and Winnicott

Winnicott wrote: 'Adults must hide among themselves what they come to understand of adolescence' (1961/1999a: 79) because the adolescent won't be told, they want to (and should) discover things for themselves, by themselves. Winnicott's psychosocial approach was dedicated to observing and evaluating the development of emotional growth, how an individual matures into an independent, autonomous being and the important role facilitating environments play in this process. His theorisation of the inner world, supported by years of psychoanalytic and paediatric clinical practice, consistently acknowledged the individual's intersubjective relationship with society, believing the health of society (and the family unit) was essential for the healthy emotional development of the individual.

He writes that adolescence is a 'stormy time' possessing 'a fierce intolerance of the false solution' (1963/1990: 244), engaging with the existential-psychosocial experience of this formative, unsettling period in our lives. The false solution, which takes many different forms, is the imposition of a cure, evident in adults trying to force-fit a way of being for the adolescent. Oftentimes this is the expectation the adolescent aligns with an authorial worldview (typically the parents'). Here we can return to Beauvoir's criticism of Freudian psychoanalysis as confusing value with authority, yet where Freud failed to account for the origins of drives in terms of existential choice, Winnicott actively explores these within the context of turbulent (specifically hateful) emotional experience.[10] He says that adolescence is something 'we always have with us' (1961/1999a: 79), a sensory state that he refers to as the 'doldrums' – a challenge society must meet, endure, but not try to solve. Where Winnicott's discussion provides insight into the internal struggle of adolescence as part of developmental and maturational processes, and its appeal for society, Beauvoir presents a more phenomenological and political interpretation on struggles specific to adolescence, placing particular emphasis on sexual difference and issues of freedom.

Beauvoir's more gender-specific view presented in *The Second Sex* sees boys and girls reaching adolescence at different times; for boys at 'about fifteen or sixteen' and girls 'at thirteen or fourteen' (TSS 329). Beauvoir makes this biological distinction in order to marginalise it in favour of highlighting the existential shock girls experience when learning of their different future from boys. The changes brought by adolescence are experienced differently by the sexes; for the boy, development becomes one of 'comparison and challenge', whereas for the girl, she 'must confine herself within the limits that her femininity imposes on her' (TSS 329). Reading this in the twenty-first century, such classification smarts a little, particularly as it ignores gender-fluid or trans identity embodied experience; but in 1949 Beauvoir's brave identification and rejection of the myth of femininity, so prevalent even now, showed how such myths yield very real embodied and emotional torment for those they affect when they go unchallenged.

By pointing out the differences of living experience between boys and girls in becoming adolescents, Beauvoir foregrounds what they share and the different futures that result due to the social and political realities of her time. Adolescents undergo 'an intimidating metamorphosis', a transformation that is met with high 'anxiety to a demanding freedom' (TSS 329) which, according to Beauvoir, is not as great a crisis for the boy as it is for the girl. The girl's future is condemned to a more limiting myth: 'the future not only moves closer: it settles into her body; it becomes the most concrete reality' (TSS 341). Beauvoir's existential-phenomenological attention on the living female adolescent body illustrates the political and emotional intention of her philosophising of women's experience. Inasmuch as *The Second Sex* provided feminism with a theory of becoming woman, Beauvoir's most famous work also delivered a philosophy that acknowledged the psychosocial elements within women's living experience by framing the affective impact of adolescence as a politicised theory of embodiment. Beauvoir spotlighted the different and disparate socio-political contexts of adolescent development between girls and boys, but also, and perhaps most relevant for the discussion at hand, she foregrounded the subsequent anxieties and their consequences for girls, women and society.

Some of the observations Beauvoir makes on the differences between boys and girls simply have to be seen as exemplifying the social and historical conditions at the time of her writing; after all, women in France were only able to vote for the first time in 1945. In *The Second Sex*, statements like: 'in many countries, most girls have no athletic training' (TSS 343) are clearly outdated but there are others that remain exceptionally valid: 'the anguish of being a woman eats away at the female body' (TSS 345). Beauvoir's ideas remain valuable when considering the affective and emotional reality of adolescence and its legacies for adulthood, especially if we take up her idea of metamorphosis more broadly.

In *The Ethics of Ambiguity*, Beauvoir treats adolescence as universal experience, and while clearly reflective of shared historical life experience – we have all been adolescents – she discusses it within ahistorical, gender-neutral terms. Her emphasis on its affective and existential changes laid the groundwork for the political and phenomenological observations she went on to make in *The Second Sex*. In this work, Beauvoir continues to show how adolescence is not a joyful period of awakening, and through many empirical as well as literary observations, highlights just how more difficult it is for girls:

> For the girl ... there is a divorce between her properly human condition and her feminine vocation. This is why adolescence is such a difficult and decisive moment for woman. Until then, she was an autonomous individual: she now has to renounce her sovereignty. (TSS 348)

The girl, unlike the boy, faces a dual crisis – the loss of her childhood omnipotence and the freedom of an open future – her autonomy is curated and stunted by patriarchy. It is hard to deny this difference between boys' and girls' embodied experience of adolescence, but it is not universal or definitive. Yet instead of focusing on the literal, and somewhat oudated, differences between a female and male adolescence, I want to emphasise the political and ambiguous aspects of the metamorphosis to which Beauvoir's philosophy points. Clearly her philosophy is specifically concerned with questions of how to be responsible for one's own freedom, the differences between ontological and moral freedoms, and how these existential changes are twinned with human development moving from childhood to adolescence to adulthood. As Beauvoir works through these issues, she proposes her ethical treatise, placing the anxious and relational aspects of ambiguity at its centre. I extend Beauvoir's philosophy to cinema, to consider how, as an aesthetic encounter, cinema has made similar political and ambiguous transitions across its histories and industries; how the evolution of a cinematic existential ethics is evident in women's independent filmmaking praxis, reflective of its struggle with finding an identity and place within a male-dominated industry.

Adolescence, as a stage of adaptation, marks a move from a situation of dependence, (and ideally) nurture and support within a protected environment to one of independence and evolving maturity. There are several ways we recognise adolescence, the most prominent being measurement of biological development and evaluation of physiological and psychological growth, that is, examining the physical, emotional and mental progression of an individual. Seen as a rebellious, complex and awkward period of life, adolescence's political and phenomenological characteristics are often side-lined in favour of foregrounding the process of individuation itself, otherwise termed a 'coming of age' or formation of subjectivity. Its existential anguish is noted rather than rigorously examined as offering a foundation for the development of an ethical orientation to the world, or as a means of establishing responsibility in our interactions with others. In this chapter, I have focused on the link between ambiguity and adolescence as a highly important, if not essential, foundation of emotional experience that structures how we relate to others in the world around us. Adolescence is not simply a period of transition or transformation, although clearly it involves both experiences. It is also a stage of experimentation, equally evoking anxiety and ambiguity – our first proper encounter with freedom is not without consequence.

Beauvoir says adolescence is the stage where we must assume our subjectivity and this involves taking responsibility for our choices, actions and behaviours in the world. Defiance is an attitude that she sees as being denied to girls but not boys, where the physical act of friendly competitive defeat (in wrestling or other sport) enables the boy to playfully practise and prepare for 'affirming one's sovereignty over the world' (TSS 343). Winnicott also observes defiance as a trait of adolescence in more ambiguous terms than Beauvoir. He associates 'defiant independence' and 'regressive dependence' as two characteristics of adolescence that alternate, even coexisting as 'two extremes at one moment of time' (1961/1999a: 81). Winnicott helps to outline why the ambiguous psychosocial life of adolescence is part of development and detachment from the parental environment, whereas Beauvoir points to ambiguity as also surfacing from the social disparities that exist for girls, but not boys. Both, however, appear to agree on the shared affective experience of adolescence, noting its anxious, ambiguous and demanding frame of mind for a body capable of acting on desires but not always able to bear or think through such intense emotion or its consequences. They also agree on the vital importance of rejecting false solutions and decisions of bad faith in order to achieve maturity, independence and freedom.[11]

Emotional Storms: Beauvoir and Bion

While Bion does not focus on adolescence[12] with the same specificity as Winnicott, he nevertheless addresses the emotional storm of encounters, emphasising choice as an orientation toward growth: 'There must be choice; this entails being tolerant enough to view the emotional turmoil' (Bion 1976/2008: 297). At first glance, 'emotional storm' evokes the idea of commotion, a state of distress visible to others, perhaps seen in the adolescent defiance referred to by both Winnicott and Beauvoir. For Bion, the storminess of the encounter is not necessarily visible in obvious ways. Instead, he indicates that everyday relationships carry such affective potential, where the storm may be present but not conscious:

> When two personalities meet, an emotional storm is created. If they make sufficient contact to be aware of each other, or even sufficient to be *un*aware of each other, an emotional state is produced by the conjunction of these two individuals, and the resulting disturbance is hardly likely to be regarded as necessarily an improvement on the state of affairs had they never met at all. (1979/2008: 321)

Bion says that the 'storm' is not immediately known, rather it is brought forth in thinking through difficult emotional experience – how to 'make the best of a bad job' by facing 'the adverse circumstance' and turning it 'to good account' (1979/2008: 321–2). Michael Eigen puts it this way:

> [the] mind uses properties of physical things to express itself, its states, its feelings: first, perception of the outside world, then emotional use of what is perceived. One experiences a physical storm [which, amongst other things, includes physical development, awakening of psychosexual drives etc.], then uses storm to express feelings: first outer, then inner. (Eigen 2005: 1)

Marso's concept of the encounter relative to Beauvoir's work is very similar, stating that choice is relational, 'crafted by our grasp on the world' (2017: 3), and it is this nexus of emotional turmoil and politics endemic to the encounter, adolescence and Beauvoir's ethics of ambiguity that I argue is embodied in Tom's character in *Leave No Trace* and in the many difficult choices she makes throughout the film.

When Tom is faced with the reality of the emotional storm within her father and of the feelings that have arisen due to having to adapt and assimilate into society, she tells Will: 'everything is different now', to which he replies with 'we can still think our own thoughts'. Will may be troubled, but he exhibits good faith in his parenting. Tom makes an effort to fit in and form friendships in the community, whereas Will finds it much more difficult, unable to evolve in the ways his daughter has, and this strains their relationship. Arriving late home one evening, Tom apologises for the worry she has caused her father and uses this moment of moral choice to explain: 'I think it might be easier on us if we try to adapt'. Tom, in her usual manner, shrewdly addresses the storm within her father, acknowledging that the freedom he seeks might be found in facing what he fears most – opening himself up again to the outside world. Tom is also telling him how difficult it is for her to bear his fear, how the 'us' of their relationship is suffering under the weight of Will's inability to make the best of a bad job in ways similar to hers.

Bion writes: 'We can be in a universe of thought, a culture, or even a temporary culture, of such a kind that we are sure to suffer the pain of feeling that our universe is not conducive to our welfare' (1979/2008: 322). This reads very similarly to Beauvoir's claim that adolescence is the moment of moral choice, where we are confronted with the emotional turbulence involved in becoming responsible for our own freedom and need to act, but also that such freedom requires the help and backing of others. Will is trapped in his 'universe of thought' but Tom can see her way out. In this exchange, and throughout the film, Tom embodies the principle of Beauvoir's existential ethics and Bion's emotional storm as she consistently looks to nurture the potential of her father's freedom as well as her own. Perhaps like other children who transition into adolescents, Tom accepts her lack of being (in the Beauvoirian sense). Her actions and words in the film show that she understands that 'the existence of others as a freedom defines my situation and is even the condition of my own freedom' (EA 97); she cannot be free unless her father is also able to be free. The ambiguity of the film (and what adolescence teaches us) is that the existential ethics of freedom is found in affective and political liberation not necessarily in the sharing of the other's facticity, but nevertheless it is imperative we recognise and work to develop it.

Sara Ahmed's concept of 'affective economies' suggests that emotions establish the 'very effect of the surfaces or boundaries of bodies and worlds' which can be said to typify the experience of the encounter (Ahmed 2004b: 117). Winnicott is attentive to the moods of adolescence, which he views as the affective expression of 'our social awareness and the special social conditions of the time we live in' (1961/1999a: 79). Like Bion, Winnicott's position is that the ambiguity within adolescence elicits anxiety and other emotional storms within us. Adults must recognise the challenge adolescence presents for them and 'meet the challenge as part of the function of adult living ... rather than set out to cure what is essentially healthy' (1961/1999a: 87). Both psychoanalysis and phenomenology agree that observation plays 'an extremely important part' in living experience, and in order to valorise the freedom of another, one must be 'sensitive to the totality of that person' (Bion 1979/2008: 325). These object relational psychoanalytic models show that such alternative psychoanalytic attention on emotion has something else to say about the affective economies within Beauvoir's (and Marso's) encounter. In this way, the specificity of the 'cinematic encounter' resonates with Marso's attention on 'the primacy of relationships' (2017: 7) and foregrounds both the storminess of the encounter and the lack of certain outcomes.

Film-going experience demonstrates a particular type of encounter that intersects political, aesthetic, historical and embodied lived experience – the messy and the sticky (Ahmed 2004a: 89–92) – and showcases the 'inability to absorb or possess; there is a distance, an appearing of the foreign, forbidden, unfamiliar, unknowable and threatening' (Marso 2017: 7). For Marso, these affective resonances are viewed as 'staging encounters' (2017: 17) demonstrating political character, what she artfully sees as a strategy within Beauvoir's work, showing that lived emotional experience is primarily embodied and relational. Ahmed also argues that emotional experience is political and that the political is emotional; by looking at the circulation and economy of emotion as transmissive sensoria, she shows that what we feel is dependent on, if not determined by, our relations with others. What object relations psychoanalysis also offers is the notion that the emotional storm of an encounter is not contained within singular experience, but reaches and spreads through the unconscious self and through our interrelational, intersubjective experience, going 'often unnoticed and misnamed' (Eigen 2005: 6). At this point, we can link the enterprise of Beauvoir's existential ethics, and the emphasis of object relations psychoanalysis on affect and emotion, to the intentions seen in *Leave No Trace*, where emotions 'create the very effect of the surfaces or boundaries of bodies and world'. In *Leave No Trace*, the emotional encounter appears outwardly gentle yet internally stormy for both Will and Tom, appearing (at times) as inchoate but coming from a place of care, respect and love. However, the threat of the other and the emphasis on the relation of self to other as a political and emotive experience is still foregrounded. The threat for Will is the dissolution of self via the conformity expected in civilisation and capitalistic self-interest; for Tom it is not knowing and not being able to be responsible for her own choices or thoughts.

The reason for bringing Beauvoir into conversation with more contemporary models of psychoanalysis is to show that phenomenological and psychosocial approaches are not always antithetical, particularly in terms of studying the experience of the encounter. The applications of psychoanalysis within 1970s film theory (feminist, apparatus and otherwise) were mainly focused on theories of identification, viewing positions and power relations, and the role of sexual difference within such paradigms of thought. Certain contemporary psychoanalytic models adopt different emphases, concerning relating to/with others and the emotion experience that yields, while sharing the main idea that psychoanalysis is about discussing what we can't face by ourselves, alone. By foregrounding psychoanalytic attention on our capacity to use objects, that is, identifying the ways in which we think with objects (like the moving-image) and the extent of our capability of doing so, we move closer to recognising that our ability to 'think our own thoughts' depends on how we relate to others. Freedom of the self, emotional and political freedom, requires acknowledging the role others play in our lives.

Freedom and the Woman Director

Leave No Trace is certainly a story about Tom and the path she finds for herself, but it is also a story about the importance of respect for others. For Beauvoir, freedom was essential to lived experience, and for it to exist it must be acknowledged and respected by others. I cannot be free if you do not share the same freedoms as I do; if my desires rob you of your freedom, then they are not desires worth having: 'Freedom realizes itself only by engaging itself in the world: to such an extent that man's project toward freedom is embodied for him in definite acts of behavior' (EA 84). Adolescence, then, is to be viewed as the foundational ambiguous, affective and embodied living experience that I suggest recurs throughout life when difficult and emotionally turbulent situations are encountered. In Granik's words, it is 'how we fare' in these situations that matters, where the drama lies.

What is the relevance of this for our consideration of ambiguous cinema? The relational experience of cinema, between audiences, cultures, histories and the intertextual connections between film objects themselves, affords repeated experience of adolescence in that we enter story worlds which explore situations of emotional anguish or tension, worlds that contain misfortunes and crises we affectively register though may not have experienced directly. In the cinema of independent women filmmakers, a key stylistic trait is willingness for experimentation, evident in breaking away from generic narrative or aesthetic form to the extent that certain styles of experimentation come to represent auteur-like signatures. When Molly Haskell asked if women directors were different, if there was 'such a thing as a "woman's point of view", a distinctly "feminine" approach to filmmaking?' (Haskell 1975/1977: 430), she was rejecting any generalisation based on essentialist argument; women filmmakers are not biologically predisposed to making films that demonstrate a 'feminine sensibility' (Haskell 1975/1977: 430). Her argument. that women directors treat sexuality (specifically the sexual act and its anxious intimacies) in a different way to their 'male counterparts', indicated such difference might be 'characterized as *feminine*' (1975/1977: 431). Her two examples were Lina Wertmüller and Liliana Cavani,[13] whose films explore sexuality which 'equalize, in subtle ways, the positions and responsibilities of their men and women' (1975/1977: 432). Toward the end of her article, Haskell questions whether there are other attributes within women's filmmaking that may fall within a 'feminine' approach:

> Are they more emotional, more intuitive? More sensitive to surroundings and décor? And while we're at it, do we observe anything – a wobbly camera, mismatched shots – that might explain why other women have such a hard time getting backing as directors? Do we notice a sudden lapse of continuity that might be explained by infirmities of a cyclical nature? (1975/1977: 434)

The danger here, of course, lies in prescription, what Haskell even catches herself doing when she asks what style is often 'expected' from women filmmakers. Yet it is undeniable, as Ivone Margulies and Jeremi Szaniawski have more recently argued, that 'woman's cinema unavoidably focuses critical attention on bodies grappling with the status of their visibility; with the burden and exposure of their exploitation; with states and affects, and how they configure identities and desiring subjectivities in flight or subjection' (2019: 8). Critical attention on the sensoria of cinema, on its aesthetic and affective resonances both as political and emotional lived experience, appears to answer Haskell's 1975 question: what else can be included within a 'feminine approach?' While women filmmakers are not solely the creators of films that examine 'the convergence and mediations between the materiality of the world and of cinema' (Margulies and Szaniawski 2019: 9), their films do engage with the 'resilient ambiguities' specific to women's lived experience more than male filmmakers, paying close attention to gesture and relations with others.

Experimentation in filmmaking is therefore an act of resistance. Similar to rebellion against social order or strategies of categorisation, its goal is to liberate. To return to Doane, the relation between aesthetics and politics mustn't rely on mimesis but it should recognise its potential within cinema's intersubjective experience; especially as an affective aesthetic encounter, it engenders reflection on our existential ethics. In many respects, Granik's film embodies Haskell's notion of a 'feminine approach' and responds to Doane's critique of mimetic representation as feminist politics, not by being avant-garde *per se*; rather, Granik's experimentation lies in avoiding prescriptive style and being precisely *of her time*, aware and authentic in the way she films the living experience of her characters. In what I am referring to as Granik's phenomenological filmmaking, there is sustained attention on texture, light, colour, gesture, body movement, emotion and intuition. There is also the 'structuring presence of the maker, her intuitive navigation of her material and story' that works as 'moving thought' (Margulies and Szaniawski 2019: 20), where female characters find themselves in situations which demand action and choice, in order to emancipate themselves from the precarity of what they are going through. Tom, for example, tries her best to show her father a different possibility of home, recognising his need for isolation but wanting it to include her need for community.

Will abruptly decides to leave the home provided for them by social services, and they hitchhike to Washington to return to the forest, although this time it lacks the security and sense of comfort first seen in Forest Park. The weather is too cold, and the pair finds shelter in a cabin. Will leaves to get more food and ends up falling and badly injuring his foot, lying unconscious on the forest floor. Tom finds and rescues Will, enlisting the help of passing quad bikers from a remote community, and gets them back to safety. At this point, usual narrative strategy dictates we might judge Will for leaving his daughter, or at least view the conflict of his accident as a precursor to forthcoming resolution of familial unification. Instead, Granik once more demonstrates a Beauvoirian tactic in her filmmaking: she uses the circumstances of the individual to engender reflective thought on collective freedom, but it isn't an easily reached thought. No-one is free without the other; and instead of positioning Will as an aberrant or harmful father to Tom, Granik illustrates that men (fathers, brothers and sons who have been psychosocially, economically and physically affected by war and socio-economic misfortune) need the support of others so that freedom itself remains possible. At the same time, we see Will's increasing incapacity to meet Tom's developing needs; principally, it is her thirst for community and social connection that Will struggles to fulfil.

Beauvoir says that leaving childhood behind and stepping into adolescence is in one way, 'a deliverance' (EA 42); childhood allows us to eschew responsibility, but it also denies political agency; we are easily dismissed as children. Adolescence, on the other hand, offers the potential for satisfaction in liberation but 'is not without great confusion' (EA 42); adolescents are not so easily dismissed, but in finding their freedom they must also decide, that is, experiment with, how to face freedom and behave as free beings. This is the underpinning ambiguity of adolescence; the possibility of freedom carries existential anguish because 'the world reflects back upon us a choice which is confirmed through this world which it has fashioned' (EA 42–3). This is why Beauvoir sees adolescence as the moment of moral choice because it is during this time that we elect to respond to the anxiety and ambiguities that come along with one's own responsibility for their freedom through the form and manner of experimentation. For object relations psychoanalysts, like Bion, it is where we demonstrate a capacity to tolerate frustration and weather emotional storms.

In the final part of the film, Tom and Will find themselves convalescing in a remote, mobile community in the Washington forest. After spending a few weeks there, Tom begins to feel settled once more. Indirectly broaching the subject of staying in the community, she asks her father, 'Have you ever seen inside a hive before?' In the following one-minute-eighteen-second sequence, Tom shows her father the bees' hive, first with the safety of gloves and then with bare hands (Figure 3.5). The close-ups on hands highlight Tom's confidence as well as her willingness to be vulnerable; she removes her gloves to gently hold the bees, illustrating her desire for autonomy and to be part of a community. The aesthetics further frame the body as a means to convey the film's politics, but a cut to medium shot also gives enough room for the audience to sense the affective ambiguity of their father-daughter relationship. Tom and Will have previously used hands to communicate their feelings and anxieties in the film (Figure 3.2); here, Tom, through gesture more than words, tells her father what she

Figure 3.5 Granik's focus on hands conveys Tom's need and want for community.

wants and needs at this point in their life together, and at the same time, acknowledges his fear and insecurity at allowing himself to become part of a group (of being touched, facing potential threat). As they both focus on the bees crawling over Tom's hand, the threat of being stung remaining unspoken between them, she says: 'you don't need to be scared'. Her words speak to her father's dread, showing that different things can possess the sense of threat but at the same time are not fated to harm you, and this is effectively conveyed through images that focus on shared gestures and the exchange of touch.

This sequence circumvents narrative expectation, particularly with respect to genre classification (as a 'teen film') but also more widely to our regard for those less fortunate and more vulnerable in society. Beauvoir says, 'One can reveal the world only on a basis revealed by other men. No project can be defined except by its interference with other projects. To make being "be" is to communicate with others by means of being' (EA 76). Tom's responsibility is evident in her facing the ambiguity of their situation and making choices that are aimed at her father's freedom as well as her own. The anguish Tom ultimately faces and must live through is also illustrative of the 'tragic ambivalence' in becoming free (EA 5). By telling her father '[t]he same thing that's wrong with you isn't wrong with me', Tom articulates the ethics of ambiguity Beauvoir proposes, one that refuses to deny our interrelationship with others or our own sense of autonomy.

Throughout this chapter, I have been interested in the existential-phenomenological experience of adolescence that Beauvoir presents in *The Ethics of Ambiguity*,[14] rather than evaluating the legitimacy of whether a film, such as *Leave No Trace*, is an example of teen cinema. Beauvoir views adolescence as a threshold of responsibility, marking the differences within lived experience between the life of the child and the life of the adult. She identifies the awareness that emerges of 'the contradictions among adults as well as their hesitations and weaknesses' (EA 41). This essential part of growing up is daunting for the child. As they begin to question adults and their lifeworld, they are faced with the task of becoming responsible for their own choices, the forming of their own subjectivity where myths are either rejected or assumed. It is no wonder Beauvoir calls this a 'crisis'; the child, in becoming an adolescent, faces 'a world which is no longer ready-made, which has to be [re]made' (EA 42).[15] It is easy to overlook the significance of adolescence in her philosophy and the foundation it offers for her notion of ambiguity, particularly the necessary role it plays in the struggle for freedom.

Notes

1 See Beauvoir's depiction of Françoise in her first novel, *She Came to Stay* (1984).
2 See Catherine Driscoll (2013, xi–xv) who discusses the importance of Beauvoir for contemporary girlhood studies. Driscoll, a formative thinker on the subject of girlhood, identifies three core legacies of Beauvoir's work on 'The Girl' from *The Second Sex*. These include her originary distinction of girlhood from childhood, where she also placed emphasis on the girl's embodied situation of lived experience; the characterisation of 'girlhood as a period of "waiting"'; and the constitution of the girl 'as an object of desire' (Driscoll 2013: xii). Driscoll's research employs a cultural studies approach elsewhere to discuss the genealogy of girlhood (2002) and varying discursive practices of feminine adolescence. Her attention on the sexual being of girls and their representation within popular culture has instructed my thoughts on the aesthetic aspects of Tom in *Leave No Trace*, especially on the distinction between 'teen' and 'adolescence' which I discuss later in the chapter. However, I deviate from Driscoll's project by concentrating on Beauvoir's notion of ambiguity as phenomenological, political, and affective experience as it relates to adolescence.
3 Understandably the predominant psychoanalytic models at the time of her writing were indeed classical. Beauvoir refers to Freud and Adler primarily in the historical section of *The Second Sex*, although in Part Two relies considerably on Helene Deutsch's work. At the time of *The Second Sex's* publication in 1949, object relations psychoanalysis via the work of D. W. Winnicott was only just being published, and of course Wilfred Bion's revolutionary models were still to come in the 1960s. I return to this later in the chapter.
4 Her other features include *Down to the Bone* (2004), *Winter's Bone* (2010), *Stray Dog* (2014, documentary).
5 Arp (2001: 45–6) notes in Beauvoir's literary work such as *The Blood of Others* (1964) and *All Men are Mortal* (1995) that female characters wrestle with ambiguous feelings in their 'attitude toward love, [which] leads to inauthentic behavior'. She identifies *The Ethics of Ambiguity* as the primary work wherein Beauvoir outlines the 'philosophical basis for her ideas about freedom' and develops her existentialist ethics. Beauvoir's own life also reflects this frustration in love, particularly in *The Prime of Life* where she writes of her jealousy regarding Sartre's affair with Marie Girard, 'jealousy is far from being an emotion of which I am incapable, or which I underrate' (PL 149), and later of Olga, whom she describes like this, '[h]er impetuous, whole-hogging nature made Olga the very epitome of adolescence' (PL 194). While Beauvoir makes assertions that she 'did not mind' (PL 193) Sartre's trysts, it is hard to dismiss their negative impact on her. This sentence is particularly telling of the frustration and sadness she must have felt: 'Little by little, however, I began to compromise: my need to agree with Sartre on all subjects outweighed the desire to see Olga through eyes other than his' (PL 194).

6 See Bolton (2016) who offers a close textual analysis of Mia in Andrea Arnold's *Fish Tank* (2009). Bolton argues that Arnold's social-realist style works as 'phenomenological experimentation' (2016: 76) as it evokes and explores Mia's lived experience, particularly emphasising cinematographic praxis as means to observe the interrelation of movement, time and space. In this way, Arnold's approach is somewhat similar to Granik's in that Tom's experiences are presented and observed like Mia's: empathically, ethically and consciously.

7 In January 2018, an amendment to the Congressional Accountability Act of 1995 revealed changes that responded to demands stemming from the #MeToo movement. These included, *inter alia*, transparency of settlement payouts, altering timeframes for filing complaints, and politicians having to pay for their own harassment settlements. <https://www.nbcnews.com/politics/congress/house-unveils-landmark-sexual-harassment-overhaul-bill-n838436> (last accessed 2 August 2020). See Qrescent Mali Mason (2018) who writes on intersectional ambiguity, discussing #BlackGirlJoy which 'centers Black women experiencing pleasure and exaltation' (2018: 60) as a series of individual acts (social media posts) that form a collective expression of resistance, 'revolt need not be lived as traumatic but can rather be experienced in the mode of celebration' (2018: 61).

8 In particular, Driscoll's final chapter, 'Which Teen/Film?', discusses the distinction between adolescence and teen cinema in transnational contexts. She argues that the increasing syndication of teen media (constitutive of transnational youth culture) has yoked cross-cultural genres and other creative industries (such as marketing and technology platforms) to 'manifesting the internationalization of adolescence' (2011: 149).

9 See Bion's (1970) notion of negative capability which refers to the removal of 'any sense of expectation from the circumstance and event of the analytic situation'. This view of negation, or negative capability, attends 'more specifically to open, intuitive observation' by being reflexive of observation as a form of embodied experience (Fuery 2018: 169), and such a conception of negation fits very well with Granik's style of filmmaking given she does not create any sense of judgement in her practice.

10 See 'Hate in the Counter-Transference', 194–203, where Winnicott specifically addresses the place and role of difficult emotions in terms of seeking emotional freedom: 'An analyst has to display all the patience and tolerance and reliability of a mother devoted to her infant; has to recognize the patient's wishes as needs; has to put aside other interests in order to be available and to be punctual and objective; and has to seem to want to give what is really only given because of the patient's needs' (1992: 202–3). This is very close to Beauvoir's notion of reciprocal recognition which is taken up later in the book (specifically Chapters 7 and 8).

11 Debra Bergoffen notes that the avoidance of responsibility is a form of bad faith 'that constitutes a permanent threat to the possibility of an existential

ethic' (1997: 82). She argues that for Beauvoir, the tensions evoked by ambiguity are historical, determined by the fantasy of nostalgia which recalls the omnipotence of childhood, a time and space of doing what we want without any real consequences in a world decided for us, 'in experiencing values and meanings as already given, [the child] experiences itself as having a clearly defined place in the world; it experiences itself as the fulfillment of its desire to be' (Bergoffen 1997: 83). Cinema, in theatrical auditorium situations, provides an environment where one can retreat into a reminiscence of nostalgic fantasy and sensibility, presenting a situation that we acquiesce as being real. In order to follow the story, for the film to become meaningful, we must submit to the order of the film. I explore the concept of bad faith in greater detail in Chapter 5.

12 In his 1976 paper on 'Emotional Turbulence', Bion writes that he does not 'stress adolescence' over other periods of life because it is a period that is 'too strong'. What he means by this is that adolescence, as a period of mental turbulence, defines its period because it is so intense, and 'latency is too weak' to hide the emotional turmoil it contains. Adolescents don't have the luxury of latency, that is, you can't hide from or avoid the emotional turbulence from the struggle of choices that are demanded from adolescence (the defence mechanism of repression is not as fully developed as in adults). Therefore, instead of adolescence being a consequence of difficulties or struggles, it *is* these things – adolescence *is* the embodiment of complex and uncomfortable proto-mental struggle, what is thought and felt.

13 See my discussion of Liliana Cavani's 1974 film *The Night Porter* with regard to Beauvoir's thinking in Chapter 2.

14 I am referring to Beauvoir's philosophical essays and not her literary works. See Fullbrook and Fullbrook (1998) for a discussion of the two unpublished chapters of *She Came to Stay* which clearly illustrate Beauvoir's view that adolescence was a significant period of life where one develops and experiments with their moral and ethical choices.

15 See Emma Wilson (2012) who writes on Beauvoir's attention toward childhood within the context of Lucile Hadžhalilović's film, *Innocence* (2004).

CHAPTER 4

Habit the Cinematic Encounter: Cheryl Dunye and the 'Dunyementaries'

In her review of Maurice Merleau-Ponty's *Phenomenology of Perception*,[1] Beauvoir makes a point concerning embodied perception, saying that 'in spite of ethics', each person knows intimately a life that is their own, where each person sees with their own eyes (1945b/2004: 159). She emphasises ambiguity within the experience of perception as a means of highlighting the more prevalent ambiguity within the human condition, supporting Merleau-Ponty's use of the phenomenological approach that facilitates authentic connections with the world: 'it is in giving myself to the world that I realize myself, and it is in assuming myself that I have a hold on the world' (1945b/2004: 160). In other words, becoming enworlded as conscious and reflexive agents requires recognition and acceptance of ambiguous experience. This philosophy is clearly personified in the 'Dunyementaries', a collection of experimental films by African American filmmaker Cheryl Duyne, whose creative practice blends various reflexive, participatory and poetic modes to destabilise established narrative and documentary genres, crafting a subtle, yet effective style that celebrates ambiguity in women's identity. In this chapter, I discuss phenomenologies of habit as a way to think through the relationship between racialised vision, situation, and freedom within film experience, ending with a consideration of how Dunye realises Alia Al-Saji's (2014) phenomenology of hesitation as ethico-political action that interrupts complacent viewing habits in the cinematic encounter.

Beauvoir states phenomenology's rejection of the opposition between subject and object opens up the possibility of seeing connections through lived experience and that this perceptive awareness is what leads to the development of an ethical existence. The result is the opportunity for an audacious life, the freedom to make oneself known and say, 'I am here' (1945b/2004: 160). Not as easy as it sounds, of course, as the audacity of ethical existence requires acceptance of responsibility, often breaking the habits of perception we have learned to use in order to navigate our life. It is when we are shown worlds of another's lived experience (those that are often ignored, forgotten or neglected), presented with embodied perceptions that are not our own, that we may learn to develop more ethical ways of being.

Beauvoir's review of Merleau-Ponty's book is short, around five pages, yet it outlines all of the major philosophical themes that came to occupy her later works: the fundamental importance of ambiguity in lived experience; the significance of the body and its role in realising freedom through responsibility; and how the embodied experience of perception involves relations with others, without which ethical existence (as a freedom) is not possible. On this note, one of Beauvoir's legacies (and other existentialists, such as Merleau-Ponty) for the study of moving-image experience, is that a phenomenological approach helps to reveal the world as it is experienced in all its diversity and complexity. Through the story worlds of cinema, television and digital media, we can be introduced to another's world of perception that we might never know otherwise; these different worlds involve our embodied perception, offering an opportunity to gain a broader, more complex, and potentially more ethical, understanding of the world. It isn't just that we might see unusual places or watch diverse stories; we are also afforded the experience of seeing how others see and live their worlds differently. A phenomenological consideration of film experience therefore positions cinema as comprising multiple other worlds that audiences negotiate between their own, embodied subjective perception and that of the story world screened.

In *The Address of the Eye: A Phenomenology of Film Experience*, Vivian Sobchack writes: 'Without an act of viewing and a subject who knows itself reflexively as the locus and origin of viewing *as* an act, there could be no film and no "film experience"' (1992: 51). By describing the act of viewing as an active, embodied engagement with the world, Sobchack foregrounds vision, more specifically, seeing the world as 'a *situated* mode of being that discovers the *self* in the world and recognizes the activity of seeing as *mediated*, as the consciousness of experience' (1992: 51).[2] Sobchack makes it clear that this activity is not innate, explaining that the ability to see is not equivalent to reflexive conscious perception, that is, knowing one is capable of seeing and thinking about what is seen, what she terms as a 'possession of our own vision' (1992: 54). Film experience, therefore, involves reflexive consciousness of seeing, knowing that you are watching a film as well as having the capacity to use moving images to negotiate meaning.[3] Further, Sobchack alludes to the ambiguity within conscious embodied perception, identifying the intentionality of seeing within the structure of film experience:

knowledge of the lived-body as both the *subject of seeing* and an *object of seeing* ... without such reflexive and reflective consciousness of vision and the latter's reversible structure, what we *mean* by film experience would not be possible'. (1992: 53)

This resonates with Beauvoir's much earlier claim that phenomenology 'restores things to us' (Beauvoir 1945b/2004: 162), implying that although we can exist in the world, it is only through reflecting on our use of and engagement with the world (its objects, like films, and people) that we can know ourselves authentically. For existential phenomenologists like Beauvoir and Merleau-Ponty, this is not a solely theoretical pursuit; it is only through sensory, embodied perception that we can communicate with and through the world.

While Sobchack does not state it in such terms, what she examines is the habitus of seeing, highlighting the repetition, reflexivity and reversibility of conscious viewing that structures our perceptual encounters. Even though embodied seeing experience is not directly discussed as a phenomenology of *habit*, her emphasis on the existential structure of seeing within film experience does affirm the notion that a habit of seeing exists as material, vital action that requires examination if we are to fully 'know ourselves as body-subjects living a perceptual encounter with the world and other that is always already communicative, always already expressive and semiotic in nature' (Sobchack 1992: 54). Habit within film experience requires careful description, but in basic terms it includes repetition in technique, content and delivery (both within the film world and the world of the audience) in order to determine a habitus specific to its perceptual encounters, including eyes, ears and body facing a screen, seated; a guided bodily orientation to the intersubjective experience between the two worlds – what Sobchack calls a '*doubled*' existential structure of seeing (1992: 57).

Habitus, a term critically developed by sociologist Pierre Bourdieu (1992a), refers to the experience of situation involving a set of structuring parameters that support and sustain actions of distinction and classification. Habitus can be identified through the categories (and sub-categories) of film genre. For example, habitus informs the ways in which people differentiate between horror and war films despite both involving gore, fighting, blood, death and traumatic scenes. Bourdieu and Loïc Wacquant state: 'Habitus is creative, inventive, but within the limits of its structures, which are the embodied sedimentation of the social structures which produce it' (1992b: 19). Habitus, then, is a term that acknowledges the range of bodily activities (gestures, perceptions, movements, and so on) that comprise living experience with the world, specifically our relations with objects and others within it. It supposes the existence of corporeal manner, a way of being that exists across and within different social situations, being at once both general and situation specific.[4]

Habit, as discussed throughout this chapter, does not refer to instinctual or libidinal response. While it may include and acknowledge 'individual, corporeal, perceptual and personal, or, on the other hand, social, cultural, collective, historical and traditional' experience (Moran 2011: 55), it does not do so prescriptively. Habit is discussed in terms of situation, embodied experience and its role in the encounter, continuing with Lori Jo Marso's definition as explained in Chapter 3. To recall, Marso interprets Beauvoir's existential phenomenology as concentrating on the politics of the encounter wherein our relations, choices and actions with others are 'the *only* way to produce and experience freedom' (2017: 2). While habit in the cinematic encounter may involve physical activities specific to viewership – sitting, facing a screen, and so on – these routine behaviours are not my main focus. I am more interested in the sensibilities and manners of habit that aesthetically inform ways of knowing and relating, as well as contributing to the formation of ethical choice, in order to recognise the variable functions that habit holds at the individual and collective levels. This means that describing what role(s) habit plays is more useful than specifying what literal or conscious habits exist in the cinematic encounter (even though these are inextricably linked). Therefore, I discuss two characterisations of habit in order to emphasise their role in the embodied perception of cinema. These are 1) the associations of habit within aesthetic experimentation; and 2) habit's affective aspects – manifested through Al-Saji's phenomenology of hesitation – as 'a situated response to the context in which the body finds itself' (2014: 145). These two characteristics of habit discussed within the context of embodied perception consider the political potential cinema offers for transformation within broader habitual behaviour.

A phenomenological study of habit within film experience questions how habit infuses the body, closely describing the orientations within the cinematic encounter that highlight how reflexivity concerning habit may lead to socio-political awareness and, potentially, freedom. As Dermot Moran puts it,

> Habit has to be located between reflexive behaviour and intellectually self-conscious deliberate action. It is not to be understood as something merely mechanical or automatic, a matter of sheer mindless repetition ... it is a kind of embodied praxis that is actually extremely individualised. Each individual has his or her own 'style'. (Moran 2011: 56–7)

Cheryl Dunye's style of filmmaking exemplifies a series of her own aesthetic habits that intentionally interrupt broader White perceptual habits of viewing through experimentation, thereby evoking an ethical challenge in the cinematic encounter. My aim in this chapter is to disclose such habits and spotlight the ethical and political value that independent women's filmmaking has for our habits of thinking and feeling, particularly in terms of film-going tendencies (and complacencies). Habit, as Beauvoir tells us, 'has more than one meaning, and we must distinguish between them' (CA 466), so that we might mine its political and affective potential. Dunye's auto-ethnographic filmmaking effectively challenges racialised habitual vision as it concerns the condition of woman. I argue that her experimental approach illuminates Beauvoir's existentialist ethics and notion of freedom through a recognition of responsibility for creating meaning in one's world. More explicitly, Dunye demonstrates a phenomenological style of filmmaking through her consistent cinematic expression of Black lesbian experience – one conscious of the power of images on the sense of embodied being. Before I discuss Dunye's films in detail, let us contextualise the significance of habit within Beauvoir's phenomenology and the ways in which it has been taken up by other feminist phenomenologists.

Kruks and Fielding on Phenomenologies of Habit

Beauvoir's discussion of habit in *The Coming of Age* informs my consideration of the conditions and circumstances of habit within film experience and the value it holds for identifying ambiguous freedom through aesthetic experimentation. For Beauvoir, taking 'refuge in habit' is a defence against the precarities of situation and the inner anxieties they manifest (CA 466). She defines the meaning of habit as repeated lived experience seen 'in the shape of attitudes and forms of behaviour' (CA 466), which increase via routine and age. Habit manifests in repetition of daily activities, despite the variations that such routines can include. Beauvoir gives the example of walking (not surprising, given her love for it)[5]; one can take a walk every day even though the route itself may change. The repetition of routine gives birth to habit and the longer habit exists, the greater its antinomy for the old: reassurance versus spontaneity. Habit, defined this way, offers 'ontological security', (CA 469) sparing one 'the effort of difficult adaptations' (CA 466). Adhering to habit wards off the existential anguish that resurfaces loudly in old age, one 'avoids having to ask himself the dreadful question, "What shall I do?"' (CA 467). Habit, in this conception, functions as a defence mechanism protecting the aged from confronting loss of social value, of failing memory and a sense of purposelessness to living. It guards against powerlessness over one's future. At first glance, Beauvoir appears to view habit in a very negative light but to read her in this way is to miss the political appeal of her phenomenological inquiry. Beauvoir reflects on the existence of habit in the lived experience of older people in order to present a political warning; *The Coming of Age* is a phenomenology of ageing for those not yet aged, a harbinger of what is to come if we do not reflect on habit's inherent ambiguity.

Sonia Kruks notes that Beauvoir's core intention in *The Coming of Age* is to identify the 'oppression and ontological crisis' of old age, a situation brought about by social forces, which furthers the aged's incapacity to live and act in 'future-oriented' ways (2014: 98). Habit, however, remains significant and meaningful, involving 'an intentional "re-presenting" of the past ... [and] produc[ing] an "integration" in which a "reanimated past" and "anticipated future" are drawn together' (2014: 99). Habit, ironically, maintains ambiguity within lived experience as we get older, and at the same time it structures the sedimentation of life. Helen Fielding, drawing on Merleau-Ponty's notion of the habit body, writes of the interrelation between situation and habit body, explaining that '[t]he other's body teaches me how to touch. This knowing is not innate; it is learned and sedimented in the habit body [...] Perception as a questioning of the world is then always already imbued with sense that belongs to the situation' (2020: 156). Habit, then, involves repeated embodied perception that affirms our orientation to the world and place within it. The ways in which we learn to see the world are continuously repeated – habitually – and any disruption to these viewing habits carries the potential for existential confrontation (often described as a 'crisis') or liberation. Fielding puts it this way:

> To disrupt someone's habitual life is to unanchor that life from the world, from an identity shaped by repetition, by the constancy of a shared reality of things, that is, from the spatial-temporal process of inhabitation, and thus from her ability to engage with others and to disclose the world. (2014: 69)

Even though Beauvoir's discussion of habit is mainly concerned with old age, feminist phenomenologists, like Kruks and Fielding, apply the notion of habit to broader existential situations, recognising that without the ontological security of habit, critical reflection on lived experience is hard to evoke.

Merleau-Ponty's Habit Body

A phenomenology of habit engages primarily with the ambiguity of lived experience, for habit is seen as an embodied expression of how the body negotiates itself with the world. Habit simultaneously involves thinking and non-thinking, the subjective and the objective. For Merleau-Ponty, it is through habit that we introject the world, that is, we form and perform habitual behaviours so that we may have and be in the world:

> In so far as I have a body through which I act in the world, space and time are not for me, a collection of adjacent points nor are they a limitless number of relations synthesized by my consciousness, and into which it draws my body. I am not in space and time, nor do I conceive space and time; I belong to them, my body combines with them and includes them. (1945/2002: 140)

Through habit we inhabit the world, one that necessarily involves the ambiguous worlds of others, and because Merleau-Ponty recognises that embodied living experience always includes 'indeterminate horizons that contain other points of view' (1945/2002: 140), habit becomes a phenomenal expression of experience that is both unique to a body and something that is shared between bodies. My habit may not be your habit but we see each other's habits and a relation is formed through recognising the possibility of similar phenomenal being-in-the-world.

As phenomenology concentrates on the bracketed off experience between the individual (their conscious intentionality) and their experience with the world, it highlights the agency within such experience. Beauvoir argued that an existentialist phenomenology didn't only allow for 'an elaborations of an ethics' but that it was the 'only philosophy in which ethics has a place' (EA 34). By describing agency within lived experience, one must face the relationship between action, responsibility and freedom; and these interrelated components always involve the body. This is significant for habit because it indicates that it is most effective when it operates at the gestural level, when we find ourselves reacting or behaving responsively, rather than reflectively (and indeed responsibly). Merleau-Ponty says that '[t]he cultivation of habit is indeed the grasping of a significance, but it is the motor grasping of a motor significance' (1945/2002: 143); put another way, the more a behaviour is practised, becoming a habit within a specific context, the more naturalised and normalised it becomes. One example he gives is that of being able to drive a car through a narrow space without needing to measure the space first, so that a behaviour that was once uncertain and unfamiliar becomes an extension of our being-in-the-world: 'Habit expresses our power of dilating our being in the world, or changing our existence by appropriating fresh instruments' (1945/2002: 144). Until a different car is driven through the same space, the habit anchors the body in the world through specific behaviour and motility.

Within the context of film experience, we can think how habit anchors our being-in-the-world through the repetition of selective representation on screen, such as seeing only White, cis-gendered heteronormative sexual relationships. Sex scenes between men and women in narrative features more often than not privilege the attractive, fit and young. It is a casting recipe so common that it is safe to refer to it as a habit of cinema, a stalwart sustaining the habitus of film experience. However, implications of this habit are manifold and phenomenology helps to describe the affective impact of such cultivated cinematic habits on the spectator's situation. At one level, the habit is formed in the repetition of such casting, but more significantly the 'visual pattern' of an audience negotiating the world with such limited images 'can evoke a certain type of motor response' (Merleau-Ponty 1945/2002: 144). The repetition of embodied perception and response to cis-het White sex scenes results in the normalisation and naturalisation of those images. A consequence of regular viewing across varied Hollywood genres shows they appear as given, inducing neutral affective response. When this habit of representation is broken and the visual pattern of cis-het White sexuality is disrupted with Black lesbian subjectivity, does it yield a different embodied response? Are audiences' bodies reacting differently to this paradigmatic shift? Merleau-Ponty reminds us that 'it is the body which "understands" in the cultivation of habit' and a phenomenological study of habit allows us to rethink what is really being understood within such habitual lived experience, not as conscious thought, but as affective embodied response (Merleau-Ponty 1945/2002: 144). This rethinking is also seen in Beauvoir's *Ethics*, where she writes of the responsibility required in thinking one's condition: 'in the very condition of man there enters the possibility of not fulfilling this condition' (EA 35). By noticing habit, assessing its normalisation (grasping its significance) and describing our embodied, affective responses, we can begin to exercise ethical action. A phenomenology of habit within the cinematic encounter is an effective first step to evaluating a cinema of ethics and recognising what our responses to images are actually telling us.

In their respective discussions of existential ethics and habit, despite offering frameworks for ways of being-in-the-world, neither Beauvoir nor Merleau-Ponty consider the specificities of racial embodied perception, unlike their contemporary, psychoanalyst Frantz Fanon, who in *Black Skin, White Masks* (1952/2008) specifically focuses on the thought and felt experiences of racialisation in terms of habit and encounters. Fanon associates the habit body, its spatiality and movement with a racialised sense of being through a critique of the White gaze. He identifies a 'historical-racial schema' as borne from myths created by the White man: 'I arrive slowly in the world; sudden emergences are no longer my habit. I crawl along. The White gaze, the only valid one, is already dissecting me. I am *fixed*' (1952/2008: 95). Fanon links body comportment with habits of perception, specifically the White gaze over Black bodies, and this manner of living becomes a habit that must be rejected if the Black man is to be free. In *America Day by Day*, Beauvoir reflects on the intersection of freedom and oppression in terms of race and class. In her 9 February entry, she describes going to the Abyssinian Baptist Church in Harlem with close friend Richard Wright, an African American writer. At times her diary entries are a little galling; she describes Reverend Adam Clayton Powell: '[he had] such light skin and aquiline features that I would never have taken him for black' (ADD 57). I read this as Beauvoir being honest in her account (acknowledging that this is a grace I often afford her in the autobiographies), as she also seeks to describe the reality of Black life against her position as a foreign witness in the United States in 1947.[6] In her less philosophical works, Beauvoir sought to offer a style of thinking that was accessible and less abstract. As Sara Heinämaa explains, 'Beauvoir presents a different view of philosophizing, an alternative notion of philosophy. In her writing, philosophical activity is seen primarily as the search for truth and evidence, and as questioning and communication with others' (1999: 119). In *America Day by Day*, her journal entries illustrate this style, couching a discussion of the links between acts of behaviour and freedom within such reflexive and uncensored expression.[7]

Wright explains to her that

> there isn't a minute in a black person's life that isn't penetrated by social consciousness. From the cradle to the grave, working, eating, loving, walking, dancing, praying, he can never forget that he is black, and that makes him conscious every minute of the whole White world from which the word 'black' takes its meaning. (ADD 57-8)

Beauvoir, a firm exponent of freedom for all, writes of the oppression she sees and addresses it throughout her four-month journey across the United States. On one outing to Café Society, she describes a performance by Josh White (an African American singer) and her reaction to the audience's reception: 'The house applauds warmly ... However, I feel uncomfortable' (ADD 71). The management had previously refused service to a Black woman a few weeks earlier and yet, at Josh White's performance, there was applause and support from White Americans in the crowd. Beauvoir is quick to observe the hypocrisy here and speaks to the cultural habitus of Black lived experience in the United States as structured through a deep awareness of White privilege and reification of otherness. She notes 'the blacks who sing and play know very well that they don't have the right to sit in the audience. They must not have much friendship in their hearts' (ADD 71). For Beauvoir, freedom is always associated with embodied being and the experience of situation. Her observations of behavioural habits are made reflexively with the intention to expose their impact on identity and freedom; habits help to determine the politics of subjectivity and these are always already embodied. By describing habits (indirectly) as she sees and experiences them, whether in American bars or within women's situation, Beauvoir's intention is to indicate how alternative ways of seeing situation function as political action and present possible pathways to futures of freedom. In many respects, her reflexive observations are expressions of hesitation regarding situations of oppression.

Merleau-Ponty's concept of the habit body has also informed important feminist scholarship on embodiment, race and perception,[8] identifying habit as a key phenomenological concept for describing the affective and negative impact of prejudice on the body.[9] Beauvoir's discussion of habit in *The Coming of Age* similarly discloses negative consequences of naturalising processes of othering, her attention, however, is directed toward the aged and their lived experience. Contemporary feminist phenomenologies of racialising vision within the context of habit, hesitation and freedom (Alcoff 2000a; Al-Saji 2014; Ngo 2016) provide an intersectional perspective on our viewing practices and the capacity to identify the links between habit, ambiguity and freedom. Despite film experience not being a shared focus between these scholars, their collective critical phenomenologies of perception and experience 'contain[s] the ground for both objectification and its critique, for racialization and for antiracist interventions into social practice' (Al-Saji 2014: 136), which is essential for thinking about habit and perceptual manners in the cinematic encounter.

Beauvoir's review of Merleau-Ponty's *Phenomenology of Perception* reveals the significant impact his ideas had on the formation of her own philosophy of existentialist ethics and the notion of ambiguity. When read next to the opening of *The Ethics of Ambiguity*, it is clear that her philosophy of ambiguity, as the foundational element of human existence, is indebted in part to Merleau-Ponty's work. In the review she writes, 'it becomes impossible to possess the world and oneself at the same time … the subject reveals itself only through the objects in which it is engaged'

(1945b/2004: 160); with this idea stated similarly in the opening of *The Ethics of Ambiguity*:

> This privilege, which he alone possesses, of being a sovereign and unique subject amidst a universe of objects, is what he shares with all his fellow-men. In turn an object for others, he is nothing more than an individual in the collectivity on which he depends. (EA 6)

A year earlier, Beauvoir's *Pyrrhus and Cineas* put forward an ontologically focused theory of freedom,[10] but between her review of Merleau-Ponty's book and the writing of *Ethics*, her elaboration of ambiguous human experience took on stronger consideration of embodiment, directing her philosophy of ethical freedom along bodily and relational lines. Her existential ethics depended on the concept of embodied situation, involving the existence and action of others, 'the freedom of one man almost always concerns that of other individuals' (EA 155) – each situation is different, requiring different ethical action, and again her emphasis on the experience of connection and relation informs her thinking on freedom.

While *The Ethics of Ambiguity* is not without its difficulties,[11] it is the primary work where we see Beauvoir's thinking shift, incorporating more affectively driven phenomenology no doubt in response to Merleau-Ponty's notions of the habit body and the body schema (body image). Her attention to ambiguous lived experience forms the basis for all our engagements with the world: 'the notion of body image is ambiguous', 'the body image is finally a way of stating that my body is in-the-world' (Merleau-Ponty 1945/2002: 98, 101). By the time Beauvoir completes *The Second Sex* in 1949, presenting her existential phenomenology on the condition of woman, she locates women's experience through her body, making it clear that the relationship a woman has with her own body is connected to the one she has with the world and other people. The body, therefore, and primarily, is ambiguous living experience; its intentionality makes itself known and felt in other bodies through our choices and actions, that is, our living experiences and connections with others of which habit plays a significant part.

The word 'habit' does not feature as a specific point of discussion in the review, *Ethics*, or *The Second Sex*. Indeed, it does not really become a direct topic of Beauvoir's attention until much later in *The Coming of Age*, but the interrelationship of lived experience, time and habit as cornerstones of ambiguity appear in different forms and with varying degrees of emphasis across her writing, particularly with regard to women's situation and character.[12] After all, what is *The Second Sex* if not a concerted attempt to shift perceptual and habitual ways of living within women's situation?

A Beauvoirian Conception of Freedom

Merleau-Ponty's work on the habit body was not Beauvoir's first encounter with a phenomenological account of the body. In *The Prime of Life*, she tells us that in 1934 she 'dipped into Husserl for the first time' (PL 162), reading a collection of Husserl's lectures and notes, *Lessons on Internal Time Consciousness*. Finding it exciting, she wrote: 'I felt I had never come so close to the real truth' (162). Later in 1935, Sartre commented that Beauvoir's command of Husserlian phenomenology was 'quicker and more precise than his own' (PL 178). Her familiarity with Husserl's rich phenomenology of the body would have therefore served her well when reviewing Merleau-Ponty's reconsideration, particularly on the issue of habit.[13] As Moran also explains, Husserl saw habit as a vital aspect of meaningful life, 'from the level of perceptual experience, through the formation of the ego, to the development of society, history and *tradition*, indeed to our whole sense of the *harmonious course of worldly life* and to the genetic constitution of worldhood as such' (2011: 53). So, while it is safe to say Beauvoir's conception of habit, embodiment and ultimately her existential ethics is highly influenced by Merleau-Ponty's thinking, it is also served by her strong command of philosophical and phenomenological theory.[14]

It is on these terms that I argue that Dunye is a filmmaker who positions a woman's body in political ways, through 'real' images via ethnographic style, involving personal, lived experience as a character in her stories about women whose lives are often marginalised or (in Dunye's words) 'forgotten' (1992: 18). The existentialist-phenomenology I see at work in Dunye's films interrupts the habitual behaviours prevalent in the cinematic encounter. Dunye's personal life is also her theoretical life; through her films she becomes 'her own text' (Dunye in Juhasz 1992: 293). Beauvoir writes:

> To exist genuinely is not to deny this spontaneous movement of my transcendence, but only to refuse to lose myself in it. Existentialist conversion should rather be compared to Husserlian reduction: let man put his will to be 'in parentheses' and he will thereby be brought to the consciousness of his true condition. And just as phenomenological reduction prevents the errors of dogmatism by suspending all affirmation concerning the mode of reality of the external world, whose flesh and bone presence the reduction does not, however, contest, so existentialist conversion does not suppress my instincts, desires, plans, and passions. It merely prevents any possibility of failure by refusing to set up as absolutes the ends toward which my transcendence thrusts itself, and by considering them in their connection with the freedom which projects them. (EA 13)

In this lengthy quote, Beauvoir shows the influence that both Husserl and Merleau-Ponty had on her philosophy of existential ethics. Here she refers to the *epoché*, Husserl's phenomenological method of bracketing off experience, to argue that bracketed experience ('in parentheses') engenders conscious reflection of one's 'true condition'. Far from denying or forgetting the materiality of the body in this activity, Beauvoir asserts that the phenomenological method is effective because it permits a questioning of the world, its 'absolutes', within the freedom of connection. This is the freedom at work in the films of Dunye – a body of work which foregrounds the connection between the audience and the screen story. Beauvoir emphasises a similar connection: by refusing 'facts' (absolutes) in the world and looking more at our experience with objects and reflecting on them, we can enact a freedom of connection. Therefore, in Beauvoir's view, it doesn't matter if things are true or not (or good or bad) in themselves, an existential ethics is formed in how we experience our connection and choose to act reflexively on such experience.

For Beauvoir, 'freedom realizes itself only by engaging itself in the world: to such an extent that man's project toward freedom is embodied for him in definite acts of behavior' (EA 84); freedom establishes existence, to exist is to be free, to be able to act and exercise agency. But freedom lies in responsibility, alive in the ways in which we live in the world with other people. Underwriting all the elements within Beauvoir's conception of freedom (responsibility, action, choice) is an understanding of relationality. The phenomenological question here, then, is not what is different about Dunye's films (although clearly that it is relevant), but rather concerns the manner in which her films explore the ways we live through the world and relate to others. By describing the connections between her films and the experimental forms they utilise and repeat, we can ask more reflectively: how does Dunye's experimentation demonstrate a critical questioning of habit (and our experiences of habit and habitus) as it affects women? Can the difference of such cinematic experience tell us something more about the condition of woman and her reality?

Now that I have outlined a phenomenology of habit via Beauvoir and Merleau-Ponty, in the following section, I examine the stylistic traits and practices within Dunye's films that I argue critique habitual modes of seeing, but also discuss how a reflexivity of habit in film experience can become 'a matter of self-growth and social justice ... [a] fresh opportunity for thinking of "assuming ambiguity" as a lifelong endeavor made up of many small projects and practices of situated resistance to stagnation' (Cuffari 2011: 535). I then draw on Al-Saji's phenomenology of hesitation to complement Beauvoir's phenomenology of habit in considering film experience and the role viewing habits play in our thinking and feeling development, concentrating on racial and sexual embodiment.

Cheryl Dunye: Unanchoring Habit through Aesthetic Experimentation

One of the reasons for selecting Dunye as a case study for critically describing a phenomenology of habit in the cinematic encounter is that her films consistently and intentionally make clear the links between personal lived experience, aesthetic and creative praxis, and political potential – in other words they are all concerned with a conscious bracketing-off of experience and connections with people. Her films play with convention (what Kathleen McHugh calls 'accessible form' (2007: 342)), using popular aesthetics (low budget; mixed media of Super 8, Hi-8 video and 16mm film;[15] comedic and narrative structure) and overlapping documentary styles (participatory, reflexive and performative modes) in order to interrupt them. Dunye's use of accessible form is intentional, establishing a sense of familiarity in the habitus of spectatorship, while at the same time slowly breaking away from previous normalising and naturalising tendencies.

Dunye's films convey a Beauvoirian quality through their interconnected themes of ethics, subjectivity and critical comment on habits of perception. In a video interview for The Criterion Collection with Grace Barber-Plentie (2020), Dunye expresses her motivation for filming a sex scene between characters Shae (Cheryl Dunye) and Margo (Wanda Freeman) in one of her early short films *She Don't Fade* (1991): 'It was a necessity because I really thought it was a political act to see two women's bodies, brown like me, in bed literally sort of rolling around.' Dunye recognised the exclusion of Black lesbian sexuality in the habitus of film experience and sought to create space for diverse representations of their subjectivity on screen, thereby taking responsibility for the 'political act' and effecting change. We perceive the world via instruction, through style, content and manners of viewing, meaning it isn't just how we are taught to see, but rather what we are taught to recognise and identify that matters. In order to change and transform habits of perception that instruct our way of being-in-the-world, to resist sedimentation and offer variable ways of being anchored in the world, we need different sets of instructions (styles as social scripts) regarding what and how to see differently.

For Dunye, 'documenting was the way it [filmmaking] began' (2020 interview), and she cites this style as the foundation for her 'theory of three's', the basis for her self-titled 'Dunyementaries'. Her audiences' attention is directed toward hearing, seeing and reading the messages within the stories in her films, making clear Dunye's existential ethical statement: 'I do exist and I'm telling you a story', which echoes Beauvoir's comment concerning the audacity of saying 'I am here'. The experimentation of the 'Dunyementaries' involves mixing the aesthetic elements of direct address which act as an appeal to the audience (Figure 4.1); a focus on bodies and gestural movement, which evoke understanding of connection and relation with others; involvement of her community peoples, and the legacy (good or bad) of history 'to create a texture of here I am, all full, all complete'. (Dunye 2020). Fielding writes that perceptual habits are formed at historical and cultural levels, they are institutional, and therefore any challenge to or resistance of habit in embodied perception must also find fresh expression so that space is generated for 'new ways of

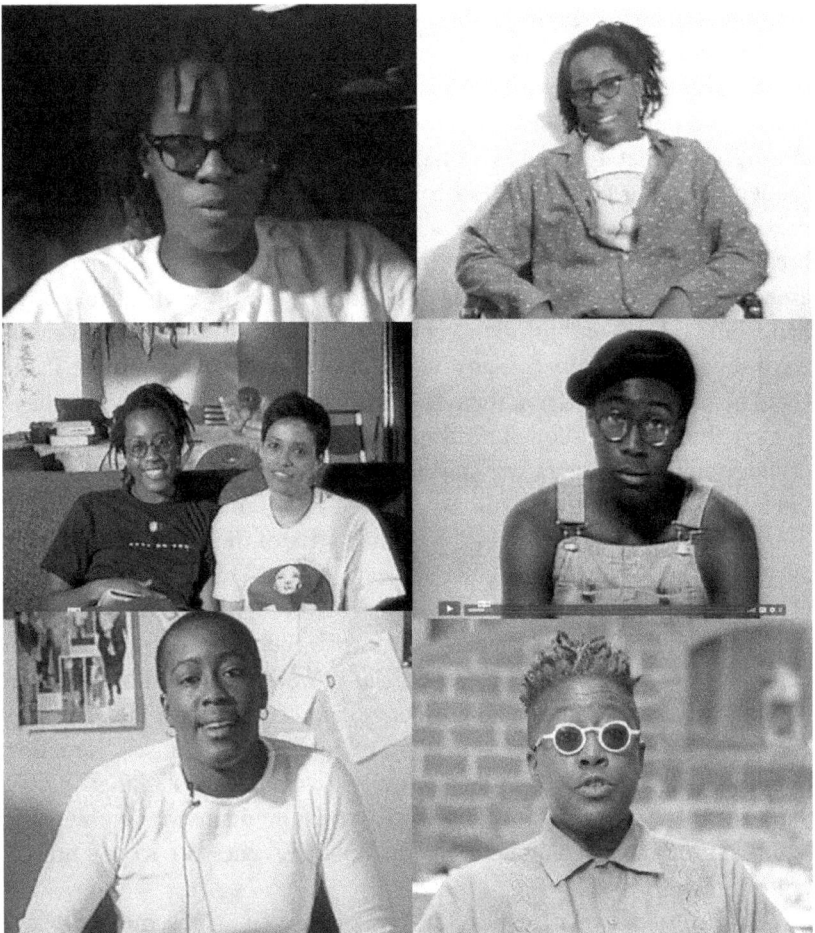

Figure 4.1 Cheryl Dunye's habit of direct address. From top left: *Janine* (1990); *She Don't Fade* (1991); *The Potluck and the Passion* (1993); *Greetings from Africa* (1994); *The Watermelon Woman* (1996); *Cheryl Dunye Interview* (2020).

moving and hence understanding' (2020: 156). Fielding also explains that if the habit body is not challenged or presented with alternative ways of existing, it may restrict its capacity for knowing and connecting: 'A world can disable certain bodies that are not accommodated in their alternative ways of inhabiting it' (2020: 157). The 'Dunyementaries' are a collection of films that unmake and remake complex and diverse portrayals of Black womanhood, breaking habits of viewing women on screen and providing new sensory, embodied perceptive experience for audiences.

The two sex scenes in *She Don't Fade* work as examples of phenomenological reduction of Black lesbian lived experience within film experience and foreground the experience of embodied perception. They are also examples of how breaking habits of perception leads to ethical action within the cinematic encounter because they present different contexts of sexuality and thereby engender varying embodied responses. The first sex scene occurs between Shae and Margo and is shot as a reflexive ethnography that appears as a 'making of an intimate lesbian sex scene' sequence. The scene begins with a close-up shot of Shae and Margo, naked and kissing in bed. There is no score or diegetic music and Cheryl breaks character and the fabric of the eroticism by joking to the off-screen crew 'just don't be all quiet please!' For the rest of the scene, shot with a hand-held camera and through a combination of close and medium shots, we hear direction from a man's voice, as well as Cheryl's friend, Paula (Paula Cronan) instructing them to 'sit up', 'caress each other', 'you have to move more'. The sequence, like the film's overall structure, combines ethnographic and narrative storytelling with humour and a sense of casualness, blurring the normative ways of classifying a sex scene within film experience. McHugh sees this as indicative of the political intentionality of French New Wave cinema, seen in Jean-Luc Godard's *Passion* (1982) or *La Chinoise* (1967), for example. Although where Godard used Brechtian alienation strategies to break with the natural attitude in film experience to reassert cinema's political power and potential for social comment (exposing filmmaking practice, direct address to the audience, conversation with off-screen crew), McHugh views Dunye's intention as being 'to make the lesbian community accessible and familiar' (2007: 348). Arguably, given the conservatism within mainstream cinematic habitus, integrating comedic moments in such scenes is part of Dunye's political action.

The second sex scene appears in 'the intense fantasy' sequence where Shae imagines having sex with Nikki, a woman Shae briefly meets and finds herself immediately attracted to while out and about. Shae is making jewellery for her vending business and begins to reimagine her intimate interactions with girlfriend Margo as being with her new interest, Nikki. Via a low-angle shot, we see the two women, naked and kissing, spliced with jumpy cuts of Shae humming and working. There is a very different tone throughout this imaginary sequence – no comedy or off-screen discussion. As the sequence progresses, the shots of Shae and Nikki are slower and longer in pace than those of Shae working. The juxtaposition of the different tempos suggests that we are seeing Shae's fantasy, but also invites a longer look at a sexual life that has previously been hidden or shown sketchily in Hollywood cinema. By alternating shot length in the sequence, Dunye inverts the habitual values attached to what is viewed and also solicits different affective embodied responses (comedic, serious). In *She Don't Fade*, each sex sequence, one emphasising the ethnographic and objective, the other fantasy and the subjective, Dunye's body remains the locus for interpreting the situation; it is through the ambiguity of Shae/Cheryl's body and its actions and movements that the audience is compelled to feel and reflect on the habit of embodied perception within the cinematic encounter. Beauvoir, paraphrasing Merleau-Ponty, says we can understand experience in the world if we are able to recognise situation as it is determined by the body. The body, through its comportment, crafts and effects a 'perceptual ground, a basis of life, a general setting for my coexistence with the world' (1945b/2004: 161) and without the body providing this sensibility, the possibility of generating new ways of seeing, such as new attitudes, styles and manners of filmmaking, and anchoring them in shared reality, is lost. Dunye's Black lesbian body is paramount in her resistance to filmmaking tradition and spectatorship. By showing different bodies depicting different expressions of Blackness (via identity, sexuality, etc.) and by using blended ethnographic and narrative form, Dunye communicates a core existential-phenomenological principle in her filmmaking. As Beauvoir puts it, '[m]y history is incarnated in a body that possesses a certain generality, a relationship with the world prior to myself, and that is why this body is opaque to reflection' (1945b/2004: 163); existence is expressed through our bodies and our interaction with others.

The Watermelon Woman (1966), arguably Dunye's most famous work, is a feature-length comedy that follows Cheryl's (Cheryl Dunye) documentary film project on faux film star Fae Richards, an actor from the 1930s and 1940s 'known' for her on-screen mammy roles. After watching the film *Plantation Memories*, and discovering that Richards is uncredited, Cheryl researches Richards's life and career, aiming to piece together her forgotten history. As Cheryl's project progresses, we also track her own relationships, platonic and romantic, their trials and tribulations; a narrative structure similar to that of her other earlier 'Dunyementaries'. Continuing Dunye's previous blurred ethnographic style seen in *She Don't Fade*, *The Watermelon Woman* revises the forgetting of Black actors in film, drawing attention to the consequences of marginalisation and lack of space afforded to Black lesbians in cinema, both on and off-screen.

In these first few moments of the film, Dunye shows her intention to disrupt, intervene and insert Black women into cinematic spaces and places that have excluded them, both in front of and behind the camera. The film begins with the fourth movement from Mozart's *Eine kleine Nachtmusik*, followed closely with the intertitle 'Bryn Mawr, PA' and a videotape of an exasperated Tamara (Valarie Walker) asking Cheryl (yet unseen): 'Where do you want it?' The scene is an interracial wedding reception (Black/Jewish), with guests milling around and waiting for their photographs to be taken. We hear Cheryl direct Tamara, telling her to move around for a better shot. Tamara brings together the wedding group for the standard family picture, only to have a Jewish man come between Cheryl's camera (the audience's POV) and the family, repeating her direction. Cheryl comes out from behind the camera and also interrupts the audience POV, explaining to the man in no uncertain terms that she is 'working with the family' and asks that he 'wait his turn'. The camera, set up as a medium shot, rests on Cheryl's back, that appears out of focus.

The classical score affectively suggests a habit of expectation and association with White, European culture, what Dunye has described as a 'safe subject' within filmmaking (1992: 18). This use of sound design at a wedding reception nods to the pervasive implicit and habitual associations embedded in such social scripts. Weddings are expressions of cultural behaviours which not only observe and maintain socio-political and socio-religious specific habitus but sustain them through capitalistic industry. To recall, Beauvoir stipulates that one meaning of habit evolves from repeated use and manifests in the 'shape of attitudes and forms of behavior', fundamentally informing human experience. This particular meaning of habit is not specific to old age; rather, such repetition of attitude and its association with behaviour exists at pre-conscious levels and is dependent on the manner of appearance. The wedding scene is followed with voiceover dialogue, set against a classic house score, between Cheryl and Tamara on their way home, who discuss the inappropriate presence of a montage of 'urban realism' shots in a wedding video. The film shifts viewing habits and moves more into Cheryl's world, examining differences within the 'screen of customs and ceremonies' which we often fail to examine (CA 467).

Dunye also uses humour to show the ways in which audiences have been habituated to the forgetting of Black lesbians throughout visual cultural history. In a later scene, Cheryl visits C.L.I.T. (the Center for Lesbian Information and Technology) looking for material on Fae Richards (Lisa Marie Bronson). She says: 'I came to find out about the Black collection on lesbians. Is that a separate collection?' to which she is told, 'It's *very* separate.' Here Dunye uses humour to gently underline the lack of inclusion of Black women's lives in traditional feminist historiography; her accessible aesthetic form offers a refuge of habit in the cinematic encounter as well as an opportunity for its poetic disruption.

Dunye's experimentation initially appears slight when compared to other experimental filmmakers (such as Maya Deren or Chick Strand); her films are rarely esoteric, violent or confrontational (despite bearing the brunt of conservative reaction).[16] Instead Dunye approximates manners in cinematic viewing by disrupting associations between content (centring Black lesbian stories and characters) and form (sound design, the use of direct address). In her article 'Building Subjects', Dunye refers to the danger of stereotypes to one's sense of being, saying they 'distort' an identity that she celebrates 'as the life I choose to live' (1992: 18), expressing the existential tension of marginalisation – how false and shallow stereotypes impact an individual's relationship to the world, to others and to their own history. Her films intentionally expose the existence and legacy of a damaging history for Black lesbians and present a more accurate and personal one via a 'visual language' that she originally saw as being 'too personal to be considered art-worthy' (1992: 18). The value of her cinematic experimentation, then, lies explicitly in its existential ethical praxis and political appeal. Dunye actively understands her role in the making of her films, seen through gentle interruptions to habitual visual storytelling, thereby displaying the ethical intentionality behind her films. By centring on personal lived experience, Dunye also demonstrates responsibility for her films as sites of resistance. She quite literally seeks to construct different viewing habits by shifting previous perceptual manners that have shaped normative cinematic attitudes. Without the familiarity of accessible form, Dunye's political and ethical challenge to normative viewing praxis loses its subtlety and efficacy.

Habit's Affective Aspects: Hesitation as Political Action

Dunye's use of direct address and conscious camera direction is a common aesthetic trait in her filmmaking. In her first short, *Janine* (1990), the camera is fixed through the entire film, static shot, close-up concentrated on Cheryl's face as she tells her story. *Janine* is an intimate recounting of Dunye's teenage crush on a high-school friend, Janine, and how Cheryl became comfortable with her own sexuality and evolving identity. Throughout the film, mixed media of still photographs from Cheryl's childhood and slow-motion video of two candles (with a partially seen naked Cheryl blowing them out – only her shoulders and the lower part of her face are visible) interrupt her address. Cheryl immediately begins her story as though the audience is known to her, creating a sense of comfort and connection. It is hard not to like Cheryl straight away and to want to know everything about her. *Janine* is a reflective coming-out story, an autobiographical account of exploring Black lesbian sexual identity, empowering in its simplicity and authenticity. It is also a clear example of cinematic existentialism, a creative statement on the relationship between responsibility and freedom, as Cheryl talks through her experience of transcending the oppression at play in the dynamic between her and Janine. In terms of Dunye's aesthetic style and filmmaking habit, *Janine* provides a good template for both the form and content of her later films.

The static close-up effects an embodied, cinematic phenomenological reduction. The audience members are (likely) seated and their consciousness is oriented to a screen, bracketed off from the external world for the 9:14 minute run time. Cheryl's story is entirely about connection and relating – not to Janine (as might first seem to be the case) – but to her Black, lesbian self, whom she is shown to have happily graduated into at the end of the film (the film ends with a still photograph of Cheryl's smiley high-school graduation photo). Throughout the film, Cheryl tells mini-stories of interactions she had with Janine that highlight the habitus of heteronormative, White culture. One example is when Janine enters the bathroom while Cheryl is showering and comments on the 'wrong way' Cheryl shampoos her hair. This memory speaks to what Al-Saji calls the 'ontological expansiveness of white habits' (2014: 144),[17] where White privilege is oblivious to its appropriation of space. Not only does Janine assume access to the bathroom while Cheryl is showering but proceeds to correct the way in which she showers.[18] As Cheryl tells this story, the camera makes a rare movement, zooming in on a still photograph of Cheryl and Janine at prom until it is out of focus. This blurring of the image is a visual interruption to habitual ways of seeing. In addition to her use of still photographs and creative cinematography, Dunye uses intertitles that repeat what Cheryl is saying. The three elements –hearing, seeing, reading – form the 'theory of three's', which is the strategy behind the 'Dunyementaries' (Dunye 2020) working as Dunye's intentional, ethical and audacious claim, 'I am here', listen to me.

Inasmuch as *Janine* can be seen as a template for Dunye's aesthetic experimentation that seeks to deviate from and challenge habits of perception within film experience, it is also a film about affective and existential change within one's situation. Like most of Dunye's films, and in particular *The Watermelon Woman*, it exposes the racialising habits of White women who assume access and recognition in all spaces, 'including those that they colonize' (Al-Saji 2014: 150). Janine hands down her old sweaters to Cheryl, an action that Dunye recalls with hesitation and disbelief saying, 'it took me a while to get to this way of thinking about it, that's why I'm doing this piece'. Al-Saji's phenomenology of hesitation describes the affective disruption to habit within situation: 'environmental change can only be effective if it is able to create a certain tension or discomfort, a fracture, at the level of habits of White privilege – what I have called hesitation' (2014: 150). Dunye uses an embodiment of hesitation as a technique to subtly disrupt the habitus of viewing, specifically racialised viewing within the cinematic encounter. Linda Martín Alcoff has discussed the entrenched links between racist perceptual habits and the visibility of racial identity, observing how 'racial consciousness works through learned practices and habits of visual discrimination and visible marks on the body' (2000a: 31). Alcoff argues that race has been shaped as a habitual way of knowing the world, entangling 'social identity' with 'visible bodily attributes' (2000a: 31). Perceptual manners are organised just as readily and routinely as bodily movements, which carry similar social expectations of discipline, adherence and conformity. They are cultivations of habits that anchor our being-in-the-world as any other physical or spatial motility.

Dunye's aesthetic experimentation incurs hesitation in our habits of viewing by thwarting expectation in a number of ways. Firstly, via dialogue and comedy (Cheryl edits herself when describing what she does for a living). In *The Watermelon Woman* she says: 'Hi I'm Cheryl and I'm a fiiii-ilmmaker, ah I'm not really a filmmaker. But I have a video-taping business that I run with my friend, Tamara and I work at a video store' (Figure 4.2). As with the aforementioned dialogue at C.L.I.T., these ambiguous expressions work as verbal hesitations that provoke affective reflexive responses. Second, via manipulation of cinematic temporal pace (slow motion to regular speed of film), disrupting the structure of temporality in cinematic viewing (an invisible spectator habit), and via montage – for example, scenes in *The Watermelon Woman* are separated with brief sequences of Cheryl dancing on top of a building. The interruptive focus on her bodily movement is an aesthetic technique that opens up different expressions of Black, lesbian authorial agency (Dunye's production company is called

Figure 4.2 Cheryl hesitates when describing what she does for a living.

'Dancing Girl Productions'). Third, via the use of mixed media (through her use of intertitles, false archival footage, still photographs, video tape). In doing so, Dunye foregrounds her Black, lesbian subjectivity, not as other but as an affirming authorial voice and corporeal presence in control of her film.

The use of hesitation introduced through aesthetics is a stylistic way in which Dunye makes habits in perception visible and felt within the cinematic encounter, evoking reflexivity 'wherein vision can become self-critical – questioning the structures of habituation and socialization that it takes for granted and yet cannot see' (Al-Saji 2014: 153). This enables a deeper hesitation to occur, illustrating blind spots within White habits of viewing. Al-Saji distinguishes between two ways of seeing: '*see with* or *according to* others' (2014: 156), which form the basis of her phenomenology of a critical-ethical vision. Developing these distinctions from Merleau-Ponty, Al-Saji outlines how habits of viewing are subject to transformation depending on our receptivity; viewing habits are able to shift if we allow 'an event to insinuate itself into our vision', becoming the feature that reframes our visual experience (2014: 155). In the context of Dunye's films, this 'event' is Cheryl's own Black, lesbian body, for without it, there is no transformation of viewing habit in the cinematic encounter.

To see with others is habitual perception; 'we always *already* see with others' (Al-Saji 2014: 156). It relies on racialised and institutionalised ways of seeing and is oblivious to other embodied perception. Beauvoir herself experienced this 'seeing with others' during a discussion she had with Jean-Paul Sartre on one of his leaves during the Second World War. It is an oft-cited conversation, usually referred to when writers discuss *The Second Sex*, and shows how Beauvoir's thinking had begun to invest far more political and ethical meaning in lived experience than Sartre's as early as 1940. In her autobiography, Beauvoir describes a conversation she had with Sartre on the relationship between situation and freedom. Her position being 'not every situation was equally valid: what sort of transcendence could a woman shut up in a harem achieve?', whereas Sartre believed that 'even such a cloistered existence could be lived in several quite different ways' (PL 346). Even though Beauvoir believes she is right, she gives in to Sartre (as often happened) whose position reflects a schema that he cannot see beyond. Al-Saji refers to such a position as a 'forgetfulness' (2014: 157) that is developed by socio-historical discourses and sustained through hegemonic adherence and practice (patriarchy). Put in the context of film experience, embodied differences (different sexual, racial or alternative physical ways of being) are not screened often enough to form part of habitual visual schemas, meaning they remain ostracised, othered and threatening. Worse, their 'abjection plays a constitutive role in how I come to see' (Al-Saji 2014: 157). What viewing habits are able to replace those that are normalising? How are new, alternative habits of perception able to be developed so that the ontological expansiveness of White privilege is resisted?[19] Al-Saji's phenomenology of hesitation registers such ways of seeing with others, and by noticing that they exist, also reflexively thinks about how to transform such viewing habits and their legacies.

Within almost all of the 'Dunyementaries', the ontological expansiveness of White privilege is reflected upon. We have seen it first introduced in *Janine*, where Janine walks in on Cheryl in the shower and where she hands down her old clothes. It also occurs in *The Potluck and the Passion* (1993), the follow-up short to *She Don't Fade*.[20] The film begins with Dunye's aesthetic technique of direct address to the camera. Linda (Dunye) and her girlfriend Nikki discuss plans for a potluck with their friends to celebrate their one-year anniversary. Other actors also use direct address throughout the film, reflexively commenting on their character and the role they play before transitioning into the character more fully. The expansiveness of White privilege is most evident in the character of Megan (Nora Breen), a White woman who believes herself to be expert on all things African.[21] Throughout the film, her controlling persona becomes more and more representative of a visual schema expectant of access and perennial possibility. Megan has invited Tracy as her guest to the dinner party, believing they are in the early stages of a relationship. Tracy, an African American woman studying nineteenth-century Irish literature, conveys a very different understanding of her relationship with Megan, both in character and via the actor's direct address. Megan does not exhibit any acts of hesitation throughout the film. She assumes she and Tracy will go dancing after the party (without asking if Tracy would like to); she tells Tracy and Evelyn she has joined the peace corps in Ethiopia to study the problems facing the Third World [*sic*]; and she later pushes past Lisa and Kendra, leaving the party, without apology. Megan demonstrates no receptivity or awareness regarding the conditions and feelings of others at the party.

In *Greetings from Africa* (1994), Cheryl is single again, having broken up with Nikki after four years (we see a photo of them as an earlier couple in the first minute of the film as Cheryl is talking about the break-up). Cheryl unexpectedly meets L (Nora Breen, the same actor who played Megan in *The Potluck and The Passion*) at a party and falls for her. The two women go out on a few dates and are intimate with each other. At one point in the film, L intrudes on Cheryl who is naked in the bathtub (an echo of the shower scene in *Janine*, and a precursor to the one *The Watermelon Woman*). L goes to the bathroom and then proceeds to get changed and get in the bath, expecting Cheryl to give her access and permission that she believes she is already entitled to. Later in the film, Cheryl is waiting for L to arrive at a party and ends up talking with another woman (Jacqueline Woodson), who turns out to be L's girlfriend. The film ends with Cheryl receiving a postcard from L who has joined the peace corps in the Ivory Coast. In Dunye's shorts, the White woman character demonstrates no hesitation in behaviour, dialogue or gesture. Al-Saji says that hesitation requires a slowing-down, an interruption to the 'totalizing sense of completeness' that White privilege demands. But how else might hesitation be recognisable within the cinematic encounter?

In my final examples, once more taken from *The Watermelon Woman*, hesitation as a destabilising intervention on viewing habits is clearly shown via Cheryl's new White girlfriend Diana (Guinevere Turner). Cheryl and Diana have been invited to a dinner party with Stacey (Jocelyn Taylor) and Tamara, but the atmosphere is tense. To assuage good relations between the four, Tamara lights a joint to share with Stacey. Before Tamara even has a chance to offer it around, Diana jumps up saying 'lemme have a hit', completely unaware of her expectation of having first offer (Figure 4.3).

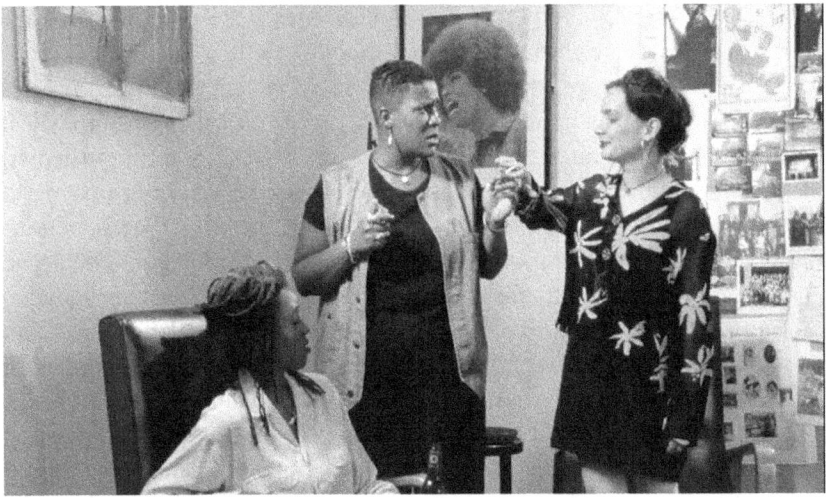

Figure 4.3 Diana (Guinevere Turner) assumes first go of the joint without invitation in *The Watermelon Woman* (Dunye 1996).

During the dinner, Diana continues to exercise her privilege, appropriating the situation so that it becomes about her own lived experience. She says that she was born in Jamaica ('I love telling people where I was born'); that her family lived everywhere: 'Germany, California, Iceland ... Bangladesh, Tel Aviv' and then tells Cheryl she has arranged an interview with the Page family for her film. (The character of Martha Page, played by Alexandra Juhasz, is a faux White film director. Cheryl has been trying to piece together the history of Fae's film career and Diana's ability to secure an interview with the Page family is a further extension of her privileged entry and acceptance in White spaces.) The racialising habit Dunye exposes here is the manner in which Diana assumes access to and recognition within Black culture. As she recounts her peripatetic childhood, we are shown Tamara and Stacey's unfavourable reactions, which can be read as gestural hesitations that intervene on the expansiveness of Diana's privilege primarily for the audience. Diana, of course, is completely unaware and undeterred by their reactions. The hesitation shown through aesthetics disrupts the 'objectifying habits' of cultural appropriation exercised by Diana (Al-Saji 2014: 155) and offers a different relationship to the film for the audience. Beauvoir writes '[t]o accept nuances is to accept ambiguity of judgement, argument, and hesitation; such complex situations force you to think' (ADD 67). The audience now must use these gestural nuances to negotiate the ambiguity of the relationships between Diana and Cheryl, and Cheryl, Tamara and Stacey.

In a later scene, Cheryl and Diana visit Mrs Page-Fletcher (Patricia Ellis), Martha Page's younger sister, hoping to find out more about Martha's relationship with Fae Richards. Mrs Page-Fletcher refuses to acknowledge Martha and Fae's lesbian relationship. The ontological expansiveness of White privilege here is seen in her 'forgetting' (denial) of their love and her condescension toward Cheryl: 'You're not trying to infer that something went on between them?' Diana intervenes, softening her tone of voice, aiming to appease Mrs Page-Fletcher. The scene is shot via wide medium lens, portraying the defensive body movements of the two White women (crossed arms, standing away from Cheryl) and the affective hesitation within the scene. Al-Saji says '[h]esitation is both the ontological ground that makes possible transformations in habit, and the phenomenological opening that can be utilized and supplemented for such change to take place' (2014: 149). As Cheryl stands her ground and insists on recognition of Martha's lesbian identity, she ontologically makes possible a transformation in habitual ways of seeing in the cinematic encounter. Diana admonishes her, an action that playfully indicates the obstructive role White women have played even when seeming to support Black lesbian identity. The scene ends on a self-reflexive ironic note, with a Black woman as modern-day mammy (Lillie Hayes) entering the room to see if Mrs Page-Fletcher is alright.

What might Beauvoir make of Al-Saji's phenomenology of hesitation? It is clear that Al-Saji's conception is an extension of Beauvoir's philosophy of ambiguity, given she argues that affective hesitation is felt as 'ambiguous and multiple' lived experience (Al-Saji 2014: 148). Beauvoir saw habit as an ambiguous combination of sedimentation and replaceability, an embodied expression of one's past behaviour and, equally, a pathway for future, possible transformation. In-between these two characteristics of habit lies a series of hesitations. Beauvoir's view on the relationship between situation and freedom was consistent, that in order for one to be free, the freedom of all must be fought for. Her closing points in *The Ethics of Ambiguity* firmly argue that an ethical, free life is dependent on the freedom of others, involving 'constructive movement ... which rejects oppression for oneself and others' (EA 170). If ambiguity is not seen to exist at the centre of human experience, Beauvoir claims that human beings will fail to achieve complete freedom. Rather than pretend that our lives are without contingency, Beauvoir proposes that we should face it head on, 'to stir up in the world the outrage' we do not want (EA 170). This suggests that Beauvoir would have agreed with Al-Saji's phenomenology of hesitation, finding a more complex and nuanced argument to the affective resonance of ambiguity in embodied perception. Despite having exercised her own ontological expansiveness of White privilege throughout her life, Beauvoir had no qualms about acknowledging when she was wrong.[22]

Beauvoir's review of Merleau-Ponty's book illustrates that intentionality of experience is one of the core phenomenological legacies that bears significance for an ethical reading of cinema, particularly with respect to independent filmmakers such as Cheryl Dunye. She writes that our body lives in the world and through living, we have a world. The body, through movement, choice and action, 'expresses our existence' (1945b/2004: 161). We are enworlded through our body and the manner in which it connects with other bodies. This movement through the world, however, is not random; rather, Beauvoir acknowledges the intentionality behind our bodily movement, or embodied perception, as 'the manner in which we stretch out toward the future through our body and through things' (1945b/2004: 161). Beauvoir is, of course, once more combining Husserl's phenomenology with Merleau-Ponty's development of his ideas. Through our experience, which is always directed toward something or someone, we combine subjective perception with the objective perceived. This is precisely the process of thinking when we watch cinema, as film experience (all experience) demands intentionality; our subjective, embodied perception is directed to the objective perceived (screen/film). For although intentionality is a conscious act, where we are aware of directing our perceiving gaze toward a film, such as 'I am going to direct my gaze toward this film', there is also another iteration, that of embodied intentionality which functions at the level of sensation where our sight and movement are guided into a relationship of connection, in order to form a situation or 'the intersensory unity of a world' (Merleau-Ponty 1945/2002: 137). For Merleau-Ponty, consciousness is thrown into the world and our understanding of the world relies on habit within our intentionality. He says 'it [consciousness] projects itself into a cultural world and has its habit: because it cannot be consciousness without playing upon significances given' (1945/2002: 137). Put simply, experience has to be repeated so that it can form a world and give it meaning. This repetition of experiencing forms routines and subsequent habitual behaviours. We should be mindful to think about breaking with such habits, or if not breaking, at least reflecting on their legacies.

Alexandra Juhasz describes Dunye's experimentation as pushing 'the representation of traditional identity' (1992: 292), action that simultaneously alerts the viewer to a habit of film experience and subtly inserts political challenge. By always casting a Black, lesbian character in the leading role (herself no less, a simple and effective paradigmatic shift), Dunye throws light on the persistent, enduring expansiveness of White privilege within cinematic stories about women. As Dunye is the filmmaker as well as the central character, her decisions are also foregrounded as informing the story and how to interpret her films. In effect, Dunye creates new cinematic habits by repeating the casting choices, aesthetic style and narrative structures in her films. An altered consciousness about womanhood is projected into the world and is given alternative habitus because it plays on the significances Dunye has given in her other cinematic appearances. The personal character of her 'Dunyementaries' are not just artistic or auteurist signatures; rather, the affect generated by Dunye's decision to incorporate personal lived experience is direct resistance to homogeneous cinematic habitus. It immediately (literally and figuratively) acknowledges the tradition of excluding women of colour from the screen in meaningful and powerful roles. Further, it also showcases the legacies of forgetting that infect, destabilise and potentially destroy communities. Habit in the cinematic encounter, then, is as much about the impact of generic principles, routines of casting, story-framing, and so on, as it is about the systemic impact on identity formation in its audiences (those who are seen and not seen). What emerges from all of Dunye's films is a solid sense of the importance of community, its ambiguous and evolving existence, and the centrality of the embodied self.

Notes

1 See 'A Review of the *Phenomenology of Perception* by Maurice Merleau-Ponty (1945)', first published in 1945 in *Les temps modernes*, 1: 2, 363–7. All references are from this text.
2 The ocular-centrism here is evident, given the emphasis on 'eyes', but as Beauvoir, Merleau-Ponty and others argue, the ability to physically see is not the same as possessing a subjective, intimate perception of the world. See Merleau-Ponty (1948/2008) *The World of Perception*.
3 Film experience is not solely dependent on vision, however. It includes audio-visual processing and here I include sound design as part of the consciousness of perception. See Michel Chion's (1994) 'Projections of Sound on Image'. Note his notion of added value.
4 Bourdieu acknowledges his debt to phenomenology, specifically the ideas of Edmund Husserl, in *The Logic of Practice*: 'The practical world that is constituted in the relationship with the *habitus*, acting as a system of cognitive and motivating structures, is a world of already realized ends – procedures to follow, paths to take – and of objects endowed with a "permanent teleological character", in Husserl's phrase, tools or institutions' (Bourdieu 1992a: 53). See also Moran (2011) for a clear and meticulous account of Husserl's discussion of habitus and habituality, which outlines the influence that his

'operative concepts' (2011: 59) of habit and habitus had on the development of Bourdieu's thought.
5 Beauvoir was a lover of walking, bordering on what some may call fanaticism. See *The Prime of Life*, where she describes many eight-to-nine-hour walks during her European holidays, often alone (PL 175, 260, 261, 297)). Beauvoir's descriptions of walking often work through the anxieties leading up to pre-war Europe, for herself, her friends and also Sartre. See, for example her discussion of Sartre and his 'lobsters' (PL 175–8).
6 See ADD 140–1, where Beauvoir also speaks of her position as foreign witness in her description of attending Chinese theatre in San Francisco, 'I know that these [Chinese masks and costumes] have a symbolic language, but I don't understand it'.
7 Beauvoir was very capable of censoring when she wanted to. *America Day by Day* hides any mention of her love affair with Nelson Algren despite describing some of their meetings in Chicago. See Beauvoir (ADD 96) and for commentary (Kirkpatrick 2019).
8 Linda Martín Alcoff's *Visible Identities: Race, Gender, and the Self* (2006) and Iris Marion Young's *On Female Body Experience* (1980/2005) are pioneering works in this regard. See also Helen Fielding (2006); Gail Weiss and Honi Harber (1999); Shannon Sullivan (2006); Alia Al-Saji (2014) and Emily Lee (2014).
9 See Helen Ngo, for example, who argues that racist behaviours and practices are guided by an ease within 'habitual bodily orientation' (2016: 848) that often goes unexamined. By identifying racism as a bodily habit, Ngo foregrounds the importance of gesture and perception as manifestation of body thoughts.
10 I discuss Beauvoir's *Pyrrhus and Cineas* in greater detail in Chapter 2.
11 See Toril Moi who writes in reference to *The Ethics of Ambiguity*, 'I find it repetitive, badly constructed and mostly unconvincing' (2010a: 169) but maintains its significance in the trajectory and development of Beauvoir's thinking.
12 See the section 'Situation' in *The Second Sex* (TSS 439–664).
13 Heinämaa (2004: 153–8) also makes this observation in her introduction to Beauvoir's review.
14 Moran notes that Husserl's work on habit is often neglected in wider philosophical accounts (2011: 54) but on the basis of Beauvoir's autobiographies and own philosophical works (especially her familiarity with Merleau-Ponty), we can be certain this is not applicable in her case.
15 Dunye explains that her use of mixed media is influenced by cost: 'I can't afford 16mm. I build work that really talks about not having access to a complete 16mm production. That kind of creative thinking – not just thinking about a political identity – is about a lot of things' (Dunye in Juhasz 1992: 300).
16 McHugh explains the negative reaction Dunye's *The Watermelon Woman* received in Congress, a reaction from Michigan Republican Peter Hoeskra

regarding the NEA funding ($31,500) due to the portrayal of lesbian sex. McHugh reads this reaction in terms of Jacques Derrida's 'signature effect' (2007: 347), who argued that the body and the text overlap (over-determine) in levels of meaning at the textual/linguistic level; McHugh develops this overlapping in the visual language of Dunye's films, which I interpret as Dunye's intentional political challenge to our habits of seeing in the cinematic encounter.

17 Al-Saji expands on Shannon Sullivan's *Revealing Whiteness* (2006) regarding the unconscious habits of White privilege to develop her phenomenology of hesitation as an interruptive response to racialised vision.

18 This scene – of Cheryl being interrupted in the bathroom – represents the conceit of the White character interrupting a Black character and appears in *Greeting From Africa* (1996) and *The Watermelon Woman*, which I discuss later on. Another interruption occurs in *The Potluck and the Passion* (1993), where Robert walks in on Nikki getting changed.

19 One clear answer to this question lies outside the cinematic praxis of film-making and rests with funding for features. See Stacy Smith et. al's 'Gender & Short Films: Emerging Female Filmmakers and the Barriers Surrounding their Careers' (2015), which statistically details the difficultly women directors encounter when securing funding for feature films.

20 Relationships with White women are not a point of focus in *She Don't Fade*.

21 It is also evident in the tardiness of Lisa and Kendra who arrive very late to the party, despite being given directions twice. They also eat the pasta salad they bought as their contributing dish on the way.

22 See, for example, *The Prime of Life* (366) where Beauvoir acknowledges how wrong she was about 'there being no such thing as a Jew'.

CHAPTER 5

A New (Ethical) Face on Love: Bad Faith and Claire Denis's *Let the Sunshine In*

In her 1946 profile of Jean-Paul Sartre, commissioned by *Harper's Bazaar*,[1] Beauvoir outlines the basic tenets of his existential philosophy: 'there are two ways of existing: in the world, one comes across inert things that remain indefinitely equal to what they are [*en-soi*]; and on the other, men who are consciousnesses and freedoms live in this world [*pour-soi*]' (2004: 229). In doing so, Beauvoir explains that existentialism is more than a type or approach of philosophy, rather it is a way of being-in-the-world, a way of life. On the face of it, the article's function was to sell Sartre to the US, speaking to his style of working and thinking, thereby attaching a personality to existential philosophy. Yet, despite Beauvoir appearing to write about Sartre, the brief article also subtly presents the contour of her existential ethics, which was outlined in greater detail the following year in *The Ethics of Ambiguity* and further elaborated on in specific relation to women's situation in *The Second Sex*.

Throughout the article, Beauvoir writes of one's fleeing from freedom and argues for the responsibility that freedom requires, implicitly characterising different versions of existence (sub-man, serious man, passionate man), and using the figure of Sartre to illustrate the writer-artist who 'as a creator of imaginary works' is able to 'escape from getting stuck in the paste of contingent life' (Beauvoir 2004: 231). 'Jean Paul Sartre: Strictly Personal', as a description of Sartre as a man, reads as a publicity love letter but, more subtly, it indicates Beauvoir's emerging emphasis on ambiguity as a foundational expression of the personal within ethical decision, appeal and the pursuit of freedom.

Debra Bergoffen has written on Beauvoir's 'muted voice',[2] found within the 'trap' or frame of Sartre's philosophy, arguing that it speaks to an existential ethics that Sartre did not foreground or craft closely in his work.[3] For Bergoffen, this muted voice identifies emotional experience, inclusive of 'joy, generosity, the gift, the erotic and the couple' (1997: 2), as the primary connection between body and consciousness. It expresses an 'erotic generosity' which Bergoffen views as the premise of Beauvoir's philosophy: an ethics of existence that juxtaposed the erotic against the patriarchal. She interprets Beauvoir's muted voice as evidence of her philosophical keystone of ambiguity, exercised throughout her writing. In Beauvoir's critique of the patriarchal systems of marriage, the social scripts of motherhood and romance were argued to be sustaining mechanisms of bad faith that subordinated love to further its own privileges, but Beauvoir also allowed room for its more positive aspects. As Bergoffen puts it, Beauvoir afforded bad faith the capacity to represent 'legitimate but betrayed, desires of the erotic subject' (Bergoffen 1992: 194). In other words, Beauvoir did not fault women for their bad faith, but saw it as a coping or defence mechanism against objectification, possession and subjugation of a woman's being-for-herself. The question of bad faith, particularly within love relationships, is in Beauvoir's view one that involves history and situation. As situation is seen as a determinant of bad faith, bad faith must also be a question of ethics where context and intersubjective relations form a part of one's lived experience.

Beauvoir's muted voice, evident in 'Jean Paul Sartre: Strictly Personal' and her more popular styled articles written for magazines as *Esquire*, *Vogue*, *Flair*, and *McCall's*, offered her readers greater accessibility to her philosophical ideas on topics such as femininity, ethics and love. Her article 'It's About Time Women Put a New Face on Love' (1950)[4] appeared in the April issue of *Flair*, and continued her discussion on the future of love for the seemingly emancipated woman, proposing an authentic and equal love between man and woman, contingent on recognising the 'double nature' within human existence (Beauvoir 2015a: 77). The article reads as a synopsis of *The Second Sex* (which had been recently published in France; H. M. Parshley's English translation was forthcoming), introducing its core themes of reciprocity, ambiguity and women's situation. Even in its brevity, the article maintains Beauvoir's equivocal position on the freedom of both men and women: 'I believe what fascinates each in the other is the discovery of a human world like its own but *different*' (2015a: 79). Beauvoir is promoting her phenomenology of women's gendered existence not as a condemnation of men but as an appeal for an existential ethical freedom based on recognition of men's and women's immutable ambiguity and vulnerability.

In *The Second Sex*, the chapter 'The Woman in Love' (TSS 683–708) describes the difference between a man's and a woman's experience of love[5] in stark terms. The man views a woman's love as submission and for the woman, love is seen as devotion. Citing Nietzsche's use of the word '*faith*', Beauvoir illustrates the subjugation involved in a woman's lived experience of the emotion 'devotion' and its place in the relation between man and woman: 'What woman means by love is clear enough: total devotion (not mere surrender) with soul and body, without any consideration or reserve ... In this absence of conditions her love is a faith; woman has no other *faith*' (Nietzsche cited in TSS 683, italics original). Beauvoir interprets faith here as a circumstance of gendered situation and argues that love (within such a context) is experienced differently by men and women; it is founded on inequality and Beauvoir argues that this inequality has been historically determined and sustained. She frames the heterosexual love relationship within Hegel's master-slave dialectic, explaining that a woman's freedom (the possibility of her transcendence) is restricted as long as her being-in-love is associated with fulfilling societal scripts of desirability, appearance, motherhood, homemaking and serving her husband.

In this chapter, I focus on Claire Denis's *Let the Sunshine In* (*Un Beau Soleil Intérieur*) (2017), a film that examines ambiguity within the heterosexual love relationship, to argue that the existentialist concept of bad faith presents as a key feature of the film, addressing our vulnerabilities within love. Throughout *Ambiguous Cinema*, it is suggested that film experience offers alternative imaginations of the world, not just portrayals of other lives, histories or situations, but also descriptions of what it is to live such lives in specific conditions. Cinema, *in potentia*, shows us the emotional living experience of the human condition, for better or worse. The moving-image describes a point of view of lived experience that is assumed by the spectator to exist somewhere, for someone. As we watch a character evolve over the course of a film, we are privy to the intimate and focused witness of another's becoming and within Denis's *Let the Sunshine In*, we observe Isabelle's (Juliette Binoche) emotional turmoil unfold as she negotiates her own bad faith in response to the bad faith of the men she becomes involved with.

A film is an appeal to watch, recognise and feel a different experience, and to notice difference that exists within experience. For Beauvoir, emotional experience was the basis for our appeal to others (EA 72), the vulnerability of emotional dependence and its risk of reciprocity forming the foundation of the ambiguous human condition. This emphasis and expression of appeal is couched within emotion, like love, and acknowledges the hazard of bad faith: 'Love is then renunciation of all possession, of all confusion. One renounces being in order that there may be that being which one is not' (EA 72). For Beauvoir, love can never be genuinely fulfilling if it fails in its appeal to the other for recognition and reciprocity. Throughout *Let the Sunshine In*, cinematography draws attention to

Figure 5.1 Close-ups of Isabelle (Juliette Binoche) focusing on her emotional state in *Let the Sunshine In* (Denis 2017).

emotion within the appeal and the risk it contains. One example is the prevalent use of appeal via the close-up, which consistently intensifies Isabelle's emotional request to be seen, for her subjectivity to be recognised and validated as equal. The camera rests on her face, closely recording every expression and gestural movement, muscle twitch, eye tearing-up, and smirk to further the appeal within her emotional experience and the request for recognition it contains (Figure 5.1).

The intertwining of emotion and bad faith in the film is one of its most critical features, a point that this chapter examines in detail. Before I discuss the film, let us consider the philosophical significance of emotion for Beauvoir's philosophy of ambiguity so as to establish its role in the mechanism and event of bad faith. Recalling from Chapter 2, in her article 'Must We Burn Sade?', Beauvoir had come to view emotion as the crucial fleshed connection between self and other. Here she argues that 'emotional intoxication' is the felt and lived experience of erotic (intimate as well as sexual) love and desire, and through it 'existence is grasped in one oneself and in the other as at once subjectivity and passivity' (MWBS 59–60). It was through sexual love that Beauvoir believed the ambiguity of human existence was at its most noticeable and felt most intensely. While the Marquis de Sade exposed the very real connections between violent sexual acts and privilege (possession and cruelty), his life was also evidence of its consequences; he was outcast on popular account of his deviant behaviour. I have discussed how Beauvoir paradoxically saw Sade as an example of moral authenticity, as he did not hide who he was or what his sexual intentions were. Indeed, Sade lauded his privileged position within society and valorised the consciousness and subjectivity of his victims so that he could find pleasure in his domination. Beauvoir's analysis of Sade's life (and stories) acknowledges the necessity of individuality (the being-for-oneself), that is, the separation between self and other, but argued that equal, authentic love was only possible through reciprocal recognition of both subjectivities.

Karen Vintges argues that Beauvoir's view of sexual love identifies a 'fusion', where '[b]ody and consciousness become a unity when consciousness is absorbed into the body' (1996: 47). During the sexual act, authentic love is expressed in the simultaneous give and take of pleasure where both partners experience themselves as subjectivity and passivity in their taking of pleasure. Sex, therefore, is much more than a corporeal encounter; as a fleshed experience it is an enworlding of body and mind (consciousnesses). Vintges explains: 'For Beauvoir, becoming "flesh" through emotion is a unification of body and consciousness' (1996: 48). 'Fusion' within sexual love must therefore include emotion, for without it there is no feasible experience of authentic or ethical love. If the sexual act remains purely physical, if one refuses to acknowledge emotional experience as an entanglement with the other's consciousness as well as their body, then the consciousness of the physical fusion becomes an act of self-deception, 'consciousness thus declines into an attitude of bad faith' (Vintges 1996: 51).[6] It is precisely emotional experience that allows us to inhabit the world, generating an embodied self-awareness that our human existence is different to that of ants and daffodils, warranting the pursuit of freedom.

Searching for Love in *Let the Sunshine In*

Let the Sunshine In is a story of Isabelle, a fifty-something, highly successful artist and divorced mother who relentlessly pursues the feeling and experience of being in love as a means for self-fulfilment. The film opens with a medium bird's-eye shot of Isabelle lying naked on her bed, the score mixed with her breathy sighs and soft electronic music. This moves to a close-up shot of Isabelle and Vincent (Xavier Beauvois), before returning to the bird's-eye shot of them mid-intercourse. Both are middle-aged; Vincent is overweight and unattractive, whereas Isabelle is beautiful and sexy. This is how the film opens, highlighting the superficiality in judging the match of the two characters, seemingly reifying the myth that the value of a woman lies in her appearance. The opening sequence moves between two types of shot, the close-up and bird's-eye view, and therefore two modes of looking. Denis's cinematographer, Agnès Godard, is contrasting modalities of perception, creating a distance that is both intimate and interrupting. This effects an ambiguity in perspective that makes one feel caught between the act of looking and wanting to look. Such cinematography is suggestive of the appeal of reciprocal recognition, telling us that looking at women and looking with women is a constant demanding interplay within women's situation, especially within love relationships. It illustrates the interdependency between looking and bad faith, our vulnerability in our pursuit of ethical freedom, the necessity of reciprocal recognition for authentic love, and, finally, the existential differences that exist in gendered loved experience.

Isabelle moves through a range of emotions in this short, opening sex scene, first appearing resigned, then engaged, then irritated and finally upset after Vincent asks her about a previous lover's sexual performance. As far as lovemaking goes, this experience hasn't gone well for Isabelle. Vincent, on the other hand, appears non-plussed in spite of the tension that has developed between them. The sequence briefly indicates what the film will go on to examine in greater detail: the complex dynamic between patriarchally gendered men and women,[7] the domination that women in particular are subject to, and the self-deceptions that both genders adhere to in love relationships. The fluctuation between Isabelle's expressive emotional states is revealing of her demeanour throughout the film; adolescent, insecure, irrational, but also ever-hopeful, warm and generous. Her emotions are always on show, calling for engagement and desperately seeking attachment. She does eventually leave Vincent, but does not appear to change her way of being, moving from one relationship to another (they do not last very long) and never asking why she cannot break away from placing 'her trust in a foreign consciousness' (TSS 704). Instead, exhausted from the anxiety and anguish of her situation, she asks 'Why, why, why?' can't she find real love. Through this question, Isabelle illuminates the ambiguity of the love relationship, a question that she quite rightly projects onto the situation, but where her bad faith limits recognition of her own role in sustaining it and in examining the social situation and scripting of patriarchal love.

We follow Isabelle's search for 'one real love' through three further encounters: with an unnamed actor (Nicolas Duvauchelle), with her ex-husband, François (Laurent Grévill), and with Sylvain (Paul Blain), a man from a different social class with whom she was getting on well. Isabelle allows herself to be persuaded by a friend (who arguably has his own self-serving interest in her) to leave Sylvain, saying they are not suited to each other. Immediately following her break-up with Sylvain, we encounter Isabelle's final liaison with Marc (Alex Descas), the only man to demonstrate self-awareness and who seems genuine in wanting a relationship. Isabelle and Marc walk down the street during the evening, close-ups wordlessly convey their attachment and their nervous intimacy. Respective close-ups of their faces cut away to one of Isabelle gingerly reaching out to hold Marc's hand. Once more the cinematography uses the intimacy of the close-up to foreground the emotion within love's appeal through gestural, emotional and embodied experience. After a gentle kiss, Marc says he wants to wait and avoid 'jumping straight into things'; Isabelle is unable to see this positively and desperately begs him to stay with her. Marc refuses but says he likes what is happening between them and that he will see her again after his month-long vacation with his daughters. Before they part, Marc points out that he likes the space and the intimacy that is growing between them – it is a brief moment that underlines one of the many ambiguities within the lover's discourse. No matter how clearly feelings are spoken or gestured, they run the risk of miscommunication if what is being said isn't what the receiver wants to hear. Isabelle's impatience and uncertainty get the better of her and she seeks clarification from David (Gérard Depardieu), a clairvoyant.

In the final scene of the film, shot via close-up in warm, soft light, Isabelle consults with David about the future promise and longevity of her relationship with Marc. The audience has just witnessed David's girlfriend break up with him, and knows that he too is unlucky in love. The conclusion of the film acknowledges that bad faith in love is not specific to a woman's situation; rather, the need for others and emotional connections, to love and be loved, is felt by all. Despite all of Isabelle's failed efforts in love, she remains consumed with longing for this existence. Beauvoir's view of love affirmed this need for others, writing in her short article for *McCall's*, 'What Love Is and Isn't',[8] that love relationships go beyond the oft-cited lovers' solitude; the exclusivity of the love relationship depends on 'the whole of society' (2015b: 100). Isabelle remains likeable, maddeningly so, precisely because she embodies the universal desire and need to love and be loved.

In her DVD interview, Denis states that *Let the Sunshine In* was originally to be loosely based on Roland Barthes's *A Lover's Discourse: Fragments* (1978/1990). Barthes's text describes various gestural, verbal and linguistic expressions, avowals and sentiments of love, all celebrating love's (and the lover's) ambiguity. The final entry, titled '*Sobria Ebrietas, vouloir-saisir/the will-to-possess*' (pp. 232–4), discusses the lover's 'non-will-to-possess', or in Beauvoirian terms, an ethical authentic love that refuses to dominate the other's freedom. Instead of developing Barthes's text specifically, Denis (2019) says she wanted to think through her own love fragments (and those of her co-writer Christine Angot). The fragments of Isabelle's love relationships show that, despite their failure, her wish for love is an anticipation that these men will gift her what she cannot gift herself – the revelation of a new world (Beauvoir 2015b: 100), the possibility of transcendence and of a future that may facilitate her freedom through multiple possibilities and relations with others. Even in these captivating closing moments, ambiguity remains strong. David tells Isabelle to be 'open' (the English word is used in the film), simultaneously prescribing a way of being for her as a view from without where only a view from within (a beautiful sun inside) can result in transcendence and be the basis for an ethical, authentic love. Ironically, David's one bit of sound advice falls on Isabelle's deaf ears. We are left with her misfortune, like Beauvoir's woman in love: 'her [need for] love disfigures her, demolishes her; she is no more than this slave, this servant, this too-docile mirror, this too-faithful echo' (TSS 704). Isabelle remains endearing, her hope for requited love continuing, simultaneously appearing doomed to fail. The film ends without any romantic conclusion, mimicking Isabelle's own inability to reach her self-determined freedom.

Beauvoir, Sartre and Bad Faith

Beauvoir's thinking on bad faith differs from Sartre's, which as Vintges, Bergoffen and Le Doeuff have discussed, engages with women's real-life experiences rather than imagined scenarios.[9] Sartre saw bad faith as the self-deception between our material existence (facticity) and our freedom (transcendence), viewing human beings as entirely responsible for the realisation of their own freedom, regardless of historical condition or circumstance. While Beauvoir agreed with Sartre in part, her attention on the appeal for reciprocity and responsibility for the other's freedom, the importance of psycho-physiological unity in fleshed encounters and the differences between social and ontological situations speaks more effectively to an ethical freedom, acknowledging ambiguity and the countenance of bad faith. For her, there are different manifestations of bad faith, just as there are different experiences of love, and these are determined by social and ontological histories.

There are many groups and peoples in the world whose voices are still disregarded or negated. The conditions and realities of their lived experiences are not acknowledged or widely considered and while it is vital that they are seen and heard, what is of equal importance is a consideration of the vectors through which they are exhibited and distributed. Utilising Beauvoir's phenomenology to examine the theme of ambiguity within film experience focuses on a fundamental aspect of human existence: how we are to recognise and realise our pursuits of freedom, the necessity of others, and how we come to terms with the anxieties its precarities yield. *Let the Sunshine In* is evocative of Beauvoir's argument that if an authentic love is to be free, it must be ethical, reciprocal and ambiguous, and if taken as an example of film-philosophy or film-phenomenology, it can be viewed as a close description of the patterns of women's experience in love, illustrating particular experience (and another's experience of that experience) which may be accepted by spectators and reflected upon. Watching the varying bad faiths in action, of Isabelle and the men that use her, particularly as patterns that recur as part of love relationships, challenges the feasibility of institutions that enable such bad faiths to exist. It compels us to look and question, thwarting avoidance of our own self-deception by showing it at work so prevalently in the film's characters.

Sartre's (1966) concept of *être en-soi*, being-in-itself (material existence), helps to position cinema as a thing; where *être pour-soi* – being-for-itself (consciousness of such materiality) identifies spectator consciousness of the film as a world that expresses another's mode of being. However, here, the significance of the film's portrayal of bad faith is made stronger if read in Beauvoirian terms. The bad faith witnessed in Isabelle's love relationships (both her own specific bad faith of dependence and the bad faith of the men's privilege) offers an ethical (and political) warning because it asks spectators to recognise the inequity within the relationships, the degradation of Isabelle as a being-for-herself, the vain transcendence of men who seek to control her and the avoidance of both parties to alter their respective modes of bad faith. The spectator's core affective state is formed of two main parts: 1) the film's own ambiguity (through style and/or story); and 2) the consciousness of this ambiguity which evokes awareness of the relationship between responsibility and an ethical life – often resulting in an emotionally turbulent and uncomfortable position. The prominence of ethics in our relations with each other is Beauvoir's contribution. Put simply, the bad faith portrayed via Denis's characters engenders audience reflection on the necessity of ethics and its inherent ambiguities in our love relationships.

Following the opening sex scene, Vincent dresses and leaves the apartment, and we are shown a shot of sunlight entering a window, between a slit of two curtains (Figure 5.2) with the intertitle: 'Un beau soleil intérieur'. To use Beauvoir's language, we are shown 'a view from within', indicating that the film is sympathetic to Isabelle, the conditions of her situation and the frustrations these incur. In an interview with *The Guardian's* Jonathan Romney (2018), Denis clarifies that the meaning of the French title is lost in the English translation. *Un beau soleil intérieur* – translated as 'a beautiful sun inside'[10] – speaks more clearly to the film's overall intention of following a woman's search for self-acceptance through confronting and avoiding her self-deceptions, as well as the failures this journey involves. Put another way, it explores the obstacle of bad faith in finding authentic

Figure 5.2 'A view from within'. Isabelle's POV of the window and outside world.

Figure 5.3 'A view from without'. Isabelle's POV of David's (Gérard Depardieu) apartment.

love, a love that requires an emotional involvement with others without sacrifice of oneself. The translation '*Let the Sunshine In*' expresses a view from without, the imposition of the other's knowledge as a deprivation or degradation of one's own freedom. Visually, it would appear as looking into the window from the outside (Figure 5.3).

As Isabelle is consistently used as a body-thing by the men in the film, denied a status of consciousness (or freedom) from the men she encounters (aside from Marc), we see that she struggles with creating a beautiful sun inside herself. Instead, the pattern of her sexual encounters suggests that her view of herself coincides with that of Vincent and the other men; she provides the context for their own sexual pleasure. The opening sequence further establishes the ambiguity regarding how we are to interpret Isabelle, to feel for her or feel frustrated by her. The opening bird's-eye shot establishes an objectifying perspective, watching Isabelle's body as a being-in-itself (*être en-soi*), foregrounding its materiality, its flesh and/as femininity. The extreme close-up brings us close, at head level, inviting recognition of her subjectivity, where spectator consciousness is directed to Isabelle's experiencing of the sex act, registering her facial expressions as evidence of her emotional state, a being-for-itself (*être pour-soi*). This cinematic intentionality is continuously emphasised through dialogue as well as cinematography. Vincent asks Isabelle: 'You cumming? Cum. Not cumming?' Isabelle replies: 'You cum. Cum. I feel good. I'm good.' She sacrifices her transcendence even at the point of orgasm, acquiescing her pleasure in lieu of Vincent's. Isabelle is resigned.

This shift in shot style combined with the ambiguity in communication between man and woman,[11] and the focus on intentionality of activity, expresses an existential ethics for women seeking love. *Let the Sunshine In* confronts bad faith in heterosexual love; the frustration of women wanting to be loved within a situation that refuses to acknowledge and support their freedom. Love, then, is examined in the film as a definitive aspect of ambiguity within the human condition, portraying the paradox between freedom and situation and how bad faith in love thwarts the pursuit and realisation of an ethical self and of authentic, reciprocal love. The film continues Denis's long-examined theme of women in situations of oppression, albeit appearing far less biting and gruesome than those of her earlier works, such as with Coré (Béatrice Dalle) in *Trouble Every Day* (2001); Maria (Isabelle Huppert) in *White Material* (2009); or Justine (Lola Créton) in *Les Salauds* (2013). In some respects, this enables the ethical sentiment to be made more effectively because of the relatability Isabelle evokes; the violence she endures is not like the horror Justine or Coré experience, nor is it exacerbated by the political turmoil in Maria's circumstance. It is hidden within the history of her social situation and, consequently, Isabelle's search for her ethical self is strong and conflicted.

Beauvoir's concern with the ethical implications of the existence of the Other is addressed in *The Ethics of Ambiguity*, notably in her discussion of joy and passion as the pathway to realising freedom. She explains that freedom is possible if one is able to convert passion for the self into passion for others without wanting to possess or limit their existence (EA 72). It is only through risking an emotional relationship with others, one that supports and promotes the ontological and emotional well-being of the other, that freedom is possible: 'No project can be defined except by its interference with other projects. To make being "be" is to communicate with others by means of being' (EA 76). In the following section, I discuss the difference between Sartre's and Beauvoir's thinking on bad faith with regard to the ways in which Beauvoir's philosophy of ambiguity specifically addresses women's situation in love.

Bad Faith, the Look and Feminist Film-Phenomenology

Sartre states that bad faith presents a unity of two contradictory concepts that combine to produce a self-deception: 'an idea and the negation of that idea' (*Being and Nothingness* [*henceforward* BN] 98), establishing the false consciousness that one is not what they are (BN 99). Bad faith, a term that identifies the practice of lying to oneself, a self-deception that we are not aware of, is different from a regular lie, as a lie carries with it a conscious intention to deceive. Bad faith is aware of its duality, as a 'duality of myself and myself in the eyes of the other' (BN 89). While it shares the similar appearance of a lie, bad faith is different because it is the self who is the one being deceived. Sartre saw bad faith as a 'metastable' concept, subject to change and transition, even being a normal way of life for most people (BN 90). His description of bad faith in *Being and Nothingness* is given its own titled section, whereas it recurs less markedly throughout Beauvoir's writing. It has been recently described as 'one of the most memorable aspects of his [Sartre's] works', 'one of the most enduring of Sartre's concepts', even stemming 'directly from [Sartre's] description of the basic structures of consciousness' (Pamerleau 2020: 122 and 123). While the former comments are as may be, the latter is certainly up for debate. Sartre's conceptualisation of bad faith not only echoes ideas from Beauvoir's earlier literary works *She Came to Stay* and its original 'Two Unpublished Chapters', it is in debt to them.

Edward Fullbrook defends Beauvoir's provenance, arguing that 'Two Unpublished Chapters' and *She Came to Stay*,[12] written in 1938,[13] are examples of philosophy, exemplifying her 'problem-oriented' approach (2004: 35), with their form representing a challenge to the institutionalisation of the discipline overall. Beauvoir's method of writing involves high description, focusing particularly on Françoise's experience and worldview, an approach emblematic of the phenomenological method, where meaning is determined via an account of individual lived experience.[14] Fullbrook compares the two texts in order to clarify that many of the existential-phenomenological concepts, originally thought to belong to Sartre, were present first in Beauvoir's novels.[15] In 'Two Unpublished Chapters', Beauvoir describes Françoise's adolescence through expressions of reflective states of consciousness: '[an old worn jacket] could not complain as Françoise complained when she had hurt herself; it has no soul ... Françoise tried to imagine what she would feel like if she could not say: "I am Françoise"' (2004b: 42). She further describes Françoise's erotic awakening and her relations with friends in a similar descriptive and reflexive voice that demonstrates the actuality of bad faith as it plays out in the lived experience of her character.

Taken together, these two chapters through literary narrative amplify what both Beauvoir and Sartre meant by 'playing a part', of feigning feelings one does not possess. For example, Françoise defends herself against Mademoiselle Vaison's accusation of plagiarising a translation: 'I am not a liar' (Françoise is in fact lying here). Later, this lie is described through a different deception that can be read as an account of bad faith: 'Françoise wrote the quotation down and wondered for a moment: how unpleasant, to think that, concealed behind their windows, other people could see you while you could not see yourself' (Beauvoir 2004b: 55). The origin of the conception of bad faith and its attribution to Beauvoir is mentioned because it highlights the insidiousness of bad faith in general, particularly the historical role gender plays in determining the social situation, as well as the objectification of others and the maintenance of patriarchal privilege. I suggest that bad faith is a cornerstone concept present in many of Denis's films, as her central characters often lie to themselves in one way or another, allowing an exploration of specific situations of conflict and consciousness, where bad faith almost becomes a character in itself. For the most part, bad faith presents as a gendered and classed quality within the social situation. One of the strategies of phenomenology is to bracket off (*epoché*) experience from the natural attitude (surrounding context) and describe concretely the consciousness of living experience. From this description, broader observations and witnessing can be made on lived experience and situation.[16] Sartre problematically[17] uses this method in *Being and Nothingness* where he employs bad faith as a concept in his development of an existentialist, ontological philosophical system. Beauvoir also used the phenomenological method of description in her use of interviews, literature and scientific research in works such as *The Second Sex* and *The Coming of Age*. In her case, however, Beauvoir was not concerned with creating a philosophy (this is worth reflecting on when thinking about her claim that she was not a philosopher, once again illustrating the ambiguity of her muted voice), but instead used existentialist philosophical systems and concepts to describe and question situations (of women, of the aged, and so on). In each case, the philosophers describe in concrete detail (for Sartre, imagined detail) examples of lived experience to craft meaning that is then utilised to form more abstract meaning.[18]

To take up a specifically feminist film-phenomenological approach involves similar methodology, wherein close description of a film, its aesthetics, the actor's performance, its reception via film reviews, and so on, shares some features of various phenomenological paradigms, blending similar aspects of methodology (bracketing off, description, identifying the experiencing of film experience) albeit with different aims. Sara Cohen Shabot and Christinia Landry argue that feminist approaches offer phenomenology a 'visibility' of bracketed lived experience, emphasising the ambiguity of embodied sexed and gendered experience that forms 'normal experience' (Cohen Shabot and Landry 2018: 2). In their view, one that is almost impossible to deny, feminist phenomenologies attend to women's alienation of their own bodies, the ambiguity at the heart of feminine comportment (which is either embraced or rejected) and the inextricable link to freedom. Beauvoir's gendered phenomenology of women's situation and Iris Marion Young's later application of her philosophy to the motility of women and their embodied existence are the primary sources for Cohen Shabot and Landry's inquiry. Their aim is to alter what 'normal experience' is for women and this, they explain, is 'one of the radical endeavors of feminist phenomenology' (Cohen Shabot and Landry 2018: 5). Even in the twenty-first century, cinema holds on to its efficacious position that helps realise this aim, exposing, critiquing and readdressing what 'normal experience' and other lived experiences that are typically shunned, such as the love relationship,[19] might be for women. A feminist film-phenomenology therefore explicitly describes the experience of witnessing stories of women's gendered and embodied lived experience, being observant to its inherent ambiguity, and describing the affective and emotional turbulence it may or may not elicit.

Post-Phenomenology: Bad Faith as A Manner of Perspective

Bergoffen asks if bad faith can be thought of as a manner of perspective, not in terms of opinion, but on the basis of intentionality, ethics and privilege. Le Doeuff interprets perspective as expressing 'a point of view or chosen theoretical position which is applied to a particular area of experience assumed to exist before the investigation whose object it is' (2007: 89). Bad faith, as a perspective that goes unchecked, is a shared experience working most effectively and efficiently in unexamined situations or areas of experience that seek to protect and hide one's vulnerabilities. Where Sartre privileges the position of the one who looks (and therefore illustrates bad faith of the perceiver; a position that denies its own vulnerability), Beauvoir honours the perspective of 'the one who is looked at' (a position all too aware of the risk of vulnerability) (Bergoffen 1992: 224) and questions the bad faith of the situation. To question the situation contextualises a number of hidden elements informing 'a manner of perspective'. The gaze, the look, attention, intention – each effects various affective resonances for embodied being and involves orientations toward something or someone other than itself. Beauvoir sought to illustrate how a manner of perspective, that is, looking at and with women in their situation, was historically determined and sustained. In doing so, she combined the experience of looking and being looked at (subject-object) as contingent on history and situation, and denied separation between a woman's body and her being-for-herself. Instead, women's situation is shown to be ambiguous and embodied, and because of this her search for freedom requires the support of others and is therefore an ethical pursuit.

Sartre's perspective, and by extension his concept of the look, is born from conflict, arguing that the gaze is about possession of the Other, forming the basis of the intersubjective dynamic between the Other and the Self. He writes: 'The Other holds a secret – the secret of what I am. He makes me be and thereby he possesses me, and this possession is nothing other than the consciousness of possessing me' (BN 475). This possession is what Sartre uses to define his being-for-others, as the basis for objectification, the look that limits the potential of one's subjectivity and reduces the self to an object. As Bergoffen has noted, it shows the entanglement of the look and bad faith. It is hardly a surprise, then, that for Sartre, 'love is a conflict' (BN 477). Beauvoir, on the other hand, viewed love in far greater moral terms, claiming that an authentic love is contingent on 'two freedoms' that 'would not mutilate themselves; together they would both reveal values and ends in the world' (TSS 706). These short references are offered to demonstrate the principle that bad faith is driven by gendered situations and that perspective is an ambiguity of its own requiring close examination. To be clear, Beauvoir never outwardly criticised Sartre in her philosophical writing or in her autobiographies, although she did clearly differentiate her philosophy of situation from Sartre's, and demonstrate the importance of relations with others (and therefore the role of emotion).[20] What does emerge clearly is that each author was capable of being ignorant of their own bad faith which manifested itself differently in line with the variations of their perspectives on love, but also that for Beauvoir, emotion was the sensory aspect of lived experience that acknowledged the ambiguous unity of body and consciousness within one's situation. Without confronting emotion, or acknowledging its significance in recognising an appeal of reciprocated freedom, bad faith is likely to thrive. What, then, is the significance of recognising another's bad faith?

For the purposes of this chapter, and the particulars of conceiving a feminist film-phenomenology, the film experience of *Let the Sunshine In* is first described here as feminist. In this way, the experiencing itself is bracketed off from other parallel embodied experiences (such as ability, class, etc.), where the experience of the experience is the qualifying position (for example, the feminist experience of film experience). However, while this suggests a critical technique for describing and identifying a particular film experience (my own), it also recognises the things themselves – *my* experience of *this* film – is open to other consciousnesses and therefore meaning is contingent. Prescription of any specificity of experience (film or otherwise) is antithetical to the phenomenological method, and a key quality of feminist phenomenology is its openness to other disciplines (Oksala 2004; Stoller 2017).

It is not my concern to try to argue that Denis is a feminist filmmaker. I do not think it is feasible to collapse stories about women, even those that explore women's situation, as being intentionally feminist by default of their sex. Rather, it is more fruitful to situate Denis as a phenomenological filmmaker, one who concentrates on the freedom of others through the lens of emotion and reciprocal recognition. In an interview with Hermione Eyre (2010), Denis acknowledged the importance of emotion and empathy in her directing but eschewed any political feminist intentionality. Her method of filmmaking is more illustrative of what Johanna Oksala has called 'post-phenomenology' (2004: 238), an evolved method that calls for a giving-up of 'the first-person perspective as the indispensable starting point of our analysis', and is instead developed through a 'critical distance from the commonly accepted meanings of various forms of experience' (2004: 240). Oksala argues that for a phenomenology of gender to be viable, phenomenological methods themselves must evolve to include awareness of lived experience and situations that are not one's own. A post-phenomenology therefore takes up the crucial Beauvoirian insistence on reciprocal recognition, starting 'with knowledge and experiences that are foreign to us' (Oksala 2004: 241). Only in this way can lived experience, one that attends to gender, be comprehensively and ethically described, inclusive of self-other experience and the ambiguities it contains.

Denis's filmmaking, as an example of a post-phenomenological method, can be viewed as a consequence of a feminist politic that has evolved historically, to the extent that the inequity of women's situation is widely acknowledged (if not resolved). She says: 'Often women as little girls are sent off on a track for them to live a perfect life and be a perfect woman. Not for boys, who can be themselves, with their mood and their temper' (Denis in Eyre 2010: np). In many respects, this exemplifies a particular Beauvoirian sensibility, rejecting any essentialist difference between female and male directors but offering a clear assessment of a persistent social situation. Denis also speaks of responsibility to her characters, which she demonstrates on screen empathetically: 'This kindness [toward her characters], yes: this is something I'm aware of ... They [her characters] exist because of me and I have responsibility for them.' The lack of judgement that we see in *Let the Sunshine In* of Isabelle's pattern of bad choices in men is an example of Denis's kindness toward her characters. By avoiding any *schadenfreude* in the narrative, Denis crafts an empathy toward Isabelle and her situation through oscillating between perceptual camera distances. This critical distance that is affected through the cinematography also facilitates disclosure, Beauvoir's term that argued for an unveiling of situation.[21]

Denis also shares Beauvoir's creative influences (William Faulkner, Virginia Woolf), noting explicitly Woolf's 'freedom in her thoughts' as being a good example of femininity. Even further, Denis often expresses irritation at being asked about being a 'woman' director, pragmatically agreeing that it is more difficult for women to make films but equivocally noting that '[i]t's not easy, in fact, being a human being' (Denis in Eyre 2010: np). Her position is that filmmaking itself responds to different social, cultural and economic situations, and she claims one shouldn't compare the Hollywood studio industry with cinema from a different culture. Beauvoir also stressed the reality of contingencies between men and women, stating that differences will always exist and ending *The Second Sex* firmly arguing that women's freedom can only be sustained if she is seen on her own ambiguous terms:

> to refuse to enclose her in the relations she sustains with man, but not to deny them ... recognizing each other as subject, each will remain an *other* for the other; reciprocity in their relations will not do away with the miracles that the division of human beings into two separate categories engenders. (TSS 766)

Returning to Bergoffen's question – is bad faith a manner of perspective? – a film-phenomenological, or post-phenomenological, approach must not simply bracket off experience and consider the elements that constitute the film experience in order to determine meaning, but also embrace a 'critical distance from certain forms of experience' (Oksala 2004: 240).

Bad faith, in this sense, does affect a manner, that is, a sensibility of style and situation, of perspective. While Oksala identifies psychological reports and ethnographical studies as the material that enables such critical distance, I can see no reason why film experience (especially cinema from outside one's own respective culture or history) should be excluded as example. In the case of *Let the Sunshine In*, Isabelle's particular set of experiences might not be known to a spectator but it does offer 'partial bracketing' (Oksala 2004: 240) that discloses something of women's experience in patriarchal love relationships, enough to create a sense of recognition and relatability in audiences. In many ways, because Isabelle's situation is distant from that of the spectator, possessing some 'foreign' elements (this might include the French language for non-French speakers, or it may be Isabelle's age, again such specificity here is not helpful or necessary; it is enough that some 'foreignness' as 'otherness' exists), her lifeworld can be 'appropriated in an attempt to make visible the presumptions and implicit ontological commitments in one's homeworld' (Oksala 2004: 204). Put another way, by witnessing the emotional turmoil Isabelle endures as a result of the bad faith in her love relationships, spectators are able to appropriate her story to think through their own situation and potential circumstances of bad faith.

This echoes Beauvoir's opening point in *Pyrrhus and Cineas*, where she uses the example of the little boy who cries empathically over the death of another little boy ('his concierge's son'; PC 92) to illustrate the necessity of others and the need for empathy in asserting the significance of being-for-oneself: 'If I myself were only a thing, nothing indeed would concern me' (PC 92). If I lack the capacity to care for another, outside the parameters of self-profit or relevance, I cannot be ethically free. In order for my freedom to exist, that is, for it to be recognised, validated and returned by others, it must also be relevant and relatable to others. Vintges outlines a 'three-level configuration' to Beauvoir's theory of existential ethics, involving a recognition of human existence as a 'given' situation, requiring a 'social freedom' that makes possible any transcendence, and through these two elements (the situation of social freedom) craft an ability to 'search out positive ties with others' (Vintges 1996: 70–1). Through this existence is moral freedom and authentic love possible.

In casting Binoche as Isabelle and foregrounding her seductiveness, attractiveness and carnality in middle age, Denis proposes an ethics specific to women's situation in (heterosexual) love. *Let the Sunshine In* contests the usual practice of casting women as leading love interests as the domain only of the young by placing the complexities and anxieties of a middle-aged woman's search for love centre stage. Isabelle's age, and by extension her ageing body, is significant because in its facticity it expresses the endurance of tyranny of men over women's carnality, in terms of appeal and fertility. Beauvoir's meticulous attention to women's bodies in her philosophy of their lived experience demonstrates the irrefutable link between the body and situation. She writes 'a situation does not depend on the body; it is rather the body that depends on it' (TSS 736), inciting a historicity to the systematic imposition that women endure either in the home or in society at large. In what could be read as a description of Isabelle's character, Beauvoir continues:

> to assert her femininity: she dresses up, goes out, and flirts, she is in love, wavering between masochism and aggressiveness. In all cases, she questions herself, is agitated and scattered. By the very fact she is in thrall to outside preoccupations, she does not commit herself entirely to her enterprise; thus she profits from it less, and is more tempted to give it up. (TSS 737)

Bergoffen notes Beauvoir's attention on 'ontology [being] infected with history' (1992: 22), showing that within patriarchy, women's situation is codified through discourses of gender. While this appears as well-trodden ground, Bergoffen uses Beauvoir's focus to illustrate how she deviates from Sartre's position regarding bad faith. As gender significantly limits the possibilities of our existence, within patriarchy, our ontologies are therefore limited by the histories and contexts that have shaped them. Gendered ways of looking determine different 'modes of being as bad faith' (Bergoffen 1992: 22) for men and women. This in turn reifies the affect and power of the look in determining or degrading the reciprocal recognition of women's freedom.

Isabelle's age further implies that the bad faith evident in her love relationships is not a new way of being for her; she hasn't just become neurotic as a consequence of her relationships with these men and, of course, patriarchal love hasn't just begun to treat women in disrespectful and subjugating ways. Isabelle's existence is a synecdoche of the history of women's oppressed situation, especially in love. Her existence is foregrounded as gendered and ageing, therefore the bad faith that Isabelle exhibits in the film is derivative of the histories that have confounded to create it. Beauvoir puts it this way:

> In accepting herself as the inessential and as total dependence, the woman creates a hell for herself; all women in love see themselves in Andersen's Little Mermaid, who, having exchanged her fish tail for a woman's legs out of love, walked on needles and burning coals. It is not true that the beloved man is unconditionally necessary and that she is not necessary to him; it is not up to him to justify the woman who worships him, and he does not let himself be possessed by her. (TSS 694)

The film also acknowledges women's capacity to act in childish and immature ways, their own acquiescence to social scripts, as being consequences of their ontological histories.[22] And yet, Denis resists an easy conclusion or prescription of what authentic love might look like or how one might achieve it.

Exasperatingly, Isabelle visits Vincent at his apartment where she first accosts him for forgetting to call her over the weekend, then tells him she is in love with him. In this scene, the use of a wide medium shot invites a different viewing engagement compared to the opening close-ups, asking us to look once more at the temperature and dynamic of Isabelle and Vincent's relationship. A medium shot, particularly when statically positioned as is the case here (Figure 5.4), asks the audience to regard the interaction of elements within the *mise-en-scène*. The circular furniture echoes Isabelle's movement around the room, as does her repetitive dialogue ('What did you say? What did you say?') – we are shown that Isabelle and Vincent are going round and round in circles in their relationship, with no suggestion of growth or evolution.

Isabelle asks that he 'take care of her, a tiny bit' and to keep his promise to call her if he says he will, otherwise 'this thing won't last much longer'. It is hardly a long list of demands but Vincent nevertheless hears a claim of possession, responding with 'Dictatorship of the proletariat!' Despite this terse exchange, it is implied that they have sex once again, confirming the pattern of Isabelle's bad faith; '[s]he imagines the man's love as the exact counterpart of the love she bears him, with bad faith, she takes desire for love' (TSS 699). This scene superficially affirms Sartre's position that 'love

Figure 5.4 Isabelle visits Vincent (Xavier Beauvois) in his apartment.

is a conflict' but to view it solely on this basis is to acquiesce to the invitation of bad faith and overlook the codification of gender and the vulnerability that is structured here through the look (Bergoffen 1992: 221). Isabelle has come to Vincent's apartment to assert her subjectivity, to ask that he give her what she is already entitled to – care, respect, love. Denis uses this interaction between the two characters to establish and expose a central modality of bad faith in love – a woman's search for validation through men, and a man's belief that his subjectivity confers the privilege of being the origin of meaning. Women request reciprocity, men decide whether or not to give it.

The value of highlighting bad faith foregrounds an avoidance of responsibility concerning self-awareness, evasion of authentic being, a desire for omnipotence, and followership without reflection or consideration. As Denis's films often portray characters in emotionally tense situations, the existentialist concept of bad faith helps to indicate the relational aspect of ambiguity, what Lewis R. Gordon observes as 'a crucial element … It is *social*' (2020: 19). In *Let the Sunshine In*, bad faith is primarily portrayed in Isabelle and her refusal to take responsibility for her own freedom. Yet it is also strikingly evident in the men she encounters, indicating that it is the institution of romance and the social scripts which sustain it that are also under examination. The ways in which we look at women and with women remain patriarchally ordered, and the recognition of a woman's vulnerability within the love relationship (and the bad faith she uses to hide it) must therefore be described by first acknowledging the historical conditions of her inessential otherness. In this way, we can begin to see bad faith in the more positive terms Beauvoir acknowledges – as an ethics of the erotic, or more simply, as a defence mechanism. The continued significance of Beauvoir's philosophy remains some seventy years later, a philosophy which, as Le Doeuff says, teaches us 'to look at the social world with a critical eye, instead of looking within ourselves for some hidden cause of an existential incapacity' (2007: 57), thus foreshadowing Oksala's notion of critical distance as a post-phenomenological method.

Let the Sunshine In is certainly a film about love, but I disagree with critics who have classified it as a 'romantic comedy' (Brody 2018). Such classification is a mistake as it misses what I see as a clear engagement with its ethics regarding women's experiences of being in love. The film's ambiguous sensibility is served much better by Beauvoir's existential phenomenology, which addresses women's oppression in love relationships and outlines the potentiality of transcendence toward freedom, positioning authentic love as the 'reciprocal recognition of two freedoms' (TSS 706). In *The Second Sex*, Beauvoir develops the ethics she proposed in *The Ethics of Ambiguity* in more precise gendered terms. Here, woman's ontology is under discussion, specifically the 'facts and myths'[23] of her existence in society, where the ethical claim of asserting her subjectivity is often met with a series of empirical and existential hurdles that impede her freedom. Beauvoir says that alongside the desire to be authentic is a 'temptation to flee freedom' to turn oneself 'into a thing' (TSS 10). Without recourse to reciprocal recognition of her freedom, the woman faces alienation; her alternative is bad faith, avoiding the 'anguish and stress of authentically assumed existence' (TSS 10). To conform as an inessential other is an easier life, to accept what is conditionally given rather than fight for a freedom that is repeatedly delayed, if not negated or ignored. Or is it? Perhaps up to a point, and in fragments, with interrupting realisations of the reality of oppression that compel us to look, to really see, before we turn away again. If *Let the Sunshine In* has a dark humour (and it certainly has its moments), this stems from the recognition of Isabelle's bad faith, that her experiences in love are all too familiar and shared by women. What Beauvoir's philosophy offers for a reading of Denis's film is the capacity to regard its comment, at a critical distance, on the condition of women and to locate its portrayal in a context that avoids judgement. Being able to laugh at, and sometimes with, Isabelle is a defence mechanism reacting to the fight against internalising the realities of domination in relationships that should be supporting women's freedom.

The predominant bad faith exposed in the film relates to the 'misogynistic systems of love and marriage' as 'societal faults' (Wilson 2019: 25) within patriarchal love relationships and creates a consciousness of the history relevant to women's situation. Like Beauvoir, however, the film does not lay blame at the feet of the oppressed; it avoids faulting Isabelle for choosing the type of man she does (selfish, demeaning, narcissistic). Rather, it sees the ambiguity within women's situation – being a subject for herself and an object for others – and responds with the possibility of authentic love and an open future either with Marc or some other future man (according to David, the clairvoyant). Beauvoir writes: 'Love, for the woman, is a supreme attempt to overcome the dependence to which she is condemned by assuming it; but even consented to, dependence can only be lived in fear and servility' (TSS 707). *Let the Sunshine In* further echoes Beauvoir's assertion that 'the simple juxtaposition of the right to vote and a job amounts to total liberation; work today is not freedom. Only in a socialist world would the woman who has one be sure of the other' (TSS 721). Isabelle's success as an artist is never questioned or jeopardised. Indeed, her creativity is one of the qualities that men find attractive about her.

Vincent tells Isabelle he admires her, would like to be her, because she does 'the best thing in the world'. He sees her artistry as preventing her from feeling alienated from the world around her, but of course Isabelle scoffs at his condescension. Vincent may admire Isabelle's creativity, her ability to generate imagination and ideas of transcendence in the minds of others so that they may avoid complacency in existence, but he does nothing to support or facilitate it. He wants to control it and possess it for himself. Isabelle continues to be career-successful throughout the film, her work is internationally represented and she gets on well with her gallery agent, yet her ethical freedom is limited by her dependence on needing to be loved by men. It appears little else fulfils her.

Beauvoir's analysis of the woman in love appears toward the end of the second volume of *The Second Sex*. In Margaret Simons and Marybeth Timmermann's (2015) *Simone de Beauvoir: Feminist Writings*, the more accurate translations of Beauvoir's shorter articles – written in her more popular voice for magazines in the late 1940s to mid-1960s – show how Beauvoir's thoughts on love were clearly directed and developed in line with her existential ethics. In addition to *The Second Sex*, these articles show that as Beauvoir continued to address the repression of women in situations of marriage, love and family planning, her voice grew to combine the political with the popular, a direction that Denis's filmmaking also appears to have taken.

Notes

1 'Jean Paul Sartre, Strictly Personal' was commissioned and published by *Harper's Bazaar* in 1946. The original article was translated by Marybeth Timmermann and printed in Simons, Timmermann and Mader (eds), *Simone de Beauvoir: Philosophical Writings* (2004: 229–35). I quote from the latter.
2 See Bergoffen (1997: 2, 190–202). See in particular Bergoffen's in-depth comparison of Beauvoir's *The Second Sex* and *The Long March* regarding women's role in society and patriarchy's possession and manipulation of love.
3 *Notebook for an Ethics (Cahiers pour une morale)* (1992) notwithstanding. Originally written in 1947.
4 'It's About Time Women Put a New Face on Love', first published in *Flair*, 1, 3, April 1950, pp. 76–7, appears in Simons and Timmermann (eds), *Simone de Beauvoir: Feminist Writings* (2015: 76–80). All quotations are from the latter.
5 See Secomb (2012) 'Simone de Beauvoir, Melodrama and the Ethics of Transcendence', pp. 81–96. Secomb discusses Beauvoir's philosophy on the woman in love in her comparative aesthetic analysis of classic and contemporary melodramas (Douglas Sirk's *All the Heaven Allows* (1955) and Todd Haynes's *Far From Heaven*, (2002)) as illuminating the transition of ethical positions in response to socio-cultural and historical changes. Secomb does not discuss

Rainer Werner Fassbinder's *Ali: Fear Eats the Soul* (1974), however her analysis of prejudice concerning interracial relationships in Haynes's film certainly applies, particularly with regard to their shared 'ambiguous and contradictory signification' in race and class situations (2012: 92).

6   See Vintges (1996: 46–66) for a closer and highly detailed discussion of the difference between Beauvoir and Sartre's thinking on emotion.

7   I find Bergoffen's (1992) terminology particularly useful in understanding bad faith as a consciousness that does not belong to one gender over another, yet concurrently acknowledges the considerable impact of gender structures in sustaining ontological histories of bad faith.

8   Written for *McCall's* magazine in 1965. References are taken from Simons and Timmermann (eds), *Simone de Beauvoir: Feminist Writings* (2015: 99–102).

9   See Vintges (1996: 22–6), Le Doeuff (2007: 96–9) and Bergoffen (1992: 221).

10 This line is spoken at the end of the film by David, when he tells Isabelle how he lives his life, how he protects himself from being used by others.

11 Film critic Glenn Kenny (2018) reads this sex scene differently, seeing Vincent as being 'avidly concerned with bringing her to orgasm'. I see Vincent's questions as evidence of his inability to intuitively know Isabelle or attend to what she wants. After all, if a woman is in the throes of orgasm, is there really any doubt? Sexual intercourse is a fleshed encounter, and it is very clear that Isabelle's body is not communicating any pleasure or enjoyment. If Vincent cares, and it is hard to believe he does, he doesn't do so with much sincerity or for very long.

12 Fullbrook specifies that Beauvoir wrote *She Came to Stay* without any input from Sartre (2004: 35). In *The Prime of Life*, Beauvoir briefly refers to her decision to jettison these two chapters that outlined Françoise's childhood after Brice Parain from Gallimard thought they 'did not measure up to her [other] stories' (PL 268). See PL 268–75 where Beauvoir discusses her writing of this novel in depth.

13 This date is supported by Beauvoir herself in her autobiography: 'I began She Came to Stay [*sic*] in October, 1938, and ended it in the late spring of 1941' (PL 295). Both *She Came to Stay* and *Being and Nothingness* were published in 1943.

14 Beauvoir clearly points out in *The Prime of Life* that her character Françoise is based on her own childhood and adolescent experiences.

15 See Margaret Simons (1981b: 25–42) for a closer analysis concerning this questioning of origin of thought between Beauvoir and Sartre. Also, Kate Kirkpatrick (2019: 127, 192) has written on this issue of attribution, questioning Beauvoir's use of 'we' in her autobiographical comment: 'we applied this term to anyone who feigned convictions or feelings that they did not in fact possess'.

16 See Gravil (2007: 17–20); Warnock (1970).

17 In *Hipparchia's Choice* (2007: 64–6), Michèle Le Doeuff discusses Sartre's 'de facto solipsism' in his philosophy of bad faith, noting that his reference

to 'woman' is only ever made 'when an actual sexual encounter is being discussed' (2007: 62). Le Doeuff further shows that his examples of women in his determination of bad faith are evidence of 'sexism in philosophical texts' (64). Using the 'frigid woman' as a case study to exemplify his concept of bad faith (he also refers to the 'homosexual' who does not publicly admit his sexual orientation), Sartre exposes his own bad faith. At no point does Sartre question the validity of his source, Viennese psychiatrist Stekel, and yet writes confidently about lived experience as broad generalisation: 'women whom marital infidelity has made them frigid' (BN 95). Sartre points out that Stekel's work bears 'witness to a pathological bad faith that the Freudian doctrine can not [sic] account for' (BN 95), also contradicting his refutation of psychoanalysis's validity in addressing self-deception. Sartre even goes so far as to claim, without irony, that women, in order to avoid experiencing pleasure during intercourse 'which they dread', distract themselves by thinking of domestic chores and 'household accounts' (BN 95). Sartre offers no example of a heterosexual man's sexual 'pathology' (for example, erectile dysfunction) as bad faith. Le Doeuff makes her point to argue that philosophy must be held to a standard that rigorously questions what is said and consider the ways in which it is said. See also Moi (2010: 147–54). See Lewis Gordon (2020: 19) who defends Sartre's imagined example of the woman on a date as an illustration of 'disembodiment'.

18 See Le Doeuff (2007: 90–1) who discusses the difference between Sartre's and Beauvoir's methods in greater detail.
19 See Jenny Chamarette (2018: 187–208) who argues that without inclusion of intersectional approaches, feminist phenomenology fails to realise its goal of making visible othered embodied experience.
20 Additionally, in her descriptions of hers and Sartre's polygamous relationships, it is difficult to overlook the hurt she felt. See *Force of Circumstance* and her discussions concerning Dolores Vanetti in particular.
21 See Chapter 2 where I discuss Kate Ince's notion of ethical vision and Beauvoir's disclosure with respect to Liliana Cavani's *The Night Porter*.
22 Denis's most recent films (*Let the Sunshine In*; *High Life*, 2018) do not focus as closely on the politics of colonialism as do her earlier ones (*Chocolat*, 1988; *White Material*, 2010; *35 Shots of Rum*, 2009) but the flippant tone of *Let the Sunshine In* underscores Isabelle's privileged class conditions. Her worries are entirely concerned with love, even her mother-daughter relationship with Cécile is a distant concern. It is precisely the lack of worries (economic, etc.) that highlights Isabelle's class and the persistence of disparity between men's and women's freedom at all social levels.
23 'Facts and Myth' is the title given to the first volume of *The Second Sex* (TSS 1–274).

CHAPTER 6

A Cinema of the Borderlands: Lucrecia Martel's *Zama*

The previous chapters have discussed various aspects of Beauvoir's philosophy of ambiguity and their role in determining her existential ethics, suggesting that the emotional turbulence that results from ambiguity holds specific significance for a phenomenology of film experience. Using selected films of independent women filmmakers (Cavani, Granik, Dunye and Denis), I have outlined how their respective films exemplify Beauvoir's existentialist ethics as involving the following: 1) the need for reciprocal recognition to enable moral freedom; 2) the significance of emotional experience in our relations with others; 3) a questioning of habit in our manners of perception; 4) the systemic assumptions they maintain; and 5) the role of bad faith in love. These features illuminate how Beauvoir's existential phenomenology offers new ways of thinking about the importance of emotional indeterminacy within the context of cinematic experience. Her specific conception of ambiguity, when considered in terms of film experience, serves to recognise how effectively independent women filmmakers investigate the emotional turbulence within contingent existence, shedding particular light on women's lived experience.

But where to from here? Can Beauvoir's notion of ambiguity continue to be relevant for the twenty-first century within the shifting parameters of womanhood, taking into consideration the polemics of identity politics that exist within the related disciplines of feminism, feminist philosophy and film studies? Can her ethics of ambiguity be satisfactorily developed in line with its initial project, and extended to include reflective thinking on our current state of being on ethical and inclusive terms for the purpose of cinematic experience? The aim of this chapter, and for those that remain, is to consider the ways in which Beauvoir's philosophy of ambiguity can be put in closer conversation with current feminist phenomenologies. Beauvoir's philosophy, while ground-breaking, was of a different time, and despite her acknowledgement of the emotional and affective tensions common to everyday existence and their connection to the pursuit of moral freedom, to answer the questions posed above, this chapter engages with other feminist phenomenologists whose work attends much more to multiplicitous lived experience in diverse and global situations. Here, I reflect on Beauvoir's Eurocentrism and engage with other phenomenologies of ambiguity, and look toward an example of cinema that acknowledges ambiguous lived experience but which also critiques Eurocentric or colonialising world views, advancing more inclusive perspectives on freedom.

Argentine director Lucrecia Martel, revered for her sensorially complex and politically shrewd films, evokes a phenomenological and inclusive sensibility through her integration of concrete lived experience from her own childhood and selected historical events in Argentina.[1] Her first three feature-length films (sometimes referred to as the Salta trilogy): *La ciénaga* (*The Swamp*, 2001), *La niña santa* (*The Holy Girl*, 2004) and *La mujer sin cabeza* (*The Headless Woman*, 2008), poetically examine the bad faith of Argentina's privileged middle-class, producing languid and (paradoxically) emotionally fraught narratives, and employing innovative use of marginal aesthetics (such as off-screen space, narrative *lacunae*, lack of dialogue and acousmatic sound) to effect disquieting and unsettling cinematic experience. Her films generate feelings of incertitude, crafting a sense of discomfort that is sustained through the entire feature. As spectators, we come to slowly notice that there is something wrong, something off in the situations of her characters (and in the characters themselves) and rarely does Martel neatly resolve such questions for her audiences.

In *La ciénaga*, for example, there is no specific narrative causality given for the drunken malaise of the adults who squander their time lying around the rundown swimming pool (Figure 6.1). The degradation of environment, the aimlessness of the adults' action and behaviour, the unexplained mess of their belongings – these are all visual evocations of indeterminacy. Gerd Gemünden notes that these work to 'create fundamental epistemological uncertainties in the service of moral fables that force viewers to question their values and beliefs' (2019: 8). Consequently, Martel has quickly become known for crafting a nuanced examination of how 'neocolonial, patriarchal and heteronormative structures are perpetuated' (Martin 2016: 9) and 'avoids the creation of a false universalism that underlies almost all mainstream productions' (Gemünden 2019: 127). In addition to her signature aesthetic of celebrating the margins of existence primarily through cinema's affective resonances, her commentary on Argentina's political events and their consequences is equally restrained.

La mujer sin cabeza, for example, is often interpreted as a metaphor for Argentina's Dirty War (1976–1983) which began with Jorge Rafael

Figure 6.1 Adults lazing around the pool in *La ciénaga* (Martel 2001).

Videla's *coup d'etat* overthrowing Isabel Perón's government. During this period under Videla's presidency, military forces violently oppressed any political dissidence against his government, enacting state terrorism and crimes against humanity such as torture, murder and the forcible disappearance of around 30,000 Argentines (called *los desaparecidos*, the disappeared ones) (Blakeley 2009: 96). However, Martel has resisted the ease of this allegorical reading, saying that her intention was to underline 'the complicity of society' as being what 'most affects us today' (Martel in Gemünden 2019: 84). Therefore, by avoiding overt representation, Martel manages to disclose the bad faith of Argentina's middle-class, implying that where other similar situations of bad faith persist, complicity in society's neoliberal oppressions is sustained (the set design, costume and music within *La mujer sin cabeza* supports the timeframe of 1970s Argentina). Deborah Martin interprets this strategy as disclosing defamiliarisation of reality and the hegemonic practices utilised by oppressive and conservative social orders. For Martin, the value of Martel's restraint is what enables her to create a very affective ambiguity within film experience, that is, the 'pervasive creation of uncertainty and doubt, their play with perception, which in turn suggests a contingent and mutable reality, and allows for the glimpsing of alternative possibilities' (Martin 2016: 9). To this I would add that Martel's films foreground the emotional cost and socio-cultural corrosion that results from the trauma and allusive horror that occurs within the story worlds of the films themselves. The films' affective disquieting and disturbing sensibility illuminates what it feels like to exist in the margins and within states of ambiguity. Audiences therefore don't simply observe the consequences of ambiguous experience in the characters' lives on screen, they feel them within their own experience of watching Martel's films precisely through the unnerving aesthetic devices she uses.

Martel's predominant aesthetic signature is her capacity to incur this shift of perception in her audiences, to make us aware of the hidden spaces and ignored aspects of life that shape our interpretation of it. Interestingly, Beauvoir also says the practice of well-made plots irritated her because of their artificiality; in her novels she wanted 'to imitate the disorder, the indecision, the contingency of life; I had let my characters and the events in the book sprawl in every direction; I left out all the "necessary scenes"; all the important things happened offstage"' (FC 249). Similarly, Martel's feature films induce a sense of waiting, looking and searching but, as she has remarked, '[t]he waiting doesn't exist if there isn't this question of identity' (Martel in Teodoro 2017). From *La ciénaga* to *Zama* (2017), audiences are invited into story worlds where characters exist in situations of stagnation, ambiguity and futility, often wrestling with existential crises indicative of the failures stemming from ineffective social systems, institutions and questionable life decisions.

Gemünden notes Martel's prevalent use of water: the swimming pool featured in *La ciénaga*, the hotel's thermal pool in *La niña santa*, the pool and the rain in *La mujer sin cabeza* and the rivers in *Zama*. For Gemünden, the symbolism of water in Martel's films is a primary signifier that emphasises 'fluidity or blurring of borders, it defies fixed, concrete identities and desires' (2019: 4). Not only do Martel's films use such recurrent symbolism to critique Argentina's fetishisation of European identity, they also explore the impact and consequences of investing in the shallowness of such bad faith. 'There is a pretentiousness here, which for me is something very Argentine – this desire, wanting to be European, being ashamed to be [Latin] American' (Martel in Gemünden and Spitta 2018: 39). Making visible the multiplicitous selfhoods within Latin American identity is a consistent theme in Martel's cinema, and equally, she explores the ambiguity of existence and the necessity to confront the possibility of failure within lived experience, to tolerate it and respond to it, in order to achieve moral freedom. In this sense, Martel's *Zama* effectively demonstrates Beauvoir's notion of ambiguity as typifying a 'lack' of being (EA 71) through her main character Zama (Daniel Giménez Cacho), by closely considering his emotional experience in the disclosure of his world.[2] Here I draw on the work of Latina feminist phenomenologists such as Gloria Anzaldúa, María Lugones and Mariana Ortega to discuss how Martel manages to foreground the multiplicity of indigenous people's lived experience, recognising the diversity and agency of Latin American peoples rather than promoting any particular singular worldview.

In this chapter, I concentrate on Martel's exploration of lived experience at the border in *Zama*, arguing the aesthetics of her filmmaking engender a consciousness of being in-between, of crossing-over, of spaces and experiences that are hybrid, or as Anzaldúa says: 'a consciousness of the Borderlands' (2012: 99). While Martel is not readily labelled or easily categorised as a feminist filmmaker, her films to-date nevertheless demonstrate very clear feminist, and as I later argue, intersectional and intermeshed politics. Though her feminist politic may not necessarily appear overtly in the narrative structure of her films, I argue it is highly evident in her style of filmmaking and treatment of film narrative, often in the celebration of the margins and what she elects to not screen. Examples include breaking the rules of the cinematic frame, where Martel's use of off-screen space is one of the ways her films draw attention to and include perspectives of those often neglected and ignored within society. Other examples are *Zama*'s anachronism of colonialist presence and the fragility of geo-political borders, and the intertwining of indigenous languages using 'different dialects of the regions of Argentina, plus Portuguese and the mixture of Spanish and Portuguese, or *Portugnol*, which is a phenomenon of the border' (Martel in Gemünden and Spitta 2018: 37). Sounds as well as images illuminate the sensory experience of existence on the periphery of dominant social orders. These examples demonstrate Martel's close attention on diversity and the mobilising of audience attitude and orientation to the reality of oppression of others, which also further acknowledges the difficult emotional burdens that are incurred in the struggle for freedom. In the next section, I discuss some of the limitations within Beauvoir's philosophy of ambiguity and put her ideas in conversation with those of feminist philosophers of colour and their close discussion of women's diverse lived experience. I then consider how these distinctive phenomenologies more effectively identify the connections of ambiguity and emotional turbulence within Martel's *Zama*.

Beauvoir's Intersectional (In)Action and the Need for Multiplicity

By situating ambiguity at the heart of her existential ethics, Beauvoir linked the struggle for freedom with a need for relationships with others as the necessary but emotionally anxious experience for an authentic, moral existence. Yet since she did not address multiplicity in identities or subjectivities, the ethical side to her analysis of freedom requires further development. As a keystone concept, ambiguity intended to address the paradox of the human condition and while Beauvoir's ethics of ambiguity continues to speak to concrete, embodied, emotional experience, it suffers from its own situation. Despite noting the tensions involved in the pursuit of freedom, Beauvoir did not identify the differences (ambiguous or otherwise) of the diverse lived experiences of women of colour as a way to rethink and remake existence on ethical terms.

To recall, Beauvoir's philosophy of ambiguity involves recognising and confronting that we are simultaneously subjects and objects, that we are conscious of the paradox of our existence as caught between a sense of self 'against which no external power can take hold' and also susceptible to being crushed by 'the dark weight of other things' (EA 5). This sense of ambiguity, and indeed the anxiety it evokes, is not something that is often conscious in our minds. Reflection on the precarity of our existence is not a common behaviour outside philosophical contexts, or aesthetic lived experience such as cinema (and other artistic forms). Rather, ambiguity as the foundational condition of human existence is felt as it becomes known; we can identify it because its affective resonance takes form in the embodied feelings of anxiety and other emotional experiences. While Beauvoir's *The Ethics of Ambiguity* develops an argument for an existential ethics that requires a recognition of ambiguity in order to determine our actions and behaviour toward others, it does not specify causalities of ambiguous lived experience beyond the categories of five types of attitude (sub-man, serious man, nihilist, adventurer and passionate man).[3] In addition, *The Ethics of Ambiguity* does not examine the intermeshed lived experience of ambiguity in any concrete specificity with regard to women of colour. And even within Beauvoir's more focused work, *The Second Sex*, where concrete examples are offered, the question of women's freedom problematically defaults to Western, White women.[4]

Kristiana Arp finds Beauvoir's ethics to further engage with 'the quest for moral freedom', linking it to 'a commitment to the political liberation of the oppressed', so making her ethics 'an anti-imperialistic ethics' (Arp 2001: 5). For Arp, Beauvoir's ethical stance was formed in response to the horrors (and Beauvoir's own passivity) of the Second World War.[5] From this experience, Beauvoir develops her position on violence as possessing a conditional moral significance, where in order to secure one's own freedom through reciprocal recognition or through the creation of a pathway to achieve such reciprocity, one is obliged to remove obstacles that thwart or prevent achieving it. In Beauvoir's view, obstruction of one's potential freedom results in the degradation of the human to a thing (as witnessed via the Holocaust), and is to be regarded as an evil. Therefore, violence as a means to secure the freedom of the self can be viewed as necessary; a moral obligation that permits one to achieve what is otherwise prevented. This leads Arp to view Beauvoir's ethics as 'an ethics that privileges action, indeed preaches activism, and scorns passivity' but she also says that Beauvoir went too far in this direction, claiming that in today's world 'no comparable evil' confronts us (Arp 2001: 5). I disagree. There are many comparable evils that persist in the world today which continue in their attempt to steal, thwart and prevent the freedom of the other and therefore of the self. This is the work that feminists of colour such as Kimberlé Crenshaw (2017) and Patricia Hill Collins (2000, 2016, 2019) have sought to do, arguing that intersectionality as a critical social practice (as well as theoretical concept) reveals comparable evils, reversing the invisibility of multiplicity in race and gender at the point of identity intersection.

Beauvoir's examples in *The Ethics of Ambiguity* are more abstract than in *The Second Sex*, used to structure her philosophy concerning the quest for freedom. As a result, statements such as 'an action which wants to serve man ought to be careful not to forget him on the way', or 'the goal is not fixed once and for all; it is defined all along the road which leads to it' (EA 165) can easily appear to apply to anyone who shares *her* view. But as Collins (2019) and Stephanie Rivera Berruz (2016) note, it is precisely Beauvoir's own view that is the problem, despite the value her philosophy of freedom holds for ethical and political action. Beauvoir's race/gender analogy makes assumptions that homogenise difference, particularly for women of colour.

Rivera Berruz notes that Beauvoir's race/gender analogy within *The Second Sex* failed to parse out a successful or inclusive phenomenology of multiplicitous identity, reifying women's situation-as-other within 'the imperceptibility of the intersection between racial and gendered embodiment and oppression' (2016: 320). For Rivera Berruz, Beauvoir's efforts to illuminate the oppression of women's situation via Hegel's master-slave dialectic resulted in a collapsed comparison. In situating woman-as-other in the same political situation of a slave, she argues that Beauvoir was unsuccessful in addressing and exploring 'the multiplicitous character of identities' (Rivera Berruz 2016: 320). To remedy this, and extend Beauvoir's *The Second Sex* to be used 'responsibly' by future feminists, Rivera Berruz looks to Latina feminist phenomenologists and their nuanced and diverse accounts of 'Latina' as referring to 'multiple axes of identity' (2016: 325). Rivera Berruz focuses on *The Second Sex* but does not discuss or engage with *The Ethics of Ambiguity*, although she does acknowledge how Anzaldúa uses a number of multidimensional terms to identify and describe the ambiguity within Anzaldúa's own concrete lived experience as Latina. Within Anzaldúa's writings, the notion of ambiguity itself is meticulously examined and awarded a range of expressions that combine embodied and emotional lived experience, consistently interrogating its liminal spaces as sites of anxiety, threat and dissociation, but also addressing their potential for transformation.

One example cited by Rivera Berruz is Anzaldúa's self-description of her Chicana, lesbian identity as *un choque*, a term chosen specifically because it does not translate easily into English: 'it can mean encounter, crash, intermeshing, clash, or collision' (Rivera Berruz 2016: 328). Anzaldúa's tactic of using Spanish words to intentionally foreground the embodied and emotional experience of ambiguity discloses the anxious tensions that are involved in such lived experience. Their multiplicity and resistance to easy translation into English is one strategy that recognises Anzaldúa's phenomenology as enhancing and critically extending the ideas within Beauvoir's philosophy of ambiguity. Anzaldúa saw her own philosophy as 'a philosophical *mestizaje*' where she purposely drew from 'different cultures ... of Latin America, the people of color and also the Europeans' (Anzaldúa 1987/2012: 277) to create the sense of multiplicity in her writing. *Mestizaje* is a term Anzaldúa draws on to develop her own notion of the new *mestiza*, which is more critical than the general reference of *mestizaje* to race-mixing (especially between Europeans and American Indians). For Anzaldúa, the new *mestiza* includes the identity politics of race but also 'material, economic, and geographic conditions' (Ortega 2016: 25). In this way, the new *mestiza* is a gestalt concept in that it situates the self materially and metaphorically in space/time/in-between, torn between them all. As a label-identifier, the new *mestiza* recognises the struggle that underwrites liminal lived experience and its complex emotional turbulence.

Similarly, Patricia Hill Collins argues that Beauvoir 'never advanced an intersectional analysis of oppression or freedom' (2019: 14) and this is true; there are no specific articles or books where Beauvoir intentionally addresses intersectional oppression. Collins, unlike Rivera Berruz, does engage with *The Ethics of Ambiguity* and acknowledges Beauvoir's claim that 'ethical freedom [is possible] by taking responsibility for lives via social action' (2019: 192). Like Rivera Berruz, Collins notes Beauvoir's failure to recognise multiplicity within the race/gender analogy she uses. Both theorists eloquently and rigorously outline the problematic issues of Beauvoir's complicity with her privilege. Beauvoir absolutely benefited from her White middle-class European situation, and despite philosophising about oppression and the ethics of freedom, she neglected to seek out and ascertain concrete examples of women of colour for inclusion in *The*

Second Sex or *The Ethics of Ambiguity*. However, given Beauvoir's own politics, it is not always easy to judge her action (or inaction) purely on the basis of her early publications. In her later years, Beauvoir did become more vocal and publicly political, recognising her privilege and the role of her fame in helping various actions of resistance and political commitment bring about genuine outcomes.

For example, Beauvoir exercised her privilege precisely to draw France's attention to the case of Djamila Boupacha, an Algerian FLN (Front de libération nationale; National Liberation Front) member who had been arrested, tortured and raped for the alleged crime of planting a bomb. Beauvoir was approached by Gisèle Halimi, an attorney 'of Jewish Tunisian birth but a French national' (Kruks 2012: 113) to help ignite French attention and support of Boupacha's case with the hope that it would further incur stronger attention and political resistance against the systemic use of torture within the Algerian war, and more broadly France's own complicity in colonial violence.

Sonia Kruks comments that Beauvoir's June 1960 article, 'In Defense of Djamila Boupacha' in *Le Monde* was 'a significant intervention in the formation of French political discourse' (Kruks 2012: 114) and Julien Murphy has noted that *Djamila Boupacha* (Beauvoir and Halimi 1962) was the 'only book Beauvoir lent her name to as co-author' (Murphy 2012: 262), so committed was she to Algerian independence.[6] The Boupacha case is noteworthy here, as one of Beauvoir's core charges in her article is an attack on France's bad faith and complicity. She writes: 'you [the French people] will come to understand why the wailing and crying and blood-curdling screams that have been emanating for so long from the land of Algeria – and that of France too – have not reached your ears, or have sounded so faint that it took but a hint of bad faith on your part to ignore them' (Beauvoir 2012c: 273). At this point, we can note a point of similarity between Beauvoir's article and Martel's films; their shared intention of calling out the bad faith involved in ignoring violence resulting from colonialism and the specific brutal consequences it has for oppressed people and society in general. Beauvoir ends her article with a very pointed incitement for political action:

> The efforts made in Djamila's case would fall short of their mark if they failed to arouse a revolt against the treatment of her brothers and of which her case represents only one very ordinary example. But this revolt will have no reality unless it takes the form of political action. (Beauvoir 2012c: 281)

Therefore, even though I agree with both Collins and Rivera Berruz's claim that Beauvoir's race/gender analogy within *The Ethics of Ambiguity* and *The Second Sex* is problematic and in need of amendment, there is evidence in Beauvoir's other writing that illustrates her strong commitment to the political freedom for all, including action for racial and gender equality.[7]

Collins illustrates the real-life consequences resulting from Beauvoir's situation in her comparative analysis of Beauvoir and Pauli Murray, a highly educated African American woman who became a lawyer, activist and priest. These two women were 'generational contemporaries' (Collins 2019: 190), born at the same time and both working to advance women's freedom within society, yet each woman experienced very different treatment in their respective countries, which Collins attributes to invisibility of intersectional identity. So, while Collins agrees that Beauvoir's *The Ethics of Ambiguity* remains 'highly useful as a tool for reimagining political behavior' (2019: 198), she views Beauvoir's inability to recognise her own biases relative to her social, historical and cultural situation within *The Second Sex* as resulting in a race/gender analogy 'more closely aligned with frameworks of oppositional difference, with important consequences for her critical theoretical analysis of women's oppression' (Collins 2019: 219). With regard to Murray, who 'never fit comfortably anywhere' (Collins 2019: 208), Collins sees her social activism as demonstrating a more concrete lived experience of existential freedom because her own freedom was a constant struggle with 'state[s] of becoming, a process of moving toward freedom' (Collins 2019: 217) that directly addressed difference in race and gender identity politics.

Intersectionality, as Collins asserts, is problematic if left as a set of ideas. Instead, it is because intersectionality informs social action and social justice activity that it can be said to have 'consequences in the social world' (Collins 2019: 2). For María Lugones, however, even if intersectionality can be theorised effectively as a critical social praxis, the main task is to rethink 'the logic of the intersection so as to avoid separability' (2007: 193). Lugones regards the conception of intersectionality as maintaining the separability of identity politics even in its efforts to disclose the layering or overlapping that occurs within women's lived experience. As she sees it, it is only at the point of intersection that the critical work is foregrounded, '[f]eminists of color have made clear what is revealed in terms of violent domination and exploitation once the epistemological perspective focuses on the intersection of these categories' (Lugones 2007: 188). In response, her term 'intermeshed' looks to avoid the separability of intersection and make visible the overlap and plurality of identity categories that consistently occur as embodied lived experience. Lugones's reflections on intersectionality precede Collins's latest work which argues that intersectionality is social action and works as a way of knowing. Collins valorises the critical significance of using descriptions of concrete lived experience as political action.

> Because experiences occur in the social world, they are windows to that world. Experiences can be theorized just as thoroughly as books, movies and texts. Individuals have experiences, yet the meaning they make of them stems from their placement within the families, groups, nations, and other collectivities that make up their social world. (Collins 2019: 13)

Collins's emphasis on experience is, in other words, a practice of observing or making visible Lugones's notion of 'intermeshed'. It is action that depends on reciprocal recognition of the situated social subject because lived experience is always in the process of becoming, of shaping and constructing being-in-the-world. The phenomenological method of describing lived experience (such as Anzaldúa's neologism *un choque* that identified her own intermeshed identity politics) by default intermeshes the embodied with the emotional, layering not only plural aspects of identity politics but also noting the moments in which they overlap.

In returning to Beauvoir's *The Ethics of Ambiguity* and reviewing her association of freedom with politics and ethics as exemplifying 'the anguish of free decision' (EA 160), we must further re-evaluate the situation of today. Phenomenologically, the intermeshing of situation and society is the foundation of human existence wherein subjectivity is crafted. We are no longer in Beauvoir's situation or society, and therefore, in order for characteristics of Beauvoir's concept of ambiguity to continue and grow, responding to contemporary ethical, political and emotional changes, they need to be placed in conversation with other ideas that similarly examine sites of ambiguous existence, ones that Beauvoir may have overlooked (or that were invisible to her). This is to highlight her attention regarding sensibility of emotional turbulence as central to ambiguous experience but also to expand the disclosure of ambiguity for experience beyond Beauvoir's predominantly Eurocentric point of view and engage more responsibly and inclusively with diverse perspectives.

To this end, and in recognition of intersectional and intermeshed relationships of situation, society and selfhood, I now turn to selected pivotal and critical concepts from the Latina feminist phenomenologies of Anzaldúa, Lugones, and Ortega, whose works have integrated ambiguity into their respective theorisations and discussions of identity politics in varying ways. While each of these Latina feminist phenomenologists have produced differing accounts of identity, the coherent themes of ambiguity, ethics and politics explicitly and implicitly unite their research, addressing existential characteristics of the self, situation and sociality, and emotional turmoil (albeit predominantly through Heideggerian phenomenology in Ortega's case).[8] A full and comprehensive consideration of the richness and significance of these thinkers clearly exceeds the scope of this chapter, and for this reason I limit my discussion of their work to the following specific concepts as identifiable points that work with and improve upon Beauvoir's foundational philosophy of ambiguity, accentuating the intermeshed, multiplicitous lived experience involving considerations of ethics, politics and emotion: Anzaldúa's new *mestiza* and associated neologisms constructive of *mestiza* consciousness and *nepantla* (1987/2012); Lugones's 'world'-travelling and notion of playfulness (1987); and Ortega's multiplicitous self (2016). In many respects Ortega's call to cultivate Anzaldúa's 'creative *mestizaje*' (2016: 220) helps to rethink and remake philosophies that are attuned to tensions and turbulences in our current social worlds, not those of Beauvoir's time, but those of the twenty-first century, so that it might be possible to 'create new possibilities within our discipline[s] and in the worlds in which we dwell' (Ortega 2016: 219).

Next, I analyse *Zama* with a view toward a multiplicitous ethics of ambiguity via feminist phenomenologists of colour.

Zama

Zama, Martel's fourth feature, is a loose adaptation of Antonio Di Benedetto's 1956 novel of the same name. Set in the late eighteenth century in Asunción, a seemingly forgotten colonial outpost of the Spanish Empire, the film follows the quest of *americano*[9] Don Diego de Zama and his desire to return to his family, to escape the exile implied by his relegation to the provinces. Zama's daily life as a local magistrate consists of enforcing Spanish colonial rule and the subjugation of indigenous peoples (either through rule, torture, rape or any other oppressive means to hand). Tasked with the responsibility of maintaining the oppression of others, Zama fulfils his duties with a resigned sense of indifference and a lack of passion; and spends his days sycophantically scouting allegiance with Spain's nobility, notably with Madame Luciana Piñares de Luenga (Lola Dueñas) to improve his chances of returning to Spain.

As the film progresses, we follow Zama's unsuccessful attempts to secure governmental and aristocratic support for his return to Lerma,[10] where his wife and children live. He does not enjoy a single fulfilling or worthwhile relationship with any other character; indeed, Zama is a man who appears existentially isolated and in limbo, despite holding an imperialist occupation. His efforts to leave become increasingly wasted and in a final desperate attempt to secure favour that might ensure the possibility of his departure/return home, Zama joins a mission to find and capture the infamous Vicuña Porto (Matheus Nachtergaele), a man whose cruelty and criminality has reached the level of myth for the Spanish colonial population – a myth not so different from the Dread Pirate Roberts from *The Princess Bride* (Reiner 1987), or Colonel Kurtz from *Apocalypse Now* (Coppola 1979). Certainly, however, Porto's character does not share the comedy of Roberts's character (although there is some humour in the moment when we see Soldado Gaspar Toledo reveal himself as Porto's secret identity). Martel's use of this myth can be read as a further criticism of European consciousness's incapacity to adapt to the environments it colonises. At one level it highlights the false assumption of superiority embedded within systems of privilege, and at another it signifies the 'alien consciousness' (Anzaldúa 1987/2012: 99) of the indigenous population unable to be colonised or dominated. I return to this later.

Throughout the film, and especially toward the end, Zama cuts a lonely and failed figure of a man, going through the motions of appeasing his superior officers with the knowledge that he is certain to fail. The purposelessness of his endeavours reaches its logical conclusion and even in the face of death, his inclination to cling to life persists, pointless, but poetic nonetheless. In the final section of the film, Porto punishes Zama for refusing to tell him where to find '*las cocos*', their word for the amethyst geodes that Porto and his men believe will make them rich. Instead, Zama says: 'I do for you what no one did for me. I say no to your hopes'. In this moment, Zama appears to reach a clarity and authenticity that he has lacked for most of the film, speaking honestly to the futility of the men's mission and the unlikelihood that it will bring them the wealth they believe the geodes hold. Yet to read him only in this way at this point in the film would be a mistake. At the heart of this confrontation is the persistent question of identity, as even in their interrogation of Zama for the location of *las cocos*, Porto's men cite his identity as '*corregidor*', as the subject who is supposed to know, indirectly once more illustrating the anxiety that oppression and dependence instils into a sense of identity.

For Porto and his men, Zama remains the embodiment of Spanish colonialism, the holder of knowledge, riches and privilege; he personifies Europe as the preferred, more valued identity, despite appearing bedraggled, worn out and lacking any future certainty for himself. The men, however, refuse to accept this reality because in doing so they would also have to accept the reality of their situation and the pointlessness of their mission. Instead, their search for *las cocos* sustains the bad faith of their nationalistic myths and their inability to confront the hopelessness and failure of their situation, a bad faith which incidentally Zama and his colonising colleagues have created. We can recall Martel's remark: 'The waiting doesn't exist if there isn't this question of identity. If someone doesn't believe, they don't hope for anything. The firmer the identity, the harder it is to satisfy that hope' (Martel in Teodoro 2017).

Zama, therefore, complicates the usual representation of colonialisation by focusing on the existential ambiguity of its central character. Zama's masculinity as coloniser, an identity normally associated with a sense of grandeur, empowered by the hidden and systemic institutions of foreign authority and possessing a voyeuristic and sadistic enjoyment of violence toward others, is undercut by his own indeterminacy and longing for a fantasy that never eventuates (a return home and validation as 'European' rather than *americano*). Instead, Martel's marginal aesthetics make concerted effort to infer the pathetic fragility and ephemerality of this character trope, consistently placing Zama on the outside of every community he comes into contact with – the government officials, the Spanish nobility, the indigenous people and even the supernatural beings in the dilapidated hut when he is sick. Zama's liminal position suggests that he is not even able to revel in the pretentiousness and incongruity of the European performativity he shares. Nevertheless, Zama continues his tragic bad faith, believing in the authority of office, of privilege, and fetishises the ideal and materiality of Europe. He cannot find happiness unless he is seen by the Establishment, and granted permission to return home (there is the question of whether or not actually returning home is half as important as the recognition of position it bestows on Zama and therefore of his social status).

The film's story world first emerges through sound. We hear a non-diegetic score of insects before the image of Zama appears: a wide shot, deep focus, with him looking out to sea (Figure 6.2). The acousmatic insect sounds denote a non-European location; this sound fades and is overlaid with the diegetic sounds of water lapping at the shore and children's voices. Zama is shown as a man isolated and longing for something that has yet to eventuate, and if we pay close attention to the audio-visual unity here, he is presented as ill-suited to his environment. Later we do indeed come to know very clearly that he is a man unable to reconcile himself with the consequences of his situation. Zama's costume is tired, dirty and torn at the sleeve, suggesting his pride has been corroded and his station is not taken all that seriously. We are given a sense this is not his first time to the beach and he appears as someone familiar with privilege, but also with being frustrated with the experience of having his expectations go unfulfilled. The absurdity of his longing is made clear visually and aurally in the opening minutes of the film.

Figure 6.2 Zama (Daniel Giménez Cacho) looks out to sea.

Zama does cut a figure of absurdity in these initial moments of the film, but I distinguish this as an ontological absurdity rather than an existential absurdity. As an ontological absurdity, Zama's appearance undercuts the overt seriousness of the colonial situation in which we find him. Subtly comical, he plainly doesn't look as if he belongs on the shores of the Paraná river, but his appearance also intimates his inability to come to terms with his own ambiguity; he *looks* as if he doesn't belong and yet incongruously seems to take himself quite seriously. On the difference between absurdity and ambiguity, Beauvoir argues that a declaration of 'existence as absurd is to deny it can ever be given a meaning; to say that it is ambiguous is to assert that its meaning is never fixed, that it must be constantly won' (EA 139). The absurdity of Zama in this first sequence is entangled with his sense of identity – the clash between his environment and his costume, and his isolation from any other similarly dressed person (we first see Zama by himself and a few indigenous children playing in the distant background). His absurdity, we come to learn, is precisely his inability to resolve or reconcile himself with the reality and ambiguity of his situation.

On his return to town, Zama overhears indigenous female voices laughing and attempts to seek them out and listen more closely to their conversation. As we are introduced to these women, the cinematography shifts, tracking in closer to them, changing from the film's opening wide, deep focus shot of Zama on the shoreline to the medium shots of Zama searching and listening for the women in the sandhills, then to a series of intimate close-ups of the women spreading mud on their skin at the beach. One of these women is Luciana's maid, Malemba (Mariana Nunes),

Figure 6.3 Zama listens to women speaking.

who reappears later in the film. She is incorrectly identified as mute by Madame Luciana, as we are shown in this scene, she is very much able to speak. The women are talking about words, of translations for 'spider' and 'wasp', the insect motif repeating here through dialogue rather than score. Not all of their conversation is translated, as is Martel's way – she often affords women's conversation and relationality the respect of existing as an alien consciousness that cannot be used, colonised or shared. Zama is shown secretly listening to the women, and even though Malemba calls him 'voyeur!', the scene highlights that Zama is in fact listening (Figure 6.3)[11] but not necessarily understanding. It is these in-between moments, of denied translation and inexplicable narrative causality, allowing the film's *lacunae* to go unexplained, that embody Martel's film with an ambiguity reflective of Anzaldúa's *mestiza* consciousness, operating as a cinema of the borderlands.

New *Mestizas*, Multiplicitous Selfhood, and 'World'-travelling

Anzaldúa distinguishes a border – as 'a dividing line, a narrow strip along a steep edge' – from a borderland, which she defines as 'a vague and undetermined place created by the emotional residue of an unnatural boundary' (1987/2012: 25). In doing so, she identifies the significant differences and connections between material and emotional marginal lived experiences of the mestizxs ('mixed-raced peoples descendant from imperial settler Iberians and American Indians' (Ruiz 2020: 217)),[12] foregrounding the pain of feeling and living an indeterminate selfhood in the in-between borderlands. From this space of conflict, Anzaldúa argues that a *mestiza* consciousness is born, a 'consciousness of the borderlands' that overlaps with other spaces, crisscrossing both geo-political and material locations and the sensory, invisible psychical spaces of belonging that involve contingent identity politics such as gender, race, ethnicity, sexuality, ability and age. For Anzaldúa personally, these specific borderlands refer to the transitory spaces along the Southwest US–Mexico border and the overlapping spaces of Latina identity (woman, lesbian, Chicana), although her evolving notions of selfhood extend far beyond her personal situation and literal geographic location. What is particularly valuable within Anzaldúa's notion of the new *mestiza* is its awareness of the emotional disruption with regard to the effort to ensure inclusivity and multiplicity. As Ortega comments, some of the core features of *mestiza* depend on acknowledgement of situation and tensions within situation 'to reveal the agonizing but also rewarding struggle of life in the borderlands' (2016: 25). Martel's filmmaking is highly indicative of this agonising struggle that appears as a reflection of her own consciousness of borderlands within Argentina. *Zama* is further representative of the affective tumult of colonialism in terms of the border and borderlands as Anzaldúa describes.

The *mestiza* consciousness encapsulates the proto-mental experience of being 'plagued by psychic restlessness' (1987/2012: 100); as a term it identifies a self-awareness of the embodied emotional experience of living in-between different social and cultural spaces and histories, which pull different parts of the self in opposing directions that effect inner disharmony. It also identifies the in-between space representative of the margin as responsible for producing such interstitial consciousness. In *Borderlands/La Frontera*, the new *mestiza* signals an early conception of selfhood in Anzaldúa's writing, which over the course of her life and accrual of lived experience evolved into other variations and incorporated neologisms such as *nepantla*, *la nepantlera*, *la facultad*, the *Coatlicue* state and *conocimiento*.[13] These terms develop from *mestiza* consciousness and when compared to Beauvoir's ethics of ambiguity, offer a more complex, nuanced and definitive expression of the emotional turbulence that results from ambiguous existence.

In Beauvoir's notion of ambiguity, freedom can only be possible 'if one destines his existence to other existences through the being – whether thing or man – at which he aims without hoping to entrap it in the destiny of the in-itself [*en-soi*]' (EA 72),[14] thereby saying that our own freedom is separate from but made possible through and with the freedom of others. But in this sharing of freedom, or rather the recognition of the other's subjectivity which makes freedom authentic and possible, Beauvoir does not make room for what cannot be shared within authentic relationships: the part of the other that cannot be known, which is the unknowable, alien part of the self. She maintains the separateness of the individual while calling for reciprocal recognition, whereas Anzaldúa concentrates on the very thing that generates a sensibility of 'alien' consciousness: 'racial, ideological, cultural and biological cross-pollinization' (1987/2012: 99), and the importance of overlapping.

> With the nepantla paradigm I try to theorize unarticulated dimensions of the experience of the mestizas living in between overlapping and layered states of different cultures and social and geographic locations, of events and realities – psychological, sociological, political, spiritual, historical, creative and imagined. (Anzaldúa in Keating 2006: 8)

Nepantla specifies the emotional uncertainty that results from ambiguous existence, of what it feels like to experience the indeterminacy of one's situation, particularly the paradoxical states to which it gives rise. Anzaldúa further defines it in this way:

> Nepantla is the Nahuatl word for an in-between state, that uncertain terrain one crosses when moving from one place to another, when changing from one class, race, or sexual position to another, when traveling from the present identity into a new identity [...] [those] who find themselves in this bewildering transitional space may be the straight person coming out as lesbian, gay, bi, or transsexual, or a person from working-class origins crossing into middle-classness and privilege. (2009: 180)

Ortega notes that *nepantla* is 'an unstable, precarious, and unpredictable space' (2016: 26) that generates the sensation of displacement and alienation, but also that this ambiguity and instability is characteristic of *mestiza* lived experience and that, without it, *mestiza* consciousness is not possible. *Mestiza* consciousness emerges from this abrasive emotional state, a capacity to critically reflect and interpret one's situation while embracing different perspectives. This is similar to Beauvoir's 'moment of moral choice' in *The Ethics of Ambiguity*, but in the light of Anzaldúa's writing, Beauvoir's identification of the 'crisis of adolescence' (EA 42) as an in-between state of emotional storms doesn't possess the same force or complexity in describing various aspects of ambiguity nor the embodied and emotional consequences of its tensions. Nor does it address the differences in lived experience that identity politics of race and gender yield.

'The new *mestiza* copes by developing a tolerance for contradictions, a tolerance for ambiguity ... She can be jarred out of ambivalence by an intense, and often painful, emotional event which inverts or resolves the ambivalence' (Anzaldúa 1987/2012: 101). In addition to painful emotional struggles that typify *nepantla* and the ambiguity of living an in-between, borderline existence, Anzaldúa regards this paradoxical space as containing transformative potential. As Anzaldúa develops her concept of the new *mestiza*, it grows to specify ways in which *mestiza* consciousness moves toward moral freedom. Once again, the difficulty of her situation is foregrounded, indeed '[h]er first step is to take inventory', to recognise the pain of her situation and the confounding role history has played in causing it.

> This step is a conscious rupture with all oppressive traditions of all cultures and religions. She communicates that rupture, documents the struggle. She reinterprets history and, using new symbols, she shapes new myths. She adopts new perspectives toward the darkskinned, women and queers. She strengthens her tolerance (and intolerance) for ambiguity. She is willing to share, to make herself vulnerable to foreign ways of seeing and thinking. She surrenders all notions of safety, of the familiar. Deconstruct, construct. She becomes a nahual, able to transform herself into a tree, a coyote, into another person. She learns to transform the small 'I' into the total Self. (Anzaldúa 1987/2012: 104–5)

This transformation comes via rupture, but is not without its perils. In the event the new *mestiza* is unable to take inventory and tolerate ambiguity and conflict within her situation, if she cannot face failure or bear the emotional turbulence within *nepantla*, she enters into the *Coatlicue* state, 'the consuming internal whirlwind' (Anzaldúa 1987/2012: 68). *Coatlicue* refers to an inability to think or tolerate emotional conflict, 'my refusal to know some truth about myself brings on that paralysis, depression – brings on the *Coatlicue* state' (1987/2012: 70).

Martel's protagonists are often depicted as wrestling with their refusal to confront a difficult truth about themselves and their situation, and such turmoil is further played out through the body, portraying a *Coatlicue* state. Vero's guilt over her hit-and-run in *La mujer sin cabeza* causes her amnesia. Throughout the film, she is shown looking away or down at the ground, dissociated from the world around her. Much has been made of Vero's change in hair colour in the latter part of the film (from blonde to brunette), its symbolism exemplifying the way the body embodies hidden (and in Vero's case, denied) emotions. If Vero's blonde hair signifies the fetishisation of European feminine beauty and the bad faith of Argentine women's idealisation of that image, her conformity with the European image is a further comment on her inability to confront the truth of her inauthenticity.[15]

Zama's descent into illness is another illustration of the cost that the body incurs in refusing to confront the ambiguity and conflict within its situation. After Zama is ejected from his rooms by the Governor, he is forced to find alternative accommodation and ends up in a dilapidated room that the local people refuse to enter, believing it is haunted. With this confirmation of his dwindling importance to the Crown, and the increasing improbability of returning home, Zama's health declines and he begins to lose his grip on reality. At this point in the film, Zama is the furthest we have seen him from the centre of the Spanish privileged community. His new rooms are located closer to where the indigenous people live and yet he appears to continue to refuse the truth of his situation. He becomes more and more ostracised and, consequently, his circumstances turn more dire. He sees ghosts of women wandering around his new home, and later, during his feverish state, we see them watching over him at his bedside, their eerie acousmatic laughter laid over the recurring insect track. In relocating Zama diegetically to be closer to the indigenous population, Martel has also slowly reoriented his narrative centrality. More emphasis is given to prioritising the voice and gaze of the indigenous peoples and this increases until the end of the film. In one scene Zama asks Emilia (María Etelvina Peredez) for a shirt, to which she sarcastically replies: 'Am I your wife?' It is not only the indigenous people's on-screen presence that increases, but their authority and comfort in expressing their agency and resistance to colonial presence.

Arrogant Perceptions and 'World'-travelling

Zama weaves two sides of colonial lived experience together: the arrogant perception of the coloniser and the imposed 'world'-travelling of the colonised. These two terms, 'arrogant perception' and '"world"-travelling', taken from María Lugones's article, 'Playfulness, "World"-Travelling, and Loving Perception' (1987),[16] help to consider how Martel constructs a story world that playfully breaks with normative habits of cinematic perception, and at the same time encourages what Lugones has referred to as 'loving perception', that is, a capacity to develop a loving attitude toward others through identification that rejects the abuses that result from a failure to identify (a common situation in colonisation). In order to find this capacity for loving perception, Lugones argues we must 'world'-travel and foster a sense of non-agonistic playfulness: 'Intimacy is constituted in part by a very deep knowledge of the other self and "world" travelling is only part of having this knowledge' (1987: 17). While Lugones's article is not focused on film experience, her idea of 'loving perception' is based on cultivating a 'pluralistic feminism' and 'cross-cultural and cross-racial' (1987: 3) love between women. Her ideas can be thought with Beauvoir's existential phenomenology of the situated self, helping to extend them in more diverse and inclusive ways. While Lugones specifically refers to a loving perception between women, I am extending her feminist phenomenology to include a broader loving perception of the other which I see as typical of Martel's filmmaking.

Lugones's pluralistic feminism is descriptive of and attentive to outsider lived experience and socio-cultural status. She argues that 'world'-travelling is necessary for those who live outside mainstream society, who are compelled to find ways of being at ease in worlds (or to use Beauvoir's term, situations) that do not locate their subjectivity as dominant. Lugones's use of the word 'travel' is polysemic, given that the leisure constitutive of vacation travel is undeniably a privilege afforded to those few who are able to move within the world in ways unavailable and unaffordable to others. Many are forced to travel through exile, diaspora, as refugee, and in seeking asylum, rather than through any wilful or playful sense of moving. As Lugones's conceives her neologism, 'world'-travelling can also be a 'wilful exercise' representative of the strategic behaviour of the outsider or of the intentional allyship of those who are 'at ease in the mainstream' (Lugones 1987: 3). As Lugones defines and layers her notion of 'world'-travelling, she includes Marylin Frye's (1983) concept of 'arrogant perception', which she uses to note 'the failure to identify with persons that one views arrogantly or has come to see as the products of arrogant perception' (Lugones 1987: 4). Both Lugones and Beauvoir regard situation as crucial in determining our behaviours and ways of being-in-the-world and it is their shared notion of situation or 'world' that helps to locate Martel's *Zama* as an effective example of intermeshed film experience, and more specifically the sense of playfulness that Lugones claims is fundamental in fostering love for the other.

The arrogant perceiver is one who views the world and their situation from the vantage point of their own interest, ignoring or neglecting the perspective and position of the other. It is easy to see Zama as fitting this description, as well as the other related colonising characters such as Madame Luciana, the governors and the implicit, invisible presence of the Spanish Crown. Their arrogance is visible in their refusing to see the world via the eyes of the indigenous people, ignoring the history of indigenous culture and instead imposing a different, parasitical socio-cultural history onto an environment where it does not belong. In one of Zama's magistral cases, he hears a complaint from one of the 'old settlers of Concepción', a settler farming family that stole land from the indigenous people, chasing and killing them to secure the property. As a result, no indigenous person is willing to work on their farm. The old settlers attempt to invoke their European privilege and request an *encomienda* for '40 tame Indians' (an *encomienda* is a grant from the Spanish government to enslave indigenous people for forced labour). The scene's score is ironically light, a happy-sounding frivolous tone juxtaposed against the vulgarity of the scene. This aesthetic clash discloses the farce of Spain's presence and any sense of justice, and subsequently highlights Zama's arrogant perception that informs his decision. As Zama listens to their request, the settler's granddaughter enters the room; her face is not shown until a few moments later (a further example of Martel's 'headless women'), but her presence is enough to disturb the scene and divert Zama's attention away from the matter at hand. He watches her lustfully and even though he becomes aware that she is indigenous, he grants the settler family the *encomienda* and they leave. Zama embraces the old man and woman but is shunned by their daughter.

His assistant Ventura Prieto (Juan Minujín) questions Zama's decision, arguing that there is no legitimate basis for his decision: 'Taking away freedom requires more than a paper with Irala's name on it.' Prieto is not being altruistic here; instead, he uses the truth of the situation as a convenience to assert superiority over Zama, declaring his Spanish identity over Zama's Latin American identity. In this scene, Martel illustrates the multiple forms arrogant perception can take (colonialisation over indigenous peoples; men over women; abuses constitutive of institutional systems of power themselves) and the absurdity it collapses into. The two men refuse to see the world from any perspective that does not serve them. Prieto's challenge of Zama's decision has little, if anything, to do with justice for the local indigenous people, rather it is vested in besting Zama and improving Prieto's own chances for promotion (which turn out to be successful – Prieto is the one who is transferred back to Lerma). The scene ends with the two men falling on the floor fighting each other.

Lugones writes: 'we are fully dependent on each other for the possibility of being understood and without this understanding we are not intelligible, we do not make sense, we are not solid, visible, integrated; we are lacking' (1987: 8). This echoes Beauvoir's position in *Pyrrhus and Cineas* where she argued that solidarity with others (when successful) rested on recognising the ambiguity of our existence as dependent on the other, 'as soon as we are thrown into the world, we immediately wish to escape from the contingence and the gratuitousness of pure presence. We need others in order for our existence to become founded and necessary' (PC 129). Lugones's concept of 'world'-travelling can be interpreted as an advancement of Beauvoir's argument, as she says it is only by travelling to the other's 'world' that we can '*be* through *loving* each other' (Lugones 1987: 8).

'Worlds' as conceived by Lugones, refer to places and spaces that are inhabited by real people, but they can also be inhabited by imaginary people, making her argument highly relevant for the story worlds audiences encounter through cinema. She specifies that she does not include possible worlds in her definition of 'world', but in the case of film experience, audiences psychically and corporeally invest in film story worlds as real in order to form meaning and attachments to films. For Lugones, 'worlds' can be imaginative, but not utopias; they can be 'an actual society' or 'a society given a non-dominant construction' (1987: 10), stipulating that these are different 'worlds' and can form part of a single society. In this sense, she continues, the size of such 'worlds' varies, being 'inhabited by just a few people' or being 'bigger than others'. 'Worlds' can be incomplete, partially constructed, or incomplete in the sense that they 'may have references to things that do not quite exist in it'. 'Worlds', therefore, are in constant states of becoming and elude easy definition or categorisation. In terms of *Zama*, we can observe Martel's crafting of multiple 'worlds' in a number of ways. For example, in the way she overlaps different Latin American dialects with each other, creating incomplete 'worlds' of communication which require 'travel' between them for meaning, and also in the way she crafts different 'worlds' of coloniser and colonised. Martel also brings different 'worlds' of class in connection with each other, usually exposing the disparity that exists between them. There is the further, more metaphysical multiplicity of 'worlds' Martel hints at between fantasy and reality, intermeshing the lived world with the supernatural world, mimicking the very experience that spectators have when watching her films. In this case, I read the supernatural world of ghosts as representing repressed histories or memories, and therefore reflecting 'worlds' that have been inhabited by flesh and blood people rather than suggesting a possible world.

'Travel' between these 'worlds' and occupation of more than one world is constitutive of the outsider's status, and Lugones maintains a highly slippery definition because her aim is to concentrate on lived experience of movement, and change in perception of another's world through 'travel', 'even if it is ontologically problematic' (1987: 11). As Lugones sees it, 'travel' denotes a shift in selfhood, 'from being one person to being a different person' (1987: 11), which occurs as a consequence of moving between 'worlds' or situations. Ortega extends Lugones's definition of 'world'-travelling in her theorisation of the multiplicitous self, arguing that we occupy and exist in multiple 'worlds' simultaneously, and in doing so she distinguishes her multiplicitous self from Lugones's pluralistic self in order to emphasise the existential aspect of her analysis of being in-between worlds: '"plurality" suggests multiple selves, while the term "multiplicity" suggests a complexity associated with one self' (Ortega 2016: 64). 'World'-travelling is therefore a concept that registers and captures the proto-mental character of ambiguous lived experience for those whose identities fall outside of the mainstream, combining the emotional tension and 'schizophrenic ... ontological confusion' (Lugones 1987: 9) of what it is to be in-between. Martel's films consistently attend to the emotion of 'world'-travelling, highlighting ambiguity as its main feature.

In a footnote, Ortega briefly observes a connection between Lugones's and Beauvoir's phenomenology, acknowledging that Beauvoir had previously developed a phenomenology 'in which ethics really matters' (Lugones 1987 fn 9: 237). I think Ortega could have been stronger on this point, recognising the legacy of Beauvoir's existentialist phenomenology in both *The Ethics of Ambiguity* and *The Second Sex*. In particular, the significance of Beauvoir's question, 'what is a woman?' (TSS 5) determined the specific difference in lived experience between a woman and a man. Ortega prefers Heidegger's existentialist position, and in doing so misses the opportunity to go beyond his abstract interpretation of human existence. The importance of Beauvoir's existentialism (and what separates her from other existentialist phenomenologists like Heidegger) is that she made the concrete distinction between man and woman and for her, this difference was fundamental if the answer to her question 'what is a woman?' was to carry any weight, particular in terms of women's freedom. However, Beauvoir's distinction also offers further important links for Lugones's and Ortega's phenomenologies of 'world' or self-travelling, which is her consideration of emotional experience within the ambiguous existence of being in-between or travelling between 'worlds', and a recognition of 'resistance that is not merely reactive or oppositional' (Ortega 2016 fn 9: 237). Lugones's concept of 'world'-travelling illuminates Beauvoir's notion of situation and its role in determining women's lived experience by foregrounding the intermeshedness of being with others in the world (*Mitsein*). Ortega's concept of multiplicitous self also extends Lugones's notion of intermeshedness, arguing that instead of us having many different selves, our self is a continuous multiplicitous being that continually exists in a process of becoming.

Ortega sees Lugones's concept of 'world'-travelling as a practice that enables the multiplicitous self's access to different worlds, foregrounding the important changes that occur in sensory lived experience. She argues that her '*existential pluralism*' better recognises how 'the self fares or *is* in worlds' (Ortega 2016: 89), and therefore regards 'world'-travelling as a conceptual tool that enables identification not just of contradictory and ambiguous existence but also of the specific sites where such turbulent emotional experience occurs (as with Anzaldúa's *nepantla*). Thus, Ortega retains Lugones's multiple senses and perspectives engendered by 'world'-travelling, creating access to different worlds, but argues that 'we can occupy the same space', given social identities. The outcome is not multiple realities or Lugones's 'plurality of selves' (1987: 14) but numerous ways of being-in-the-world that illuminate the ambiguity of being in-between and the affective resonances of such lived experience.

These Latina feminist phenomenologies help to review Beauvoir's notion of reciprocal recognition occurring not just at the level of the singular self but at the level of multiplicitous selves, asking that contradictions of selfhood, such as Anzaldúa's *mestiza* consciousness, be acknowledged but not solved. Further, they help to show how Beauvoir's notion of reciprocal recognition can be used as a basis for resistance that allows for contradiction. 'Resistance involves having access to other worlds in which the self is constructed differently and thus can see resistant possibilities that lead to resistant practices' (Ortega 2016: 99). This leads Ortega to regard Lugones's 'world'-travelling as an opportunity for allyship, to acknowledge the multiplicity within lived experience and to bear the contradictions that occur even within one's own selfhood. Reflective of her own 'world'-travelling, Lugones discusses her attitude of playfulness as a means to confront the difference between her selfhoods in different 'worlds', and positions it as the method to develop a 'loving perception'.

Like 'world' and 'travel', playfulness has alternative meanings for Lugones who distinguishes between the agonistic sense of play (the need to win, to control, to dominate) and the sense of play as a means for 'self-construction': '*the attitude that carries us through the activity, a playful attitude, turns the activity into play*' (1987: 16). The creativity in play here is reminiscent of Donald Winnicott's psychoanalytic theory, wherein he argues that it is only through playing that 'the child or adult is free to be creative' (1971/1999b: 53), and within play a paradox must be tolerated, contained and not try to be solved. In order for a successful search for the self to occur, Winnicott argues that play must be given good enough space and time to occur, for 'on the basis of playing is built the whole of man's experiential existence' (Winnicott 1971/1999b: 64). Playing forms the active basis for his psychoanalytic model of creativity, a term loosely applied to the 'colouring of the whole attitude to external reality'

(Winnicott 1971/1999b: 65). There is a strong compatibility between Lugones's and Winnicott's ideas on the role of playfulness and a creative attitude toward life, recognising that 'creative apperception' (1971/1999b: 65) indicates one's emotional orientation in their being-in-the-world.

While Winnicott's ideas of play and creativity are psychoanalytically focused, examining the workings of inner infant life, they also contain phenomenological implications, given that his attention on creativity is taken as 'a universal. It belongs to being alive ... [creativity] belongs to the approach of the individual to external reality' (Winnicott 1971/1999b: 67). In Lugones's definition, playfulness is open-ended, not just tolerant of ambiguity but courting of it, being as much about experiencing one's self across 'worlds' (or situations) as it is about finding out what the conditions for play are that might facilitate stronger self-reflection. Despite their different methodologies, both Lugones and Winnicott view playfulness (as a manner of being) and play (as an expression of the proto-mental state of being) as key behaviours and attitudes that go some way to addressing the aetiology of how the self fares in the world. Winnicott also acknowledges Freud's 'basic concept of ambivalence as an aspect of individual maturity' (1971/1999b: 70), noting the importance of all aspects of emotional experience (the destructive as well as the formative) in the search of the self, but this is not developed in terms of his theory of creativity. Instead, and perhaps more significantly for the argument here, his theory of playing and reality forms the foundation for his theory of object-relating and object-use. In the Winnicottian context, the use of an object reflects 'a *capacity* to use objects' (1971/1999b: 89), and this capacity, or rather the efficacy of one's capacity to use objects, is a developmental feature – 'another example of the maturational process' (1971/1999b: 89) – which identifies the ways in which we think (or do not think) with objects. I have written elsewhere (Fuery 2018: 150–2) on Winnicott's use of an object, and Christopher Bollas's (1987) concept, the transformational object, so for now I simply note that the conception of play that is shared between the phenomenology of Lugones and the object relations psychoanalysis of Winnicott suggests further study and extends Lugones's non-agonistic idea of play and its place in facilitating loving perception.

By now, I hope I have made it clear that the alternative phenomenologies of ambiguity offered by Latina feminist phenomenologists such as Anzaldúa, Lugones and Ortega offer a stronger and more definitive conception of proto-mental lived experience across and in-between 'worlds', and that such experience can be extended to the context of film experience. Rather than deny the import of Beauvoir's argument in *The Ethics of Ambiguity*, that one's moral and ethical freedom is dependent on recognition of the freedom of the other, the Latina feminist phenomenologies enhance the ways in which we might identify specific emotional turbulence within our own situation and that of the other. The playfulness of words and terms discloses the in-betweenness and contradictory nature of being outside or at the margins of society; such disclosure recognising 'The Other is multiple, and on the basis of this new questions arise' (EA 155).

Zama showcases the ambiguity of being in-between and the significant burden it places on the body and the mind. Martel's film doesn't simply observe this state of being through one character; her film uses the character of Zama to disclose the consequences of failing to 'world'-travel successfully – his existential crisis only deepens the more he refuses to playfully exist in Asunción. Increasingly though, we enter the indigenous world, albeit always at a respectful distance. In the last thirty minutes of the film, when Zama is part of the group of men pursuing Vicuña Porto, we see an inversion of world orders in the film. Where the film opened with Zama looking out to sea, the bearer and surveyor of a European gaze, the film now offers a different perspective, a 'world'-travel to the location and life of the indigenous population. We have seen slaves and servants standing along the peripheries of the houses and rooms, ordered around by the Spanish officials and nobility, but now, it is Zama and the group of men who must take orders and acquiesce to what the indigenous people demand.

One evening, a community of indigenous people move through the men's camp, touching their faces, and take their horses. There is no threat here, save the projected sense of fear that comes from Zama himself. I read this scene as an example of Martel's playfulness, or rather her capacity to effect 'world'-travel in her films and to expose the arrogant perception of the European gaze. Lugones says:

> travelling to other people's 'worlds' we discover that there are 'worlds' in which those who are the victims of arrogant perception are really subjects, lively beings, resistors, constructors of visions even though in the mainstream construction they are animated only by the arrogant perceiver and are pliable, foldable, file-awayable, classifiable. (1987: 18)

A woman touches Zama's face, plays with his beard and whispers something over him as she moves through the camp. Again, Martel does not translate this dialect, or much of the indigenous dialogue for the remainder of the film, thereby challenging the dominance of arrogant perception and enabling a different identification to occur through her audio-visual cinematic 'world'-travelling.

Martel's film, in its critique of colonialising institutions and paternalistic behaviours, engenders the type of identification Lugones advocates for in her phenomenology of 'world'-travelling. There is the 'disloyalty to arrogant perceivers' (Lugones 1987: 18) shown in almost every character's attitude toward Zama, but most obviously in the constant refusal of his request to return to Spain, and there is the final scene where we intuit that Zama recognises the arrogant perceiver in himself when he says he wants to live, finally aware that he will never return home or even to the station of *corregidor* he once held. He has transitioned (perhaps transformed is too idealistic here) from a figure whose existential ethics were wanting at best, unable to confront or accept the ambiguity of his situation, to becoming a man who has been compelled to recognise the situation of others. The film ends with Zama having to acknowledge that his freedom is dependent on the freedom of the indigenous people, without whom he could not survive. In being asked by the indigenous boy, 'Do you want to live?', there is the sense that he accepts he must face up to the responsibility required for his own existence.

In her interview with Gemünden and Spitta about the film, Martel speaks about the shift in casting a male protagonist as *Zama's* central character. She comments that an emphasis on the impact of oppression in women's lives is a strong focus of the film, despite it not occupying narrative centrality:

> the lesson of *Zama* is a lesson we women have learned long ago. This is a transference of wisdom that we could make to the world of men. Because if you're not prepared for failure, the frustration and violence are enormous. (Martel in Gemünden and Spitta 2018: 36)

Despite the film's story world focusing on Zama's existential longing for his European home, its message remains strongly political in its critique of patriarchal systems and the consequences for those marginalised when it fails. In this respect, Martel's mastery of aesthetics belies her feminist, and what I would also argue as phenomenological, filmmaking praxis, as her use of off-screen space, tight framing and disquieting sound generates an ambiguous, affective and anxious cinematic manner. From the start of the film, Zama is shown as an anxious man, constantly on edge and waiting, aware of the futility of his hope but hoping, nonetheless. By 'world'-travelling between social orders within the film, Martel discloses (in the Beauvoirian sense of the word) the arrogant perception of colonial and patriarchal systems of thought and manner of being, and also demonstrates Beauvoir's core claim regarding moral freedom in *The Ethics of Ambiguity* that in order to authentically and ethically be free, we must confront and tolerate the tension involved in willing oneself free: 'To wish for the disclosure of the world and to assert oneself as a freedom are one and the same movement ... To will oneself moral and to will oneself free are one and the same decision' (EA 23–4). Therefore, what *Zama* shows us is that the desire for freedom always involves a disclosure of the world which further reveals the consequences of arrogant perception and its inhibiting of loving perception. While Beauvoir's philosophy of ambiguity alerts us to the fact that our freedom is dependent on the other and their freedom, Latina feminist phenomenologies further help to reveal the nuances of ambiguity, and specifically the embodied and emotional turmoil that such disclosure entails.

Notes

1 Gloria Anzaldúa might have viewed Martel's filmmaking as a derivative form of *autohistoria*, a term that Anzaldúa coined to identify the method of drawing on her personal history to critically reflect on her lived experience and situation. As AnaLouise Keating explains: '*Autohistoria* focuses on the personal life story but, as the autohistorian tells her own life story, she simultaneously tells the life stories of others' (2009: 319). This echoes Beauvoir's practice of using her childhood and adolescent experience to inform the narratives of her novels, and the praxis of other Latina feminist phenomenologists (see Ortega (2016: 1–11, 215–20) and Lugones (1987) who draw on their personal experience to critically theorise being-in-between. See also Moi (2010a: 139) who speaks to Beauvoir's character of Françoise in *She Came to Stay*, and see Beauvoir's own account in her memoirs, *The Prime of Life* and *Force of Circumstance*.

2 Beauvoir takes the idea of the 'lack' of being from Sartre's *Being and Nothingness*, which she quotes from early on in *The Ethics of Ambiguity* (EA 10). Using Sartre's ontological definition of freedom, Beauvoir argues that one's own freedom is determined through intentionality: 'this lack of being *in order that* there might be being. The term *in order that* clearly indicates an intentionality' (EA 11). From here, Beauvoir proposes two aspects to intentionality, where consciousness makes visible being and at the same time brings about a desire for 'this disclosure' (EA 11). See Arp (2001: 51) and Bergoffen (1992: 79) who discusses the two moods that Beauvoir identifies within intentionality.

3 Beauvoir identifies five attitudes of being (EA 45–75) to illustrate situations of bad faith that are common in achieving or realising one's moral freedom. While each attitude is seen as an improvement on the other, each ultimately fails in effecting an authentic and ethical existence (and therefore moral freedom) because they fail to properly recognise the freedom of the other. See Chapter 5 where I discuss this with regard to Claire Denis's *Let The Sunshine In*.

4 Of course, this was always Beauvoir's intention – to write of her own experience of being, as a woman. In *Force of Circumstance*, Beauvoir reiterates that *The Second Sex* came about through '[w]anting to talk about myself' (FC 185). Nevertheless, she also acknowledges that in order to do so, she needed 'to discuss the condition of woman in general' (FC 185) and it is on these terms that a homogeneity of women's experience defaulting to White French women occurs and becomes problematic.
5 See Moi (2010a: 144) who also discusses Beauvoir's historical and situated context when writing *The Ethics of Ambiguity* and *The Second Sex*.
6 Beauvoir wrote the introduction, but the majority of the book is Halimi's own meticulously researched account of Boupacha's case.
7 Poignantly, Lewis R. Gordon notes the marginal (if any) acknowledgement of Beauvoir's influence in Frantz Fanon's writing: 'I cannot, however, excuse Fanon's failure to articulate his indebtedness to Beauvoir. Although he acknowledges the psychoanalytical contributions of Anna Freud, the existential philosophical domains appear squarely in the hands of men such as Jaspers and Sartre when it is clear that Beauvoir not only offered much intellectual sustenance for Fanon's thought but also that he was well aware of at least two of her major contributions at the time of writing *Black Skin, White Masks*, as the presence of these books in his home library attest' (Gordon 2015: 32).
8 See Ortega on her reasons for employing a Heideggerian framework (2016: 4; and fn 4, page 222–3).
9 An identity marker for those born in the Americas rather than Spain. It further denotes Zama's in-between position, his perennial experience as a 'world'-traveller and the conflation of the metaphysical and material lived experience at the borderlands.
10 Martel changes the location from Benedetto's novel, and this is further evidence of her *autohistoria*. Lerma is a city in Salta, a reference to Martel's hometown. 'The period in which I developed Zama were years where I had a lot of anguish about returning to Salta. I had such a strong desire to return, but it took time to decide, and my inability to decide linked me to Zama and that's why I changed the place where he longs to be transferred to Lerma' (interview with José Teodoro 2017).
11 Martel specifies that Zama is listening rather than watching in her interview with Teodoro: 'But it was important to me that Zama wanted to listen to the women' (Martel in Teodoro 2017).
12 Mestizxs, a gender neutral plural term, is refused italicisation here following Anzaldúa, who in her later work also declined to italicise 'the language of the Borderlands'. For Anzaldúa, holding onto the primacy of her 'Chicano Spanish' was a first step in countering the reaches of Anglo colonialisation, 'we Chicanos no longer feel that we need to beg entrance, that we need always to make the first overture – to translate to Anglos, Mexicans and Latinos, apology blurting out of our mouths at every step' (1987/2012: 20).

13 Anzaldùa uses the term *la facultad* to refer to a 'capacity to see in the surface phenomena the meaning of deeper realities, to see the deep structure below the surface. It is an instant "sensing," a quick perception arrived at without conscious reasoning. It is an acute awareness mediated in images and symbols which are the faces of feelings, that is behind which feelings reside/hide. The one possessing this sensitivity is excruciatingly alive to the world' (1987/2012: 60). *La facultad*, then, acknowledges the complexity and ambiguity inherent in embodied emotional experience. It is a conceptual cornerstone which identifies the transformative potential within Anzaldùa's phenomenology. Anzaldúa's term *conocimiento* is offered as an alternative pathway of knowing our lived experience, and is demarcated by seven steps of an inner journey to self-awareness and transformation. *Mestiza* consciousness is an aspect of *conocimiento* in that it privileges sensory lived experience and acknowledges emotional turmoil rather than avoiding or negating it.
14 See Chapter 5 where I discuss *pour-soi* and *en-soi* in further detail.
15 See Gemünden (2019: 85) who views the symbolism of Vero's hair colour change as 'a call to break the silence' that complicity in oppression engenders.
16 Lugones uses quotation marks for her terms 'world' and 'travel' to denote the particular way in which she uses them. I have maintained her practice here.

CHAPTER 7

Sensuous Co-Performance: Lynne Ramsay's *We Need to Talk About Kevin* and Beauvoir's Aesthetic Attitude

A characteristic of Beauvoir's *oeuvre* is the way her philosophy diffuses throughout her many works, to the extent that it can be hard to point to neatly formed theories on specific topics, particularly in terms of aesthetic experience. Michèle Le Doeuff regarded Beauvoir's philosophy as being 'tremendously well-hidden' and asks 'what definition of philosophy' we should apply when reading Beauvoir's work, especially as Beauvoir saw herself more as a writer than a philosopher (Le Doeuff 2007: 139). Margaret Simons addresses Beauvoir's own misrepresentation of her philosophical innovation, identifying her self-censure beginning in her first biography, *Memoirs of a Dutiful Daughter* (2005). When comparing the posthumously published *Wartime Diary* (2009) and *Letters to Sartre* (1991) to earlier works, a different Beauvoir emerges – a highly original philosophical thinker with a complex sexuality (Simons 2009: 3).[1] There are a few ways to situate these indeterminacies and fluidities in Beauvoir's work. Firstly, to acknowledge that Beauvoir's style of philosophy is dispersed across her writings, often changing its voice, recognising the fluid and evolving character of her thinking; and secondly, to recognise that Beauvoir's philosophy is precluded from disciplinary recognition as a consequence of epistemic sexism, which indirectly highlights the importance of situation both as a phenomenological concept but also as a determinism of philosophy itself.

As one reads through Beauvoir's enormous catalogue of writing, it becomes abundantly clear that her ideas regarding aesthetic experience received different considerations in various forms, housed in different literary modes of writing, especially her novels. Her re-evaluations of previously held philosophical notions and political positions are often highly emotive (particularly in her autobiographies and letters) and she revisited concepts in later works that indicate how her thoughts on aesthetic experience were constantly evolving. It is clear that Beauvoir's own philosophies embraced a certain kind of ambiguity within them.

For example, *The Ethics of Ambiguity* is rightly lauded as a work that puts forward a theory of existentialist ethics based on Beauvoir's philosophy of ambiguity but it is not often discussed as an early philosophy on existentialist aesthetics, even though the 'writer-artist' is fundamental to Beauvoir's argument on how one faces and assumes responsibility for an ethical freedom. In fact, her critique of the aesthetic attitude not only sketches out an alternative phenomenological approach regarding aesthetic experience, but it also forms the basis for her notion of reciprocal recognition, the importance of relationship with others and the role emotion plays in facilitating such connections.

In this chapter, I look at two of Beauvoir's essays in relation to *The Ethics of Ambiguity* – 'Literature and Metaphysics', and 'What Can Literature Do?' – to show how her philosophy of ambiguity consistently incorporated a strong sensuous understanding of aesthetic experience. While Beauvoir spoke mainly about literature, her ideas speak to the ethical role of cinema's emotional turbulence regarding the question of freedom. Beauvoir's thinking on aesthetic experience within these three essays becomes more apparent, moving from abstract to clear expression. In 'What Can Literature Do?'[2] she acknowledges that even popular artistic expressions (such as television and radio) could be seen as activity that exercised disclosure (WCLD 197), although she makes a very firm distinction between literature and information. And of course, there is her famous essay for *Esquire* on Brigitte Bardot (1959) where, like other French feminist intellectuals such as Marguerite Duras,[3] Beauvoir analysed the myth and representation of Bardot's sexuality against the reality of a free woman. Where Beauvoir argues that literature is a 'privileged place of intersubjectivity' (WCLD 201) expressing our embodied ambiguous situation in the world, I argue that cinema, which emphasises its sensory aesthetic qualities (sound, image, light, colour, performance) over dominant narrative elements (dialogue, narrative structure), similarly reveals truths of situation, and therefore our own, in the world.

In order to consider how Beauvoir's ideas on aesthetic experience and her questioning of the aesthetic attitude impact film experience, I discuss Lynne Ramsay's film *We Need to Talk About Kevin* (2011) as an example of cinema operating as an ambiguous object, blurring the arbitrary separate categories of cinema: as representational art, as mode of sensory perception, and as affective or expressive instrument. Ramsay's filmmaking certainly exemplifies a feminist style of storytelling similar to that of her filmmaker peers listed in this book: utilising off-screen space to suggest rather than show traumatic events (similar to Lucrecia Martel); focusing on close gestural movement to show emotion (like Debra Granik);

privileging visual elements of colour, light and shadow to convey feeling, and stitching ambiguity into the audio-visual design of her films (like Liliana Cavani and Claire Denis), and effectively complicating the designation of sound as an isolated 'cinematic object'. Such stylistic choices purposefully extend what aesthetic experience might mean within the wider context of cinema. The shared but variable ambiguities evident across these women filmmakers' films illustrate how 'aesthetic experience' is a term that envelops situations of emotional turbulence in more ethical and moral configurations. Through the variance of characters' experiences of joy, love, pain, anxiety and anger, cinema discloses an identifiable, emotionally tense way of being-in-the-world.

Kate Ince notes how Beauvoir's concept of disclosure from *The Ethics of Ambiguity* 'fits the actions of the female film characters' (2017: 90) in the films of Sally Potter, Catherine Breillat and Andrea Arnold (three further women filmmakers whose work also exemplifies 'ambiguous cinema'), temporarily revealing our ambiguity as a necessarily positive, uncomfortable and difficult but also a way to resist cultural myths and suggest a way of being genuinely authentic. Ince sees Beauvoir's concept of disclosure as intimately linked to situation, revealing an enworlded intermediation through vision, and while she doesn't refer to Beauvoir's critique of the aesthetic attitude directly, Ince nevertheless uses the idea of disclosure to unveil cinema's 'aesthetically ethical potential' (Ince 2017: 91).[4] Disclosure as a form of action illustrates how reciprocal recognition of the other might occur within aesthetic experience. Later in the chapter, I discuss how this concept of disclosure evolved into a more nuanced expression of situation in Beauvoir's 'What Can Literature Do?'

Rethinking Beauvoir's question, 'what can literature do?' as 'what can cinema do?' I consider how the aesthetic experience relevant to literature helps illuminate how film experience creates 'a theatre of co-performance' (Casey 2010). Edward Casey states that aesthetic objects are never fully separate from us, recognising, as Beauvoir did, that they exist in terms of situation (Casey 2010: 5). He notes that Jean-Paul Sartre 'tended in this direction with his idea of "situation" in *L'être et le néant* [*Being and Nothingness*]' but does not refer to any of Beauvoir's writings.[5] Casey's emphasis on situation is significant here because he is saying that as an existentialist idea, situation can better answer what is 'the place of "experience" in art?' (Casey 2010: 5). More specifically, he says that if we are to answer this question by going beyond Kant's pleasure/displeasure dichotomy, the role of situation demands a rethinking of what constitutes 'aesthetic experience' outside human experience, indeed establishing a 'theatre' that demands co-performance from both spectator and artwork indicative of an intersubjective area of experience.

Casey's main point of reference is Mikel Dufrenne's *The Phenomenology of Aesthetic Experience* (1973) which discusses 'the larger dimensions of feeling' in the experience of art (Casey 2010: 6).[6] By attending to 'feeling' in order to acknowledge work by 'non-phenomenological aestheticians' (Baensch 1958; Collingwood 1938; Langer 1953), Casey points to the importance of emotional experience in forming an aesthetic engagement. Specifically, it is R. G. Collingwood's notion of 'spectator as co-performer' that Casey sees as critical to rethinking aesthetic experience as 'co-immanent feeling' (Casey 2010: 6). The themes Casey identifies are examined at length by Beauvoir across her *oeuvre*, principally the role of situation as enveloping the subject. She writes: 'Each situation is open onto all the others and it is open onto the world, which is nothing other than the swirling [*tournoiement*] of all these situations which envelop each other' (WCLD 199). Here, the entanglement or 'co-performance' between author and reader can be read via Beauvoir's philosophy as 'living discovery for the author as for the reader' (LM 271). While it is beyond the scope of this work to follow this line of argument more closely, it is important to note that Beauvoir had previously reached Casey's conclusion that rethinking the role of emotion and feeling within aesthetic experience 'not only ties subject to object but melts down their very difference' (Casey 2010: 6).[7] With Beauvoir's position on literature in mind, I argue that cinema, specifically independent women's cinema, invokes a creative collaborative entanglement between work and spectator, and through the example of Ramsay's film, discuss how Beauvoir's attention on situation is fundamental to her counter-model of the aesthetic attitude where she insists on the collapsed division between subject and object. I close the chapter with a sustained reading of *We Need to Talk About Kevin*, exploring how Beauvoir's critique of the aesthetic attitude rethinks the foundation of aesthetic experience as being dependent on feeling, that is, feeling as interested and invested contemplation. Most significantly, Ramsay's filmmaking illustrates how such investment leads to a capacity to develop a reflexive awareness of the impact of tense and ambiguous situations so that we may realise our freedoms. This shift from a detached contemplative spectator position to a reconceived perspective of the aesthetic object, as transcending its status as material or finite, allows us to identify what is actually happening when we watch films. Registering the significance of difficult or uncertain aesthetic experience affords us the opportunity to see and engage with aspects of the human condition that otherwise go unseen, uncommented on and ignored.

Throughout *Ambiguous Cinema* I have discussed the limits that exist within Beauvoir's *The Ethics of Ambiguity*: its expression is difficult,[8] it shows Beauvoir's philosophy of ambiguity at an early, formative stage, and even within her ground-breaking claim that human existence is ambiguous and in order to realise our freedom we must accept failures and contingency, there is not a clear or specific taxonomy of what ambiguous experience might specifically look or feel like, rather she says we should simply assume such failures (EA 12). She had yet to link moral freedom with historical situation; this was indeed a focus in *The Second Sex* (for women's situation) and in her later works such as *The Coming of Age* (the situation of older people). Yet *The Ethics of Ambiguity* shows Beauvoir's thinking on aesthetic experience, as embodied and intersubjective thought and felt experiences of ambiguity were part of her philosophy from very early on in the timeline of her work. In *Ethics*, she associates ambiguity with the turmoil that results from emotional uncertainty, or situations of indeterminacy, where it is at its most embodied and affective. It is this conception of ambiguity that underwrites Beauvoir's philosophy and that is the reason for her emphasis in linking situation, emotion and reciprocity when proposing an ethical freedom.

In Ramsay's films, lived trauma is indirectly conveyed as the aetiology of her protagonists' indefinite situations. In *Morvern Callar* (2002), Morvern (Samantha Morton) wakes up on Christmas morning to find her boyfriend, James, lying dead on the floor, having committed suicide. Instead of falling apart, Morvern benefits by reinventing herself; she appropriates authorship of James's novel and finds freedom through its success.[9] In *You Were Never Really Here*, Joe (Joaquin Phoenix) struggles to overcome the post-traumatic stress of his abusive childhood by seeking salvation in greater turmoil. We encounter Joe as a man who is hired to find and rescue young girls who have been abducted and sold into child prostitution. Unlike Morvern, Joe doesn't find liberation or a way out of his trauma; his body literally becomes more and more battered and scarred by the horrors of his experiences. His efforts to rescue young girls from danger prolong rather than nullify his pain and existential hurt. In the end, it is the words of his latest rescue, Nina (Ekaterina Samsonov), when she says 'It's a beautiful day', that appears to connect with him most authentically in turning toward a potentially brighter and more positive future. These are words spoken from one traumatised person to another, offering Joe an alternative path away from the terror of his usual, shocking life.

The trope of resilience being borne from traumatic experience remains cinematically limited (even if within patriarchal societies there is always some truth to this concerning women). It fits the three-act structure and rarely articulates anything specific about women's circumstance or situation. Such metonymic devices suggest that women's strength only results from negative experience or that freedom is always tied to such tumultuous lived experience rather than the pursuit of freedom being the stormy experience itself. Ramsay, however, does not capitalise or exploit traumatic experience in this way. Instead, her treatment of trauma is contextualised wholly by aftermath, compelling the spectator to piece together what caused the present situation in their own journey with the film. The result is that her filmmaking illuminates the ways in which cinematic ambiguity (if accepted) can yield a more ethical experience for the spectator, appealing to their own autonomy (and freedom) to reconstruct the respective character's unseen experience through imagination. In other words, by looking more closely at aftermath, Ramsay does articulate something of situation and circumstance, particularly concerning ambiguity and the unsettling emotions that demand negotiation. On these terms, Ramsay's filmmaking appears to exemplify a similar perspective on situation to the one Beauvoir put forward in *The Second Sex*, which she clarified later in *The Prime of Life* as 'femininity is neither a natural nor an innate entity, but rather a condition brought about by society, on the basis of certain physiological givens' (PL 291). Ramsay's films, then, are regarded here not solely as aesthetic objects, but more loosely as landscapes of ambiguous co-performances between filmmaker, film and audience. Before I look more closely at Ramsay's *We Need to Talk About Kevin*, let us briefly situate the terms 'aesthetic attitude' and 'aesthetic experience' in Beauvoir's thinking.

Beauvoir's Phenomenology of the Aesthetic Attitude and Aesthetic Experience

The notion of the aesthetic attitude is not specific to Beauvoirian phenomenology, rather it refers to the frame of interest that structures a relationship to and with reality. Attitude refers to a frame of consciousness; it has meaning (when and only when) we consciously regard it aesthetically. Beauvoir's distinction between an ontological and moral attitude (or what we might call detached and engaged aesthetic attitudes, respectively) presents a paradoxical position, identifying ambiguous experience within which we are compelled to consciously determine our intention and attention. In the third part of *The Ethics of Ambiguity*, Beauvoir claims that the positive aspect of ambiguity is the incitement to action, where our freedom can be given 'a concrete content' (EA 79) as active engagement with others through disclosure. An expression of freedom must beget further opportunities for freedom, as disclosure is not a single event but an action that necessarily instils future further disclosures – for the self and for others. Only through such action for others does freedom become possible for the self and take on meaning in the world. This insistence on action, movement and engagement with others is the foundation of Beauvoir's phenomenological counter-model to the aesthetic attitude as it refutes the 'detached contemplation' in the Sartrean claim that man simply '*is* free, he can not [*sic*] will himself free' (EA 80). For Beauvoir, the positive aspect of ambiguity of willing oneself free through concrete action involves a sensuous entanglement of both body and mind, including the intention to support the other's freedom.

For most of Beauvoir's life, this action-as-sensuous entanglement was exercised through her literary writing, although philosophically (and outside France), *The Second Sex* has had the greatest reach and recognition. It remained Beauvoir's firm belief that literature was the most sophisticated art form to disclose being in an efficacious way: 'A metaphysical novel that is honestly read, and honestly written, provides a disclosure of existence in a way unequaled by any other mode of expression' (LM 276). I like to imagine that Beauvoir may have changed her mind after watching Ramsay's films, particularly as she viewed creative work as the fundamental way to produce disclosure, far more effectively than criticism. One of the ways she illuminates this engagement with others is through the example of the festival, which she saw as providing a situation for the 'passionate assertion of existence in a more durable way' (EA 137). The festival establishes an environment of interactivity and through the performance of story (in multiple forms) within a temporal structure (having a beginning and an end), its unique meaning is given life. The finite period of the festival expresses the ambiguity of human existence, confirming that acceptance of ambiguity is a discovery of 'every movement toward death is life' (EA 137). This view of the festival lends a different interpretation to the film industry's terminology 'theatrical release' and may even speak more directly to the importance of resisting the dominance of streaming platforms and the isolated viewing experience they require.

The ambiguity that cinema discloses, inviting us to confront and sit with it throughout the length of a film (regardless of the actual duration), echoes the spirit of Beauvoir's notion of the festival. She doesn't specifically speak of the collective audience, as she is more concerned with the concrete action of individual experience (at this point) of the festival but her conception nevertheless implies group experience. Similarly, she describes the creativity of painting as a 'movement toward its own reality' (EA 140); its indeterminacy becomes an example of the paradox in ambiguity, both a failure and success. Therefore, with regard to cinema, we might view the action and entanglement of disclosure as exemplified through the emotional and affective impact films have on their audiences, not just through the ocular-centric act of watching but more sensorially and intuitively as feeling the film, the potential here being a raising of consciousness about specific social situations, particularly in terms of bringing to light certain experiences of the human condition that often go unseen.

As discussed in Chapter 2, Beauvoir did not regard disclosure as a literal action of exposure – something that we consciously see (although it might very well include this). Rather, the first form of action identifying disclosure is the recognition of the other and an affective acknowledgement that the other's presence 'defines my situation' (EA 97). The freedom that is incurred through disclosure, making visible the truth of the world, takes two forms according to Beauvoir: ontological freedom and moral freedom. Where ontological freedom discloses being, 'freedom realizes itself only by engaging itself in the world' (EA 84), this is not the ultimate freedom Beauvoir seeks. Disclosure as a form of action must look toward moral freedom, and, as Kristiana Arp asks, 'what relation to the world is involved in moral freedom? How is the world disclosed through it?' (2001: 67). Another way to understand the distinction between these two types of freedom is to locate them within Beauvoir's version of the aesthetic attitude.

An ontological freedom can be acknowledged as detached contemplation, 'disclosure implies a perpetual tension to keep being at a distance' (EA 23).[10] The point of distance is important; I see your freedom over there, and I see mine here but I am not moved to identify with you. Beauvoir's moral freedom, however, involves a desire for the disclosure of being, a desire that does move one to identify and therefore act. It isn't enough to acknowledge or recognise another's freedom; it must incur continuous action that results in the creation of other future possible disclosure and freedom:

> The goal toward which I surpass myself must appear to me as a point of departure toward a new act of surpassing. Thus, a creative freedom develops happily without ever congealing into unjustified facticity. The creator leans upon anterior creations in order to create possibility of new creations ... It discloses being at the end of a further disclosure. At each moment freedom is confirmed through all creation. (EA 28)

How might this work within film experience? One of the main qualities shared in the cinema of each woman filmmaker discussed in this book is the willingness to evoke narrative *lacunae* through foregrounding sensory elements of cinema. Refusing the ease of narrative explanation, where the film is effortlessly explained for the audience so that no reflection or thought is required to make meaning, produces a tension in aesthetic experience because it generates an appeal to the spectator to participate in the unfolding of a film's story. This appeal works as an incitement of a moral aesthetic attitude. Some spectators will flee from this appeal, but others will respond. For Beauvoir, moral freedom is possible by accepting the tension of such uncertainty, and with respect to cinema, the viewer must see their 'collaboration as necessary' given that such cinematic ambiguity is an 'appeal to [their] freedom' (LM 276). The collaboration marks a shift from an ontological to moral aesthetic attitude, recognising but overcoming the separation of the other so that reciprocal recognition is possible. For Beauvoir, this occurs through identification with characters, but most significantly through an emotional identification: 'it must speak of anguish, solitude, and death because those are precisely the situations that enclose us most radically in our singularity' (WCLD 205). The appeal is also a further recognition of the right to speak, as narrative *lacunae* within Ramsay's films create space for spectators to speak/think for themselves in response to the film story world they have been invited to participate in. Her films do not speak or think for their audiences, but instead look to engage them through haptic visuality (Marks 2000).

For argument's sake (and because Beauvoir identifies the documentary as part of 'information' in 'What Can Literature Do?'), we can say that the documentary genre has developed a range of narrative structures and expressive modalities wherein audiences expect to discover a type of disclosure about something or someone in the world, either through a shift in understanding, or the presentation of an alternative (usually marginalised) perspective. This is similar to Stella Bruzzi's theorisation of approximation within documentary, which registers the 'transition from one state (of innocence, of not knowing) to another (of experience and knowledge), as the process of watching metamorphoses' into different modes of being (2020: 4). This type of disclosure as a transition does not share Beauvoir's emphasis on emotional identification, so we might further ask, is this transition or metamorphoses the same as the disclosure of existence that occurs in other artistic forms such as the feature films of independent women's cinema?

Given the practice of detached observation, more traditional documentary modalities exemplify an ontological aesthetic attitude, aiming to objectively screen historical, political and cultural events that may have been forgotten, ignored or unresolved. Newer forms, however, have established documentary traditions that investigate situation and ambiguity, promoting moral engagement through more poetic, experimental aesthetics. The intention of a documentary is an appeal to inform, to challenge the knowledge or perspective we may have on the world. This is the point that Beauvoir takes up in 'What Can Literature Do?', distinguishing between literature and information on the basis of appeal: even if information can present a world as it is revealed to an author (or filmmaker), unless it grips the reader (or spectator) and intersects with their world, it will not realise a moral freedom (WCLD 201). Read as an evolution of her early thoughts on the aesthetic attitude in *The Ethics of Ambiguity*, Beauvoir's discussion of the relationship between literature and information can be seen as a nuanced distinction between an ontological (detached) and a moral (engaged) aesthetic attitude.

She asks if literature is still important, if it can still effectively appeal and facilitate moral freedom, responding affirmatively by identifying the subjectivity of the world as a 'detotalized totality' (WCLD 198).[11] This is not the first time Beauvoir makes such a claim. Compare her expressions from *The Ethics of Ambiguity* with those from 'What Can Literature Do?':

> If I were really everything there would be nothing beside me; the world would be empty. There would be nothing to possess, and I myself would be nothing. (EA 76)

> If we first considered the world as an object to be manifested, if we thought that it was saved by this destination in such a way that everything about it seemed justified and that there was no more of it to reject, then there would be nothing to say about it, for no form would take shape in it; it is revealed only through rejection, desire, hate and love. In order for the artist to have a world to express he must first be situated in this world, oppressed or oppressing, resigned or rebellious. (EA 83–4)

> If the world were a given totality, if it were a being, something immutable that we could examine or survey as we do a world map, if this were the case and we saw the totality of the world in its unity, [then this would only increase] our objective knowledge of the world. (WCLD 198)

In these quotations, made almost twenty years apart, Beauvoir is distinguishing between the ontology of the world, something that exists independently from us, and our subjective experience of it (the 'detotalized totality'), which is dependent on the specificity of our own situations as they relate to the world. In *The Ethics of Ambiguity*, Beauvoir identifies reciprocal recognition as involving communication between people as the means to realise one's projects in the world: 'No project can be defined by its interference with other projects' (EA 76). In her later work, this evolves into an enveloping of situation that expresses the assembled phenomena of our situation: 'implicitly enveloping the world does not mean that one knows it, but that one reflects it, typifies it, or *expresses* it' (WCLD 199). Artistic or creative production, then, as a form of communication between people, is a vehicle for recognising each other's projects and situation, and for Beauvoir, literature is best placed to realise this. In the twenty-first century, we can consider time-based media as an equivalent realisation. As Moi puts it, 'our projects relate to the same world and because each project always opens onto the projects of others' (2009: 192). But what is critical to Beauvoir's interpretation of 'detotalized totality' is the acknowledgement of the difference between ontological (detached) and moral (engaged) attitudes. For Beauvoir, literature represents a subjective, moral and engaged communication, '[a] truth that is *other* becomes mine without ceasing to be an other' (WCLD 201), whereas information is distant, and does not advance an 'I' that invites one into a different view of the world to 'change universes' (WCLD 201).[12]

Returning to women's cinema, there is a much stronger and overt style of foregrounding sensuous experience. Martine Beugnet describes the relation between cinema and sensation in this way:

> Rather than establish an informative context and give viewers the elements necessary to orientate themselves and piece together the beginnings of a story, [sensuous cinema like Ramsay's] focus[es] on those fundamental qualities of the cinema that come before, yet tend to be overruled by its representative and narrative functions; those variations in movement and in light, in colour and sound tonalities that make up film's endlessly shifting compositions. (Beugnet 2007: 3)

When Beauvoir likens the ontological (detached) contemplation to the aesthetic attitude, she is simultaneously rejecting the idea that our existence as separate individuals legitimises isolation from other beings in the world, claiming that freedom cannot occur independently of others: 'outside of time and far from men, he faces history, which he thinks he does not belong to' (EA 80). The traditional aesthetic attitude of detached, unentangled being in body, history and situation is bad faith that ignores or denies the cost of achieving freedom. This is why Beauvoir says, 'the lover of historical works is present at the birth and downfall of Athens, Rome and Byzantium' (EA 80), for if we only observe and refuse to get our hands dirty we cannot expect any change in the atrocities of humanity. 'Each moment of that tormented history is contradicted by the following one' (EA 81). Beauvoir's criticism of the aesthetic attitude identifies its distant regard as an act of bad faith, 'a position of withdrawal, a way of fleeing the truth of the present' (EA 81). Therefore, Beauvoir's ideas on the aesthetic attitude inform her thoughts on willing one's self free, and that human freedom is realised 'only by engaging itself in the world: to such an extent that man's project toward freedom is embodied for him in definite acts of behavior' (EA 84). The aesthetic attitude was not simply an idea or interpretative position for Beauvoir, it was to become a way of being and a critical part of her creative practice, a form of practical action that was wedded closely to her position concerning literature. More broadly, she saw art as revealing 'existence as a reason for existing', as facilitating the 'constructive activities' (EA 86) that become meaningful as they assume responsibility and intention for one's freedom.

Through the production of concrete, creative works such as 'discoveries, inventions, culture, paintings, and books' (EA 86) (a list to which we can add cinema), possibilities for freedom can be made visible and become real for others. Without a wide-ranging practice of linking creative production to projects of freedom, Beauvoir argued that 'transcendence is condemned to fall uselessly back upon itself' (EA 87). If we are denied the space and the time to produce or engage with creative works that intend to realise our ethical freedom, we will be trapped by our situation. When writing *The Ethics of Ambiguity*, Beauvoir problematically says 'man is never oppressed by things' (EA 87),[13] a point she uses to establish the necessity of creativity as an internal and intentional response to our ambiguity and the pursuit of freedom. If we cannot accept that there will be setbacks or failure within our constructive activities, then we will not achieve moral freedom. For Beauvoir, 'withdrawals and errors are another way of disclosing the world' (EA 87), that is, making visible our situation in the world and our relationships to others within it. By the time she delivers 'What Can Literature Do?', Beauvoir states more clearly that it is through recognising and identifying with the emotional anguish within another's situation that moral freedom is possible. One of cinema's greatest potentialities is its capacity to 'render us transparent to one another in what is most opaque about us' (WCLD 205).

Perhaps it is most clear in Beauvoir's autobiographies that aesthetic experience governed her perspective on the world. Whether her experiences or encounters were good, bad or ugly, they especially helped to form her thoughts on the concepts of disclosure and situation. In her memoirs she is most candid about the varied receptions her novels and plays received, paying very close attention to describing her emotional response to critics reviews: 'Here was a review [of *L'Invitée*], written by a real critic, printed in a real paper, to assure me in black and white that I had written a real book – that I had become, overnight, a real writer. I could not contain my joy' (PL 440).[14] She also linked her life experiences to her narrative expressions: 'It is my own feelings I am expressing in *The Mandarins* when I make Anne say ... "Everything had been either worse or more unbearable ... The real tragedies hadn't happened to me, and yet they haunted my life'" (PL 396). In *The Prime of Life* she also turns to aesthetic experience to explain how her attitude was formed precisely through artistic works, describing the American novel as showing her 'something of America', and that through the 'distorting lenses' of jazz and Hollywood films, she gained some understanding of the diversity within American life (PL 114).[15] While she abhorred the United States' racist policies, 'its lynchings, its twin evils of exploitation and unemployment', it was through literature, jazz music and the cinema that she claimed to recognise 'something vast and unencumbered ... beyond all questions of right or wrong' (PL 115). Interestingly, Beauvoir notes the paradox in her attraction to American arts and disgust for 'its regime, while the USSR, the scene of a social experiment which we wholeheartedly admired, nevertheless left us quite cold' (PL 116). The description of her attitude here of not being 'actively *for* anything' (PL 116) is reminiscent of an ontological aesthetic attitude, adopting a way of perceiving the world from a disinterested position so that one's contemplation can occur without any subjective involvement or consequence for the observer and their situation. However, within the timeline of Beauvoir's thinking and publications, this position preceded *The Ethics of Ambiguity*.

Beauvoir's critique of the aesthetic attitude plays a key role in the development of her philosophy of ambiguity, particularly its attention on the intersubjective relationship between spectator and situation, offering an alternative perspective on aesthetic experience. I agree with Peggy Zeglin Brand (2002) who regards Beauvoir's work on art and aesthetics as being overlooked in terms of offering a critical and counter-phenomenological position concerning the aesthetic attitude. Beauvoir's critique presents an early and distinctively phenomenological view of aesthetic experience, and while her intention was not to outline a new aesthetic theory, nonetheless her philosophy of ambiguity does put forward a model that connects ethics, emotions and aesthetics within lived experience. Her emphasis on action, that is, of relating to others, and the movement of disclosure within the aesthetic attitude shows how she viewed aesthetic experience as the foundation for our entry to the world and its meanings; she says 'the present is not a potential past; it is the moment of choice and action; we can not [sic] avoid living it through a project; and there is no project which is purely contemplative since one always projects himself toward something' (EA 82); and elsewhere: 'Man's inner life is nothing but his apprehension of the world, and it is by turning toward the world and leaving the hero's subjectivity in the background that a writer manages to express that inner life with the greatest truth and depth' (ADD 263).

If we see the novel as 'an authentic adventure of the mind' (LM 272), it forms a way for both the author and reader to discover together how 'truths appear that were previously unknown to him, questions whose solutions he does not possess' (LM 272). In *America Day by Day*, where Beauvoir included more casual references to cinema than in any other work, she often remarks on the incongruence between the situation of society and the bad faith of Hollywood:

> Hollywood isn't suffering only from an economic crisis or from an overly extreme division of labor and other contingencies; its ills are much deeper – America no longer knows how to express itself or dares to admit anything ... Movies show a conventional, papier-mâché America in which only the landscapes and the material details have some reality. (ADD 172–3)

Let us now turn to Ramsay's *We Need to Talk About Kevin* as a work which falls within Beauvoir's view of cinema as a 'screen of platonic heaven where I grasp the Idea in its purity once more, an Idea that is only approximately embodied in the stone houses and neon lights' (ADD 74).

We Need to Talk About Kevin

In *We Need to Talk About Kevin* (hereafter *Kevin*), Eva Khatchadourian (Tilda Swinton) exists in a state of isolation, effecting a haunting existence that is positioned as a result of past trauma. She wrestles against the violence within her that emerges full force as she becomes a first-time mother, and she struggles to manage the later guilt she feels in not having been able to establish an authentic and loving connection with her son, Kevin (Ezra Miller), which leads to tragic and fatal outcomes. The film is an innovative adaptation of Lionel Shriver's 2003 novel of the same name, yet the title is somewhat misleading in terms of the film's intention. At first glance, the title suggests the point of contention rests with Kevin and his behaviour, something that requires a conversation, yet Ramsay's adaptation questions the intentionality behind it, electing to reveal Eva's inner turbulent world and the isolated, dissociated place it puts her in. The film shows that who we really need to be talking about is Eva and therefore what it really is to experience motherhood.[16]

We are first taken into the film's story world through score; the oscillation of a lawn sprinkler and an almost undiscernible twang of an archery bow, followed by overlaying cheerleader chanting voices, rising to a climax of white traffic-sounding noise. For audience members who have not read the book, the significance of this soundtrack will not be made clear until later in the film. The first image we see is of a white curtain in a suburban family home, blowing in the wind against a darkened background; a sliding patio door is open, making the curtain look like a veil separating fantasy and reality. The screen fades to white and immediately transitions to another time and place, a bird's-eye shot overlooking a completely chaotic and crowded scene, full of people jostling in a festival atmosphere (Figure 7.1). The colour red saturates the frame and initially fuels a sense of joyous excess and moment of celebration. While the colour red remains a constant motif throughout the film, it takes on different connotations, becoming a signifier of Eva's anxiety, tension and overwhelming feelings. In this first sequence, we see Eva as a hedonistic world-traveller, enjoying the Spanish tomato-throwing festival, *La Tomatina*. She smiles as she crowd-surfs, revelling in her freedom, before being lowered into the red soupy mess of the crushed tomatoes; the ecstasy of being anonymous in a sea of people turns into something more sinister as we hear a different soundtrack of sirens, screams, and objects being thrown. Eva's existence here represents a 'bad faith' freedom – the idea that being free is equitable with having no responsibility, confusing licence to do what you want, when you want, with being free. The shift in sound design, from celebratory to abrasive noise, is a further evocation of the anguish and anxiety that responsibility brings. The sound bridge of the thrown objects brings us back into Eva's present situation – rousing from sleep in a foggy state, she discovers that the front of her house has been vandalised with red paint. The opening sequence allegorically conveys the shift in Eva's mentality from pre- to post-motherhood.

Ramsay does not rely on dialogue in her films, and this is certainly the case with *Kevin*. Instead, we are thrown into the sensoria of Eva's world

Figure 7.1 Scene of the chaotic *La Tomatina* festival at the beginning of *We Need to Talk About Kevin* (Ramsay 2011).

and the opening sequence is crucial in setting up the unreliability or, perhaps more forgivingly, the subjectivity of her perspective. Either way, the film's emphasis on Eva's sensory experience of the world (through sound, light and colour) confirms that this story is much less about Kevin than it is about the unravelling of Eva as a mother. The disparate, evocative elements of cinema are given for the audience to piece together, and here we see a connection with Beauvoir's notion of 'journey' that exists between author and reader, although clearly here it occurs between filmmaker and spectator.

In 'Literature and Metaphysics', Beauvoir writes that the author's presence must be well-hidden if the appeal in the work is to succeed and grip the reader's imagination (LM 270). If the work is too on the nose, that is, if its 'intrusion of philosophy' is too obvious, the fragile potential of identification is lost and the reader may not enter the author's world. As a classification of aesthetic experience, Beauvoir seeks to highlight the potential for appeal in the intermeshed space of literature and philosophy specific to the metaphysical novel and break down the barriers that separate them (LM 270), something the field of film-philosophy has similarly sought to achieve with respect to cinema. Critic Miranda Sawyer describes Ramsay's films as 'immensely watchable, gripping studies of damaged people; but there is also an aesthetic, often an intimate focus, a mood painted by the pictures' (Sawyer in *The Guardian* 2018). Elena Lazic similarly observes that 'few [filmmakers] are as consistent and innovative as Lynne Ramsay in crafting absorbing sensory experiences and making us feel like we've experienced something alongside her characters' (Lazic 2018). Such remarks suggest that Ramsay's concentration on intense emotional experience resonates with Beauvoir's thoughts on the metaphysical novel, as her films share in the creative endeavour of linking 'the totality of the world ... and its fundamental ambiguity' (LM 276). In *Kevin*, this occurs with respect to the specific situations of women and motherhood, not from Ramsay's own singular perspective, but as collective recognition (particularly in terms of conveying the embodiment of Eva's experience). Toril Moi points out that Beauvoir is not interested in privileging form over content, rather she is more concerned with 'a way of telling a story ... to find a rhythm and a subject matter' (2009: 194), and this opening sequence concretises Ramsay's style of swiftly establishing a highly subjective character story world through closely cohered cinematography and sound design.

The stylistic choice to use a split structure narrative intermeshes Eva's past and present and runs the risk of prioritising style over substance, where the artifice of the film moves away from an appeal of intersubjective entanglement between audience and film, fleeing into pure entertainment. Yet, the film intimately focuses on the ambiguity of Eva's recollections, enabling the audience to become entangled with the meticulous expression of her character, identifying with the confusion that envelops Eva's situation. We are invited into Eva's world precisely because the film moves so swiftly and repeatedly between memories of her past and her present. Within the first fifteen minutes of the film, we traverse different temporalities within Eva's life around seventeen times as she recollects recent horrors amidst fonder memories of early love and moments of joyous freedom. These two types of memories (the distant and recent past) are spliced into her present, showcasing Eva's highly fragmented but sensuous state of mind. Eva's recollections throw us into the emotional ambiguity of her world, and we are never sure if we are witnessing only her perceptions of Kevin, her daughter Celia (Ashley Gerasimovich), and husband Franklin (John C. Reilly), or witnessing them as they really happened. Ultimately, this indeterminacy prevents detached contemplation (an ontological aesthetic attitude) as Ramsay's *Kevin* successfully evokes the specific sensoria of Eva's world – separate from its audiences, yet communicative of her complex intimacy (WCLD 201). Ramsay does not idealise Eva's efforts to reclaim her life, rather the intention of *Kevin* is to communicate the unavoidable ambiguity that exists within emotional experience that might evoke expressions of anguish, fear, disappointment and uncertainty in being a mother. Ramsay uses the indifference Eva initially feels toward motherhood to build a shared experience between film and audience.

In the sequence where we learn of Eva's first pregnancy, the past and present of her situation are tightly woven in a montage of sound and image to convey the sense of shock and despondency she felt on discovering the news. Because the sequence packs together a sense of then and now so strictly, Ramsay is able to layer and intermingle the further emotion of guilt that exists separate from the event but present in Eva's recollection. Blurred red traffic lights and noises dissolve into the flashing alarm clock lights and beeps of 12:00 turning to 12:01 (a new day, an extra person). This image is accompanied with a descending score and interwoven track of a photocopier; the sound design affectively interlacing past and present of Eva's situation (Eva is photocopying papers at her new job, ironically conveying the monotony of her new living situation without children). The sound of a heartbeat follows with a black-and-white image suggestive of Kevin's conception, the biological rendition emphasising Eva's detachment. The audio-visual intensity of this scene evokes a strong sense of Eva's disorientation, and we soon learn that this is portraying her anxiety as she is to visit Kevin in prison that afternoon. Eva's inarticulate demeanour conveys a numbness of her character but the highly evocative use of sound and image also points clearly to the chaotic, swirling ambiguity of emotions that exist under the level of her skin. While Eva may not speak much dialogue, her silences are combined with sensuous filmmaking to effect a 'co-performance' with audiences, engendering a recognition of what she feels as well as her inability to articulate it verbally.

Beauvoir is clear on the difference between entertainment and collaborative 'co-performance' regarding artistic work, saying that participation is a shared enterprise between creator and participant that constitutes a knowing of experience existing beyond ourselves. One of the things Beauvoir says literature can do is craft an 'intermingling' that communicates something that 'cannot be communicated, capable of giving me the taste of another life' (Moi 2009: 193).[17] For Moi, this 'taste of another life' is the recognition of another's sensuous experience that we cannot know directly, similar to Anzaldúa's recognition of alien consciousness that I discussed in Chapter 6 in the context of Martel's *Zama*. Beauvoir does not mean that a taste of another life is the same as knowing it, a position that appropriates through assumed understanding; rather it is her way of once again indirectly placing aesthetic experience at the centre of her philosophy of ambiguity. 'Taste' (perhaps 'engaged reflection' is a better term) is another example of Beauvoir's distinction between a detached, ontological aesthetic attitude and an engaged, moral aesthetic attitude that is attentive to sensuous and emotional experience. 'I do not annex it to myself; it remains separate from it and with whom I communicate, through books [or films], in their deepest intimacy' (WCLD 201). One of Ramsay's most effective traits as a creator of ambiguous film experience is her ability to craft a highly tense, sensory and embodied situation – as a taste (or engaged reflection) of women's lives – which cannot be reduced to any other type of aesthetic experience. So, one of the things that cinema can do is facilitate the sensuous search for freedom by communicating anxious and ambiguous emotional experience that is not always easy to articulate, but can be seen, heard and felt.

While there is the peripheral echo of social commentary on US school shootings in *Kevin*, and the whisper of causality between Eva's coldness as a mother to Kevin and his murderous act at the school, this is not what the film is concerned with. Rather, *Kevin* is a psychological study of the existential costs motherhood has on women, and examines the aftermath of traumatic experience through a singular character – Eva is the only person who appears seriously affected throughout the film. There is the aftermath of Kevin's many horrible actions (defacing Eva's study with paint, killing Celia's guinea pig, maiming Celia's face, murdering his father, sister and high-school children), but there is also the intimated trauma that results from Franklin's lack of support. Franklin refuses to recognise Eva's maternal crisis as legitimate and this is another cost Eva is expected to bear. Because Ramsay limits the amount of dialogue within the film and accentuates the complex and textural interrelatedness between sound, colour and image, audience attention is directed effectively to the sensory elements of the film, and this creates time and space for self-awareness in reflection and response. This is a film that is felt first. Throughout the film, it is hard not to think what your own responses would be in Eva's situation; whether you are a parent or not, the ambivalence of parenthood and the sense of isolation it can incur are presented for reflection. *Kevin* solicits spectator co-performance that sustains an examination of the way in which society shapes our experience and understanding of motherhood.

In 'Literature and Metaphysics', Beauvoir doesn't explicitly discuss the aesthetic attitude, but she does reject the 'false naturalistic objectivity' (LM 275) that an ontological (traditional) aesthetic attitude espouses in favour of the requisite subjectivity that facilitates disclosure of meaning within our aesthetic experiences. She begins her essay by acknowledging her own difficulty in separating her love of fiction from her love of philosophy, 'I felt torn apart' (LM 269). This entanglement of subjectivity and objectivity can be seen as the formative thinking for the collapsed division between subject and object that followed in *The Ethics of Ambiguity*, and indeed the distinction between an ontological and moral freedom. While Beauvoir's focus throughout 'Literature and Metaphysics' is again the metaphysical novel, many of her comments are well-suited to a reading of cinematic experience, particularly with respect to the role ambiguity plays in the formation of meaningful, disclosed experience. For example, Beauvoir writes that 'a work always signifies something; even one that deliberately seeks to refuse all meaning still conveys this refusal' (LM 270). Despite Beauvoir's strong advocacy of the novel (she saw the metaphysical novel as unrivalled in terms of providing 'a disclosure of existence in a way unequaled by any other mode of expression' (LM 276)), I think it is fair to argue that the cinema in 1945 is incomparable with the audio-visual sophistication seen in films today. In particular, Ramsay's capacity to explicitly evoke an 'imaginary plane' of existence, such as Eva's inner world, mirrors Beauvoir's view on how a metaphysical novel is best placed to assist the discovery of meaning rather than prescribe what is meaningful.

In terms of subjective engagement with art, a metaphysical film like Ramsay's also reconstitutes lived experience with which the audience must engage in order to know (knowing in a thought and felt embedded sense): 'Its meaning is the object as it is disclosed to us in the overall relation we sustain with it, and which is action, emotion, and feeling' (LM 270). The 'opacity, ambiguity and impartiality' of Eva's world, as Ramsay creates it, echoes the story world of Beauvoir's version of the metaphysical novel, and as a consequence, we as the audience are enriched in a philosophical way 'that no teaching of doctrine could' (LM 270). By being with Eva and discovering the ambiguity she feels as a mother, her negotiation of the violence it produces in her toward Kevin, the spectator can 'undergo imaginary experiences that are as complete and disturbing as lived experiences' (LM 270). In other words, watching and feeling Eva's emotional turbulence offers us the potential space to think, or at least begin to discover, our own.

In the final part of the film, elements from the opening sequence return (cheerleaders chanting, archery bows twanging, oscillating garden sprinklers and the billowing white curtain) to piece together the horrific events that occurred and address the complexity behind Eva's disturbed emotional state. As well as being a repetition of signifiers, this creates shared previous experience with Eva's situation, as even at the most basic level we can say 'we've been here before'. We note her guilt in terms of being the only surviving family member, as we learn that Kevin had murdered Franklin and Celia before his rampage at his high school, but there is a deeper expression of Eva's guilt here as well. Throughout the film we have seen Eva make solid efforts to tidy up and decorate her current house, cleaning up the paint splatter from the vandals, seemingly actions of getting on with her life as though she were making the best of a bad situation. But as the film draws to its conclusion, we see Eva at her most domestic maternal self, ironing Kevin's T-shirts, making his bed and preparing his room for a possible (desired) return. This is one of the very few shots in the film where there is no colour red (Figure 7.2), awash instead with the colour blue. As Eva leaves the house to visit Kevin in prison for the last time in the film, we see a train pass by behind her house, symbolising the movement and journey of her motherhood; persistent but uncharted.

If taken as an expression of Ramsay's voice and as a synecdoche of ambiguity within women's situation concerning motherhood, *Kevin* fulfils Beauvoir's requirement of a 'language that bears the mark of somebody' (Beauvoir in Moi 2009: 194) who is capable of disclosing a reality of the world. Particularly, it is the ambivalent feelings within parenthood embodied in Eva's character that audiences are able to identify with. This is not

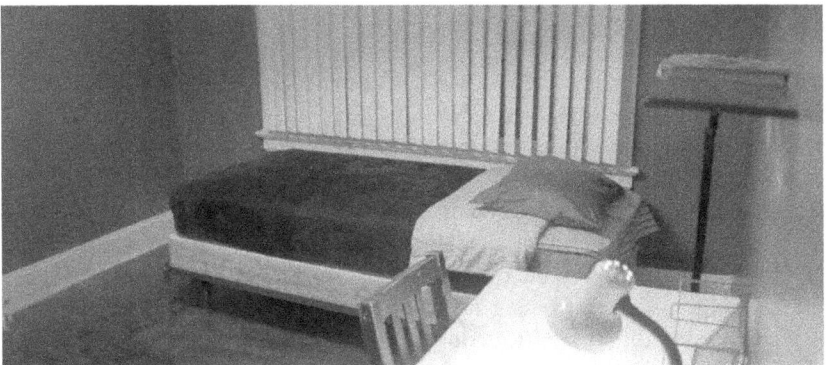

Figure 7.2 Kevin's (Ezra Miller) new bedroom, all in the colour blue.

necessarily with Eva herself (although it might be) but rather an identification that results from recognising an ambiguous orientation to motherhood, specifically the anguish and anxieties in Eva's world as separate but linked to their own.

Ramsay's cinema, exemplified here through *Kevin*, purposefully disrupts normative attitudes of spectatorship, foregrounding sensuous aesthetic experience that appeals to an engaged reflection on the situation of women. Her films revolve around morally contentious situations, stories of women (or men who look after women as with *You Were Never Really Here*) and their lived experience of traumatic situations. Ramsay's films privilege characters that are disconnected to others, possessing morally ambiguous attitudes toward the people and world which surrounds them, yet at the same time she does not judge their characters or establish any moral position with regard to their actions. This is left up to the spectator to determine, or in Beauvoirian terms, to disclose for themselves. Ramsay's films are particularly helpful in explicating Beauvoir's notion of ambiguity and her distinction between aesthetic attitudes, that human beings are equally dependent on each other as much as they are separate from them. Ramsay's films also centre on women's experience as being particularly ambiguous and, in this chapter, I have examined how Beauvoir's philosophy on aesthetic experience helps to disclose cinema's capacity to rival literature as an expression of the emotional turbulence within women's situation. Moi says that through writing, 'women convey the unique taste of their own lives' (2009: 196), and that women's creative works had philosophical insight for Beauvoir's preparation in writing *The Second Sex*. There is every reason to see Lynne Ramsay's cinema fulfilling a similar role with regard to women's emotional experience, as offering expression of women's lives that is frequently invisible.

Notes

1 Beauvoir never identified as lesbian despite having multiple affairs with women. See Deirdre Bair (2019: 264–6) who writes of Beauvoir's anger in response to her relationship with Sylvie le Bon de Beauvoir potentially being described as a lesbian. 'We are not *lesbian*!' (2019: 265). Bair places the emphasis on the word 'lesbian' in her bio-memoir and insinuates that Beauvoir's emotional rejection of the word harboured a form of prejudice. I do not view it in this way, but once again, see it as a further example of Beauvoir refusing easy categorisation of highly complex and intimate relationships, much as she did with Sartre, Aldgren and Lanzmann.

2 Beauvoir delivered 'What Can Literature Do?' as a part of a panel discussion in 1964 organised by Yves Buin (the editor of student communist journal *Clarté*) held at the Mutualitié Theatre in Paris. The speakers included Beauvoir, Sartre, Jean Ricardou, Jean-Pierre Faye and Yves Berger who spoke on the role and future of literature in turbulent times. Beauvoir and Sartre defended 'committed literature' (*littérature engagée*), a provocative style of writing that appealed to the reader's freedom, where Ricardou, Faye and Berger defended the opposite position, of the 'new novel' which supported a poststructuralist and critical semiotic position, a position that was on the precipice of reaching intellectual dominance post-May 1968. Beauvoir's talk was published a year later in 1965. See Moi (2009: 190) who notes the historical significance of this meeting. References listed in this chapter are taken from Simons and Timmermann (eds), *Simone de Beauvoir: 'The Useless Mouths' and Other Literary Writings*, pp. 197–209; and Toril Moi (2009) 'What Can Literature Do? Simone de Beauvoir as a Literary Theorist', pp. 189–98.

3 Elizabeth Fallaize writes: 'In the late 1950s and the 1960s Beauvoir was far from the only intellectual, or even the only female intellectual, to interest herself in Bardot: Marguerite Duras had published an article on Bardot the previous year, in 1958; the French critic François Nourissier was to publish a study in 1960, and even the heavyweight British critic Bernard Levin was sufficiently interested to write a review of Beauvoir's study in *The Spectator* in 1960' (2015: 109).

4 See Chapter 2 where I discuss Ince's concept of ethical vision in more detail with regard to Liliana Cavani's *The Night Porter* and Beauvoir's essay 'Must We Burn Sade?'.

5 Margaret Simons shows how Beauvoir's thoughts on situation pre-existed Sartre's and further provides evidence of his initial rejection of her position regarding situation, citing an anecdote of Heinrich Heine's biography. Simons explains that Beauvoir was struck by Heine's biography as 'showing a life "in situation" and "penetrated" [...] by the social' (Beauvoir in Simons 2009: 20), whereas Sartre criticised the biography for sacrificing 'a bit too much of the person of Heine to his situation' (Sartre in Simons 2009: 21). See

'Introduction' in Simons, *Simone de Beauvoir: Wartime Diary*, pp. 1–35 for a meticulous account of Beauvoir's trajectory of thought regarding situation based on her *Wartime Diary*.
6. For an excellent discussion on the relevance of Dufrenne's ideas for cinema, see Yacavone (2016) *Film Worlds: A Philosophical Aesthetics of Cinema*.
7. Simons attributes Beauvoir's acknowledgement of the influence of emotions as being 'essential to a full life' (2009: 10) to Jeanne Mercier, an early mentor of Beauvoir's.
8. The written expression in 'Literature and Metaphysics', published in April 1946 (*The Ethics of Ambiguity* followed in 1947), is more readable. 'What Can Literature Do?', published in 1965, delivers more nuanced and user-friendly consideration of earlier concepts present in the other two essays.
9. For a closer reading of *Morvern Callar* as an interpretation of woman's desire see Ince (2017: 137–42) and Bolton (2011: 128–66).
10. Given Beauvoir's strong grasp of Kantian aesthetics, her notion of detached contemplation appears to reference Kant's concept of disinterestedness, which also deals with the removal of the sense of self from aesthetic judgement.
11. In 'What Can Literature Do?' Beauvoir attributes this concept to Sartre (1943). However, in *Letters to Sartre*, Beauvoir writes that she had already been influenced by Hegel's 'idea of *enveloping totality* within our individual becoming – because when one is concerned with creating a work, it is certain that one regards the work as itself a moment of the total becoming in which the entire past is achieved and which is the effective liaison with the entire future' (1991: 181–2, my emphasis).
12. Beauvoir's remark that literature enables a reader to 'change universes' is similar to María Lugones's notion of 'world'-travelling that I discuss in greater detail in Chapter 6 with regard to Lucrecia Martel's film *Zama*.
13. As discussed in earlier chapters, this was a point Beauvoir later revised in *The Second Sex* where she noted the role that history and situation play in sustaining systems of behaviour and thought that oppress women.
14. Beauvoir also writes frankly of her intentions behind *Le sang des autres* (*The Blood of Others*): 'my characters became reduced to mere ethical viewpoints' and *Les bouches inutiles* (*The Useless Mouths*): 'My mistake was to pose a political problem in terms of abstract morality. The idealism which permeates *Les bouches inutiles* I find embarrassing, and I deplore my tendency to didacticism' (PL 465).
15. Beauvoir often refers to her love of African American jazz (see ADD 263; PL 115): 'Because they were born of huge collective emotions, common to each and every one of us, these songs touched us individually, at that point of deep intimacy common to us all. They dwelt in our hearts, nourishing us just as certain words and cadences of our own tongue did; and through their medium America came to exist within us.'

16 For a sustained discussion and in-depth psychoanalytic reverie of motherhood, its socio-cultural idealisation and existential ambiguity, see Jacqueline Rose's *Mothers: An Essay on Love and Cruelty* (2018).
17 Moi (2009: 193) translates: '*C'est une confusion sans cesse ébauchée, sans cesse défaite et c'est la seule forme de communication qui soit capable de me donner l'incommunicable, qui soit capable de me donner le gout d'une autre vie*' as 'It is an intermingling ceaselessly begun and ceaselessly undone, and it is the only kind of communication capable of giving me that which cannot be communicated, capable of giving me the taste of another life.' By contrast, Marybeth Timmermann translates it as: 'This confusion is continually initiated and continually undone, and is the only form of communication capable of giving me the incommunicable – the taste of another life' (WCLD 201). Both translations convey Beauvoir's point on affective transmission within the space of intersubjectivity, what I am referring to as 'sensuous co-performance'. However, in this instance I prefer Moi's translation as to my mind, 'intermingling' better expresses the sense and feeling within emotional experience.

CHAPTER 8

Femme Desire and the Reciprocal Gaze in Céline Sciamma's *Portrait of a Lady on Fire*

Céline Sciamma's films consistently display stories of girls' and women's experience in ways that implicitly challenge historical myths and social scripts relative to the erasure of women and their experiences from history. Where filmmakers like Cavani, Denis, Martel and Ramsay engage with ambiguity in a predominantly darker sense, Sciamma's filmmaking appears closer to Granik's, expressing a gentler, but no less powerful, statement on the importance of emotional turbulence within ambiguous lived experience suggestive of future ethical freedoms.

In this regard, Sciamma reflects an 'erotic generosity' (Bergoffen 1997: 2) in her filmmaking, describing the intersubjective connections between eroticism, freedom, ethics and joy.[1] Beauvoir's evolving notion of ambiguity was the key 'way of acknowledging the body; her [Beauvoir's] unique contribution to the phenomenological-existential tradition's insistence that as humans we are situated subjects whose first, primordial and most crucial situation is the body' (Bergoffen 1997: 4). In Chapter 5, I discussed Bergoffen's concept of erotic generosity, which she explains through the inherent power of Beauvoir's muted voice, as typifying an ethics that involves recognition of the other's ambiguity that enables acceptance of one's own. As Bergoffen describes, Beauvoir's muted voice as erotic generosity 'provides us with the beginnings of a feminist ethic' (1997: 7) and we see it demonstrated in Sciamma's films consistently via the female bond, as a way of being with women that is not always effortless but nevertheless shown as a highly valued pathway to freedom.

The ambiguity expressed in and through the female body in Sciamma's films is most evidently exercised through what she describes as the 'female gaze', here argued as 'the reciprocal gaze' given its emphasis on recognising the subjectivity of the other and the intermeshedness of power, ethics, freedom and desire in our relationships with others. The bond between girls or women that is created within each of Sciamma's film diegeses is further established between screen and audience. As discussed in previous chapters, Beauvoir rejects the solipsistic position in her existentialist philosophy of freedom, which is arguably a view shared by Sciamma and one which instructs her cinematic aesthetic. In an interview with Maria Garcia for *Cineaste* (2019), Sciamma speaks of the difference between a conventional (male) and revolutionary (female) gaze, where the latter is a withdrawal from a heteronormative framing of the female body, its sexuality and erasure of agency. In *Portrait of a Lady on Fire* (*Portrait de la jeune fille en feu*, 2019),[2] there is a concerted effort to create a sense of sharing and mutual respect modelled in the interactions of the women characters, but there is no false equivalence of their situations. Instead, Sciamma forms their bond by negotiating hierarchies of power, recognising the difference in their class positions without the need for confrontation, control or domination. The respective social positions these women occupy are not homogenised or assimilated into each other, as this would break the realist fabric of the film. Rather, the differences between them are noted but not othered; they are seen and valued as being elements of women's situation in this particular historical period that are separate but connected. Therefore, like Beauvoir, Sciamma's filmmaking shows that 'if individuals recognize themselves in their differences, individual relations are established among them, and each becomes irreplaceable for others' (EA 116). It is through our connections to others, which acknowledge and preserve difference, that we are enabled to act morally. This is not identification but instead an observation of connection and distinction.

As men and women can equally adopt either a male or female gaze, throughout this chapter the term 'reciprocal gaze' more effectively concentrates on the moral function of looking, that is, what constitutes the departure to which Sciamma refers to as a way to 'share the experience of the character ... it is about inventing new stories and new emotions' (Garcia in *Cineaste* 2019: 11). Further, the reciprocal gaze echoes Beauvoir's notion of reciprocal recognition, which she sees as rejecting the objectification of the other, instead valorising the paradox of being both subject and object, separate and connected. Later I discuss how this is exemplified through *Portrait's* erotic encounters and its revolutionary depiction of women's experience regarding abortion. Additionally, the idea of a reciprocal gaze demonstrates a concrete action of how, in a non-patriarchal society, 'the value of the bond will be recognized by both men and women and will become for both sexes, the source of a new vision of reciprocity, sexuality, love and the couple' (Bergoffen 1997: 7). Firstly, however, I briefly outline Sciamma's three feature films made prior to *Portrait* and examine the interrelationship between ambiguity, desire and female body movement. I end the chapter situating the concept of erotic generosity as a foundational ethical practice that belongs to a reciprocal gaze through an analysis of *Portrait of a Lady on Fire*.

Water Lilies, Tomboy, Girlhood

In Sciamma's earlier films, there is a clear distinction between girlhood and womanhood, where each experience of becoming is discreetly associated with social, historical and political causalities in girls' and women's respective situations, particularly their embodied experiences of becoming woman. Her first three feature films, *Water Lilies* (*Naissance des pieuvres*, 2007) *Tomboy* (2011), and *Girlhood* (*Bande de filles*, 2014) attend specifically to the slow burn (or awakening) of desire, body movement (through dance, violence, exercise), and anxiety of intimacy, all of which seek to amend different aspects of female or trans experience that have been previously depicted on screen. For these reasons, Beauvoir's phenomenology is particularly well suited to evaluating the ways in which Sciamma expresses various aspects of feminine becoming. Beauvoir's famous claim that '[o]ne is not born, rather one becomes, a woman' (1953: 267)[3] establishes her revolutionary position that woman is not a fixed or determined situation, but one that is constantly negotiated and disclosed through embodied experience involving power and behaviour. She begins the second part of *The Second Sex*, 'Lived Experience', by stating that women (in 1949) were beginning to overthrow 'the myth of femininity' (TSS 279), thereby suggesting that the experience of becoming woman begins with a close re-evaluation of her situation and the historical forces that have contrived to determine it. Beauvoir meticulously describes how specific myths are sustained through real experiences (of marriage, motherhood, etc.), scientific attitudes (such as classical psychoanalysis) and class position to disclose to her readers 'how woman is taught to assume her condition, how she experiences this, what universe she finds herself enclosed in, and what escape mechanisms are permitted her' (TSS 279). The intent is, of course, to raise awareness of the political and economic causalities regarding women's situation so their future lived emotional experiences might change and become more fulfilling, satisfying and free.

Beauvoir's foundational claim that sexual difference is not determined by innate biology, but rather by historical situation, was a paradigm shift in sexual theory. The idea profoundly influenced many thinkers, including Iris Marion Young (1980/2005), who emphasised that the many relationships girls and women have with their bodies are often distorted and very different when compared to those of boys and men. Young states that the idea of the lived body 'refuses the distinction between nature and culture that grounds a distinction between sex and gender', and that the living of the body involves an accumulation of cultural habits relative to 'comportment distinctive to interactional settings' (1980/2005: 17). While Young does not address the sexual being and its movements respective to the female body, her focus on women's corporeal orientations in everyday motility helps to define the ways in which 'situation' includes ambiguous experience. As such, situation contains 'orientation of the body as a whole toward things and its environment that initially defines the relation of a subject to its world' (1980/2005: 30).[4] For girls and women, such orientation is a paradox specific to patriarchy, 'as human she is a free subject who participates in transcendence, but her situation as a woman denies her that subjectivity and transcendence' (Young 1980/2005: 32). Female body movement and subjectivity is therefore out of alignment, disoriented, with the expectations embedded within gendered social scripts, what Young describes as a dissonance between an 'I can' and 'I cannot' body (1980/2005: 37). Through the 'I can/I cannot' binary, Young addresses the connections between 'any lived body' and an awareness of 'its own limits and frustrations' (1980/2005: 37) to analyse the gendered difference of feminine bodily experience. The ambiguity of 'I can' and 'I cannot', when introjected, signals an unconscious inhibition that impairs authority and agency over feminine embodied experience.[5] I comment on how Sciamma addresses this differently with respect to Mikäel/Laure's trans identity in *Tomboy* below.

A foundational element of Sciamma's filmmaking is the close attention she gives to girls' and women's body movement as a form of queer visibility, in that a queering of perspective takes place through reflexive looking and being seen.[6] With respect to Beauvoir's (and Young's) phenomenology, specifically their thoughts on women's embodied situation, Sciamma's films modify the supposed dissonance within female comportment and motility by portraying girls' movement in harmony with their intentions. She does this in each of her films through her characters' physical activity, such as competitive swimming, playing leisure games, dancing and fighting. The girls and women in Sciamma's films therefore display an 'uninhibited intentionality' similar to Young's concept (Young 1980/2005: 37) that links their psychical project with their physical motion. In Sciamma's films, rarely if ever do the girls' or women's projects fail in their physical movement. Rather their bodies are shown as being capable of realising their intentions through achieving their projects, thereby refuting Young's observation:

> [f]eminine motion often severs this mutually conditioning relation between aim and enactment. In those motions that when properly performed required the coordination and directedness of the whole body upon some definite end, women frequently move in a contradictory way. (1980/2005: 37)

In *The Ethics of Ambiguity*, Beauvoir argues that ethical action is dependent on recognising how situations emerge, that is, the role cultural behaviours and ideologies play in determining the context of the present. By being attentive to the past, we can make more informed (and for Beauvoir, more ethical) decisions in our future: 'To assert the reign of the human is to acknowledge [wo]man in the past as well in the future' (EA 99). Therefore, in order for the possibility of ethical action to emerge, there must first be an acceptance of the appeal from the past: '[the past] is an appeal toward the future which sometimes can save it only by destroying it' (EA 102). Her main claim is that before we can exercise ethical action, we must first recognise and respond to the politics of situation embedded in the appeal for freedom. This is crucial because without it we cannot identify the reasons behind the need for a change in behaviour or thought; we cannot alter the 'general pattern' of oppression (EA 95).

By positively showing girls and women as being successful in their physical movements, a success that is embodied as much as it is conceived, Sciamma's films propose the possibility that unity between body and subjectivity can be plural, queer and continuous. Put simply, her films acknowledge the past by breaking a general pattern of oppressive cinematic representation and countering previous ways in which girls' and women's bodies have been portrayed. As standalone texts, Sciamma's films exemplify a tactic of filmmaking in telling women's stories, a non-combative but very pointed illustration of how coordination, strength and physical capability does not rest on avoidance of ambiguous or emotionally turbulent experience. Instead, such experience is integrated into stories of girls and women willing their way to freedom. Let us look at some specific examples where this modification occurs, illuminating what can be regarded as a Beauvoirian practice of placing politics before ethics.

In *Water Lilies*,[7] Sciamma explores emerging adolescent female sexuality in a world that appears dissociated from adult concern or care. Set in Cergy, France,[8] *Water Lilies* revolves around the interconnected coming-of-age experience of three girls: Floriane (Adèle Haenel), Marie (Pauline Acquart) and Anne (Louise Blachère), all of whom are connected to the local community's synchronised swimming team in one form or another. Girls' body movement is a fulcrum for the film, with the camera observing the swim team in practice and competition and through close observation of the girls' movement in sexual scenes (minimal as they are). The sequences of synchronised swimming effectively convey the situational paradox of being separate yet connected, with the local community of a girls' swim team acting as a synecdoche for girls' bodies and sexualities in this period of life.

Floriane is the captain of the swim team, attractive and more physically mature than either Marie (who is petite) or Anne (who is older, larger and not athletic). Floriane's body movements in the water are assured and confident, juxtaposed against the (justified) anxiety she feels outside the pool, and particularly when subjected to the unseen sexual actions of men. When she is in command of her team and performing her sport, Floriane's movements are continuous, in unison and successful. Outside of her sport, Floriane encounters the persistent invasion of masculine desire in her phenomenal space. She confides in Marie the many hostile experiences she has experienced – her older swimming teacher massages her and tries to kiss her; the pool attendant exposes his erect penis to her under water while she trains alone; and her boyfriend pressures her to have sex with him. Even though Floriane describes such encounters in a nonchalant manner to Marie, there is a resigned and somewhat sad acceptance that such masculine oppressive behaviour is a reality to be endured. She tells Marie: 'That's life' and that Marie should feel lucky not to have had similar experiences.

Floriane, Marie and Anne exemplify Beauvoir's conception of adolescence as being a difficult, tumultuous and anxious stage, with respect to experiences of friendship, sexual awareness and their requisite moral responses. *Water Lilies* focuses on the girls' sharing of experience (between Floriane and Marie; Marie and Anne) but not with parents or any other authorial figure. As the film follows each girl's exploration of her sexuality in a hesitating, nervous and often non-verbal manner, it invites audiences to look at specifically girls' rather than general adolescent sexuality. Sciamma manages their anxiety, which is predominantly embodied, in a positive, non-judgemental way, making it an active propulsive component of the characters' story rather than a sensation to avoid or flee from. An example of this is the film's emphasis on the judgement Floriane experiences from her peers, who believe her to be promiscuous and sexually active with boys when she is not. Instead of staging a climactic confrontation against this accusation, Sciamma elects to leave it as a threatening aspect for Floriane. If the film were to try to clarify it or have Floriane correct this false belief, it would destroy the political comment being made – which is that girls' bodies are always under surveillance and that their sexual being in particular is used to define their value (or lack of) in the world. Instead, Floriane is left to negotiate this conflict for herself, particularly the threats within her heterosexual experiences against her gentle sexual encounter with Marie.

Adults are absent for much of the film, and as a result their authorial presence is weakened and usurped by the teenage girls' search for their selves in their own reality. While Marie is clearly in love with Floriane and might be conventionally categorised as lesbian, Sciamma (as is the case in all her films) does not force this classification. Instead, her focus is on the emergence of femme desire, the sexual awakening of erotic sensibility within girls that transcends the easy binary of gay/straight. The ambiguity of Floriane's sexuality in particular embodies the complex tensions that are awakened during adolescence, which Sciamma places alongside the assumption of sexual subjectivity. In this way, the rhizomatic links between sexual politics, moral decision and ethical behaviour are connected in the film through the girls' physical motility in their sexual being.

In *Tomboy*, Sciamma similarly addresses the ambiguous sexual coming-of-age experience and moral panic of trans identity through the character of Mikäel/Laure (Zoé Héran). Laure, 10 years old, introduces themself as Mikäel to a group of children in their new hometown. The film follows Laure's actions in becoming Mikäel, an intentional emphasis of Sciamma's: '*Tomboy* is not built around "why" she's doing things; it is all about "how" she's doing it' (Sciamma in Bendix 2011). As such, *Tomboy* continues Sciamma's positive and progressive attention on body movement, here looking at Mikäel/Laure's concrete lived experience of emergent adolescent sexuality *and* how they manage the ambiguity and open-ended sensibility it prompts. *Tomboy*, in many respects, counters Young's argument that girls' embodied experience is condemned as fractured or alienated by foregrounding certain steps Laure takes in physically becoming and being Mikäel.

Wanting to participate in a day of swimming with friends, Mikäel modifies a girl's one-piece red bathing suit (an echo of Floriane's and Marie's swimming costumes in *Water Lilies*) into a set of swimming trunks. Refusing to accept their body as object (and therefore any impediment to their capacity to play and be active), Mikäel forms a fake penis from play doh to use as a prosthetic in their swimming trunks so that they may pass as a boy when swimming with friends. In dominant cinematic narratives, we might expect a conflict to occur at the lake, such as the play doh being discovered, thereby revealing that Mikäel is anatomically female. Instead, Mikäel's actions are a great success, and they are able to swim, play and wrestle with friends (Figure 8.1). Mikäel experiences their body in an active and continuous way that realises their preferred subjectivity and corporeality as a unified way of inhabiting the world, and most significantly, this means the audience is invited to do so as well. What is often perceived as a narrative conflict (trans identity) is instead revised as an expression of empowered agency through innovative activity.

Figure 8.1 Mikäel (Zoé Héran) wins a wrestle with a friend in *Tomboy* (Sciamma 2011).

In an interview with Trish Bendix, Sciamma states that her aim was to foreground the complexity of ambiguity in Mikäel/Laure's character:

> I wanted to keep all the hypotheses open when I was building the character. Not to avoid the answers, but to make it more complex and accurate ... I made it with several layers, so that a transexual person can say 'that was my childhood' and so that an heterosexual woman can also say it. (Sciamma in Bendix 2011)

As with *Water Lilies*, for most of the film, adults are separate from the world of children, although in *Tomboy* they are the main characters who express fear over Mikäel/Laure's identity, particularly the mother (Sophie Cattani), who compels Mikäel to reveal themself as Laure to friend Lisa (Jeanne Disson). This act suggests fear of sexuality is learned[9] and we see such fear further performed through the group mentality of the other children who also force Lisa to confess that she found her kiss with Mikäel 'disgusting'. Unlike *Water Lilies*, however, *Tomboy* expresses an innocence in the emergence of adolescent sexuality and desire as a tender confidence by allowing it to find whichever expression it takes (Floriane, Marie and Anne express more obvious anxiety in their later adolescent sexual experiences). The anxieties which materialise stem from the adults who fail to accept Mikäel/Laure's sexual ambiguity and therefore impede Mikäel/Laure's freedom. The theme of willing one's self free is portrayed through Mikäel/Laure's character, with the message of the film being pointedly Beauvoirian: 'Only the freedom of others keeps each one of us from hardening in the absurdity of facticity' (EA 77). The queering of existence is also to be read as an issue of freedom, since being other for Beauvoir is first experienced through transcending social expectations and stories (such as the myth of femininity). This is what Beauvoir means when she says, 'no behavior is ever authorized to begin with, and one of the concrete consequences of existentialist ethics is the rejection of all the previous justifications which might be drawn from the civilization, the age, and the culture' (EA 153). Recognising the other as other before society has the chance to turn subject into object is part of the political appeal that past historical situations offer us.

Tomboy expresses Mikäel/Laure's trans lived experience and the different emotional realities it contains. Sciamma's film works as a concrete feminist phenomenological action because *Tomboy* manages to convey a significant and fundamental truth of trans identity at a personal and political level. The vehicle of a single film engages with the broader ambiguous politics of trans body movement, sexual identity, desire and freedom in such a way that the individual situation presents a truth that 'might be bearable' and is evidently 'more complex [as] the freedom of one man almost always concerns that of other individuals' (EA 155). If read as an example of Beauvoir's argument concerning existential ethics, *Tomboy* can be seen to call upon its audience to piece together the issues involved in Mikäel/Laure's embodied situation. Beauvoir makes it clear that for an ethics to come into being, we must first agree that each situation is different and requires different ethical decisions, and that each is historically relative and contingent on context. By treating each other 'as a freedom so that his end may be freedom' (EA 154), reciprocal recognition serves as a political action that responds to the situation of the subject (such as Mikäel's trans identity), specifically noting the historical reasons (prejudice) that have contrived to require new ethical decisions. And of course, at the centre of this is Young's notion of the 'I can' body – as a continuous, unified and active existence, not as object but as subject. The ambiguity of the 'I can/I cannot' binary is therefore not denied, rather the intentionality of the 'I cannot' body is kept separate, that is, external to Mikäel/Laure's inner world. Indeed Mikäel/Laure's actions show they do not simultaneously project an 'I can' and 'I cannot', only an 'I can' intentionality.

Sciamma continues her engaged exploration of 'the risky, reckless exuberance' (Scott 2015) of adolescent experience in terms of desire and voice in *Girlhood*, a story of French African teenager Marieme (Karidja Touré) who searches for her sense of self through sisterhood and community. In this film, Sciamma turns to the intersected situations of gender, race and class, although sexuality is also intermeshed with the evolution of Marieme's character as she becomes Vic (Vic is for victory – a nickname she receives from her friend Lady (Assa Sylla)). Becoming Vic is Marieme's way of finding power and assertiveness to make decisions that affect her situation. As with *Tomboy*, *Girlhood* offers a modification to Beauvoir's and Young's argument regarding female motility, comportment and spatiality.

The film opens with an upbeat electronic score as a line of footballers, medium shot, out of focus, run out on to a field ready to play. In these first moments, the players' gender initially appears ambiguous. As they begin the game, we see glimpses that disclose their female gender – eyeliner, short and long ponytails, and finally the players take off their helmets and we see that all players are girls in their later adolescence (Figure 8.2). The game ends with both teams celebrating and congratulating each other, foreshadowing a positive energy for the film and the importance the female bond will later hold for Marieme/Vic and her pursuit of freedom. Football is an emphatically more arduous sport than Young's more feminine examples of volleyball and softball, a clear contestation of the way in which women and sport are normally considered. Even though Young acknowledges that her observations about female motility are not applicable 'to all women all of the time', she maintains that they 'sensibly speak of a general feminine style of body comportment and movement' (1980/2005: 35). Sciamma's opening sequence shows women moving in powerful, strategic and coordinated ways, countering Young's view that for women in sport 'our movement is restricted in space', our bodies seen as a 'fragile encumbrance, rather than the medium for the enactment of our aims' (1980/2005: 34). My intention here is not to discount or disprove Young, especially as her work on the phenomenology of feminine movement has disclosed the very hidden and embedded consequences

Figure 8.2 Footballers in *Girlhood* (Sciamma 2014); an example of female motility, comportment and spatiality in unison, continuous.

of oppression in girls' and women's bodies in everyday life. Rather, the point is to show how Young's observation of the contradictory correlation between what women can do and what they think they are physically capable of doing is altered through the project of Sciamma's filmmaking. I agree with Young (and Beauvoir) that as long as a woman or girl thinks of herself as a thing (or is thought of as a thing by others),[10] not only is her freedom existentially limited but so is her body movement. In Sciamma's films, girls and women, if they ever do think of themselves as objects, overcome this through their physical motility, comportment, and how they take command of their spatiality.

Throughout *Girlhood*, movement is vital to Vic's capacity to pursue her freedom and change her situation. Her habits of comportment are different to those of Young's girl, who learns to 'hamper her movements' (1980/2005: 43). For example, dancing is a physical movement that *Girlhood* uses in multiple ways to revise the assumptive modalities of feminine existence as reflective of timidity, fragility and uncertainty. Firstly, as a mirroring activity to begin a female bond, Marieme (not yet Vic) mirrors Lady's dancing on the train home from Paris. Secondly, dance functions as an embodiment of a concretised bond. At the point in the film where Marieme becomes Vic, her membership in the girl gang is solidified and celebrated through dancing with her friends to Rihanna's song 'Diamonds' in a hotel room. Thirdly, dance is witnessed as an expression of social and community bonding when the girl group participates in a friendly street dance competition in an urban district of Paris. And lastly, dance is presented as a rejection of possession – Vic slow dances with Monica (Dielika Coulibaly) at crime boss Abou's (Djibril Gueye) party. An ambiguous intimacy arises between them, as they recognise each other as an autonomous sexual being for themselves if nothing else. Vic and Monica's dance movement is juxtaposed against the swift intrusion of Abou, whose own dance movements are threatening, possessive and objectifying. He demands Vic dance with him, kiss him: 'When I tell you to kiss me, you do it!', asserting his masculinity and role as her boss. Despite the threat in Abou's menace, Vic slaps him defiantly and leaves.

We can compare this freedom expressed in Marieme/Vic's dancing with Lucia's theatre of performance and domination in *The Night Porter*, discussed in Chapter 2. Cavani's film uses Lucia's dance to counter the tension and negative reality of masculine privilege in her situation, whereas Sciamma's use of dance is a more positive expression of resilience and fleeing from bad faith as a forward movement to ethical freedom. This occurs not only in *Girlhood*, but also in *Water Lilies* (as synchronised swimming) and to a certain extent in *Portrait*, when women gather and sing around a fire. Each film navigates the imbalance of power, asking the spectator to take up a critical distance and move to new possibilities resistant to patriarchal systems that seek to manage women's bodies. In the case of Sciamma's films, dance is used to not simply denote resistance but also indicate successful outcomes. Vic finds a future for herself because she is able to break free from a past dictated by Abou's control, whereas Lucia is condemned to her past because she can't escape Max's domination.

Young asks if her interpretation of the phenomenology of everyday feminine movement is applicable to physical activity such as dance or 'movement that is sex-typed' (2005: 45). What is missing from her essay are the issues of race and class, and in order to comprehensively address her question, feminist phenomenologies must include these intermeshed identity politics in their critical description, given their role in forming the natural attitude.[11] Vic's final movement in the film is to reject the lure of bad faith that offers marriage and family as her future. After electing not to return to the family home, she cries before finding her resilience and walking from screen right to left. The hesitation she exhibits in these final moments of the film echoes the disruption of habitual cinematic viewing discussed in Chapter 4 with regard to Cheryl Dunye's films. The film ends with Vic acknowledging that she cannot will herself free if she chooses to stay in situations that attenuate her movement (her efforts to masculinise her appearance and behaviour are a manifestation of this).

Within each of these films discussed, and in addition to Sciamma's more positive, albeit ambiguous, description of female motility, comportment and spatiality, there is the exercising of a reciprocal gaze. In her essay accompanying the *Portrait of a Lady on Fire* DVD, critic Ela Bittencourt writes of an 'intense looking' that is a trademark of Sciamma's films, as an expression of femme desire that is markedly different to the lens of 'conquest and possession' present in the patriarchal gaze. In the following section I continue by exploring aspects of Beauvoir's philosophy of ambiguity as it relates to women's freedom with regard to *Portrait*. I end with a discussion of Bergoffen's concept of erotic generosity as an illumination of the reciprocal gaze in *Portrait* that prioritises literal and emotional consent as an expression of ethical action.

Portrait of a Lady on Fire

For Beauvoir, marriage is 'a rotten institution', (1998: 128) a social act that dethrones women 'by the advent of private property ... her history is intertwined with the history of inheritance' (TSS 90). Beauvoir's dismal view of marriage is based on her recognition of its limitations of freedoms for both parties (unquestioningly more severe for women), and of the continuance of arranged marriages in France in 1949 (TSS 445). She acknowledges that marriage, as an institution 'perverted at its base' (TSS 521), is changing as women are able to hold jobs and share housework, but notes that while 'the man has economic responsibility for the couple, it [women's independence] is just an illusion' (TSS 521). Even today Beauvoir's observations hold and in the example of *Portrait*, Sciamma uses the historical idea of marriage to gently question its validity for audiences of the twenty-first century. The institution of marriage and the behaviours that surround and support it, including the use of women's image as an advertisement of her value, is brought under examination, questioning marriage's capacity to give women meaning and direction in their lives. Therefore, rather than look to *Portrait* as being a film only about lesbian desire, it is more fruitful to recognise its comment about the awakening of desire and eroticism within women more broadly, and the possibility of women exploring it for themselves outside of prescriptive and freedom-limiting (unethical) institutions and situations.

With *Portrait*, Sciamma moves on from the moral contingency of teenagehood and shifts her focus to the ambiguous situation of women's adulthood, specifically that of marriageable age in the eighteenth century.[12] *Portrait of a Lady on Fire* explores the erotic and romantic relationship that slowly grows between painter Marianne (Noémie Merlant) and wealthy noble Héloïse (Adèle Haenel). Set in eighteenth-century France on the northern Brittany coast, the film explores the intermeshed experience of femme desire, body and freedom in a specific historical setting, evoking reflection on the relationship between past and present in terms of the politics of women's freedom. The film's story is told by Marianne as a recollection to her art students; she narrates her relationship with Héloïse, beginning with the invitation to come and paint Héloïse's portrait. Marianne's task is to covertly observe Héloïse and secretly paint her portrait so that it can be sent to a Milanese aristocrat, confirming her arranged marriage. Marianne is the second painter to be asked to complete the portrait, as Héloïse, angry at the loss of her freedom and chosen life as a Benedictine nun, has already refused to sit for portraiture. On the surface, her anger is directed at the expectation and inevitability of the marriage and also at the death of her sister, the original betrothed who committed suicide to avoid it. However, a more Beauvoirian interpretation of Héloïse's antagonism is her lack of emotional consent regarding the politics of the situation.

As the film pays close attention to Héloïse's emotional countenance, via Marianne's observation of Héloïse and also Héloïse's own embodied feelings (Marianne finds it hard to paint her face because she has not seen her smile), the lived experience of the women in the film is not only understood perceptually but sensually, erotically. This emphasis is one way in which *Portrait* exemplifies 'the erotic as a philosophical category' (Bergoffen 1997), and it is also where we see Beauvoir's philosophy clearly influenced by Merleau-Ponty.[13] Flesh, in the Merleau-Pontyan context, refers to how we encounter the world, what we share with others:

> It is the coiling over of the visible upon seeing the body, of the tangible upon the touching body ... We must not think the flesh starting from substances, from body and spirit – for then it would be the union of contradictories – but we must think it, as we said, as an element, as the concrete emblem of a general manner of being. (1968: 146–7)

Flesh then, structures situation and the body is the lived experience, the becoming of relations with others.

Bergoffen states: 'Where Husserl, Sartre, and Merleau-Ponty save us from Cartesian dualism and solipsism by appealing to the experiences of perceiving subjects, Beauvoir saves us by appealing to the possibilities of the erotic subject' (1997: 13). She explains that Beauvoir's philosophy adapted the classical phenomenological arguments of Husserl and Hegel alongside 'Sartre's moral concerns without ignoring Merleau-Ponty's insights regarding ambiguity, the flesh and the erotic' (1997: 28), the result being that Beauvoir's existential ethics evolved to integrate embodied sexual desire and situated existence to examine women's lived experience. Gender therefore becomes a critical element of Beauvoir's philosophy of embodiment, its political aspects determined by historically sustained systems of patriarchy which are more felt than seen. In *The Second Sex*, gender is the foundational concept that Beauvoir uses to discuss the difference between women's lived (fleshed) and represented experience, where the ambiguity of her embodiment is used to identify erotic experience that ultimately disrupts the power and privilege of patriarchal systems.

Beauvoir's *The Second Sex* develops her existentialist ethics by claiming that our recognition of the other is more sensuous than perceptual, that is, sexuality is always already embedded within our perception. The consequence of this is that erotic experience is politically charged, ontologically and existentially. For women, their embodied sexual desire and fleshed ambiguity, simply by existing, are destabilising threats to patriarchy, which is why patriarchy works so hard to devalue, oppress and marginalise women's subjectivity and bodies. This is part of Beauvoir's concluding statement in *The Second Sex*, where she reminds her readers how myths of femininity have 'stifled' women's possibilities (TSS 751) and that:

> certain differences between man and woman will always exist; her eroticism, and thus her sexual world, possessing a singular form, cannot fail to engender in her a sexuality, a singular sensitivity: her relation to her body, to the male body, and to the child will never be the same as those man has with his body, with the female body, and with the child; those who talk so much about 'equality in difference' would be hard put not to grant me that there are differences in equality. (TSS 765)

We can trace a similar perspective in Sciamma's *Portrait* if we regard Marianne's action of painting Héloïse, and the representation of Sophie's (Luàna Bajrami) abortion, as a retrieval of the erotic dimensions of women's bodies. Put another way, *Portrait* focuses on women's experience not often screened; lesbian sexual desire between two women in the eighteenth century, and a woman wanting an abortion precisely because she doesn't want children at a specific moment in her life. This attention is a cinematic example of Bergoffen's concept of erotic generosity because it intentionally seeks to disclose experience that is otherwise ignored. As such it is cinema that proposes 'an ethic that warrants our attention' (Bergoffen 1997: 2). Audiences are asked to reflect on the difference between 1) lived bodies, via the erotic relationship between Marianne and Héloïse, and the sorority between Marianne, Héloïse and Sophie; and 2) represented bodies via the roles the women portray and occupy in the film – wife, daughter, maid.

By stressing the emotionality of women in the film, *Portrait* takes up a very subtle but highly significant Beauvoirian position, which claims that perception, as the principal means by which we become enworlded, is secondary to sensuous recognition. Further, the ethical implications are also different, with the former indicative of possession and the latter of ambiguity and freedom. Marianne and Héloïse's lesbian love is an expression of the fleshed ambiguity of women's bodies and a resistance to the possessive patriarchal attitudes over women and their bodies. It is specifically their lesbian eroticism that resituates their position and invites audiences to reflect on its political significance for the women's freedom. The historical period in which Sciamma chooses to situate *Portrait* is important. Beauvoir writes that European women's independence in the eighteenth century grew, although their futures were limited to the convent or the home. Yet, as the upper middle class lost its secure position in society, 'neither convent nor conjugal home can contain the woman ... [women] limit themselves to the pursuit of pleasure' (TSS 120). Even though European women's (that is, White) social activities increased in artistic and scientific experimentation, women remained economically dependent on men (and therefore marriage).

Sciamma's choice to employ a period genre, then, is an effective staging of ambiguity regarding women's desire. Given the lack of economic freedom (and slowly expanding social conditions) associated with women's situation in eighteenth-century France, we are lured into recognising how marriage curtailed women's freedom in the service of greater familial fortune then, rather than now, in our more global, developed and 'progressive' era. Héloïse's refusal of the marriage is primarily, and most significantly, an emotional one – the question of her willingness to acquiesce to the situation is moot, as whether or not the marriage goes ahead is dependent on the Milanese man's approval of her portrait. This is indeed the obvious purpose of Héloïse's marriage, to secure the longevity of her family's social situation as well as her mother's return to Italy. Marriage is therefore portrayed as an institution that seeks to legitimise the existence of patriarchy, carrying the illusion that women find reason, purpose and adventure through it. However, like the men in *Portrait*, this point is known but unseen (both her mother the Countess and Marianne say they 'know' Héloïse's anger, even though Héloïse rarely shows it), despite the tension it creates for the women in the film.[14] Sciamma's realism makes the political point simply and clearly: within a society that privileges men, marriage (if chosen) is a bondage, a possession. The matter-of-fact way in which Sciamma treats this situation through period genre allows her to foreground the emotional tensions that result from it and to indicate the ways in which the ambiguities of women's situation, so evident in the past, continue in our present.

Marianne and Héloïse first discuss the topic of marriage on the beach. The scene is shot in medium close-up via static frame (Figure 8.3). Each woman is positioned similarly, suggesting an equality between them. Héloïse asks Marianne what she knows of her impending marriage and expresses her own anxiety at knowing very little about the Milanese man she is betrothed to. Marianne explains that she is unsure if she will marry, that her future will be to take over her father's portraiture business. Héloïse accuses Marianne of not being able to understand her situation because she is able to choose her own fate. Marianne, because of her possible economic independence, can face her ambiguity and recognise the bad faith of marriage and even Héloïse's other option, the convent. Héloïse's only choices are to maintain the bad faith of man (or god) as absolute subject or of woman (or nun) as essential object.

Figure 8.3 Marianne (Noémie Merlant) and Héloïse (Adèle Haenel) discuss the inequality of marriage on the beach in *Portrait of a Lady on Fire* (Sciamma 2019).

Later in the film, the women return to the topic of marriage when discussing music. Héloïse longs to be moved by music and it is evident that it transforms her while she hears it. Learning of Héloïse's love of music, Marianne plays a little of Vivaldi's *Four Seasons* (poorly) for her on a harpsichord. She tries to comfort Héloïse (per the Countess's instructions), telling her that Milan will be a city of music. Héloïse remains unconvinced, replying, 'You're saying that, now and then, I'll be consoled', proving that she is very aware that her emotional anger is a direct correlation to the patriarchal restrictions that limit her.

In *The Ethics of Ambiguity*, Beauvoir links a capacity to confront ambiguous existence with the historical and social contexts of how we experience ourselves in the world – which in terms of the specific example of *Portrait of a Lady on Fire* refers to how contemporary audiences experience female desire, abortion, class and the institutions of marriage and family today. Additionally, she associates the sensibility of ambiguity with the political consequence of history and situation, concentrating on the ethical relations with others as a criterion for willing one's self free. Eva Gothlin has argued that while Beauvoir's use of ambiguity as a term appears less frequently in *The Second Sex*, as a concept it evolved from its focus on ethics in *The Ethics of Ambiguity* into one 'related to the female body and desire' (2006: 133). Sciamma's choice, then, in employing the period genre can be read as political given that it critically discloses 'romantic' institutions (such as marriage, but also family) and their impediments to women's freedom, particularly in the ways it portrays embodiments of female desire and choice, revising previous artistic expressions and inventing 'new images, new narratives' (Sciamma in VanDerWerff, 2020). The significance of Beauvoir's philosophy is seen through its identification of patriarchy's bad faith institutions that impede people's freedom; women are seen as embodying ambiguity more so than men. If such ambiguity is not recognised as a way to discover possibility within existence, the imperialism of the patriarchal gaze is assured.

Beauvoir writes of the heterosexual woman: 'in salons where she tries to attract the gaze of others, she does not separate man's desire from the love of her own self' (TSS 350), and of the lesbian: 'she recognizes herself in her acts, not in her immanent presence: male desire reducing her to the limits of her body shocks her as much as it shocks a young boy' (TSS 423). Here the patriarchal gaze is equivalent to an emotional possession that is a violent and limiting mechanic of desire because it is an obstacle for reciprocal recognition. Beauvoir's idea of ambiguity alerts us to options, specifically the possibility of escaping paternalistic and determinist paths (marriage, family); and registers the appeal of feminine desire, which Beauvoir sees as belonging to the experience of becoming a woman who comes to recognise her own desires (TSS 397). Recognising ambiguity, for the women characters in the film as well as the audience, is one way that we make space for the emotional turbulence it produces – recognition creates relation and therefore situation, and enables a revision of the social myths we draw on to articulate our existence.

Portrait of a Lady on Fire and *The Piano*: A Comparison

Jane Campion has also used the period genre to disclose the oppressive mechanisms of arranged marriage for women, questioning history as situation and establishing ambiguity as a condition of embodied feminine desire. In *The Piano* (1993), set in the mid-nineteenth century, Ada McGrath (Holly Hunter) is sold by her father into marriage with a man, Alisdair Stewart (Sam Neill), whom she has not yet met. Campion's film begins with a musical score and an extreme close-up of a woman's fingers, blurry, which cuts to an in-focus extreme close-up of Ada's face, covered with her hands.[15] Through Ada's voiceover, laid over the first few shots of the opening sequence, we learn that it is her perspective that opens the film. Similarly, Sciamma's *Portrait* begins with a number of different women's hands beginning their charcoal drawings on white canvas. There is no score or voiceover that accompanies these first few opening images; instead, we initially hear the sketching sound from the charcoal strokes on paper before Marianne's voice says: 'First, my contours. The outline. Not too fast. Take time to look at me.' Both films link the female voice to its body, immediately indicating that each character's experience and memory is lived through her body, not separate from it. Here the respective characters of Ada and Marianne establish their recounting of experience as corporeal rather than simply mnemonic. This emphasis on their fleshed subjectivity is also a recognition of our interdependence on each other; as Ada looks out between her fingers, so we look with her; as Marianne's students are instructed to slowly observe and sketch her contours, so we are instructed to observe her body movement as indicative of her situation and being-in-the-world.

The significant parallels between Sciamma's *Portrait* and Campion's *The Piano* are formal as well as thematic. Formally, both are period features that concentrate on a woman's arranged marriage to a man in another country; each follows the woman's reticence regarding the marriage and the tribulations that inevitably result from it. There is also a shared attention on the control and coercion of the patriarchal gaze, although where this is suggested and alluded to in Sciamma's film, it is more forcefully foregrounded in Campion's, with literal and physical violent consequences. Both women filmmakers evoke history as situation to demonstrate the impediment to freedom caused by a legacy of myth. In Sciamma's case, she uses a critical discussion of the myth of Orpheus and Eurydice to underwrite and affirm the necessity of a reciprocal gaze in cinematic and narrative space; whereas Campion exposes the very real consequences of denying the patriarchal gaze its myth of dominion and control (Alisdair, destroyed by his envy, cuts off Ada's finger after discovering her affair with Banes (Harvey Keitel)).

Both films, however, centre their stories on the importance of women's experience and the existential cost of the marriage myth, identifying the ambiguity of existence as an expression of dependence on others – a particularly Beauvoirian position. From *The Ethics of Ambiguity* to *The Second Sex* and beyond, Beauvoir's notion of ambiguity is welded to the female body, its movement and its desires in order to argue an ethical freedom. Sciamma and Campion locate authenticity and freedom within the action of creative production (understandably, given their own situation as film directors). For Marianne it is through painting; for Héloïse it is through music; for Sophie it is through needlework; and for Ada it is through playing piano. The creative act encapsulates a cornerstone principle within Beauvoir's philosophy of ambiguity, that as humans, we are both subject and object, separate and connected: 'each one depends on others, and what happens to me by means of others depends upon me as regards its meaning' (EA 88). Without intersubjectivity, the creative act, as action and as outcome, is not realised. Its contingency on being seen (painting), being heard (music) and being played (instrument) in order to generate affect and emotion within the aesthetic experience is dependent on being with others and being recognised by others.

Although each film conjures a strong sensibility of ambiguity in the women's respective situations, Sciamma's film can be said to convey the more positive message, one that avoids the issue of possession in erotic desire. *Portrait*'s offer of a more pluralistic and expansive statement of ambiguity than *The Piano* is seen in the sequence where Marianne travels to Héloïse's estate. Her journey by boat is rocky, but there is no indication via audio, lighting or other aesthetic that Marianne is in any way troubled. The camera pans to the wooden container of canvases that falls overboard and to the inaction of the men on the boat. Marianne quickly takes off her coat and jumps into the water, swimming to the wooden box and securing it. Compared with Ada's self-destructive, quasi-suicidal plunge in *The Piano*, Marianne's attachment to her artistry and creative production literally and metaphorically keeps her afloat.

The use of the period genre for both filmmakers functions as a Beauvoirian appeal, in that the historical revisions presented by each film call upon its audiences to link the (supposed) differences in women's situation from the past to the present. As each film is a negotiation of the past, it invites spectators to confront its ambiguity, specifically women's ambiguity (and the tensions it includes) so that reflection might yield ethical action. The oppressive politics of Ada and Héloïse's respective situations are mostly focused on the coercion of marriage, with each film negotiating the purpose and politics of marriage in the different contexts of its representation. Audience negotiation of the historical situation of marriage in the eighteenth century and mid-nineteenth century occurs in the contemporary context of the twenty-first and twentieth centuries respectively, therefore petitioning its audiences for a reflexive and responsible response. Beauvoir insists that the significance of the past is to alert us to its oppressions so that we may not sustain them. By depicting the denial of consent to which both women are subject with regard to their marriage, both Sciamma and Campion emphasise the interrelationship between women's consent, both emotional and literal, and their ethical freedom. The period genre, as used here, is a political appeal disclosing the social and temporal limitations of marriage throughout history, pressing comparison with today's situation.

Sciamma explains that her intention behind making *Portrait* was to show the cyclical nature of awareness concerning women's creativity, that it is contingent on visibility and not a continual myth of progress.[16] She says:

> [*Portrait of a Lady on Fire*] talks about how women are erased from art history because at this particular moment, the second half of the eighteenth century, there were hundreds of women painters. We are always told that with women's rights and opportunities for women there's been constant progress, and it isn't true. It works in cycles. (Sciamma in Aguilar 2020)

Sciamma creates an ethical dialogue between the oppressive situation of women's past (in terms of sexuality and marriage) and uses the period genre in a precisely political way to solicit an ethical response. In this respect, her filmmaking is also an example of Beauvoir's rejection of the aesthetic attitude, given that Sciamma seeks to interweave subjective historical standpoints (of the audience) with her characters' erotic experience. Marianne and Héloïse's lesbian love is a pointed rejection of the myths about women, not just in art history but also in patriarchal institutions such as marriage and motherhood.

The Reciprocal Gaze

After learning that Marianne has been asked to paint her portrait, Héloïse inspects the completed painting and rejects it, saying it has no presence or life to it. She asks Marianne if the image reflects how she sees her, discreetly questioning the veracity of the eroticism that has been growing between them. Marianne replies explaining that she has used 'the rules, conventions, ideas' of portraiture to direct the mechanics of the work, but even as she says this it becomes evident she is disturbed by Héloïse's insightful criticism. Marianne has not captured the truth of Héloïse's subjectivity, there is no reciprocal recognition of their bond in the painting. Instead, what Héloïse rightly observes is the invocation of an imperialist patriarchal gaze rendering her as object. What she had expected, and what Marianne does indeed end up creating, is a portrait that expresses an eroticism as 'a movement toward the *Other*' (TSS 467).

Sciamma's *Portrait* crafts a theme as well as a reflective aesthetic experience of the gaze. She describes the film as a 'manifesto to the female gaze' (Sciamma in VanDerWerff 2020), constructing a 'grammar that develops within the film' (Sciamma in Garcia 2019: 11), where the question of possession is considered against an embodied and erotic experience within the context of the appeal in femme desire. Marianne, upset at Héloïse's emotional refusal of her artwork, erases her painted face. This act wins back Héloïse's favour and emotional consent to sit for the portrait. It marks a moment in the film that moves closer to collective experience between women, where emotional consent and reciprocal recognition is present.

In the following discussion of the reciprocal gaze, I do not review classical psychoanalytic film theory's consideration of the gaze, which has been examined *ad infinitum*.[17] I am more interested in the ethical experience involved with looking at cinema and within its story worlds, as well as the consequences this might have for thinking about women's stories and their freedoms. Bergoffen, referencing a Lacanian perspective, links the '*méconnaissance* of the body' with 'its objectification under the gaze' and argues that the 'embodied subject must transcend these alienations' (1997: 158). Similarly, Ince says '[a] feminist phenomenological enquiry into film must start from and focus on screen women as embodied subjects of their own experience and desire' (2017: 42). And as Audre Lorde puts it: '[the erotic] is a resource within each of us that lies in a deeply female and spiritual plane, firmly rooted in the power of our unexpressed or unrecognized feelings' (2007: 53). Therefore, the idea of the reciprocal gaze is firmly located here within the context of femme erotic experience as embodied and emotional, not as an imperialist or possessive act.

It is not just lesbian desire that exemplifies the reciprocal gaze in *Portrait*. It is also present in the sequences that follow Sophie's efforts at aborting her unwanted pregnancy. Sciamma repeats that '[t]he female gaze is mostly about sharing the experience of the character and having a very active gaze' (Sciamma in Garcia 2019: 11), what might otherwise be expressed as underscoring the ambiguity of women's condition. Sophie's own attempts at abortion are humorous – she runs up and down the beach; drinks a foul-tasting herbal tea; and suspends herself from the ceiling. Not only has abortion rarely been treated positively in cinematic stories, but it is also almost always never funny, calm or uncomplicated. The fearlessness (and therefore effective humour) of such scenes in *Portrait* is the acknowledgement that women's desire and experience of childbearing has been ambiguous throughout history, and that this is a shared embodied knowing between women.

Sophie is not condemned for seeking the abortion. Her reason that she does not want children at this precise moment in her life is accepted and actively supported by Héloïse and Marianne. Perhaps even more than the lesbian love affair, the abortion demonstrates the women's authority over their own bodies, subjectivities and desires. The capacity to make and execute decisions about one's own body and to have this filmed by women filmmakers is innovation within cinematic form. Sciamma's films show the benefit of involving women in creative production, where the authenticity of women's experience, of lesbian love, can lead to complex and ethical art. After all of Sophie's efforts have failed to work, she visits a woman abortionist to undergo the procedure. The scene is tenderly shot in low, warm light, attentive to Sophie's paradoxical emotions, where the physical pain of the abortion is not denied, rather it is placed alongside Sophie's desire for future children (Figure 8.4). Héloïse instructs Marianne to watch the abortion, a reminder that this experience is not to be denied or hidden from view, rather to look is to honour Sophie's experience.

This respect is repeated later that evening, when Héloïse reconstructs the earlier events of the day (Figure 8.5). As with the previous scenes of playing cards, cooking dinner and reading out the Orpheus and Eurydice myth, Marianne's sketch of Sophie's abortion experience illustrates the necessity of ambiguity in facilitating the other's freedom. The three women involved in the making of this portrait, Marianne as painter, Héloïse as actor and director, and Sophie as actor, demonstrate how an emphasis on women's erotic experience equates freedom with command over one's body. This is not a painting that stands in for objectification like Héloïse's betrothal portrait; it is an image of erotic generosity that respects an intimate, carnal and deeply ambiguous female experience. It is an erotic representation of women's flesh but entirely outside any imperialist or possessive gaze.

Figure 8.4 An expression of ambiguity during Sophie's (Luàna Bajrami) abortion.

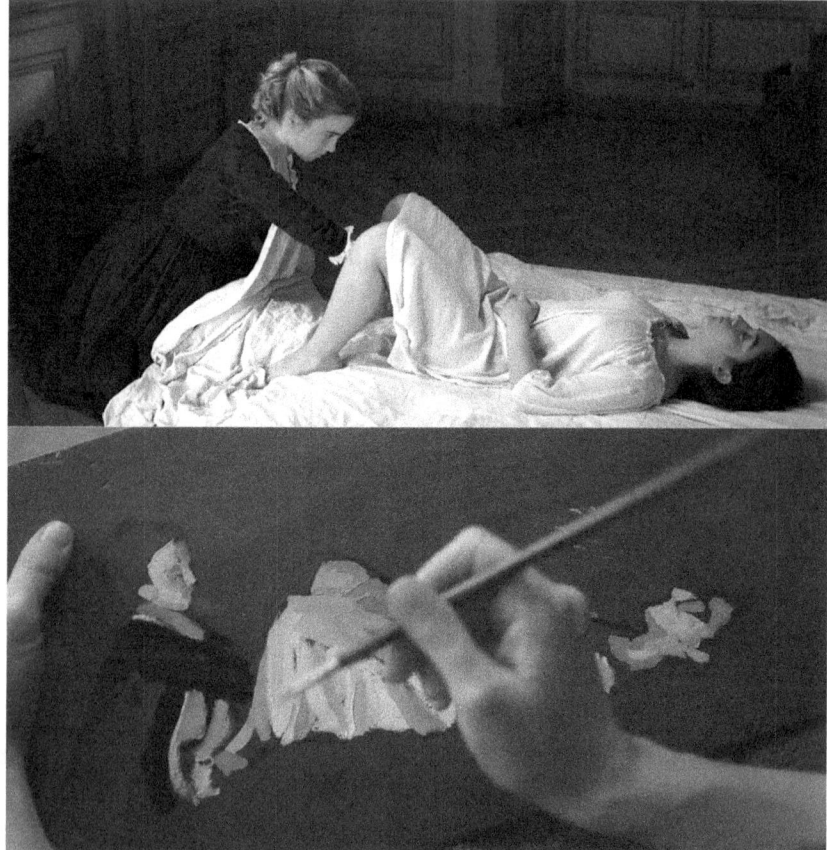

Figure 8.5 Héloïse reconstructs Sophie's abortion so that Marianne can document it via painting.

Beauvoir argues that erotic experience affords the possibility of revealing our ambiguous condition to ourselves (TSS 416). Through reciprocal recognition, as exemplified in Sciamma's filmmaking, the paradox and tensions of ambiguous existence are integrated into embodied, erotic experience so that more ethical and free living might occur. Beauvoir's philosophy of ambiguity begins as a general comment on the human condition but as the concept evolves over the course of her later writing, ambiguity becomes more specific and attuned to erotic, fleshed, and gendered lived experience. Applying Beauvoir's philosophy of ambiguity as a frame of interpretation regarding Sciamma's films discloses the ways in which women's filmmaking exemplifies ethical aesthetic experience. Additionally, it discloses the political and moral importance of authentic storytelling involving erotic, carnal and reciprocally recognised human beings. Indeed, this is the ethical action of Sciamma's filmmaking, locating an erotic generosity in the bond between women that expands beyond sexuality and includes emotional warmth and turbulence in embodied lived experience that embraces rather than negates the difference of otherness.

Notes

1 See Chapter 5 where I introduce Debra Bergoffen's concept of erotic generosity with regard to Claire Denis's *Let the Sunshine In*.
2 Céline Sciamma's fourth feature, *Portrait of a Lady on Fire* (*Portrait de la jeune fille en feu*, 2019) cements her position as a breakout innovative filmmaker whom critics have referred to as 'a blazing master' (Carlos Aguilar, Roger Ebert, February 2020) combining 'the erotic together with the cerebral' (Peter Bradshaw, *The Guardian*, May 2019), reflecting a 'thrillingly versatile' (Mark Kermode, *The Guardian*, March 2020) style of filmmaking that leads by example (Raphael Abraham, *Financial Times*, 2020). There is no debate that Sciamma's films have been positively recognised by both industry (mainly outside France) and popular audience, and yet the artistic revisions behind her deserved critical reception perhaps hold the greatest political comment.
3 In the 2010 translation, this is rendered as 'One is not born, but rather becomes, woman' (TSS 283).
4 This is derivative of Merleau-Ponty's *Phenomenology of Perception* (2002), but it is also a view Beauvoir expresses in *The Ethics of Ambiguity* (equally influenced by his ideas, linking situation to actions of politics and ethical decision), '[the body] expresses our relationship to the world, and that is why it is an object of sympathy or repulsion' (EA 44).
5 See Chapter 2, where I address this sense of embodied ambiguity with respect to Lucia's dance sequence in *The Night Porter*.
6 This is very much a paraphrase of Sara Ahmed's point that '[t]o queer phenomenology is also to offer a queer phenomenology' (2007: 4). While queer can be taken to refer to non-dominant expressions of sexuality, its meaning here is intentionally ambiguous, inclusive of LGBTQI identity and a different way of perceiving and sensuously experiencing. For example, Sciamma's double portrayal of abortion (which I discuss later in the chapter) is a form of reorientation that Ahmed's concept of queer phenomenology helps to describe as something that might take us by surprise, allowing us to think it differently because it reorients our awareness of it as a lived experience. In witnessing Sophie's experiencing of abortion in the film and its later staging (so that Marianne can paint it), *Portrait* reorients the strongly embedded orientation of woman's body as bearer of children as being wedded to the desire to want to bear them.
7 See Tim Palmer (2011: 225–6 fn 38) who discusses the translation of Sciamma's title. *Naissance des pieuvres* directly translates as *Birth of Octopuses*

and is a metaphor used to refer to the growing awareness of multiple, conflicting emotions and their tensions inside of oneself. As Palmer notes, for non-French speaking audiences this implication is likely to go unnoticed, yet I think the English translation 'Water Lilies' does evoke the long fleshy rhizomes as root structures which hold nutrients for their blooms, like the adolescent girls' legs in their synchronised swimming. The metaphor, while different from octopuses' legs, still holds as connotation of adaptation to environment, development of conflicting emotions and the sense of entanglement hidden from view.

8 Cergy is Céline Sciamma's hometown, another example of Anzaldúa's *autohistoria* in women's creative work (which I discussed with regard to Martel's film *Zama* in Chapter 6).

9 For a general discussion on the relationship between shame and sexuality see Phil Mollon (2008). For a more focused discussion on the experience of shame, gay identity and global culture, see Sally Munt (2019), and on shame/pride dichotomies see Munt (2000). For a more literary focus on shame and transgender sexuality, see Simona Giordano (2018).

10 The phenomenology of 'thingness' is too complicated to explore here, but in terms of what Beauvoir and Young are describing – the internalised thingness of the feminine – there is also the 'enforced', hegemonic thingness of the feminine within patriarchy. This is important as a distinction, because within this context of physicality, boys and men are also made a 'thing', and see themselves as 'things', but the processes through which this happens are different and work differently, operating with different consequences.

11 See Frances Smith (2020) for a more in-depth discussion of race in *Girlhood*.

12 Sciamma has noted that Marianne and Héloïse are around 30 years old (interview with Carlos Aguilar, February 2020).

13 For a far more sustained discussion of Merleau-Ponty's phenomenology and its relevance for cinematic experience, see Barker (2009) and Walton (2016).

14 The audience is never shown the marriage, although we do see Héloïse trying on her white wedding dress, and as an apparition that appears three times to Marianne over the course of the film.

15 See Sobchack (2004: 61–6) who also discusses this opening of Campion's film from a phenomenological perspective, highlighting corporeality and sensoria in the film experience.

16 See Claire Hemmings's (2005) 'Telling Feminist Stories' on the issues involved with the Western narrative of 'progress' regarding feminism.

17 Further study on more contemporary models of psychoanalysis (from object relations psychoanalysts such as Bion) may be of interest and challenge ocular-centrist positions. However, this is not a focus of this book.

Conclusion: Make Your Choice – Ambiguity Beyond Beauvoir

In *Hipparchia's Choice*, Michèle Le Doeuff interrogates the relationship that exists between women and philosophy, accentuating the political significance of Hipparchia's transformative decision. Hipparchia of Maroneia (c. 350–280 BCE) was a Greek philosopher, and the audacity of her choice was to determine how she spent her time for her own benefit. Instead of wasting it at the loom, she chose to seek knowledge and realise her epistemophilia. Using Hipparchia's choice as exemplar, Le Doeuff queries the potential and possibility for a feminist philosophy or 'a philosophy which will allow men and women to come together in a common task' (2007: xii). She asks how feasible, diverse or successful can such a philosophy be if its foundations are built upon epistemic prejudice? Perhaps unsurprisingly, Le Doeuff singles out existentialism, specifically via an in-depth consideration of Simone de Beauvoir's work and the way in which it subtly transformed the existentialist project: '[Beauvoir] explicitly approaches her investigation from the perspective of existentialist morality' (Le Doeuff 2007: 89). While cinema is not a consideration within *Hipparchia's Choice*, Le Doeuff's argument about the invocations that exist between women and philosophy, in light of Beauvoir's thought, have propelled the unspoken thrust of *Ambiguous Cinema*.

At the start of the book, I stated that I would not situate Beauvoir's philosophy of ambiguity within the parameters of Sartre's or Merleau-Ponty's respective philosophical systems. This was, in part, to action one of film-philosophy's core concerns, which seeks to decentre disciplinary binaries and broaden 'the horizon of where we philosophize, with whom, and in what way, by engaging with a world of philosophies via a world of cinemas' (Martin-Jones 2016: 8). If Beauvoir's idea of ambiguity is to be argued as a means of disclosing ethical vision and thereby indicate the political and existential significance of emotional turbulence for mental growth and the appeal for freedom, why return to philosophical thinkers whose systems of thought do not propose an existentialist ethics? In bringing Beauvoir's idea of ambiguity within the context of film-philosophy, the aim has been to identify its contours as a phenomenological concept, considered through a specific set of women's films. The speculative nature of the project was not without its obstacles.

To define ambiguity solely within Beauvoirian phenomenology would be to ignore philosophy's wanderings and claim for a system that does not exist. Le Doeuff's argument is powerfully rousing; she releases the traditions, expectations and ritualism crusted onto philosophy by foregrounding its inherent evolutionary and adaptative qualities:

> No philosophical thought is self-contained. Because it cannot stick to its programme, it proceeds by detours, lateral explorations and assorted digressions, including some related to contemporary life. There is no thinking which does not wander, and any serious work should have etc. in its title and honestly state that it will not stick to the topic. (Le Doeuff 2007: xii)

Reading this invitation, it is hard to avoid the excitement that Le Doeuff sees and practises through philosophy. Not only does Beauvoir's own philosophy wander throughout her large body of writing, but her specific concept of ambiguity is central to the evolution of her existentialist ethics. As she navigates the parameters of moral values in relationship to freedom, she also alters the existential project during her reflection. This is what Le Doeuff means when she speaks of the transformation of Beauvoir's thinking: 'It is also the case that this work does not change its object of study alone: in grappling with something, thought itself is transformed' (Le Doeuff 2007: 91). Therefore, the appeal of Beauvoir's thought for a study of cinema, specifically women's cinema in this case, was exactly its wandering and transformative qualities. While her focus remains consistent on the ethics and moral components of freedom, Beauvoir's work reflects a roving character that demonstrates a living philosophy that also presented many connections with the ideas of contemporary feminist phenomenologists. It goes without saying that scholarship which has ignored Beauvoir's contribution to phenomenology, and by extension her legacy for film-phenomenology, has not been able to extrapolate such links.

Therefore, I encourage the reader to view my decision to concentrate only on independent women filmmakers throughout *Ambiguous Cinema* as a first step – locating Beauvoir's idea of ambiguity and showcasing the significance of her widespread phenomenology as a fundamental aspect of film experience. It has also been an intention that the study and prioritising of intermeshed emotional, ethical and gendered film experience will evolve and transcend the specificity of Beauvoir's writing, seen in my discussions of Al-Saji's phenomenology of hesitation, Lugones's 'world'-travelling and Anzaldúa's philosophical *mestizaje*, for example. Indeed, a study of ambiguity within world cinemas would elaborate on the distinctions that exist between ways of seeing and embodied ways of being-in-the-world today, responding more successfully to social issues that require pressing attention. The importance of recognising ambiguity within cinema as a fundamental part of film experience helps acknowledge the persistent call for expressions of hope and the emotional difficulty embedded in such socio-cultural and socio-political issues. These objects cry out for collective resolution and require our urgent attention, if for no other reason than that confronting ambiguity also appeals to our becoming responsible for our choices and the freedom of others.

That said, there is of course a certain selfishness in the films I have chosen; they are all films that I have personally found transformative in challenging, powerful and sometimes disturbing ways. In reference to Hipparchia's choice, these were not a waste of my time, rather they furthered my own ways of knowing, thinking and feeling the world. Although not written about in the same sequence as I watched them, each film in its viewings unlocked a perspective about women's experience and situation, either in terms of erotic experience, individuation, moral choices, national identity or motherhood. Combined, they represent a synecdochic collection of films, which I came to see as illuminating a pattern of ambiguous filmmaking and reflecting a feminist and existential film-phenomenology. Or put more simply, they help me think and feel the emotional turbulence of my own lived situation, while concurrently compelling reciprocal recognition of others.

As Christopher Bollas tells us: '[t]ransformation does not mean gratification' (2011: 12), and like Wilfred Bion, Bollas views emotional and mental growth as dependent on a tolerance for frustration. Beauvoir may not have used the word 'transformation' in her philosophy of ambiguity, but she often spoke to the ways in which cinema deeply affected her. In a rare lengthy discussion of her thoughts on film in *All Said and Done*, Beauvoir voices her own world of cinemas, recalling viewings of Buster Keaton films, James Bond films, Sergio Leone's *The Good, The Bad and The Ugly* (1966), Pasolini's *Medea* (1969), Masaki Kobayashi's *Hara-Kiri* (1962), among others. She writes: '[images] offered by the cinema have all the fullness of perception – they *are* perceptions, and perceptions grasped as the analogon of an absent reality' (ASD 176); '[t]here are some ambitious directors who try to communicate their vision of the world to me; and mine is enriched if they succeed in doing so' (ASD 180). Her summary of *Five Easy Pieces* (Rafelson, 1970) ends by identifying the power of cinema to illuminate 'fine psychological shades and subtleties ... it shows them very well indeed' (ASD 186). For Beauvoir, the difference between the book and the screen was cinema's ability to 'bring a period or a society back to life; they tell of adventures; they show us the feelings that bind people together' (ASD 187) – a nascent sentiment that might be said to have evolved more fruitfully in the discipline of film-philosophy and its engagement with themes of embodiment, empathy, global politics, and their role in theorising struggles for freedom.

Each of the protagonists I discuss within *Ambiguous Cinema* faces difficulties determined by the boundaries of their situation. There is no heroism or cathartic rebellion to their respective evolution (or devolution in the case of Cavani's Lucia or Martel's Zama); instead, the cinema of their everyday lives replaces previous representations in women's cinema that have tended to concentrate on domestic spaces and patriarchal myths of girlhood or womanhood. The girls and women in these films (and those who disrupt such gender identifications) are not contextualised by such traditional spaces of home or family despite still being implicated in the reach and shadows of patriarchy. For the most part, we meet characters who are quite happy to reject such prescribed gendered social scripts, wrestling with how they are treated by others and how they choose to respond considering that treatment. As we watch such films, we participate in determining the potentiality of freedom and the behaviour it requires of us. In *The Ethics of Ambiguity*, Beauvoir wanted her philosophy to describe an existentialist ethics and at the heart of this lay her idea of ambiguity – not only as an abstract philosophical concept but also as embodied way of being. As she saw it, in our pursuit of freedom we must reach out and depend on others, meaning that we must relinquish our fetishised individualism and acknowledge that we exist only and because of other human beings. In doing so, we flirt with failure – we may not succeed – but equally, we might be able to make visible something authentic of our existence, indeed recognise the precarious and ambiguous reality that structures our freedom.

To gain a moral freedom is to disclose the situation of the present as it links to the past, so that the situation of the future can transcend current hurdles and limitations. This is what I see as one of the greatest political strengths of cinema, to which Beauvoir's idea of ambiguity effectively speaks: its capacity to illustrate what obstacles face a person in developing their moral freedom, and at the same time affectively appeal to their sense of freedom and a desire to pursue it. I have commented on how the women filmmakers examined in this book do not judge their characters, even if they may implicitly question their bad faith or dubious choices. Through specific aesthetic practice (such as the use of off-screen sound; breaking the frame; attention on gesture via close-ups; and so on), the women filmmakers refuse a sensibility of oppression and audiences are left with the invitation to reflect on the lived realities of the characters' situation and consider moral freedom – not only their own, or of the characters, but of others in their own respective situations. This is because the cinematic emphasis is placed on its sensory elements, where its storytelling relies much more on audio-visual experience than the usual determinacy of narrative or dialogue in mainstream films. The films become cinematic experiences that need to be thought as they are felt.

Is this a utopian vision of Beauvoir's idea of ambiguity and its applicability for cinema? Perhaps. Although, it has been repeatedly stressed that ambiguous lived experience is abrasive – despite it signalling moments of moral choice, it not an easy or comfortable emotional space in which we can reside. The real proof of any film-philosophy rests in determining how effective any film experience is in political and existential terms. Writing about Beauvoir's ideas and thinking about how they might relate to or investigate specific film examples can never replace the actuality of watching films themselves, feeling and/or taking up their affective appeals. On these terms, Marso's theorisation of the encounter in Beauvoir's phenomenology (specifically the affective reach of her politics) has been particularly instructive, as she argues: 'we see that freedom cannot be experienced other than in encounter, where it also risks destruction or diminution' (Marso 2017: 204). Marso places bodies at the centre of her study on political freedom, 'and their meaning to reject systems, mechanisms, and moments of oppression' (2017: 206), noting the role ambiguity plays in disclosing the many ways we might reciprocally recognise others. Therefore, while the films discussed within *Ambiguous Cinema* have facilitated such reflection and freedom for me, the aim has been to foreground enough of the main aspects of Beauvoir's idea of ambiguity so that the reader may find their own stable of similarly ambiguous cinema that facilitates their own transformative experience.

There are many other filmmakers whose work fits very well within the scope of what I am terming 'ambiguous cinema', where themes of existential uncertainty, our dependence on others and the need for reciprocal recognition, and the anxieties of negotiating our inner and outer worlds are often explored. To limit a study of ambiguity to the experiencing of only women's cinema would, therefore, be short-sighted, especially as Beauvoir's own idea of ambiguity did not develop along gendered lines, even if at times it attended critically to the emancipation of women. Kristiana Arp writes that those attracted to Beauvoir's philosophy might be lured precisely because there is little in her work that presents a strict philosophical system. Rather, it is the very pervasiveness of her phenomenology – its ambiguity – that draws one in 'to join in the project' (Arp 2001: 148). This returns us to the importance of wandering philosophical thought – which Le Doeuff argues is the way to avoid its stagnation.

The project of *Ambiguous Cinema* has been to closely investigate the film aesthetics of women's cinema, particularly the attention given through form to the gestural, sonic and framed aspects that embody such cinematic sensoria. What drew me to these women filmmakers was the way in which their films purposefully explored the sticky and messy moral aspects of women's lives. In each film, the aesthetic experience consistently turns to confront the complex, ugly, harsh and maddening experiences of girl's and women's everyday lives, although not always in the violent ways we might expect. It isn't just women's lives that are sticky, messy, oppressed or turbulent, despite the content of the films discussed throughout this book. I encourage readers to seek and create their own worlds of ambiguous cinema, with the hope that future film experience develops as an intentionally emotionally turbulent embodied expression.

Filmography

Arnold, Andrea, dir., *Fish Tank*, 2009
Campion, Jane, dir., *The Piano*, 1993
Cavani, Liliana, dir., *The Night Porter*, 1974
Chabrol, Claude, dir., *The Blood of Others*, 1984
Chaplin, Charlie, dir., *The Kid*, 1921
De Jong, Ate, dir., *All Men Are Mortal*, 1995
Denis, Claire, dir., *Chocolat*, 1988
Denis, Claire, dir., *Trouble Every Day*, 2001
Denis, Claire, dir., *35 Shots of Rum*, 2009
Denis, Claire, dir., *White Material*, 2009
Denis, Claire, dir., *Les Salauds*, 2013
Denis, Claire, dir., *Let the Sunshine In*, 2017
Denis, Claire, dir., *High Life*, 2018
Dunye, Cheryl, dir., *Janine*, 1990
Dunye, Cheryl, dir., *She Don't Fade*, 1991
Dunye, Cheryl, dir., *The Potluck and the Passion*, 1993
Dunye, Cheryl, dir., *Greetings from Africa*, 1994
Dunye, Cheryl, dir., *The Watermelon Woman*, 1996
Fassbinder, Rainer Werner, dir., *Ali: Fear Eats the Soul*, 1974
Granik, Debra, dir., *Down to the Bone*, 2004
Granik, Debra, dir., *Winter's Bone*, 2010
Granik, Debra, dir., *Stray Dogs*, 2014
Granik, Debra, dir., *Leave No Trace*, 2018
Godard, Jean-Luc, dir., *La Chinoise*, 1967
Godard, Jean-Luc, dir., *Passion*, 1982
Hadžihalilović, Lucile, dir., *Innocence*, 2004
Haynes, Todd, dir., *Far From Heaven*, 2002
Hogg, Joanna, dir., *The Souvenir*, 2019
Kobayashi, Masaki, dir., *Hara-Kiri*, 1962
Leone, Sergio, dir., *The Good, The Bad and The Ugly*, 1966
Martel, Lucrecia, dir., *La ciénaga*, 2001
Martel, Lucrecia, dir., *La niña santa*, 2004
Martel, Lucrecia, dir., *La mujer sin cabeza*, 2008

Martel, Lucrecia, dir., *Zama*, 2017
Pasolini, Pier Paolo, dir., *Medea*, 1969
Rafelson, Bob, dir., *Five Easy Pieces*, 1970
Ramsay, Lynne, dir., *Morvern Callar*, 2002
Ramsay, Lynne, dir., *We Need to Talk About Kevin*, 2011
Ramsay, Lynne, dir., *You Were Never Really Here*, 2017
Sciamma, Céline, dir., *Water Lilies*, 2007
Sciamma, Céline, dir., *Tomboy*, 2011
Sciamma, Céline, dir., *Girlhood*, 2014
Sciamma, Céline, dir., *Portrait of a Lady on Fire*, 2019
Seitz, George B., dir., *Love Finds Andy Hardy*, 1938
Sirk, Douglas, dir., *All the Heaven Allows*, 1995
Von Trier, Lars, dir., *Antichrist*, 2009

Bibliography

Abraham, Raphael (2020), 'Céline Sciamma on defying convention with the all-female Portrait of a Lady on Fire', *Financial Times*, 13 February 2020, ft.com: <https://www.ft.com/content/288ce7fa-4cc6-11ea-95a0-43d18ec715f5> (accessed 17 May 2021).

Aguilar, Carlos (2020), 'Love Dialogue: Céline Sciamma on Portrait of a Lady on Fire', *RogerEbert.com*, 12 February 2020, <https://www.rogerebert.com/interviews/love-dialogue-c%C3%A9line-sciamma-on-portrait-of-a-lady-on-fire> (accessed 17 May 2021).

Ahmed, Sara (2004a), *The Cultural Politics of Emotion*, Edinburgh: Edinburgh University Press.

Ahmed, Sara (2004b), 'Affective Economies', *Social Text*, 22: 2, 117–39.

Ahmed, Sara (2007), *Queer Phenomenology: Orientations, Objects, Others*, Durham, NC: Duke University Press.

Alcoff, Linda Martín (2000a), 'Habits of Hostility: On Seeing Race', *Philosophy Today*, 44: 30–40.

Alcoff, Linda Martín (2000b), 'Phenomenology, Post-Structuralism, and Feminist Theory on the Concept of Experience', in Linda Fisher and Lester Embree (eds), *Feminist Phenomenology*, Netherlands: Kluwer Sions Publishers.

Alcoff, Linda Martín (2006), *Visible Identities: Race, Gender and the Self*, Oxford: Oxford University Press.

Al-Saji, Alia (2014), 'A Phenomenology of Hesitation', in Emily S. Lee (ed.), *Living Alterities: Phenomenology, Embodiment and Race*, Albany, NY: SUNY Press.

Anzaldúa, Gloria [1987] (2012), *Borderlands/La Frontera: The New Mestiza*, Fourth edition, San Francisco: Aunt Lute Books.

Arendt, Hannah [1963] (2006), *Eichmann in Jerusalem: A Report on the Banality of Evil*, New York: Penguin.

Arp, Kristiana (2001), *The Bonds of Freedom: Simone de Beauvoir's Existential Ethics*, Chicago and La Salle, IL: Open Court Publishers.

Baensch, Otto (1958), 'Art and Feeling', in Susanne K. Langer (ed.), *Reflections on Art: A Source Book of Writings by Artists, Critics and Philosophers*, Oxford: Oxford University Press.

Bair, Deirdre (1990), *Simone de Beauvoir*, London: Vintage.

Bair, Deirdre (2019), *Parisian Lives: Samuel Beckett, Simone de Beauvoir and Me: A Memoir*, New York: Anchor Books.

Bakewell, Sarah (2017), *At the Existentialist Café: Freedom, Being & Apricot Cocktails*, London: Vintage.
Barker, Jennifer (2009), *The Tactile Eye: Touch and the Cinematic Experience*, Berkeley: The University of California Press.
Barthes, Roland [1978] (1990), *A Lover's Discourse: Fragments*, translated by Richard Howard, London: Penguin.
Bauer, Nancy (2006), 'Beauvoir's Heideggerian Ontology', in Margaret A. Simons (ed.), *The Philosophy of Simone de Beauvoir*, Bloomington: Indiana University Press.
Beauvoir, Simone de [1945a] (2004), 'Existentialism and Popular Wisdom', in Margaret A. Simons, Marybeth Timmermann and Mary Beth Mader (eds), *Simone de Beauvoir: Philosophical Writings*, Urbana: University of Illinois Press.
Beauvoir, Simone de [1945b] (2004), 'A Review of the *Phenomenology of Perception* by Maurice Merleau-Ponty', in Margaret A. Simons, Marybeth Timmermann and Mary Beth Mader (eds), *Simone de Beauvoir: Philosophical Writings*, translated by Marybeth Timmermann, notes by Stacy Keltner, Urbana: University of Illinois Press.
Beauvoir, Simone de (1955), *Privilèges*, Paris: Gallimard.
Beauvoir, Simone de (1959), 'Brigitte Bardot and the Lolita Syndrome', *Esquire*, translated by Bernard Fretchman, 1 August 1959.
Beauvoir, Simone de (1960), 'In Defense of Djamilla Boupacha', *Le Monde*, 3 June 1960.
Beauvoir, Simone de (1964), *The Blood of Others (Le sang des autres)*, translated by Yvonne Moyse and Roger Senhouse, Harmondsworth: Penguin.
Beauvoir, Simone de [1972] (2015), 'The Rebellious Woman – An Interview by Alice Schwartzer', in Margaret A. Simons and Marybeth Timmermann (eds), *Simone de Beauvoir: Feminist Writings*, Urbana: University of Illinois Press.
Beauvoir, Simone de [1943] (1984), *She Came to Stay*, translated by Yvonne Moyse and Roger Senhouse, London: Harper. Original publication, *L'Invitée*.
Beauvoir, Simone de (1991), *Letters to Sartre*, translated by Quintin Hoare, Preface by Sylvie Le Bon de Beauvoir, New York: Arcade Publishing.
Beauvoir, Simone de [1946] (1995), *All Men are Mortal*, translated by E. Cameron based on original translation by L. M. Friedman, London: Virago Press. Original publication, *Tout Les Hommes Sont Mortels*.
Beauvoir, Simone de (1998), *A Transatlantic Love Affair: Letters to Nelson Aldgren*, translated by Ellen Gordon Reeves, New York: The New Press.
Beauvoir, Simone de [1946] (2004a), 'Jean Paul, Strictly Personal', in Margaret A. Simons, Marybeth Timmermann and Mary Beth Mader (eds), *Simone de Beauvoir: Philosophical Writings*, translated by Marybeth Timmermann, Urbana: University of Illinois Press. Original article published in *Harper's Bazaar*.
Beauvoir, Simone de (2004b), 'Two Unpublished Chapters from *She Came to Stay* [1938]', in Margaret A. Simons, Marybeth Timmermann and Mary Beth Mader (eds), *Simone de Beauvoir: Philosophical Writings*, translated by Sylvie Gautheron, Urbana: University of Illinois Press.

Beauvoir, Simone de [1954] (2005a), *The Mandarins*, translated by L. M. Friedman London: Harper. Original publication, *Les Mandarins*.

Beauvoir, Simone de [1958] (2005b), *Memoirs of a Dutiful Daughter*, translated by James Kirkup, London: HarperCollins.

Beauvoir, Simone de (2012a), 'Right-Wing Thought Today', in Margaret A. Simons, Marybeth Timmermann (eds), *Simone de Beauvoir: Political Writings*, translated by Véronique Zaytzeff and Frederick M. Morrison, Urbana: University of Illinois Press. Foreword by Sylvie Le Bon de Beauvoir.

Beauvoir, Simone de (2012b), 'Merleau-Ponty and Pseudo-Sartreanism', in Margaret A. Simons, Marybeth Timmermann (eds), *Simone de Beauvoir: Political Writings*, Urbana: University of Illinois Press. Foreword by Sylvie Le Bon de Beauvoir.

Beauvoir, Simone de (2012c), 'Preface to Djamila Boupacha', in Margaret A. Simons, Marybeth Timmermann (eds), *Simone de Beauvoir: Political Writings*, translated by Marybeth Timmerman, Urbana: University of Illinois Press. Foreword by Sylvie Le Bon de Beauvoir.

Beauvoir, Simone de (2015a), 'It's About Time Women Put a New Face on Love', in Margaret A. Simons and Marybeth Timmermann (eds), *Simone de Beauvoir: Feminist Writings*, Urbana: University of Illinois Press. Original work published in *Flair*, 1, 3, April 1950.

Beauvoir, Simone de (2015b), 'What Love Is – and Isn't', in Margaret A. Simons and Marybeth Timmermann (eds), *Simone de Beauvoir: Feminist Writings*, Urbana: University of Illinois Press. Original published in *McCall's*, August 1965.

Beauvoir, Simone de and Gisèle Halimi (eds) (1962), *Djamila Boupacha: The Story of the Torture of a Young Algerian Girl which Shocked Liberal French Opinion*, translated by Peter Green, New York: The Macmillan Company.

Bendix, Trish (2011), 'Céline Sciamma talks "Tomboy," "Water Lilies" and why LGBT film festivals are still necessary', *AfterEllen.com*, 16 November 2011, <https://archive.is/20130116142955/http://www.afterellen.com/movies/celine-sciamma-talks-tomboy-water-lillies-and-why-lgbt-film-festivals-are-still-necessary> (accessed 17 May 2021).

Bergoffen, Debra (1992), 'The Look as Bad Faith', *Philosophy Today*, 36: 3, 221–7.

Bergoffen, Debra (1997), *The Philosophy of Simone de Beauvoir: Gendered Phenomenologies, Erotic Generosities*, Albany, NY: SUNY Press.

Bergoffen, Debra (2012), 'Introduction', in Margaret A. Simons and Marybeth Timmermann (eds), *Simone de Beauvoir: Political Writings*, Urbana: University of Illinois Press. Foreword by Sylvie Le Bon de Beauvoir.

Beugnet, Martine (2007), *Cinema and Sensation: French Film and the Art of Transgression*, Carbondale: Southern Illinois University Press.

Bion, Wilfred Ruprecht (1970), *Attention and Interpretation: A Scientific Approach to Insight in Psycho-Analysis and Groups*, London: Karnac Books.

Bion, Wilfred Ruprecht [1965] (1977), '*Transformations*', in *Seven Servants*, New York: Jason Aronson.

Bion, Wilfred Ruprecht [1976] (2008), 'Emotional Turbulence', in *Clinical Seminars and Other Works*, London: Karnac.

Bion, Wilfred Ruprecht [1979] (2008), 'Making the Best of a Bad Job', in Francesca Bion (ed.), *Clinical Seminars and Other Works*, London: Karnac.

Bittencourt, Ela (2020), '*Portrait of a Lady on Fire:* Daring to See', *The Criterion Collection*, 23 June 2020, <https://www.criterion.com/current/posts/6991-portrait-of-a-lady-on-fire-daring-to-see> (accessed 8 June 2021).

Blakeley, Ruth (2009), *State Terrorism and Neoliberalism: The North in the South*, London and New York: Routledge Publishers.

Bléandonu, Gérard (1994), *Wilfred Bion: His Life and Works, 1897–1979*, translated by Claire Pajaczkowska, New York: Other Press.

Bollas, Christopher (1987), *The Shadow of the Object: Psychoanalysis of the Unthought Known*, New York: Columbia University Press.

Bolton, Lucy (2011), *Film and Female Consciousness: Irigaray, Cinema and Thinking Women*, London: Palgrave Macmillan UK.

Bolton, Lucy (2016), 'A Phenomenology of Girlhood: Being Mia in Fish Tank', in Fiona Handyside and Kate Taylor Jones (eds), *International Cinema and the Girl Local Issues, Transnational Contexts*, Basingstoke: Palgrave Macmillan.

Bolton, Lucy (2019), *Contemporary Cinema and the Philosophy of Iris Murdoch*, Edinburgh: University of Edinburgh Press.

Boulé, Jean-Pierre and Enda McCaffrey (eds) (2011), *Existentialism and Contemporary Cinema: A Sartrean Perspective*, Oxford: Berghahn Books.

Boulé, Jean-Pierre and Ursula Tidd (eds) (2012), *Existentialism and Contemporary Cinema: A Beauvoirian Perspective*, Oxford: Berghahn Books.

Bourdieu, Pierre (1992a), *The Logic of Practice*, translated by Richard Nice, Stanford, CA: Stanford University Press.

Bourdieu, Pierre (and Loïc Wacquant) (1992b), *An Invitation to Reflexive Sociology*, Chicago: University of Chicago Press.

Bradshaw, Peter (2019), 'Portrait of a Lady on Fire review – burning desires and flashes of Hitchcock', *The Guardian*, 20 May 2019, <https://www.theguardian.com/film/2019/may/20/portrait-of-a-lady-on-fire-review-celine-sciamma> (accessed 17 May 2021).

Brand, Peggy Zeglin (2002), 'The Aesthetic Attitude in "The Ethics of Ambiguity"', *Simone de Beauvoir Studies*, 18, 31–48.

Brody, Richard (2018), 'The Exquisite Talk of Claire Denis's *Let the Sunshine In*', *The New Yorker*, 2 May 2018, <https://www.newyorker.com/culture/richard-brody/the-exquisite-talk-of-claire-deniss-let-the-sunshine-in> (accessed 7 June 2021).

Butler, Judith (2021), *The Force of Non-Violence*, London and New York: Verso Books.

Canby, Vincent (1974), '*The Night Porter Is Romantic Pornography*', *The New York Times*, 13 October 1974, <https://www.nytimes.com/1974/10/13/archives/the-night-porter-is-romantic-pornography-porter-is-romantic.html> (accessed 7 June 2021).

Casebier, Allan (1991), *Film and Phenomenology: Toward a Realist Theory of Cinematic Representation*, Cambridge: Cambridge University Press.
Casey, Edward. S (2010), 'Aesthetic Experience', in Hans Rainer Sepp and Lester Embree (eds), *Handbook of Phenomenological Aesthetics*, London and New York: Springer.
Chamarette, Jenny (2012), *Phenomenology and the Future of Film: Rethinking Subjectivity Beyond French Cinema*, Basingstoke: Palgrave Macmillan.
Chamarette, Jenny (2015), 'Embodied Worlds and Situated Bodies: Feminism, Phenomenology, Film Theory', *Signs: Journal of Women and Society*, 40: 2, 289–95.
Chamarette, Jenny (2018), 'Overturning Feminist Phenomenologies: Disability, Complex Embodiment, Intersectionality, and Film', in Christinia Landry and Sara Cohen Shabot (eds), *Rethinking Feminist Phenomenology: Theoretical and Applied Perspectives*, Lanham, MD: Rowman & Littlefield.
Chion, Michel (1994), 'Projections of Sound on Image', in *Audio-Vision: Sound on Screen*, translated by Claudia Gorbman, New York: Columbia University Press.
Clouzot, Claire (1974), 'Liliana Cavani: Le Mythe, le sexe et la révolte', *Ecran*, 26, 36–46.
Cohen Shabot, Sara and Christinia Landry (2018), *Rethinking Feminist Phenomenology: Theoretical and Applied Perspectives*, Rowman & Littlefield Publishers.
Collingwood, Robin George (1938), *Principles of Art*, Oxford: Oxford University Press.
Collins, Patricia Hill (2000), *Black Feminist Thought: Knowledge, Consciousness, and the Politics of Empowerment*, New York: Routledge Publishers.
Collins, Patricia Hill (2016), and Silma Birge, *Intersectionality: Key Concepts*, First edition, Cambridge: Polity Press.
Collins, Patricia Hill (2019), *Intersectionality as Critical Social Theory*, Durham, NC: Duke University Press.
Considine, David (1981), 'The Cinema of Adolescence', *Journal of Popular Film and Television*, 9: 3, 123–36.
Crenshaw, Kimberlé (2017), *On Intersectionality: Essential Writings*, New York: The New Press.
Cuffari, Elena (2011), 'Habits of Transformation', *Hypatia*, 26: 3, 535–53.
D'Angelo, Mike (2014), 'Despite risible subject matter, *The Night Porter* is more tedious than vile', *The AV Club*, 17 December 2014 <https://www.avclub.com/despite-risible-subject-matter-the-night-porter-is-mor-1798182232> (accessed 7 June 2021).
De Lauretis, Teresa (1976), 'Cavani's Night Porter: A Woman's Film?', *Film Quarterly*, 30: 2, 35–8.
Denis, Claire (2019), 'Claire Denis on Let The Sunshine In', *Let The Sunshine In*, produced by Olivier Delbosc, *The Criterion Collection*. DVD.
Di Benedetto, Antonio (1956), *Zama*, translated by Esther Allen, New York: New York Review Books.

Doane, Mary Ann (2004), 'Aesthetics and Politics', *Beyond the Gaze: Recent Approaches to Film Feminisms*, Special Issue, Kathleen McHugh and Vivian Sobchack (eds), *Signs*, 30: 1, 1229–35.

Driscoll, Catherine (2002), *Girls: Feminine Adolescence in Popular Culture and Cultural Theory*, New York: Columbia University Press.

Driscoll, Catherine (2011), *Teen Film: A Critical Introduction*, Oxford and New York: Berg Publishers.

Driscoll, Catherine (2013), 'Foreword', in Kate Harper, Yasmina Katsulis, Vera Lopez and Georganne Scheiner Gillis (eds), *Girls' Sexualities and the Media*, New York: Peter Lang Publishers.

Dufrenne, Mikel (1973), *The Phenomenology of Aesthetic Experience*, translated by Edward. S. Casey, Evanston, IL: Northwestern University Press.

Du Graf, Lauren (2018), 'Cinema in the Eyes of Simone de Beauvoir', *Screen*, 59: 3, 381–90.

Dunye, Cheryl (1992), 'Building Subjects', *The Movement Research Performance Journal*, 4, 18.

Dunye, Cheryl (2020), 'Cheryl Dunye Interview Clip – Criterion Channel', *YouTube*, uploaded by criterioncollection, 21 September 2020, <www.youtube.com/watch?v=GW-sQbnCj6k> (accessed 12 October 2020).

Ebert, Roger (1975), 'The Night Porter', *The Chicago Sun Times*, 10 February 1975, <https://www.rogerebert.com/reviews/the-night-porter-1975#:~:text=%22The%20Night%20Porter%22%20is%20as,memories%20of%20persecution%20and%20suffering> (accessed 7 June 2021).

Eigen, Michael (2005), *Emotional Storm*, Middletown, CT: Wesleyan University Press.

Eyre, Hannah (2010), 'Claire Denis on filmmaking and feminism', *Prospect Magazine*, 21 June 2010, <https://www.prospectmagazine.co.uk/magazine/loving-the-lost-and-monstrous> (accessed 7 June 2021).

Fallaize, Elizabeth (ed.) (1998), *Simone de Beauvoir: A Critical Reader*, London: Routledge.

Fallaize, Elizabeth (2015), 'Introduction', in Margaret A. Simons and Marybeth Timmermann (eds), *Simone de Beauvoir: Philosophical Writings*, Urbana: University of Illinois Press.

Fanon, Frantz [1952] (2008), *Black Skin, White Masks*, translated by Richard Philcox, New York: Grove Press.

Fielding, Helen (2006) 'White Logic and the Constancy of Color', in Dorothea Olkowski and Gail Weiss (eds), *Feminist Interpretations of Merleau-Ponty*, State Park: Pennsylvania State University Press.

Fielding, Helen (2014), 'The Poetry of Habit', in Silvia Stoller (ed.), *Simone de Beauvoir's Philosophy of Age: Gender, Ethics and Time*, Berlin and Boston: Walter de Gruyter GmbH.

Fielding, Helen (2020), 'The Habit Body', in Gail Weiss, Ann. V. Murphy and Gayle Salamon (eds), *50 Concepts for a Critical Phenomenology*, Evanston, IL: Northwestern University Press.

Fielding, Helen and Dorothea Olkowski (eds) (2017), *Feminist Phenomenology Futures*, Bloomington: Indiana University Press.

Freud, Sigmund (1914), 'Remembering, Repeating and Working-Through', in *The Standard Edition of the Complete Psychological Works of Sigmund Freud, Volume XII (1911–1913): The Case of Schreber, Papers on technique and Other Works*, translated by James Strachey, London: The Hogarth Press.

Freud, Sigmund (1920) 'Beyond the Pleasure Principle', in *The Standard Edition of the Complete Psychological Works of Sigmund Freud, Volume XVIII (1920–1922): Beyond the Pleasure Principle, Group Psychology and Other Works*, translated by James Strachey, London: The Hogarth Press.

Frye, Marilyn (1983), *The Politics of Reality: Essays in Feminist Theory*, Trumansburg, NY: Crossing Press.

Fuery, Kelli (2018), *Wilfred Bion, Thinking, and Emotional Experience with Moving Images: Being Embedded*, London and New York: Routledge Publishers.

Fullbrook, Edward (2004), 'Introduction', in Margaret A. Simons, Marybeth Timmermann and Mary Beth Mader (eds), *Simone de Beauvoir: Philosophical Writings*, Urbana: University of Illinois Press.

Fullbrook, Edward and Kate Fullbrook (1998), *Simone de Beauvoir: A Critical Introduction*, Cambridge: Polity Press.

Gaine, Vincent (2011), *Existentialism and Social Engagement in the Films of Michael Mann*, London and New York: Palgrave Macmillan.

Garcia, Maria (2018), 'Thinking Her Own Thoughts: An Interview with Debra Granik', *Cineaste*, 43: 4, 36–40.

Garcia, Maria (2019), 'Deconstructing the Filmmakers' Gaze: An Interview with Céline Sciamma', *Cineaste*, 45: 1, 8–11.

Gemünden, Gerd (2019), *Lucrecia Martel*, Urbana: University of Illinois Press.

Gemünden, Gerd and Silvia Spitta (2018), '"I Was Never Afraid," An Interview with Lucrecia Martel', *Film Quarterly*, 71: 4, 33–40.

Giordano, Simona (2018), 'Understanding the emotion of shame in transgender individuals – some insight from Kafka', *Life Sciences, Society and Policy*, 14: 23, Online: <https://doi.org/10.1186/s40504-018-0085-y> (accessed 12 December 2020).

Gordon, Lewis. R. (2015), *What Fanon Said: A Philosophical Introduction to His Life and Thought*, New York: Fordham University Press.

Gordon, Lewis. R. (2020), 'Bad Faith', in Gail Weiss, Ann. V. Murphy and Gayle Salamon (eds), *50 Concepts for a Critical Phenomenology*, Evanston, IL: Northwestern University Press.

Gothlin, Eva (2006), 'Beauvoir and Sartre on Appeal, Desire and Ambiguity', in Margaret A. Simons (ed.), *The Philosophy of Simone de Beauvoir*, Bloomington, IN: Indiana University Press.

Gravil, Richard (2007), *Existentialism*. Humanities E-books.

Haskell, Mary [1975] (1977), 'Are Women Directors Different?', in Karyn Kay and Gerald Peary (eds), *Women and the Cinema: A Critical Anthology*, New York: E. P. Dutton.

Heinämaa, Sara (1999), 'Simone de Beauvoir's Phenomenology of Sexual Difference', *Hypatia*, 14: 4, 114–32.
Heinämaa, Sara (2003), *Toward a Phenomenology of Sexual Difference: Husserl, Merleau-Ponty, Beauvoir*, Lanham, MD: Rowman and Littlefield.
Heinämaa, Sara (2004), 'Introduction', in Margaret A. Simons, Marybeth Timmermann and Mary Beth Mader (eds), *Simone de Beauvoir: Philosophical Writings*, Urbana: University of Illinois Press.
Hemmings, Claire (2005), 'Telling Feminist Stories', *Feminist Theory*, 6: 2, 115–39.
Hengehold, Laura (2011), 'Introduction to "What Can Literature Do?"' in Margaret A. Simons and Marybeth Timmermann (eds), *Simone de Beauvoir: 'The Useless Mouths' and Other Literary Writings*, Urbana: University of Illinois Press.
Herman, Judith (1992), *Trauma and Recovery: The Aftermath of Violence – From Domestic Abuse to Political Terror*, New York: Basic Books.
Hole, Kristin Lene (2016), *Towards a Feminist Cinematic Ethics: Claire Denis, Emmanuel Levinas and Jean-Luc Nancy*, Edinburgh: Edinburgh University Press.
Holveck, Eleanore (2004), 'Introduction to Existentialism and Popular Wisdom', in Margaret A. Simons, Marybeth Timmermann and Mary Beth Mader (eds), *Simone de Beauvoir: Philosophical Writings*, Urbana: University of Illinois Press.
Ince, Kate (2011), 'Bringing Bodies Back In: For a Phenomenological and Psychoanalytic Film Criticism of Embodied Cultural Identity', *Film-Philosophy*, 15: 1, 1–12.
Ince, Kate (2012), 'Feminist Phenomenology and the Films of Sally Potter', in Jean-Pierre Boulé and Ursula Tidd (eds), *Existentialism and Contemporary Cinema: A Beauvoirian Perspective*, Oxford: Berghahn Books.
Ince, Kate (2017), *The Body and The Screen: Female Subjectivities in Contemporary Women's Cinema*, London and New York: Bloomsbury Academic Press.
Ince, Kate (2019), 'Whose Identification? A Brief Meditation on the Relevance of Jean-Pierre Meunier's The Structures of the Film Experience to Contemporary Feminist Film Phenomenology', in Julian Hanich and Daniel Fairfax (eds), *The Structures of the Film Experience: Historical Assessments and Phenomenological Expansions. Film Theory in Media History*, Amsterdam: Amsterdam University Press.
Juhasz, Alexandra (1992), *Women of Vision: Histories in Feminist Film and Video*, Minneapolis and London: University of Minnesota Press.
Kael, Pauline (1974), 'The Current Cinema: Stuck in the Fun', *The New Yorker*, 7 October 1974.
Keating, AnaLouise (2006), 'From Borderlands and New Mestizas to Nepantlas and Nepantleras: Anzaldúan Theories for Social Change', *Human Architecture: Journal of the Sociology of Self-Knowledge*, 6: 5–16.
Keating, AnaLouise (2009), *The Gloria Anzaldúa Reader*, Durham, NC and London: Duke University Press.

Kenny, Glenn (2018), 'Let the Sunshine In', *Roger Ebert.com*, 27 April 2018, <https://www.rogerebert.com/reviews/let-the-sunshine-in-2018> (accessed 7 June 2021).

Kermode, Mark (2020), 'Portrait of a Lady on Fire review – mesmerized by the female gaze', *The Guardian*, 1 March 2020, <https://www.theguardian.com/film/2020/mar/01/portrait-of-a-lady-on-fire-review-celine-sciamma> (accessed 17 May 2021).

Kirkpatrick, Kate (2019), *Becoming Beauvoir: A Life*, London and New York: Bloomsbury Academic.

Kruks, Sonia (1990), *Situation and Human Existence: Freedom, Subjectivity and Society*, London: Unwin Hyman Ltd.

Kruks, Sonia (2012), *Simone de Beauvoir and the Politics of Ambiguity*, Oxford and New York: Oxford University Press.

Kruks, Sonia (2014), 'Beauvoir's The Coming of Age and Sartre's Critique of Dialectical Reason', in Silvia Stoller (ed.), *Simone de Beauvoir's Philosophy of Age: Gender, Ethics and Time*, Berlin and Boston: Walter de Gruyter GmbH.

Langer, Susanne (1953), *Feeling and Form: A Theory of Art*, London: Routledge and Kegan Paul.

Lazic, Elena (2018), *You Were Never Really Here Special Issue* ebook, Seventh Row, <https://seventh-row.com/product/you-were-never-really-here-special-issue-ebook/> (accessed 17 November 2020).

Le Doeuff, Michèle (2007), *Hipparchia's Choice: An Essay Concerning Women, Philosophy, Etc.*, translated by Trista Selous, New York: Columbia University Press.

Lee, Emily S. (2014), *Living Alterities: Phenomenology, Embodiment and Race*, Albany, NY: SUNY Press.

Lindner, Katharina (2012) 'Questions of Embodied Difference: Film and Queer Phenomenology', *European Journal of Media Studies*, 1: 2, 199–217.

Lindner, Katharina (2017), *Film Bodies: Queer Feminist Encounters with Gender and Sexuality in Cinema*, London: I. B. Tauris.

Lorde, Audre (2007), *Sister Outsider: Essays and Speeches*, Trumansburg, NY: Crossing Press.

López-Corvo, Rafael E. (2005), *The Dictionary of The Work of W. R. Bion*, London: Karnac Books.

Lugones, María (1987), 'Playfulness, "World"-Travelling, and Loving Perception', *Hypatia*, 2: 2, 3–19.

Lugones, María (2007), 'Heterosexism and the Colonial/Modern Gender System', *Hypatia*, 22: 1, 186–209.

Lundgren-Gothlin, Eva (1998), 'The Master-Slave Dialectic in *The Second Sex*' in Elizabeth Fallaize (ed.), *Simone de Beauvoir: A Critical Reader*, London and New York: Routledge.

McHugh, Kathleen (2007), 'The Experimental Dunyementary', in Robin Blaetz (ed.), *Women's Experimental Cinema: Critical Frameworks*, Durham, NC: Duke University Press.

Margulies, Ivone and Jeremi Szaniawski (2019), *On Women's Films: Across Worlds and Generations*, London and New York: Bloomsbury Academic.

Marks, Laura (2000), *The Skin of the Film: Intercultural Cinema, Embodiment and the Senses*, Durham, NC and London: Duke University Press.

Marrone, Gaetana (2000), *The Gaze and the Labyrinth: The Cinema of Liliana Cavani*, Princeton, NJ: Princeton University Press.

Marso, Lori Jo (2016), 'Must We Burn Lars Von Trier?: Simone de Beauvoir's Body Politics in *Antichrist*', in Bonnie Honig and Lori J. Marso (eds), *Politics, Theory and Film: Critical Encounters with Lars Von Trier*, Oxford and New York: Oxford University Press.

Marso, Lori Jo (2017), *Politics with Beauvoir: Freedom in the Encounter*, Durham, NC: Duke University Press.

Martin, Adrian (1994), *Phantasms*, Ringwood, Vic: McPhee Gribble.

Martin, Deborah (2016), *The Cinema of Lucrecia Martel*, Manchester: Manchester University Press.

Martin-Jones, David (2016), 'Introduction: Film Philosophy and a World of Cinemas', *Film-Philosophy*, 20: 1, 6–23.

Mason, Qrescent Mali (2018), 'Intersectional Ambiguity and the Phenomenology of #BlackGirlJoy', in Sara Cohen Shabot and Christinia Landry (eds), *Rethinking Feminist Phenomenology: Theoretical and Applied Perspectives*, London: Rowman and Littlefield International.

Merleau-Ponty, Maurice (1968), *The Visible and the Invisible, Followed by Working Notes*, translated by Alphonso Lingis, Evanston, IL: Northwestern University Press.

Merleau-Ponty, Maurice (1969), *Humanism and Terror*, translated by John O'Neill, Boston: Beacon Press.

Merleau-Ponty, Maurice [1945] (2002), *Phenomenology of Perception*, translated by Colin Smith, New York: Routledge.

Merleau-Ponty, Maurice [1948] (2008), *The World of Perception*, translated by Oliver Davis, Abingdon and New York: Routledge Publishers.

Moi, Toril (2009), 'What Can Literature Do? Simone de Beauvoir as a Literary Theorist?', *PMLA*, 124: 1, 189–98.

Moi, Toril (2010a), *Simone de Beauvoir: The Making of an Intellectual Woman*, Second Edition, Oxford: Oxford University Press.

Moi, Toril (2010b), 'The Adulteress Wife', *London Review of Books* 32: 3, <https://www.lrb.co.uk/the-paper/v32/n03/toril-moi/the-adulteress-wife> (accessed 7 June 2021).

Mollon, Phil (2008), 'The Inherent Shame of Sexuality', in Claire Pakaczkowska and Ivan Ward (eds), *Shame and Sexuality: Psychoanalysis and Visual Culture*, London and New York: Routledge Publishers.

Moran, Dermot (2011), 'Edmund Husserl's Phenomenology of Habituality and Habitus', *Journal of the British Society for Phenomenology*, 42: 1, 53–77.

Mulvey, Laura (1975), 'Visual Pleasure and Narrative Cinema', *Screen*, 16: 3, 6–18.

Munt, Sally (2000), 'Shame/Pride Dichotomies in *Queer As Folk*', *Textual Practice*, 14, 531–46.
Munt, Sally (2019), 'Gay Shame in a Geopolitical Context', *Cultural Studies*, 33: 6, 1–26.
Murphy, Julien S. (2012), 'Beauvoir's Preface to Djamila Boupacha', in Margaret A. Simons and Marybeth Timmermann (eds), *Simone de Beauvoir: Political Writings*, Urbana: University of Illinois Press.
Mussett, Shannon M. (2006), 'Conditions of Servitude Woman's Peculiar Role in the Master-Slave Dialectic in Beauvoir's *The Second Sex*', in Margaret A. Simons (ed.) *The Philosophy of Simone de Beauvoir*, Bloomington: Indiana University Press.
Ngo, Helen (2016), 'Racist Habits: A Phenomenological Analysis of Racism and the Habitual Body', *Philosophy and Social Criticism*, 42: 9, 847–72.
Oksala, Johanna (2004), *Feminist Experiences: Foucauldian and Phenomenological Investigations*, Evanston, IL: Northwestern University Press.
Ortega, Mariana (2016), *In-Between: Latina Feminist Phenomenology, Multiplicity, and the Self*, Albany, NY: SUNY Press.
Palmer, Tim (2011), *Brutal Intimacy: Analyzing Contemporary French Cinema*, Middletown, CT: Wesleyan University Press.
Pamerleau, William (2020), 'Bad Faith in Film Spectatorship', *Film Philosophy*, 24: 2, 122–39.
Penley, Constance (1989), *The Future of an Illusion: Film, Feminism and Psychoanalysis*, London: Routledge.
Reed, Susan A. (1998), 'The Politics and Poetics of Dance', *Annual Review of Anthropology*, 27, 502–32.
Rivera Berruz, Stephanie (2016), 'At the Crossroads: Latina Identity and Simone de Beauvoir's The Second Sex', *Hypatia*, 31: 2, 319–33.
Romney, Jonathan (2018), 'Claire Denis: 'I couldn't care less about the Weinstein affair', *The Guardian*, 22 April 2018, <https://www.theguardian.com/culture/2018/apr/22/claire-denis-let-sunshine-in-binoche-weinstein-bourgeois-metoo> (accessed 7 June 2021).
Rose, Jacqueline (2018), *Mothers: An Essay on Love and Cruelty*, New York: Farrar, Straus and Giroux.
Ruiz, Elena (2020), 'Mestiza Consciousness', in Gail Weiss, Ann. V. Murphy and Gayle Salamon (eds), *50 Concepts for a Critical Phenomenology*, Evanston, IL: Northwestern University Press.
Sartre, Jean-Paul [1943] (1966), *Being and Nothingness: An Essay on Phenomenological Ontology*, translated by Hazel Barnes, New York: Washington Square.
Sartre, Jean-Paul (1992), *Notebook for an Ethics* (*Cahiers pour une morale*), translated by David Pellauer, Chicago: University of Chicago Press.
Sawyer, Miranda (2018), 'Interview: Director Lynne Ramsay: "I've got a reputation for being difficult – it's bullshit"', *The Guardian*, 25 February, <https://www.theguardian.com/film/2018/feb/25/lynne-ramsay-director-you-were-never-really-here-observer-interview> (accessed 7 June 2021).

Schwartzer, Alice (2015), 'The Rebellious Woman – An Interview by Alice Schwartzer', in Margaret A. Simons and Marybeth Timmermann (eds), *Simone de Beauvoir: Feminist Writings*, Urbana: University of Illinois Press.

Scott, A. O. (2015), 'Exploring the Limits in a Man's World', *The New York Times*, 29 January 2015, <https://www.nytimes.com/2015/01/30/movies/in-girlhood-a-french-adolescent-comes-out-of-her-shell.html> (accessed 8 June 2021).

Secomb, Linnell (2012), 'Simone de Beauvoir, Melodrama and the Ethics of Transcendence', in Jean-Pierre Boulé and Ursula Tidd (eds), *Existentialism and Contemporary Cinema: A Beauvoirian Perspective*, New York and Oxford: Berghahn Books.

Setoodeh, Ramin (2017), '"Wonder Woman" Director Patty Jenkins on Equal Pay, Hollywood Sexism and James Cameron's Nasty Words', *Variety*, 10 October 2017, <https://variety.com/2017/film/features/patty-jenkins-wonder-woman-hollywood-sexism-equal-pay-james-cameron-1202583237/> (accessed 29 April 2020).

Shaw, Daniel (2017), *Movies with Meaning: Existentialism Through Film*, London and New York: Bloomsbury Academic.

Simons, Margaret A. (1981a), 'Beauvoir and Sartre: The Philosophical Relationship', *Yale French Studies*, 72, 165–79.

Simons, Margaret A. (1981b), 'Beauvoir and Sartre: The Question of Influence', *Eros*, 8: 1, 25–42.

Simons, Margaret A. and Sylvie Le Bon de Beauvoir (2009), *Simone de Beauvoir: Wartime Diary*, translated by Anne Deing Cordero, Urbana: University of Illinois Press. Foreword by Sylvie Le Bon de Beauvoir.

Simons, Margaret A. and Marybeth Timmermann (eds) (2011), *Simone de Beauvoir: "The Useless Mouths" and Other Literary Writings*, Urbana: University of Illinois Press.

Simons, Margaret A. and Marybeth Timmermann (eds) (2012), *Simone de Beauvoir: Political Writings*, Urbana: University of Illinois Press. Foreword by Sylvie Le Bon de Beauvoir.

Simons, Margaret A. and Marybeth Timmermann (eds) (2015), *Simone de Beauvoir: Feminist Writings*, Urbana: University of Illinois Press. Foreword by Sylvie Le Bon de Beauvoir.

Simons, Margaret A., Marybeth Timmermann and Mary Beth Mader (eds) (2004), *Simone de Beauvoir: Philosophical Writings*, Urbana: University of Illinois Press. Foreword by Sylvie Le Bon de Beauvoir.

Singh, Greg (2009), *Film After Jung: Post-Jungian Approaches to Film Theory*, London and New York: Routledge Publishers.

Smith, Frances (2020), *Bande de Filles: Girlhood Identities in Contemporary France*, London: Routledge Publishers.

Smith, Stacy, Katherine Pieper, Marc Choueiti and Ariana Case (2015), *Gender and Short Films: Emerging Female Filmmakers and the Barriers Surrounding their Careers*, Report for LUNAFEST, Media, Diversity, & Social Change Initiative.

Sobchack, Vivian (1992), *The Address of the Eye: A Phenomenology of Film Experience*, Princeton, NJ: Princeton University Press.

Sobchack, Vivian (2004), *Carnal Thoughts: Embodiment and Moving Image Culture*, Berkeley: University of California Press.
Stoller, Silvia (2017), 'What is Feminist Phenomenology? Looking Backward and Into the Future', in Helen Fielding and Dorothea Olkowski (eds), *Feminist Phenomenology Futures*, Bloomington: Indiana University Press.
Sullivan, Shannon (2000), 'Reconfiguring Gender with John Dewey: Habit, Bodies, and Cultural Change', *Hypatia*, 15: 1, 23–43.
Sullivan, Shannon (2006), *Revealing Whiteness: The Unconscious Habits of Racial Privilege*, Bloomington: Indiana University Press.
Teodoro, José (2017), 'Interview: Lucrecia Martel', *Film Comment*, 26 September 2017, <https://www.filmcomment.com/blog/interview-lucrecia-martel/> (accessed 7 June 2021).
VanDerWerff, Emily (2020), 'Portrait of a Lady on Fire director Céline Sciamma on her ravishing romantic masterpiece', *Vox.com*, 19 February 2020, <https://www.vox.com/culture/2020/2/19/21137213/portrait-of-a-lady-on-fire-celine-sciamma-interview> (accessed 8 June 2021).
Vintges, Karen (1996), *Philosophy as Passion: The Thinking of Simone de Beauvoir*, Bloomington: Indiana University Press.
Walton, Saige (2016), *Cinema's Baroque Flesh: Film, Phenomenology and the Art of Entanglement*, Amsterdam: Amsterdam University Press.
Warnock, Mary (1970), *Existentialism*, Oxford: Oxford University Press.
Weiss, Gail (1995), 'Ambiguity, Absurdity, and Reversibility: Responses to Indeterminancy', *Journal of the British Society for Phenomenology*, 26: 1, 43–51.
Weiss, Gail and Honi Fern Harber (1999), *Perspectives on Embodiment: The Intersections of Nature and Culture*, London and New York: Routledge Publishers.
Wilson, Emma (2012), 'Beauvoir's Children: Girlhood in Innocence', in Jean-Pierre Boulé and Ursula Tidd (eds), *Existentialism and Contemporary Cinema: A Beauvoirian Perspective*, New York and Oxford: Berghahn Books.
Wilson, Emma (2019), 'Love Me Tender: New Films from Claire Denis', *Film Quarterly*, 72: 4, 18–28.
Winnicott, Donald [1963] (1990), *The Maturational Processes and the Facilitating Environment*, London: Karnac Books.
Winnicott, Donald [1947] (1992), 'Hate in the Counter-Transference' in *Through Paediatrics to Psychoanalysis: Collected Papers of D. W. Winnicott*, Brunner/Mazel Publishers.
Winnicott, Donald [1961] (1999a), *The Family and Individual Development*, London and New York: Routledge.
Winnicott, Donald [1971] (1999b), *Playing and Reality*, London and New York: Routledge Publishers.
Yacavone, Daniel (2016), 'Film and the Phenomenology of Art: Reappraising Merleau-Ponty on Cinema as Form, Medium, and Expression', *New Literary History*, 47: 1, 159–85.
Young, Iris Marion [1980] (2005), *On Female Body Experience: "Throwing like a Girl" and Other Essays*, Oxford: Oxford University Press.

Index

Note: bold indicates illustrations

abortion, 11, 202, 215, 217, 222–3
absolutes, 26, 102–3
absurdity, 159–60, 167
accessible form, 104, 109
acousmatic sound, 147, 159, 165
Acquart, Pauline, 205
action
  capacity for, 19–22
  and choice, 48–54, 85, 189
  collective action, 11–12, 16
  as entanglement, 183–4
  ethical action, 2, 6, 17, 23, 37, 38, 47–9, 98, 101, 106, 152, 205, 220, 225
  and freedom, 17, 25–7, 49–50, 61, 97, 151–2, 182–4, 187–8
  inaction, 3, 9, 22, 49, 220
  political action, 9–10, 11–12, 14, 47, 63, 69, 91, 100, 104, 106, 152, 154–6
  and responsibility, 17, 23, 26, 65, 68, 97
adolescence, 23–7, 28–9, 61–87, 133, 163, 205–11
aesthetic attitude, 30–1, 178–80, 182–90, 193, 194, 195, 197, 221
aesthetic experience, 32, 177–90, 192, 194, 195, 197, 220, 221, 224
aesthetic experimentation, 94, 95, 104–9
affective economies, 81
aftermath, 182, 194–5
agency, 6, 43, 85, 97, 103, 111–12, 165, 202, 204, 207
Ahmed, Sara, 81–2
Algeria, 154
Algerian War, 154
alien consciousness, 158, 161, 163, 194
alienation, 106, 134, 142, 163
All Men Are Mortal (Beauvoir), 13

All Said and Done (Beauvoir), 229–30
America Day by Day (Beauvoir), 4, 99–100, 190
Angot, Christine, 127–8
Antichrist (2009), 29
anxiety, 29–32, 63, 68–9, 77–9, 85–6, 126, 128, 151, 153, 158, 173, 191, 194, 197, 206, 208, 231
Anzaldúa, Gloria, 3, 15, 30, 149, 150, 152–3, 156–7, 161–4, 170, 171, 194
Apocalypse Now (1979), 158
appeal, 5, 37, 55–6, 123–4, 185–6, 192, 205, 220, 221
appropriation, 110, 114–15
Arendt, Hannah, 56
Argentina, 147–50, 162, 164
Arnold, Andrea, 179
Arp, Kristiana, 66, 151–2, 184, 231–2
arranged marriage, 213, 216–21
arrogant perception, 165, 166–7, 172–4
audacity, 91, 105, 110, 227
Audry, Colette, 9
authenticity, 10–11, 19, 23, 29, 36, 53, 91, 93, 124–31, 135, 138, 140–2, 163, 179, 219, 223, 230
autonomy, 11, 64, 76, 78, 86–7, 182
avant-garde film, 15, 74, 84

bad faith, 6, 21–2, 24, 26, 29–30, 54, 57, 79, 122–42, 146–9, 154, 158–9, 164, 187, 190–1, 211–12, 216, 218, 230
Bajrami, Luàna, 215, **223**
Barber-Plentie, Grace, 104
Bardot, Brigitte, 178
Barthes, Roland, 127
Bauer, Nancy, 53

INDEX 249

Beauvoir, Simone de
  and adolescence, 23–7, 28–9, 61–79, 85–7, 163, 206
  and the aesthetic attitude, 30–1, 178–80, 182–90, 194–5, 197, 221
  and bad faith, 6, 24, 26, 29, 122–5, 128–36, 142, 146, 154, 187
  and collectivity, 11–12, 16
  conversations with Sartre, 113
  and disclosure, 31–2, 38, 55–6, 137, 178–9, 183–5, 188–9, 195–7
  existential ethics, 2, 37, 47–8, 62, 66, 81–2, 95, 98, 100–3, 121–2, 138, 143, 146, 150–2, 178, 209, 214–15, 227–8, 230
  and existentialism, 11–12, 27, 37, 61–2, 66, 72, 77, 92–4, 97, 101, 121–2, 133, 141, 146, 169, 178, 202, 227–8
  and feminism, 2–3, 10–12, 16, 146–7
  and freedom, 2, 9–11, 23–7, 49–54, 61–3, 66, 75–9, 83–6, 92, 95, 99–103, 113, 116, 121–2, 128–42, 146–56, 162–3, 172–4, 178, 181–78, 195, 202, 205, 208–9, 217–19, 228, 230
  and habit, 29, 95–103, 108, 116, 146
  interviews, 10–12
  and literature, 3–4, 26, 178, 180, 183, 186–90, 192, 194–7
  and love, 29, 66, 121–5, 127–32, 135, 139, 141–3, 146
  and phenomenology, 2–3, 7, 10, 12, 14–15, 29, 38, 61–2, 72, 77, 91–103, 116–17, 133, 141, 146, 169, 182–90, 201, 203, 227–32
  and political action, 9–10, 11–12, 47, 152, 154–6
  popular essays, 10, 13, 121–2, 127, 143, 178
  and psychoanalysis, 61–2, 75–83
  and race, 3, 7–8, 99–100, 147, 150–7
  and reciprocal recognition, 2, 4, 6, 8, 28, 40, 52–8, 62, 124–6, 136, 139–42, 146, 151, 156, 162–3, 170, 178–9, 184–6, 202, 209, 214, 218, 221–2, 224, 229, 231
  reviews, 91–2, 100–1, 117
  works *see individual titles*
Beauvois, Xavier, 125

becoming, 13–14, 18, 24, 27, 28, 31, 61–3, 69–70, 72, 123, 156, 203
Being and Nothingness (Sartre), 132, 133, 135, 179
being-for-itself, 129, 131, 135, 138, 162
being-in-between, 21, 27, 30, 73, 150, 161–4, 169–72
being-in-itself, 129, 131
being-in-the-world, 19, 23, 30, 38, 53, 97–8, 104, 121, 156, 166, 170, 219
Bendix, Trish, 208
Bergoffen, Debra, 15, 31, 46–7, 69, 121–2, 128, 134, 135, 139, 201, 222
Beugnet, Martine, 187
Binoche, Juliette, 13, 29, 123, **124**, 138
Bion, Wilfred, 6–7, 8, 45–6, 62, 68–9, 75–6, 79–81, 86, 229
bird's-eye shots, 125, 131, 191
Bittencourt, Ela, 212
Blachèrek, Louise, 205
Blain, Paul, 126
Blood of Others, The (Beauvoir), 13
body, the
  adolescent body, 24, 66, 69, 74, 77, 205–9
  alienation of, 134
  authority over, 222–3
  Black bodies, 99, 104–7
  body image, 101
  body movement, 31, 37–8, 42–4, 68–9, 84, 93, 99, 105, 111, 115–17, 202–7, 210–12, 219
  body-thoughts, 68–9
  and consciousness, 121, 125, 136
  embodied emotions, 63, 151, 162, 164–5, 214
  embodied experience, 3, 12, 14–15, 17, 32, 37–8, 46, 62, 92–103, 117, 127, 134, 153, 162, 203–4, 219, 221–4
  embodied perception, 17, 91–101, 105–7, 113, 116–17
  female body, 12, 31, 37–8, 42–4, 69, 77, 101–7, 138–9, 201–7, 210–15, 217–19, 222–4
  and habit, 93–5, 96–102, 106
  lived body, 203–4, 215
  materiality of, 12, 17, 103, 130–1
  phenomenology of, 17, 91–103, 201

body, the (cont.)
  represented bodies, 215
  and situation, 12, 21, 24, 66–7, 139, 201, 203–4, 214, 219
  and transgender identity, 207–9
  visibility of, 12, 84, 111, 204
Bogarde, Dirk, 28, 36, **51**
Bollas, Christopher, 171, 229
Bolton, Lucy, 66
Bond films, 229
borderlands, 150, 161–4
Boulé, Jean-Pierre, 7
Boupacha, Djamila, 154
Bourdieu, Pierre, 93
bracketed experience, 97, 102–3, 104, 133, 134, 136, 138
Brand, Peggy Zeglin, 189
Brecht, Bertolt, 106
Breen, Nora, 113–14
Breillat, Catherine, 179
Bronson, Lisa Marie, 109
Bruzzi, Stella, 185
'Building Subjects' (Dunye), 109
Burke, Tom, 19
Butler, Judith, 8
Byrne, Honor Swinton, 18, **20**, **22**, **25**

Campion, Jane, 218–21
capitalism, 74, 82, 108
Casey, Edward, 179–80
casting, 98, 117–18, 138–9, 173
catastrophic change, 45–6
Cattani, Sophie, 208
Cavani, Liliana, 5, 12, 28, 36–58, 83–4, 179, 201, 211
censorship, 4, 74
Chamarette, Jenny, 14–15
change, 6, 45–6, 70, 76–8, 104, 111, 116
childhood, 24, 65, 69, 85
children, 24–5, 170–1, 215, 222–3
Chinoise, La (1967), 106
choice, 2, 4, 8, 18, 22–7, 38, 45, 48–54, 62–5, 68–9, 74, 79–82, 85–7, 94, 163, 189, 218, 227, 229, 231
Ciénaga, La (2001), 147, **148**, 149
Cineaste, 202
class, 19, 99, 126, 133, 147–8, 153, 168, 202–3, 209–10, 212, 217

close-ups, 43–4, 51, 53, 64, **65**, 67, 71, **72**, 86, **86**, 109–10, **124**, 124–7, 131, 140, 160, 216, 231
Clouzot, Claire, 40
Coatlicue state, 30, 162, 164
Cohen Shabot, Sara, 134
collective action, 11–12, 16
collective freedom, 75, 85
collectivity, 11–12, 16, 17, 75
Collingwood, R. G., 180
Collins, Patricia Hill, 152, 153–6
colonialism, 22–3, 111, 147, 148, 150, 154, 157–74; *see also* imperialism
colour, 51, 84, 178, 179, 187, 191–2, 195, 196
comedy, 5, 104, 106, 107–8, 111, 141–2, 158
Coming of Age, The (Beauvoir), 95–6, 100, 101, 133, 181
community, 27, 70, 73, 80, 85–7, 211
complacency, 29, 91, 95, 143
consciousness, 23, 28, 38, 58, 117, 121, 125, 132, 133, 136, 161–4
Considine, David, 73
contingency, 53, 75, 116, 136, 149, 181
contraception, 11, 143
convents, 213, 215, 216
conversion, 23, 24, 102
co-performance, 179–80, 182, 194, 195
costume, 40, 42, 148, 159, 160
Coulibaly, Dielika, 211
Crenshaw, Kimberlé, 152
Créton, Lola, 131
critical distance, 136–8, 141, 142
critical reception, 28, 39–40, 45, 47, 134, 188
Cronan, Paula, 106
cruelty, 35–6, 38–40, 42, 44, 47, 56–8, 158

Dalle, Béatrice, 131
dance, 37–8, 41–4, 203, 204, 211–12
deep focus, 42, 53, 64, 159
dehumanisation, 43, 45, 54, 57, 151
democratic values, 47
Denis, Claire, 6, 12, 13, 22–3, 29, 123–32, 136–43, 179, 201
Depardieu, Géerard, 127
Deren, Maya, 109

Descas, Alex, 126
desire, 19, 31, 41, 53, 61, 140, 202–3, 206, 207, 209, 213–23
Deutsch, Helene, 75
Di Benedetto, Antonio, 157
dialogue, 18–21, 41, 53, 108, 111, 131, 140, 147, 161, 178, 194, 195, 231
direct address, 24, **25**, **105**, 105–6, 109–10, 113–14
Dirty War, 147–8
disappearances, 148
disclosure, 31–2, 38, 55–6, 137, 178–9, 183–5, 188–9, 195–7
Disson, Jeanne, 208
Djamila Boupacha (Beauvoir and Halimi), 154
Doane, Mary Ann, 74, 84
documentary, 5, 29, 91, 104, 107–8, 185–6
Driscoll, Catherine, 72–4
Dueñas, Lola, 157
Dufrenne, Mikel, 180
Dunye, Cheryl, 12, 29, 91, 95, 102–18, **105**, **112**, 212
'Dunyementaries', 29, 91, 104–18, **105**, **112**, **115**, 212
Duras, Marguerite, 178
Duvauchelle, Nicolas, 126

economic freedom, 216
egotism, 35–6, 41, 63
Eigen, Michael, 80
Ellis, Patricia, 116
embodied emotions, 63, 151, 162, 164–5, 214
embodied experience, 3, 12, 14–15, 17, 32, 37–8, 46, 62, 92–103, 117, 127, 134, 153, 162, 203–4, 219, 221–4
embodied perception, 17, 91–101, 105–7, 113, 116–17
emotional consent, 213, 220, 221–2
emotional growth, 24, 76, 229; *see also* psychological growth
emotional identification, 82, 165–6, 172–3, 185, 192–3, 196–7
emotional storms, 8, 62, 68, 79–82, 86
emotional tension, 6, 15, 21, 26, 83, 216
emotional turbulence, 4–7, 8, 12–13, 17–27, 31, 39, 62, 73, 75–6, 79–83, 123, 129, 134, 138, 146, 156, 163–4, 170, 172, 174, 178–82, 196–7, 201, 205, 218, 227, 229, 232
empathy, 26, 66, 70, 136, 137, 138
encounters, 14, 29, 39, 75, 79–82, 94, 99, 231
entanglement, 125, 180, 183–4, 193
environment, 64, 66, 76, 79, 160, 204
epoché, 103, 133; *see also* bracketed experience
erotic experience, 8, 28, 35–43, 56–8, 124–5, 201, 202, 213–15, 221–4, 229
erotic generosity, 31, 122, 201–3, 215, 223, 225
Esquire, 122, 178
ethical action, 2, 6, 17, 23, 37, 38, 47–9, 98, 101, 152, 205, 220, 225
ethical choice *see* moral choice
ethical ambiguity, 12, 24, 27–8, 29, 31, 40
ethical existence, 37, 39, 91–2
ethical freedom, 4, 6, 25–8, 66, 78, 122, 126–9, 143, 146–7, 151, 153, 156, 164, 172–4, 178, 181, 184–8, 195, 201, 211, 219, 220, 230–1
ethical vision, 5, 38, 55–6, 227
Ethics of Ambiguity, The (Beauvoir), 14, 23, 29, 48–9, 54, 65–6, 69–70, 77–8, 87, 98, 101, 116, 121, 131–2, 141, 151–6, 163, 169, 171–4, 178–9, 181–3, 186, 188–9, 195, 205, 217, 219, 230
ethnographic style, 95, 102, 106, 107, 108
Eurocentrism, 147, 156, 151, 156
European gaze, 172; *see also* White gaze
existentialism
  Beauvoir's, 11–12, 27, 37, 61–2, 66, 72, 77, 92–4, 97, 101, 121–2, 133, 141, 146, 169, 178, 202, 227–8
  cinematic existentialism, 110
  existential aesthetics, 178
  existential ethics, 2, 17, 37, 47–8, 62, 66, 78, 81–2, 95, 98, 100–3, 121–2, 131, 138, 143, 146, 150–2, 173, 178, 209, 214–15, 227–8, 230
  existential phenomenology, 12, 13, 22, 61–2, 72, 77, 87, 93–4, 97, 101–2, 107, 133, 141, 146, 169
  Heidegger's, 169
  Merleau-Ponty's, 17, 92–3, 227

existentialism (*cont.*)
  Sartre's, 27, 66, 121, 133, 179, 227
experimentation, 29, 69, 79, 83–4, 86, 94–5, 103, 105, 109, 111
exploitation, 12, 38–9, 42, 47, 69, 155, 189
Eyre, Hermione, 136

failure, 23, 24, 30, 149, 158–9, 181, 188, 230
Fairbanks, Douglas, 4
false reciprocity, 36, 38–9, 43–5
false solutions, 76, 79
Fanon, Frantz, 2, 98–9
fantasy, 106–7, 159, 167
fascism, 9, 42, 49–50, 54, 57
Faulkner, William, 137
female body, 12, 31, 37–8, 42–4, 69, 77, 101–7, 138–9, 201–7, 210–15, 217–19, 222–4
female bond, 31, 201–2, 210, 211, 221, 225
female gaze, 201–2, 221–2; *see also* reciprocal gaze
femininity, 19, 69, 77, 122, 131, 134, 137, 139, 164, 203, 209, 215
feminist film, 74, 136, 150, 173, 178
feminist historiography, 109
feminist politics, 3, 11, 84, 136–7, 150
feminist theory, 2–3, 8, 10–17, 25, 30, 37, 96, 100, 134–7, 146–57, 161–74, 212, 228–9
femme desire, 31, 207, 212
festival, 183–4, 191
fetishisation, 42–3, 149, 159, 164
Fielding, Helen A., 17, 96, 105–6
film-phenomenology, 8, 14–17, 25, 37, 92, 129, 134, 137, 149–50, 228–30
Five Easy Pieces (1970), 229–30
Flair, 122
flashbacks, 41–2, 51
flesh, 17, 35, 38, 41, 47, 125, 131, 214
Foster, Ben, 63
France, 77, 154, 213
freedom
  and action, 17, 25–7, 49–50, 61–2, 97, 151–2, 182–4, 187–8
  and adolescence, 23–7, 61, 63, 66, 70, 75–9, 81, 83, 85–7

Beauvoir on, 2, 9–11, 23–7, 49–54, 61–3, 66, 75–9, 83–6, 92, 95, 99–103, 113, 116, 121–2, 128–42, 146–56, 162–3, 172–4, 178, 181–78, 195, 202, 205, 208–9, 217–19, 228, 230
collective freedom, 75, 85
and creative production, 184, 188, 219–20
economic freedom, 216
ethical freedom, 4, 6, 25–8, 66, 78, 122, 126–9, 143, 146–7, 151, 153, 156, 164, 172–4, 178, 181, 184–8, 195, 201, 211, 219, 220, 230–1
and love, 122–3, 127, 128–32, 135
ontological freedom, 184, 195
political freedom, 10, 155, 156, 231
pursuit of, 3, 6, 25, 70, 75, 87, 121, 128–9, 146–7, 150–2, 182, 187–8, 194, 210–11, 230
and race, 99–100, 155
and responsibility, 4, 9, 11, 14, 17, 24–7, 53–4, 81, 85–6, 92, 95, 97, 103, 110, 121, 128, 141, 173, 178, 188, 191, 229
Sartre on, 49, 66, 128, 183
sexual freedom, 10
situated freedom, 35, 38, 50, 113, 116
social freedom, 138
as theme for women filmmakers, 3, 6, 14, 83–7
and violence, 48, 151–2
willing oneself free, 174, 183, 187–8, 205, 208–9, 212, 217
Freeman, Wanda, 104
French New Wave, 106
Freud, Sigmund, 45, 46, 61–2, 75, 76, 171
Front de libération nationale (FLN), 154
frustration, 66, 68, 75, 86, 129, 131, 229
Frye, Marilyn, 166
Fullbrook, Edward, 132–3
funding, 12, 13

Garcia, Maria, 65, 202
gaze, 31, 42, 44, 54, 56, 99, 117, 135, 165, 172, 201–3, 212, 218, 219, 221–5
Gemünden, Gerd, 147, 149, 173
gender (in)equality, 10, 55, 123, 137, 155
genre, 13, 14, 73–4, 87, 91, 93
Gerasimovich, Ashley, 193

gesture, 19–21, **20**, 24, 41, 43, 66–7, 69, 84, 86–7, 93, 105, 115–16, 127, 178, 231, 232
Giménez Cacho, Daniel, 30, 149, **160**
Girlhood (2014), 203, 209–12, **211**
Godard, Agnès, 125
Godard, Jean-Luc, 106
Good, The Bad and the Ugly, The (1966), 229
Gordon, Lewis R., 141
Gothlin, Eva, 217
Granik, Debra, 6, 12, 28–9, 61–74, 80–7, 178, 201
Greetings from Africa (1994), **105**, 114
Grévill, Laurent, 126
Griffith, D. W., 4
Gueye, Djibril, 211

habit, 29, 91–118, 146
habit body, 96–101, 106
habitus, 93–4, 98, 100, 103, 104, 110, 118
Haenel, Adèle, 205, 213, **217**
Halimi, Gisèle, 154
Hara-Kiri (1962), 229
Harper's Bazaar, 121–2
Haskell, Molly, 83–4
Hayes, Lillie, 116
Hegel, G. W. F., 123, 152, 214
Heidegger, Martin, 157, 169
Heinämaa, Sara, 12, 15, 99
Henry V (1944), 4
Héran, Zoé, 207, **208**
Herman, Judith, 45
hesitation, 29, 87, 91, 94, 100, 103, 109–16, 212, 228
heteronormativity, 5, 21, 98, 110, 147, 202
High Life (2018), 13
Hipparchia of Maroneia, 227, 229
Hogg, Joanna, 12, 18–23
Hollywood, 13, 70, 98, 107, 137, 189, 190
Holocaust, 151
Holveck, Eleanore, 27
horror films, 93
Humanism and Terror (Merleau-Ponty), 17
Hunter, Holly, 218
Huppert, Isabelle, 22, 131
Husserl, Edmund, 15, 102–3, 117, 214

I can/I cannot binary, 204, 209
identification, 82, 165–6, 172–3, 185, 192–3, 196–7
identity politics, 2, 11, 15, 146, 153, 155–7, 162, 163, 212
imperialism, 151, 157, 221; *see also* colonialism
'In Defence of Djamila Boupacha' (Beauvoir), 154
inaction, 3, 9, 22, 49, 220
Ince, Kate, 37–8, 55–6, 179, 222
indigenous peoples, 149–50, 153, 157–74
individualism, 22, 38, 47, 230
individuation, 3, 63, 65–6, 74, 78–9, 229
information, 185–6
inner world, 19, 23, 48, 76, 189, 195, 231
intentionality, 92–3, 97, 101, 106, 109, 117, 131, 134, 190, 204, 209
interdependence, 28, 47–8, 50, 55, 126, 219
intermeshedness, 15, 17, 32, 150–1, 155–6, 166–7, 169, 201, 212, 213, 228
intersectionality, 14–15, 17, 75, 99, 100, 150, 152–6, 209–10
intersubjectivity, 22, 26, 38, 42, 62, 64, 75–6, 82, 84, 93, 122, 178, 181, 189, 192–3, 201, 220
intertextuality, 83
intertitles, 110, 112, 129
isolation, 50, 64–5, 85, 157–60, 165, 190, 195
'It's About Time Women Put a New Face on Love' (Beauvoir), 122

Janine (1990), **105**, 109–11, 113, 114
'Jean-Paul Sartre: Strictly Personal' (Beauvoir), 121–2
Juhasz, Alexandra, 115, 117

Kant, Immanuel, 179
Keaton, Buster, 229
Keitel, Harvey, 219
Kid, The (1921), 73
Kierkegaard, Søren, 21
Kobayashi, Masaki, 229
Kruks, Sonia, 15, 16, 23, 25, 36, 49, 50, 54, 96, 154

Labourdin, Simone, 9
Lacan, Jacques, 222
Landry, Christinia, 134
Latina feminist phenomenology, 3, 8, 15, 30, 149–50, 152–7, 161–74, 228–9
Lauretis, Teresa de, 28, 39, 40, 45, 50
Lazic, Elena, 192
Le Doeuff, Michèle, 128, 134, 141, 177, 227–8, 232
Leave No Trace (2018), 6, 28–9, 61–74, **65, 67, 71, 72**, 80–7, **86**
Leone, Sergio, 229
lesbianism, 29, 95, 98, 104–12, 116, 153, 207, 215, 218, 222
Lessons on Internal Time Consciousness (Husserl), 102
Let the Sunshine In (2017), 6, 13, 29, 123–32, **124, 130**, 136–43, **140**
Letters to Sartre (Beauvoir), 177
light, 21, 84, 178, 179, 187, 192
liminality, 73, 153, 159
literature, 3–4, 26, 149, 178, 180, 183, 186–90, 192, 194–7
'Literature and Metaphysics' (Beauvoir), 178, 192, 195
lived body, 93, 203–4, 215
looking at, 125–6, 135; *see also* gaze
looking with, 112–13, 125–6, 135
Lorde, Audre, 222
love, 29, 66, 82, 121–32, 135, 138–43, 146, 165–6
Love Finds Andy Hardy (1938), 73
Lover's Discourse, A (Barthes), 127
loving perception, 165–6, 170, 171, 174
Lugones, María, 3, 15, 30, 149, 155–7, 165–74, 228–9
Lyotard, Jean-François, 74

McCall's, 122, 127
McDonough, Michael, 66
McHugh, Kathleen, 104, 106
McKenzie, Thomasin Harcourt, 63
magical thinking, 6
male gaze, 202; *see also* patriarchal gaze
Mandarins, The (Beauvoir), 13, 188–9
Margulies, Ivone, 11, 12, 84
marketing, 72, 74

marriage, 29, 45, 122, 143, 203, 212–13, 216–21
Marrone, Gaetana, 37, 39, 40, 43–4, 54
Marso, Lori Jo, 15, 29, 37, 75, 80–2, 94, 231
Martel, Lucrecia, 5, 12, 13, 30, 147–50, 154, 157–69, 172–4, 178, 194, 201
Martin, Adrian, 73
Martin, Deborah, 148
Martín Alcoff, Linda, 15, 29, 30, 111
master–slave dialectic, 39, 123, 152
materiality, 12, 17, 103, 129, 130–1
Medea (1969), 229
medium shots, 41, 50, 53, 57, 66–7, 69, 71, 86, 108, 140, 160
Memoirs of a Dutiful Daughter (Beauvoir), 177
Merlant, Noémie, 213, **217**
Merleau-Ponty, Maurice, 2, 7, 15, 17, 91–3, 96–102, 112, 117, 213, 227
mestiza consciousness, 30, 153, 157, 161–4, 170, 229
metamorphosis, 77–8, 185
metaphysics, 13, 183, 192, 195–6
Mexico, 162
Miller, Ezra, 190
mimesis, 74, 84
Minujín, Juan, 167
misogyny, 48, 142
mixed media, 104, 110, 112
Moi, Toril, 23, 24, 187, 192, 194, 197
Monde, 154
montage, 51, 108, 111, 193
moral choice, 18, 24–7, 62–5, 68–9, 74, 79–82, 85–7, 94, 163, 229, 231
moral freedom *see* ethical freedom
Moran, Dermot, 94, 102
Morton, Samantha, 181
Morvern Callar (2002), 181
motherhood, 122, 123, 190–7, 203, 221, 229
Mouvement de Libération des Femmes (MLF), 11
movement, 31, 37–8, 42–4, 68–9, 84, 93, 99, 105, 111, 115–17, 202–7, 210–12, 219
Mujer sin cabeza, La (2008), 147–8, 164

multiplicitous self, 149, 157, 168–70
multiplicity, 15, 30, 32, 147, 149–50, 152–3, 157, 162, 168–70
murder, 148, 195, 196
Murray, Pauli, 155
music, 51, 108, 125, 148, 189, 217, 218, 219–20
'Must We Burn Sade?' (Beauvoir), 14, 28, 35–6, 38, 40–1, 46–7, 49, 56–8, 124
muted voice, 121–2, 133, 201
myths, 10, 27, 69, 77, 87, 99, 142, 158, 178, 179, 201, 203, 209, 215, 218, 219, 230

Nachtergaele, Matheus, 158
Nadylam, William, 22
narrative *lacunae*, 147, 161, 185
narrative structure, 21, 31, 39, 104, 118, 149, 150, 178, 185, 192–3
Nazism, 39, 41–4, 49–50, 53–4, 57
Neill, Sam, 218
neoliberalism, 148
New Wave cinema, 106
Nietzsche, Friedrich, 122–3
Night Porter, The (1974), 5, 28, 36–58, 51–2, 211–12
nepantla, 30, 157, 162, 163–4, 170
Niña santa, La (2004), 147
Nouvel Observateur, 10
Nunes, Mariana, 160

object relations psychoanalysis, 5, 8, 62, 72, 76, 81–2, 86, 171
objectification, 35, 42, 53, 100, 115, 122, 131, 133, 202, 211, 222
off-screen space, 147, 150, 173, 178
Oksala, Johanna, 136, 138, 141
old age, 95–6, 100, 108, 181
Olivier, Laurence, 4
Olkowski, Dorothea E., 17
ontological freedom, 184, 195
oppression, 30, 37, 41–5, 49–50, 54–8, 75, 99–100, 110, 131, 139–42, 148–58, 173, 205–6, 214–15, 218–21, 231
Ortega, Mariana, 3, 15, 30, 149, 156–7, 162, 163, 168–71
otherness, 17, 35, 49, 82, 100, 113, 131–2, 135, 141, 172, 221

painting, 184, 213, 215, 219–20, 221–2, 223
Pasolini, Pier Paolo, 229
Passion (1982), 106
patriarchal gaze, 212, 218, 219, 221; *see also* male gaze
patriarchy, 5, 29, 43, 45, 54, 57, 78, 122, 126, 133, 138–42, 147, 173, 181–2, 204, 212–21, 230
Pattinson, Robert, 13
Penley, Constance, 15–16
perception, 17–18, 80, 91–107, 110–13, 116–17, 125, 135, 146, 165–7, 172–4, 214–15, 229
Peredez, María Etelvina, 165
period genre, 215–21
Perón, Isabel, 148
perspective, 134–8, 185–6
phenomenology
  and aesthetic experience, 182–90
  Beauvoir's, 2–3, 7, 10, 12, 14–15, 29, 38, 61–2, 72, 77, 91–103, 116–17, 133, 141, 146, 169, 182–90, 201, 203, 227–32
  and the body, 17, 91–103, 201
  existential phenomenology, 12, 13, 22, 61–2, 72, 77, 87, 93–4, 97, 101–2, 107, 133, 141, 146, 169
  feminist phenomenology, 2–3, 8, 10–17, 25, 30, 37, 96, 100, 134–6, 146–57, 161–74, 209, 212, 228–9
  film-phenomenology, 8, 14–17, 25, 37, 92, 129, 134, 137, 149–50, 228–30
  of habit, 29, 91–103
  of hesitation, 29, 91, 94, 103, 109–16, 228
  Husserl's, 15, 102–3, 117, 214
  Latina feminist phenomenology, 3, 8, 15, 30, 149–57, 161–74, 228–9
  Merleau-Ponty's, 2, 7, 15, 17, 91–3, 96–102, 117, 214
  of perception, 17, 91–101, 116–17
  phenomenological filmmaking, 66–7, 84–5, 95, 136, 173
  phenomenological method, 103, 132–3
  post-phenomenology, 134–43
  relation to psychoanalysis, 5–6, 82–3
  Sartre's, 2, 7, 214

Phenomenology of Perception (Merleau-Ponty), 91–2, 100–1, 117
Phoenix, Joaquin, 181
Piano, The (1993), 218–21
playfulness, 30, 157, 165–6, 170–2
political action, 9–10, 11–12, 14, 47, 63, 69, 91, 100, 104, 106, 152, 154–6
political freedom, 10, 155, 156, 231
popular cinema, 4, 13; *see also* Hollywood
popular magazines, 10, 13, 121–2, 127, 143, 178
Portrait of a Lady on Fire (2019), 6, 202–3, 211–25, **217**, **223**, **224**
possession, 58, 122–3, 127, 131–2, 135, 140, 211, 215–16, 218, 220–1
post-phenomenology, 134–43
Potluck and the Passion, The (1993), **105**, 113–14
Potter, Sally, 179
power, 31, 37, 38, 41, 50, 56, 82, 167, 201, 202, 203, 212
Powell, Adam Clayton, 99
Prime of Life, The (Beauvoir), 9, 13–14, 102, 182, 189
Princess Bride, The (1987), 158
privilege, 5, 19, 35–8, 42, 44, 47, 55–7, 98, 100, 110–18, 124, 133–4, 147, 153–4, 158–9, 166–7, 211
psychoanalysis
  and adolescence, 61–2, 68–9, 72, 75–83, 86
  Beauvoir's view of, 61–2, 75–83
  Bionian, 6–7, 8, 45–6, 62, 68–9, 75–6, 79–81, 86
  Freudian, 45, 46, 61–2, 75, 76, 171
  and the gaze, 222
  Lacanian, 222
  object relations psychoanalysis, 5, 8, 62, 72, 76, 81–2, 86, 171
  relation to phenomenology, 5–6, 82–3
  and sexuality, 62, 75
  and trauma, 45–6
  Winnicottian, 8, 62, 75–6, 79, 81, 170–1
psychological growth, 6, 78, 79, 227, 229; *see also* emotional growth
Pyrrhus and Cineas (Beauvoir), 9, 14, 23, 28, 38, 47–9, 55–6, 101, 138, 167

queer perspectives, 15, 204, 205, 208–9

race, 3, 7–8, 15, 29, 32, 91, 95, 98–100, 104–18, 150–7, 161–4, 189, 209–10, 212
racialisation, 29, 91, 95, 99–100, 111, 113, 115
racism, 48, 111, 189
radio, 9, 178
Ramsay, Lynne, 6, 12, 30–1, 178–9, 180, 181–2, 183, 185, 190–7, 201
Rampling, Charlotte, 28, 36, **51–2**
rebellion, 69, 70, 74, 78, 84
reciprocal gaze, 31, 201–3, 212, 219, 221–5
reciprocal recognition, 2, 4, 6, 8, 28, 40, 52–8, 62, 124–6, 136, 139–42, 146, 151, 156, 162–3, 170, 178–9, 184–6, 202, 209, 214, 218, 221–2, 224, 229, 231
reciprocity, 4, 6, 24, 38, 48–9, 62, 122–6, 128, 141, 151, 202; *see also* false reciprocity; reciprocal gaze; reciprocal recognition
Reed, Susan A., 38, 42–3
reification, 53, 74, 100
Reilly, John C., 193
relationality, 5, 7, 8, 48–50, 66, 83, 103, 141, 161, 178
repetition, 45–6, 93, 95–6, 98, 108, 117
resistance, 12, 69, 70, 84, 107, 109, 154, 170, 212, 215
respect, 67, 83
responsibility, 4, 9, 11, 14, 17, 22–7, 53–4, 57, 65, 68, 79, 81, 85–7, 91–2, 95, 97, 103, 110, 121, 128, 141, 173, 188, 191, 229
responsive materiality, 12
Richards, Fae, 107–9, 115, 116
Rivera Berruz, Stephanie, 152–3, 154
Romney, Jonathan, 129
Rose, Jacqueline, 62

Sade, Marquis de, 28, 35–7, 38, 40, 41, 45–7, 53, 55–8, 124
sadomasochism, 36, 40, 44, 46, 49, 51, 55, 58
al-Saji, Alia, 29, 91, 94, 103, 110–16, 228
Salauds, Les (2013), 131

Samsonov, Ekaterina, 181
Sartre, Jean-Paul
  and bad faith, 24, 128, 129, 132–5
  Being and Nothingness, 132, 133, 135, 179
  Beauvoir's profile of for *Harper's Bazaar*, 121–2
  and collectivity, 16
  conversations with Beauvoir, 113
  être en-soi and *être pour-soi*, 129, 131
  existentialism, 27, 66, 121, 133, 179, 227
  and freedom, 49, 66, 128, 183
  and love, 135, 140–1
  phenomenology, 2, 7, 214
  and situation, 179
Sawyer, Miranda, 192
Schwartzer, Alice, 10, 11–12
Sciamma, Céline, 6, 12, 31, 201–25
score *see* music; sound
Second Sex, The (Beauvoir), 10–11, 14, 23, 31, 35, 49, 54, 61, 69, 70, 75–8, 101, 113, 121–3, 133, 137, 141–3, 151–3, 155, 169, 181–3, 197, 203, 214–15, 217, 219
Second World War, 3–4, 9, 48, 49–50, 151
security, 19, 64, 85, 95–6
self-annihilation, 25, 44, 57
self-awareness, 125, 126, 141, 162, 195
self-deception, 47, 125, 126, 128, 129, 132–3
sensation, 117, 183, 187, 191–7, 214, 215, 231
sexism, 48, 177
sexual difference, 61, 76–9, 82, 122–3, 137, 203–4, 215
sexuality
  and adolescence, 74, 205–9
  desire, 19, 31, 41, 53, 61, 140, 202–3, 206, 207, 209, 213–23
  erotic experience, 8, 28, 35–43, 56–8, 124–5, 201–2, 213–15, 221–4, 229
  femme desire, 31, 207, 212
  heteronormativity, 5, 21, 98, 110, 147, 202
  lesbianism, 29, 95, 98, 104–12, 116, 153, 207, 215, 218, 222
  and psychoanalysis, 62, 75
  in Sade, 35–7, 38, 46–7, 56–7, 124

sex scenes, 98, 104–7, 125–6, 131, 205
sexual freedom, 10
sexual love *see* love
  and violence, 35–43, 47, 53, 55–8, 124
  women filmmakers' treatment of, 83–4, 104–7
shallow focus, 53, 64, **65**, 71, **72**
She Came to Stay (Beauvoir), 13, 23, 132–3
She Don't Fade (1991), 104–7, **105**
Shriver, Lionel, 190
silent films, 4
Simons, Margaret, 10, 11, 143, 177
situated freedom, 35, 38, 50, 113, 116
slavery, 167; *see also* master–slave dialectic
Sobchack, Vivian, 92–3
social expectations, 12, 76, 82, 84, 108, 111, 204, 209, 213
social freedom, 138
socialism, 10, 142
sound, 21, 71, 108–9, 147, 150, 159, 165, 167, 173, 178–9, 187, 190–5, 218–19, 230, 232
Souvenir, The (2019), 18–23, **20**, **22**, 24, **25**
Soviet Union, 189
space, 19–21, 42, 44, 97, 99, 110–11, 161–2
Spain, 157–9, 166–7, 191
spectacle, 35, 36, 38, 39, 42
spectatorship, 22, 26, 29, 31, 94, 104, 107, 185, 189, 197
Spitta, Silvia, 173
sport, 79, 203, 205–6, 210–11
Steinbeck, John, 4
stereotypes, 109
still photographs, 110, 112
Strand, Chick, 109
struggle, 14, 25–7, 30, 55, 69, 70, 75, 76, 150, 153, 162, 164
Sunderland, 18–19
Swinton, Tilda, 190
Szaniawski, Jeremi, 11, 12, 84

Taylor, Jocelyn, 114
teen cinema, 63, 72–4, 87
television, 9, 92, 178
temporality, 17, 26–7, 97, 111, 193
Tidd, Ursula, 7
Timmermann, Marybeth, 143

Tomboy (2011), 203, 204, 207–9, **208**
torture, 36, 41, 45, 56, 148, 154, 157
totality, 186–7, 192
Touré, Karidja, 209
transgender identity, 207–9
transcendence, 43, 49, 102, 113, 123, 127–8, 131, 138, 141, 143, 188, 204
transformation, 27, 46, 77–9, 94, 116, 153, 164, 229
trauma, 5, 22, 31, 45–6, 47, 49, 63, 67, 148, 181–2, 190, 194–5, 197
Trouble Every Day (2001), 131
Turner, Guinevere, 114
'Two Unpublished Chapters' (Beauvoir), 132–3

United States, 4, 28, 39, 45, 47, 64, 73, 99–100, 121, 162, 189, 190, 194
universality, 47, 55, 77–8, 147, 171

Videla, Jorge Rafael, 147–8
viewership *see* spectatorship
Vintges, Karen, 125, 128, 138
violence, 28, 35–42, 47–8, 53–8, 74, 124, 131, 148, 151–2, 154, 159, 195–6, 203, 219
visibility, 12, 55–6, 84, 111, 204, 221
Vogue, 122
voiceover, 108, 218
von Trier, Lars, 29
voting rights, 77, 142
vulnerability, 16, 21, 42, 63, 86–7, 141

Wacquant, Loïc, 93
waiting, 149, 159
Walker, Valarie, 108
war films, 93
warfare, 3, 48, 49–50, 151, 154
Wartime Diary (Beauvoir), 177
Water Lilies (2007), 203, 205–7, 208, 211
Watermelon Woman, The (1996), **105**, 107–9, 111, 114–16, **115**
Wayward Bus, The (1957), 4
We Need to Talk About Kevin (2011), 6, 30–1, 178–9, 180, 190–7, **191**, **197**
Weiss, Gail, 15, 26
Wertmüller, Lina, 83–4
'What Can Literature Do?' (Beauvoir), 178, 185–7, 188
'What Love Is and Isn't' (Beauvoir), 127
White, Josh, 99–100
White gaze, 99; *see also* European gaze
White Material (2009), 22–3, 131
White privilege, 100, 110–11, 113–18
wide shots, 42, 64, 70–1, **71**, 159
Winnicott, Donald, 8, 62, 75–6, 79, 82, 170–1
Winter's Bone (2010), 74
women filmmakers, 3, 4, 6, 7, 12–18, 22, 27, 32, 56, 63, 69–70, 78, 83–7, 95, 137, 146, 178–9, 184–5, 224, 228–32
Woodson, Jacqueline, 114
Woolf, Virginia, 137
'world'-travelling, 30, 157, 165–6, 167–70, 172–3, 229
Wright, Richard, 99

You Were Never Really Here (2017), 31, 181, 197
Young, Iris Marion, 15, 38, 42–4, 134, 203–4, 207, 209–12

Zama (2017), 5, 13, 30, 149–50, 157–62, **160**, **161**, 165–8, 172–4, 194

EU representative:
Easy Access System Europe
Mustamäe tee 50, 10621 Tallinn, Estonia
Gpsr.requests@easproject.com